Management Mistakes

& Successes

Management Mistakes
& Successes

Third Edition

Robert F. Hartley
Cleveland State University

JOHN WILEY & SONS, Inc.
New York • Chichester • Brisbane • Toronto • Singapore

Acquisitions Editor	*Cheryl Mehalik*
Copy Editor	*Richard Blander*
Production Manager	*Joe Ford*
Production Supervisor	*Savoula Amanatidis*
Illustration Coordinator	*Sigmund Malinowski*
Manufacturing Manager	*Lorraine Fumoso*

Library of Congress Cataloging in Publication Data:

Hartley, Robert F., 1927–
     Management mistakes and successes / Robert F. Hartley. — 3rd ed.
        p.   cm.
     Rev. ed. of: Management mistakes. 2nd ed. 1986.
     Includes bibliographical references.
     ISBN 0-471-50762-8
     1. Management—Case studies.   I. Hartley, Robert F., 1927–
Management mistakes.   II. Title.
HD38.H3488   1991
658.4—dc20   90-20034
                                                                                        CIP

Printed in the United States of America

10 9 8 7 6

Printed and bound by Courier Companies, Inc.

Preface

I would like to welcome back past users of *Management Mistakes*. I hope you will find this new edition and format, which still retains some of the most popular cases, a worthwhile change from the earlier editions.

For new users, I hope the book will meet your full expectations and be an interesting and effective learning tool.

In addition to certain additions and deletions to the cases of earlier editions, another significant change has been made. Certain notable management successes have also been described; thus, we can identify practices that differentiate unsuccessful from successful firms. The hypothesis is that we can learn from mistakes, we can learn from successes, and we can learn more by comparing the unsuccessful with the successful, especially when the firms are in the same or similar industry.

The book presents a blend of both classic and current cases. Some of these cases are so current, such as the Savings and Loan industry and Campeau's eroding retail empire, that the final outcomes are still evolving. Admittedly, we have not been able to achieve perfect symmetry in matching the mistakes and successes of sufficiently similar firms. However, each section includes both perspectives. One case of particular interest today is that of the Yugo, manufactured in Eastern Europe, which graphically depicts the contrasts of socialistic and capitalistic economies, their work ethics and managerial effectiveness. The organization of cases is described in Chapter 1.

While we have tried to classify the cases under the various managerial functions, such as planning, organizing, leading and controlling, with many cases it was not possible to truly compartmentalize the mistake or the success strictly according to each management function. The patterns of success or failure tend to be more pervasive. Still, whenever applied, the functional delineation should bring order to the subject matter.

At the end of each chapter a number of learning insights are presented. Some of these will be common to several cases, and illustrate that certain successful and unsuccessful practices tend to cross company lines. In the final chapter, the various learning insights are summarized and classified so that general conclusions from the mistakes and successes are described.

As a supplemental text, this book can be used in a great variety of courses, both undergraduate and graduate, ranging from principles of management to strategic management to business policy. It can also be useful in ethics and organizational theory courses.

A number of persons have provided encouragement, information, advice, and constructive criticism. I thank in particular Dean Ephraim Smith and Chairman Ram Rao of Cleveland State for their generous contributions to this book. Further, I thank the following reviewers who have given me their valuable suggestions and insights: W. Jack Duncan, University of Alabama–Birmingham; Mike Farley, Del Mar College; Joseph W. Leonard, Miami University (OH); Abbas Nadim, University of New Haven; William O'Donnell, University of Phoenix; Howard Smith, University of New Mexico; and James Wolter, University of Michigan–Flint.

Finally, I express my gratitude to Cheryl Mehalik, my sponsoring editor at Wiley, for her support and encouragement, and to Richard Blander, Senior Copy Editor, for his helpful input and careful review of the manuscript.

Robert F. Hartley

Contents

CHAPTER 1

Introduction

In this third edition we take a somewhat different approach from the other editions. Although we still examine classic and contemporary management mistakes for what can be learned—insights that are transferable to other firms, other times, and other situations—now we seek additional insights through comparisons.

We also study successful firms, some of these having similar resources and opportunities in the same industries as the blundering firms. What key factor(s) produced monumental mistakes for one and resounding success for another? Through such contrasts, we may learn to improve the "batting average" in the intriguing challenge of decision making.

We will encounter many examples of the phenomenon of organizational life cycles, with an organization growing and prospering, then failing (just as humans), but occasionally resurging. Success usually is not forever, whereas even the most serious mistakes can be (but are not always) overcome.

A variety of firms, industries, problems, mistakes, and successes are presented. You will be familiar with most of the firms, although perhaps not with the details of their situations. Whereas the book explores fairly recent events, it covers more than three decades. For scenarios occurring several decades ago—such as the Edsel, Harley Davidson, and Penney—the circumstances and what can be learned are far from dated.

These cases have especially been chosen to bring out certain points or caveats in the art of management decision making. They have been selected to give a balanced view of the spectrum of management problems. We have sought to present examples that provide somewhat different learning experiences, where at least some aspect of the mistake or success differs from other aspects described in the book. Still, we see similar mistakes occurring time and again. Ant the universality of some of these mistakes casts doubt about the extent that decision making has improved over the decades.

At present, let us consider what learning insights one should gain from examining the mistakes and successes of well-known firms. What can be learned with the benefit of hindsight that may help increase the success factor?

LEARNING INSIGHTS

Analyzing Mistakes

In looking at sick companies, or even healthy ones that have experienced failures of certain parts of their operations, the temptation is to be unduly critical. It is easy to criticize with the benefit of hindsight. Mistakes are inevitable, given the present state of the art of decision making and the dynamic environment facing the business organization.

Mistakes can be categorized as errors of omission and of commission. *Mistakes of omission* are those in which no action was taken, and the status quo was contentedly embraced amid a changing environment. Such errors, which often characterize conservative or stodgy management, are not as obvious as the other category of mistakes. They seldom involve tumultuous upheaval. Rather, the company's fortunes and competitive position slowly and unspectacularly fade, until years later the sudden realization comes that mistakes having monumental impact have been allowed to happen. The firm's fortunes often never regain their former luster. A number of examples in this book evidence such mistakes of omission: Woolco, Harley Davidson, Adidas.

Mistakes of commission are more spectacular. They involve bad decisions, wrong actions taken, misspent or misdirected expansion, and the like. Although the costs of the erosion of competitive position coming from errors of omission are difficult to calculate precisely, the costs of errors of commission often are fully evident. The write-offs associated with the Edsel, for example, were estimated to be $100 million in operating losses and another $100 million in unrecoverable investment. (The losses would have been still greater except that $150 million of plant and tools were recovered and used in other Ford divisions.) But such costs pale before the billions of dollars of losses due to the excesses in the savings and loan industry, costs to be borne by the federal government and taxpayers.

Granted that mistakes of omission and commission will occur, alert and aggressive management is characterized by certain actions or reactions when probing their own mistakes or problem situations.

1. Looming problems or present mistakes should be quickly recognized.
2. The causes of the problem(s) should be carefully determined.
3. Alternative corrective actions should be evaluated in view of the company's resources and constraints.
4. Corrective action should be prompt. Sometimes this may require a ruthless axing of the product, the division, or whatever is at fault.
5. Mistakes should provide learning experiences, the same mistakes should not be repeated, and future operations should be improved.

Slowness to recognize emerging problems leads us to think that management is lethargic and incompetent, or that controls have not been established to provide prompt feedback at strategic control points. For example, a declining competitive position in one or a few geographical areas should be a red flag to management that something is amiss. To wait months before investigating or taking action may mean a permanent loss of business. Admittedly, signals sometimes get mixed and information may not come as complete as desired, but procrastination cannot be easily defended.

Just as problems should be quickly recognized, the causes of these problems—the "why" of the unexpected results—must be determined as quickly as possible. It is premature to take action before knowing where the problems really lie. To go back to the previous example, the loss of competitive position in one or a few areas may occur because of circumstances beyond the firm's immediate control, such as an aggressive new competitor who is drastically cutting prices to "buy sales." In such a situation, all the competing firms in that area will likely lose some market share, and little can be done except to remain as competitive as possible with prices and servicing. However, closer investigation may disclose that the erosion of business is due to unreliable deliveries, poor quality control, or a lost technological advantage.

With the cause(s) of the problem defined, various alternatives for dealing with it should be defined and evaluated, and the corrective choice of action made as objectively and prudently as possible. This may require further research, such as obtaining feedback from customers or from field personnel. If drastic action is needed, there usually is little rationale for procrastination. Serious problems do not go away by themselves; they tend to fester and become worse.

Finally, some learning experience should result from the misadventure. A vice president of one successful firm said:

I try to give my subordinates as much decision-making power as possible. Perhaps I err on the side of delegating too much. In any case, I expect some mistakes to be made, some decisions that were not for the best. I don't come down too hard usually. This is part of the learning experience. But God help them if they make the same mistake twice. There has been no learning experience, and I question their competence for higher executive positions.

Analyzing Successes

Successes deserve as much analysis as mistakes, although admittedly the urgency is less than with an emerging problem that requires remedial action lest it spread.

Any analysis of success should seek answers to at least the following questions:

Why were such actions successful?

Was it because of the nature of the environment, and if so, how?

Was it because of marketing research, and if so, how?

Was it because of any particular element of the strategy—such as products and/or services, promotional activities, or distribution methods—and if so, how?

Was it because of the specific elements of the strategy meshing well together, and if so, how was this achieved?

Was the situation unique and unlikely to be encountered again?

If not, how can we use these successful techniques in the future, or in other operations at the present?

ORGANIZATION OF BOOK

We have endeavored to classify the cases under the important management functions of planning, organizing, leadership and strategy implementation, controlling, and, finally, ethical and social responsibility. Admittedly, however, some of the cases cannot be neatly compartmentalized into, for example, errors or successes of planning or organizing, because they involve broader and more pervasive situations.

Cases in Planning

The first case in the planning section involves not a single company, but an entire industry—the savings and loan, or thrift industry. As of the beginning of 1990, the full extent of the debacle is still unraveling, and the final bailout figure is estimated at over $200 billion dollars. This case represents the ultimate repudiation of management for prudence in planning and sober responsibility to stockholders and depositors. Admittedly, management is not alone in culpability: state and federal regulators and an easily influenced and naive Congress must also share the blame. Although the issue is complex, we have focused our attention primarily on the managerial aspects.

At the other extreme, the J. C. Penney Company showed a planning so conservative that no changes could be contemplated from what had been successful in the past, even though the environment for doing business represented a whole new ball game. Only the audacious action of a staff executive—who bypassed his superior in going to the board of directors, thereby violating one of the sacred dictums of organizational theory—opened the eyes of the company to the need for change.

Then there is Adidas. Here was a firm in the catbird seat, utterly dominating its industry at the beginning of the running boom. But somehow, incredibly, it let its advantage slip away. And hungry interlopers—Nike, in particular—starting from scratch, carved up the burgeoning market, while Adidas in its planning continued to underestimate the strength and durability of running's popularity, as well as the growing strength of its aggressive American competitors.

The miscalculation of Coca-Cola in changing the flavor of its traditional and major product shows planning flaws even with the use of extensive evaluation and research. Although things turned out well, a major improvisation had to be made by embarrassed executives.

The last case in this section describes a contrasting success, that of Hyatt Legal Clinics. Joel Hyatt found a strategic window, an untapped sector of the market for legal services, and parlayed this to one of the nation's largest law firms.

Organizational Cases

We may not always realize the importance of an organization in paving the way for growth, but its failure can cause monumental mistakes, whereas the right organization can be a powerful conduit for profitable growth.

The Edsel case could also have been placed under the planning section, because it provides us with the thoughtful realization that even the most detailed planning does not guarantee success. We have placed this case in the organizational section because it graphically illustrates the fallacy of creating an organization suited for the most ambitious plans and expectations without sufficient evidence that such expectations are likely to be realized. We also examine the major contrast by the same firm in the space of less than five years—the Mustang. How could the Edsel have been such a monumental failure and the Mustang the most successful new car introduction to that time? Here we have the proof that a firm can learn from its mistake.

Next we turn our attention to three famous failures of discount-store operations—Korvette, Woolco or Woolworth, and W. T. Grant—and compare them with the success of K mart, destined to become the biggest discounter of them all and one of the largest retailing organizations in the United States. How could these three fail so miserably (W. T. Grant, when it went into bankruptcy and eventual liquidation, was the second biggest U.S. company ever to do so) when they had more experience and greater resources than K mart? But come today, and the fortunes of K mart are being threatened by Wal-Mart, illustrating again the life cycle that seems as operative with organizations as with biology.

The last case in this section deals with the most current example of misguided leveraged buyouts (LBOs) using heavy financing. Robert Campeau acquired two major department store corporations, Allied and Federated, through heavy financing in the "raider" tradition of the 1980s. But his greatly expanded organization was too highly leveraged to handle both the operational expenses and the interest costs, and like a house of cards began tumbling down. Campeau could not digest what he had swallowed.

Cases Dealing with Strategy Execution

The Coors case at first poses the question of whether a firm can be virtually invulnerable to competition. Coasting on a mystique that had somehow been built up for the product, Coors enjoyed great success, only to find it diminishing. With little advertising, no concern with competition, and aloof public and employee relations, the company's fortunes faltered badly in the face of more aggressive competition. The mystique of Coors had proven ephemeral.

As the decade of the 1980s began, U.S. industry found itself faced with a problem never before encountered in such severity. Foreign firms, especially those of Japan and West Germany, were producing better quality products for less cost than we were able to do. They were invading our domestic markets and placing many of our firms at a competitive disadvantage, resulting in hundreds of thousands of U.S. workers being laid off. In few industries was this invasion of foreign products more severe and disruptive than in the auto and steel industries.

Chrysler in the late 1970s and early 1980s epitomizes the dilemma facing many other U.S. firms, although the financial straits of Chrysler, brought on partly by bad management decisions in the past, made its position the more precarious. In this case we examine the background that made such foreign incursions possible and effective, and describe the situation facing the savior, Iacocca, when he took over.

The A. C. Gilbert Company is a case of a firm unable to handle a crisis. Although this old toymaker should have recognized the environmental factors leading to its crisis long before it did, the greatest mistake was frenzied reactions that made matters worse. This case illustrates practically every mistake imaginable: successive rash decisions aimed at correcting the problem with no weighing of consequences or prudent evaluation of alternatives, along with a continued upheaval of the formerly stable organization. In the space of only 5 years, bad crisis leadership caused the 58-year-old company to fail.

In the early 1960s, Harley Davidson dominated a static motorcycle industry. Suddenly, Honda, a newcomer from overseas, burst on the scene and vastly changed the industry. Harley Davidson's market share dropped from 70 percent to 5 percent in only a few years. The inroads by Honda were a precursor of what was to happen with Japanese imports of all kinds. At the time, Japanese products did not have the image of quality and dependability that they have today, making the quick success of Honda all the more remarkable.

In the last case in this section—a success—the business is not a product but people: celebrities and famous athletes. Mark McCormack of International Management Group executed a strategy of promoting the most famous athletes and other celebrities of the world to business firms eager for their sponsorship and association with their products and firms. The "hand-holding" of such temperamental people represents an unqualified success in executing an innovative strategy.

Cases Dealing with Control

Part Four deals with firms that represent great contrasts in their monitoring and controlling of certain aspects of their operations. The fast-food franchise operation, Burger Chef, showed unwise expansion even though it was under the auspices of a large and seasoned firm, General Foods. But the irresistible temptation to open hundreds of additional outlets over a few years' time, without proper operational fundamentals and without imposing strict controls over a far-flung organization, soon forced severe retrenchment. The Burger Chef division of General Foods never became a money maker, and was finally sold in 1982. The strict and rigorous standards and controls of McDonald's contrasts sharply with the looseness of Burger Chef.

The Osborne Computer case represents perhaps the most extreme example of success and failure in the annals of American business. First on the scene with an inexpensive portable computer packaged with an abundance of software, sales rose to $100 million in only 18 months, only to come plummeting down as lack of systematic controls and feedback resulted in major miscalculations and huge and unexpected losses. Contrast this with one of the greatest success stories of the early 1980s, Apple Computer.

The last case in this section concerns a foreign product from a socialist economy, Yugoslavia, that for a few years sold the Yugo in the United States. At the time, this was the lowest-priced automobile obtainable. But the flaws inherent in socialist environments showed up starkly in poor quality, shoddy workmanship, and other problems.

Ethical and Social Responsibility Problems

No firm today can violate social and environmental constraints with impunity. The reputation or public image of a firm—how it is perceived by its various publics—can play a crucial role in success and failure. Even more so, the vulnerability to litigation if a firm is guilty of causing injury can bring any firm to its knees. In this last section we examine three cases: A. H. Robins and the Dalkon Shield catastrophe, Nestle and its infants formula controversy, and the successful handling by Johnson & Johnson of its Tylenol scare.

Where possible in these cases, we have depicted the major personalities involved at the time. We invite you to imagine yourself in their positions, confronting the problems and decisions they faced at their points of crisis or just-recognized opportunities. What would you have done differently, and why? We invite you to participate in the discussion questions and role-playing episodes appearing at the end of each chapter. We urge you to consider the pros and cons of alternative actions.

FOR THOUGHT AND DISCUSSION

1. Do you agree that is it impossible for a firm to avoid mistakes? Why or why not?
2. How can a firm speed up its awareness of emerging problems so that it can take responsive action? Be as specific as you can.
3. Large firms tend to err more often on the side of conservatism and are slower to take corrective action than smaller ones. Would you speculate as to why this is so?
4. Which do you think is likely to be the more costly to a firm, errors of omission or errors of commission? Why?
5. So often we see the successful firm eventually losing its pattern of success. Why cannot success have more durability?

PART **One**

PLANNING GONE
AWRY

CHAPTER 2

The Savings and Loan Disaster—Repudiating Prudence in Planning

In the 1980s, a financial disaster of monumental proportions suddenly emerged on the public consciousness. That it involved the savings of ordinary people, and that the long-term consequences would be borne by all taxpayers, made it all the more consequential. That it involved management incompetence and violation of depositor and shareholder trust in excesses of spending and lending brought widespread media attention.

Our savings and loan (S & L) industry, the source of home ownership for millions of Americans, was on the verge of total collapse; indeed, hundreds of institutions would go bankrupt. But the savings of the depositors were protected by the federal government, and were not at risk, though the government bailout would be the costliest in history.

How could this have happened? What can we learn from it? What management mistakes were made that other managers in other times and places, with awareness, can avoid? And what were the keys to the S & L's success that survived and prospered during this time?

A SAMPLING OF FIASCOS

Sunbelt Savings

Edwin T. McBirney III was 29 years old when he began his run to a vast fortune in the savings and loan business. The year was 1981. While still in college he had shown unusual business acumen, starting his own business of leasing refrigerators to college students. Upon graduating he turned to real estate, becoming a broker and investor in the booming Dallas market.

In December 1981, he formed an investment group that began buying small S & Ls. One of these was Sunbelt Savings, an obscure S & L in Stephenville, Texas. McBirney was to merge these holdings into one large S & L, which he named Sunbelt Savings Association. In less than four years, Sunbelt was the nucleus of a $3.2 billion financial empire. Its growth came mostly from commercial real-estate loans that were so risky Sunbelt gained the nickname, "Gunbelt," for its shoot-from-the-hip lending policies. As one example, Sunbelt lent $125 million (secured only by raw land) to an inexperienced Dallas developer in his 20s, who went on to lose $80 million.[1] In its heyday, Sunbelt owned mortgage and development-service companies, had a commercial-banking division, and made real-estate loans to developers from California to Florida.

McBirney and his executives soon were covering Texas in the company's fleet of seven aircraft. McBirney liked to throw sumptuous parties. He would serve lion and antelope to hundreds of guests at his palatial Dallas home. In 1984 and 1985, Sunbelt footed $1.3 million Halloween and Christmas galas, including a $32,000 fee to his wife for organizing the parties. No end seemed to be in sight for these Texas big spenders. But it was there, just around the corner.

In 1984, the Empire Savings and Loan of Mesquite, Texas, collapsed after funding massive high-risk investments. Its demise raised troubling questions about the entire industry. Edwin Gray, chairman of the Federal Home Loan Bank Board, a regulation of S & Ls, became fearful of a disaster and slammed on the brakes. He forced reappraisals based on current market values, increased capital requirements, limited direct appraisals, and hired hundreds of new examiners and supervisory agents. And appraisers found that the collateral backing billions of dollars of loans had been overvalued by up to 30 percent. Many thrifts had to lower the book value of their loans, in so doing reducing their already weak capital positions. And then real estate values plummeted as Texas' economy began collapsing, led by declining oil prices. The domino effect took over as a rash of loan delinquencies led to one foreclosure after another.

Now the excesses of McBirney's heyday came to roost. Hundreds of examiners descended on the Dallas home-loan office in the spring of 1986, and the bulk of the Sunbird S & Ls were declared insolvent. While Sunbird was spared temporarily, McBirney was forced to resign as chairman by June. Of the foreclosed real estate on Sunbelt's books, only a few million out of its $6 billion portfolio of troubled assets could be sold off. By late 1988, the Fed-

[1] Howard Rudnitsky and John R. Hayes, "Gunbelt S & L," *Forbes*, September 19, 1988, p. 120.

eral Home Loan Bank Board estimated that it would cost as much as $5.5 billion just to keep Sunbelt alive over the next ten years.[2]

To add to the insult, a lawsuit filed against McBirney and other insider shareholders charged that nearly $13 million in common and preferred dividends had been taken out in 1985 and 1986, this at a time when Sunbelt's capital was rapidly evaporating because of wild expenditures and devaluation of assets.

Shamrock Federal Savings Bank

In Shamrock, Texas, the little savings and loan on the corner went belly-up. The collapse of the Shamrock Federal Savings Bank left a bitter pill for this town of 3,000 in the Texas panhandle. It was a common story for many Texas communities: a small-town thrift taken over by an outsider; fast growth followed by sudden insolvency; a trail of incompetent management and soured high-risk ventures in places far beyond the limits of the town. "We made a mistake selling it. We should have kept it under local control, making loans in our community," declared one of the original directors of the town's only savings and loan.

Back in 1977, Phil Cates, a state representative and head of the local Chamber of Commerce, had a vision of a financial institution that would serve Shamrock and other small towns near the Oklahoma line. He started pushing townsfolk to start their own savings and loan association in view of the oil and gas boom that was bringing hundreds of people into the town. Shamrock's two family-owned banks shunned long-term home mortgages and refused to pay competitive interest rates. Cates sold the idea of a local S & L to hundreds of local residents. When the Red River Savings and Loan Association opened in 1979, it had more than 350 stockholders in a town of 2,834. Community pride ran high.

These were the days of S & L deregulation, and small-town thrifts like Red River were hot properties, targets of opportunity for promoters and speculators. One such was Jerry D. Lane. He offered $21 a share, more than double the original price. And the townspeople jumped at the opportunity.

The name was changed to Shamrock Savings Association, and in three years deposits rocketed from $11.6 million to $111.3 million. This was mainly accomplished by shifting the thrift's focus far beyond the small town of Shamrock, with offices opened as far away as Amarillo and Colorado Springs, Colorado. Lane also began buying some of other thrifts' outstanding loans.

---

[2] For more detail, see "Why Our S & Ls Are in Trouble," *Reader's Digest*, July 1989, pp. 70–74.

Disaster struck in 1987 when the Federal Savings and Loan Insurance Corporation filed a $150 million racketeering suit against Lane and others after the 1985 failure of State Savings of Lubbock, Texas, when Lane had been chief executive officer there. Federal regulators had found a pattern common to the S & L industry, and would soon find at Shamrock: fraudulent loans to developers, concentrating an "unsafe" amount of credit with one client, basing loans on inflated property appraisals, and making them without proper credit documentation. "Loans were made over lunch with a handshake."

Shamrock was closed by federal regulators in November 1987; it owed $16.6 million more than it was worth. But its betrayal of the local community occurred before that. It had been conceived to make loans locally for homes and other projects that could help the community. But with its buyout and the shift of emphasis far beyond the local community, it had little interest in providing less lucrative but less risky local loans.

Shamrock characterized a large segment of S & Ls, especially in the heady days of the oil boom when Texas and other southwestern states thought there was no stopping the runaway building boom built on the belief that oil prices could only go up. But they dropped to $14 a barrel in the early 1980s, destroying the cash supports from under commercial real estate projects all across the Southwest.[3]

Lincoln Savings and Loan: Political Scandal

Charles Keating is the former owner of California's Lincoln Savings and Loan. He purchased Lincoln in 1984, and switched it from investing in safe, single-family mortgages to raw land speculation, junk bonds, and huge development projects like the $900-a-night Phoenician Resort in Scottsdale, Arizona.

Keating was a heavy campaign contributor, giving to five prominent U.S. senators: Glenn, Cranston, McCain, Riegle, and De Concini. In total, these influential politicians received $1.3 million. As his failing S & L came under the scrutiny of the Federal Home Loan Bank Board, which found enough bad loans and shaky business practices to shut it down, he sought help from these senators, and action was delayed for two years because of their intervention. During this time, the federally guaranteed cost of paying back Lincoln's depositors went up $1.3 billion to $2.5 billion, making this one of the costliest thrift failures.[4]

---

[3] Adapted from "Small Town's Dreams Vanish," *Cleveland Plain Dealer*, August 13, 1989, p. 3C.

[4] Margaret Carlson, "$1 Billion Worth of Influence," *Time*, November 6, 1989, pp. 27–28.

Now Keating is a defendant in a lawsuit involving racketeering, fraud, and conspiracy in using the institution's funds. And the senators' complicity is under investigation.

So we see in this sampling of S & L blunders a repudiation of any systematic planning, with megabuck deals made on the spur of the moment, without investigation, heedless of risks and probable consequences. The following box summarizes the *desired strategic planning process* for coping with long-range environmental changes and opportunities.

INFORMATION SIDELIGHT

THE STRATEGIC PLANNING PROCESS

Strategic planning is the managerial process of planning to cope with an ever-changing environment over the long run. Strategic planning is very much forward looking. One manager described it as "an eager seizing of opportunities." This type of planning should permeate an organization and not be limited to top executive suites and ivory towers.

Strategic planning begins with determining the company's fundamental mission. Usually this involves deciding "What business should we be in?" The answer may or may not be the same as that of "What business are we presently in?"

After the mission has been determined, objectives or performance goals should be established. Firms may have multiple goals, although in many, especially smaller firms, these may be implicit or ill-defined. Goals may be stated too vaguely or smack of the flavor of public relations. Nevertheless, there are important benefits of stating goals and objectives in explicit language and in order of priority, because some may conflict. Goals that are well communicated and understood by all units of the organization can provide criteria for making policy decisions and introduce consistency into planning and decision making.

The final step of the strategic planning process is to assess environmental opportunities or potential—this is often called *environmental scanning*—which should be guided by the more generally stated objectives and goals of the firm. The firm's present business is the starting point for this assessment, commonly called *portfolio analysis*. Then other potential customers should be considered and perhaps verified as offering opportunity as a result of previous business with them, similarity of their operations to those of present customers, intriguing growth possibilities, or simply that competitors are disregarding them or seem vulnerable.

In this assessment of environmental opportunities or potential, a risk/reward ratio should be carefully considered. That is, are the risks of seeking the new business opportunities sufficiently modest compared with the possible gains? Are these risks manageable? As many savings and loans learned, to their profound dismay, the risks in their new endeavors far outweighed the short-term gains.

THE FULL FLAVOR OF THE S & L DEBACLE

By 1988, of the nation's 3,178 so-called thrift institutions, 503 were insolvent. Another 629 had less capital on their books than regulators usually require. In 1987, 630 thrifts had lost an estimated $7.5 billion, half again as much as the earnings of all the rest combined.[5] Most of the "terminal" S & Ls got into trouble making risky loans. But fraud also contributed to the failures of nearly 50.[6] More than half the troubled thrifts were to be found in Texas. But other Sunbelt thrifts were also crashing: Beverly Hills Savings & Loan in California, which had much of its $2.9 billion in assets invested in dicey real estate ventures and junk bonds, closed in 1985; Sunrise Savings & Loan of Florida, with $1.5 billion in assets, was liquidated in 1986; in Arkansas, First South Federal Savings & Loan was closed in 1986 after 64 percent of its $1.4 billion in loans were found to be speculative. (See Table 2.1 for a sampling of Sunbelts on the "deathwatch" as of September 30, 1988.) Still, the worst excesses occurred in Texas. And there were suspicions that some of the insolvent Texas S & Ls were shuffling bum loans from one to another a step ahead of the bank examiners.

Table 2.1   S & L's on the "Deathwatch" as of September 30, 1988[a]

State	Thrift	Negative Net Worth (millions)
Texas	Gill Savings, Hondo	($542.7)
	Meridian Savings, Arlington	($387.7)
New Mexico	Sandia Federal, Albuquerque	($482.6)
Arizona	Security S & L, Scottsdale	($351.6)
Arkansas	Savers Federal, Little Rock	($286.5)
California	Westwood S & L, Los Angeles	($222.7)
	Pacific Savings, Costa Mesa	($206.6)
Florida	Freedom S & L, Tampa	($231.6)

[a] This is only a sampling.
Source: SNL Securities, Inc., and Fortune, January 30, 1989, p. 9.

Undeniably, part of the motivation for taking wild risks with deposits was that individual accounts were insured up to $100,000 by the Federal Savings and Loan Insurance Corporation (FSLIC). But even the resources of this

[5] John Paul Newport, Jr., "Why We Should Save the S & Ls," Fortune, April 11, 1988, p. 81.
[6] Robert E. Norton, "Deep In the Hole in Texas," Fortune, May 11, 1987, p. 61.

government agency were to be insufficient to cope with the problem without massive congressional appropriations in the billions of dollars.

The lurking danger, of course, was that depositor panic could create a devastating run on the nation's $932 billion in thrift deposits, and bring down scores of S & Ls; threaten the $14 billion of capital in the 12 regional Federal Home Loan Banks, which would have to supply emergency funds to the thrifts; and potentially swamp the FSLIC. The most simple solution would be to write off the insolvent thrifts and pay off their depositors. But this would exceed the original resources of the FSLIC, and could cost more than $100 billion. Taxpayers will eventually have to foot the bill.

HISTORY OF THE SAVINGS AND LOAN INDUSTRY

At first they were called building and loans; and they filled a real need. Before the Great Depression, many commercial banks would not lend on middle-class residential property. Working class people were eventually forced to band together to form cooperative associations to take their deposits and lend those funds out as home mortgages. The Depression saw the failure of thousands of banks and building and loans, and the Roosevelt administration created the two deposit-insurance funds we know today, the FSLIC for S & Ls, and the Federal Deposit Insurance Corporation (FDIC), which insures commercial bank deposits.

In the late 1960s, the S & Ls began experiencing some troubles. By law the federally regulated S & Ls were required to lend long with home mortgages, but they borrowed short, with most of their lendable funds coming from passbook savings accounts. This situation of long-term loans and short-term lendable resources posed no problem at first—until inflation. With this scenario the value of the S & L portfolios, like that of all fixed-rate long-term debt, fell. In 1971, the S & L industry had a negative net worth of $17 billion. But the inflation rate in the 1970s worsened, and the industry faced ever larger losses on its loan portfolios.

The environment was changing in other ways as well. In particular, money-market mutual funds came on the scene, aided by computer technology. These money-market funds accumulated high-yielding financial instruments such as jumbo certificates of deposit (CDs), commercial paper and government notes, and then allowed the small investor to own a piece of the high-yielding package. Technology enabled customers to write checks on these money funds, while still receiving high interest. Computers made possible extremely complex bookkeeping for such transactions.

The effect on banks and S & Ls was, of course, substantial. Money flowed out of them and into money-market funds by the hundreds of billions of dollars. This combined with the double-digit inflation of the late 1970s brought the industry, with its long-term loans at low-interest rates, seemingly to the point of disaster. By 1981, 80 percent of the thrifts were losing money, and fully 20 percent were below the minimum capital requirements set by regulators.[7] (See Table 2.2 for a summary of the worsening S & L situation during the 1980s.)

In order to save the thrift industry from a potentially devastating outflow of funds, Congress in 1980, in the Depository Institutions Deregulation and Monetary Control Act, gradually phased out interest rate ceilings on deposits and allowed S & Ls to make various kinds of consumer loans. The Federal Savings and Loan Insurance Corporation's (FSLIC) insurance coverage was also raised from $40,000 to $100,000—essentially, the government deregulated the industry. But now a rate war developed among the thrifts, with some paying depositors double-digit interest rates.

Table 2.2   Summary of the Worsening S & L Situation During the 1980s

1980–82: Congress begins phasing out interest-rate limits. Banks and S & Ls are allowed to offer new savings accounts that compete with market interest rates. Federal deposit insurance is boosted from $40,000 to $100,000 per account. Money that flowed out of S & Ls in 1980, when deposit rates were capped at 5.5%, begins flowing back. But the new deposits cost more than S & Ls can earn on the old fixed-rate mortgages made in the 1960s and 1970s at rates as low as 6% and even lower. Now S & Ls are losing billions of dollars, and hundreds fail. The Garn-St. Germain bill is passed in 1982, allowing S & Ls new lending and investment freedom.

Mid–1980s: A lending spree develops, with billions of dollars loaned for apartments, office buildings, and other projects, especially in the booming Southwest. Many S & Ls are seeking high-profit investments to make up for the low rates on old mortgages. In a climate of drastically loosened controls, wild speculation and outright fraud characterize the operations of hundreds of thrifts.

1986: Oil prices plunge, and the Texas economy collapses, and the overbuilding comes home to roost as developer loans are defaulted and the properties foreclosed are worth only fractions of building costs. More S & Ls are brought to insolvency. The Federal Savings and Loan Insurance Corporation finds its capital depleted by earlier S & L failures, and needs massive infusions of capital. Prospective acquirers are attracted to take over the dead and dying thrifts under most favorable terms.

1988–89: A massive government bailout is prepared and enacted.

Congress acted again to "remedy" the situation, only the remedy led to worse abuses. In 1982, the Garn-St. Germain Act was passed. This further loosened the restraints on S & Ls, now giving them lending powers to write

[7] John J. Curran, "Does Deregulation Make Sense?" *Fortune*, June 5, 1989, pp. 184, 188, and 194.

acquisition, development, and construction loans; form development subsidiaries; and make direct investments. If properly handled, the new freedom should have enabled S & Ls to better match assets and liabilities and find a sounder footing. Now they could begin lessening their dependence on mortgage lending and instead seek higher yielding investments. Figure 2.1 shows the decline in mortgage lending by S & Ls over the last 20 years.

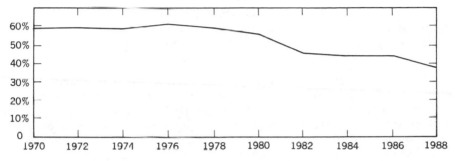

Percent of mortgage debt for 1–4 family homes held by savings and loans, excluding mortgage securities.

Figure 2.1. Decline in mortgage lending by S & Ls over the last 20 years. (*Source·* Federal Reserve).

By now, with constraints of regulation mostly unraveled and a new business environment in place, S & Ls needed to give careful attention to their strategic planning. Most important, they needed *to reevaluate their company mission* (as discussed in the following Information Sidelight)

The deregulatory "solution" to S & L problems did not reckon with the unbridled greed that was soon to take place with this greater freedom. It was particularly inviting for schemers and eager speculators in Texas. Previously, Texas regulations had limited lending power of S & Ls to the lesser of the purchase price or the appraised value of any project. But the new federal regulations overrode this requirement, permitting S & Ls to lend 100 percent of appraised value, even if the actual purchase price was much lower. And it was not difficult to find appraisers who would greatly inflate the value of property.

At this point, using federal deposit insurance the developers got low-rate debt to put into their housing and shopping center developments. If the projects were successful, fortunes were made. If unsuccessful, the Federal Home Loan Bank Board and the Federal Savings and Loan Insurance Corporation absorbed the loss. As Art Soter, a bank analyst at the Morgan Stanley

INFORMATION SIDELIGHT

WHAT SHOULD OUR MISSION BE?

As we noted in the earlier box, strategic planning should begin with an assessment of the company's current mission, and whether this fundamental mission should be changed in light of changing circumstances. Usually this involves deciding "What business should we now seek to be in?" A mission determination should involve the following factors:

1. Assessing the environment and how it is changing or is expected to change.
2. Appraising competitive factors and how these may be changing.
3. Weighing the particular strengths and weaknesses of the company—what it does best and where it has been deficient.

Mission statements can be too broad—for example, "to make a profit"—or too narrow, focusing on a particular product or service that may become obsolete as technology and customer requirements change. Narrow definitions restrict perspectives and the grasping of different opportunities, just as too broad a definition is useless as a guide for definitive action. An example of a definitive and useful mission statement of a manufacturer is the following:

> The mission is to serve the industry and government with quality instruments used for the primary measurement, analysis, and local control of fluid flow, level, pressure, temperature, and fluid properties. . . . Markets served include instrumentation for oil and gas production, gas transportation, chemical and petro-chemical processing, cryogenics, power generation, aerospace, Government and marine, as well as other instrument and equipment manufacturers.[8]

But a company's mission, whether formally stated, or merely in the top executive's mind, can be distorted to a reckless abandonment of former successful and durable practices. It can repudiate community best interest and trust, as we saw with Shamrock and with Sunbelt. Government deregulation in the early 1980s provided S & Ls with a vastly expanded arena for doing business. Far too many saw their mission now one of wild growth, unrestrained by cost considerations and risk potential.

investment banking firm noted: "What regulators failed to see is that the current system of deposit insurance increases the propensity to take risks."[9]

A further error of deregulation occurred: equity capital standards were lowered. For years, thrifts had to have capital equal to at least 6 percent of their deposits. Then as industrywide losses caused capital to deteriorate—in only 2 years, 1980–82, the value of capital in the industry fell from $32 bil-

---

[8] John A. Pearce II, "The Company Mission as a Strategic Tool," *Sloan Management Review,* Spring 1982, p. 17.

[9] Curran, p. 188.

lion to less than $21 billion—thrifts were allowed to expand by taking as many deposits as they could.

Soon, brokered deposits moved in. These are funds collected by stock-brokers and sent in large amounts to the highest-yielding thrifts. With this, there was nothing to slow the growth of the reckless S & L operators. Phenomenal growth was possible, as described in the following example:

> American Diversified Savings was a small thrift in a rural town, Lodi, California. In June 1983, it had $11 million in assets. In only 18 months its assets totaled $792 million, mostly from brokered deposits attracted by its high yielding certificates of deposit. The owner, Ranhir Sahni, a former commercial pilot, put the money into his favorite projects: geothermal plants, wind-driven electric generators, as well as a venture to supply local manure to a fertilizer business. In 1988, the government had to find $1.1 billion to pay off the depositors and liquidate the thrift.[10]

So the seeds for disaster were laid. Washington aggravated the problem and the potential for disaster by failing to hire adequate regulatory staff or replenish the reserves of the Bank Board or FSLIC. And all this time S & Ls in the Southwest continued to slide into bankruptcy.

THE GOVERNMENT BAILOUT

Thus we had a situation of thrifts with billions of dollars of losses, while governmental agencies responsible for them had not nearly the resources to bail out the insolvents. In August 1989, a costly bailout measure was enacted by Congress and signed by the President. Upward of $166 billion was expected to have to be spent to close or sell hundreds of insolvent S & Ls over the next decade.

An obvious solution was to attract would-be acquirers to take over the dead and dying thrifts and rejuvenate them. So Congress allowed acquirers to use the great bulk of the accumulated tax losses of the previous owners. Thereby, federal income and other taxes would be greatly reduced, while taxpayers absorbed the losses through a larger deficit, reduced government services, and new taxes. The Federal Home Loan Bank Board made the deal even better. Not only would it guarantee the losses on the nonperforming portfolios, but it also guaranteed the performing portfolios against losses. For example, should interest rates move adversely and lower the value of the performing assets (i.e., those assets still viable and paying interest), the Bank Board would make up the loss if the S & L later found itself illiquid.

[10] Ibid.

This was an El Dorado for acquirers. As *Barron's* noted:

> From the moment an acquirer signed the papers, he would be able to deduct already acquired losses of, say, $1 billion. Against a combined corporate tax rate of about 40%, he would be saving about $400 million in year one. For his out-of-pocket outlay of $50 million, he would have made a return of eight times.[11]

In December 1988, Robert Bass, a Texas billionaire, age 40, took over the crippled American Savings and Loan of Stockton, California. This represents perhaps the consummate gilt-edged deal to one of America's richest men.

American Savings was once the largest thrift in the United States, but it got into the same trouble as many others, with brokered deposits and high-risk loans. The Bank Board seized American in 1984, and installed fresh management. But the new team gambled and failed, and the Bank Board eventually granted exclusive bargaining rights to Bass.

In the deal, American Savings was split into two entities: a healthy S & L with $15.4 billion of good assets, and a "bad" one that will liquidate $14.4 billion in sour loans. For a total investment of only $500 million, the Bass Group got 70 percent ownership of the good thrift, a huge, healthy S & L with 186 branches. As another sure thing, more than half of this thrift's assets consist of a $7.8 billion loan to the "bad" S & L that is fully guaranteed by FSLIC to pay a handsome 2 percent more than the cost of the funds. Also as part of the deal, Bass is rewarded with some $300 million in tax benefits.

Taking all this into account, Bass stands to make $400 to $500 million in straight profits over the next four years, and this is roughly equal to his original investment of $500 million.[12]

WAS THE S & L ENVIRONMENT IN THE 1980s, IMPOSSIBLE FOR MANAGEMENT?

As we have seen, more than one third of the nation's S & Ls were either insolvent, or on the verge of insolvency by 1988. In 1987, the losses were so prodigious for 630 thrifts—$7.5 billion—that these were half again as much as the meager earnings of the other 2,500.

In such a catastrophic environment, can we find any success stories, any S & Ls that had effectively bucked the trend? And the answer is a resounding yes.

---

[11] Described in Benjamin J. Stein, "Steal of the Century?" *Barron's*. February 20, 1989, p. 7.

[12] Described in S.C. Gwynne, "Help Your Country and Help Yourself," *Time*, February 20, 1989, p. 72.

Suncoast Savings and Loan Association

Suncoast of Hollywood, Florida is one of the largest originators and servicers of mortgages in the Southeast. Its strategy has been to reduce the interest rate risk inherent in rate fluctuations. As we have seen before, many of the devastated S & Ls blamed their demise on rising interest rates in which the costs of funds increased while the return remained low because of long term mortgage commitments.

How did Suncoast reduce such risks? By the purchase and resale of mortgages complemented by its loan servicing capability. Suncoast and its subsidiaries purchase and originate mortgage loans for resale into the secondary market. In the process of reselling, however, Suncoast retains servicing rights on these mortgages, and these fees comprise a major part of its income. These two activities—purchase and resale of mortgages, and its loan servicing capability—are complementary. For example, in declining interest rates, mortgage lending increases as more people buy property during such favorable conditions. But when interest rates rise and loan volume decreases, loan servicing increases in importance as more borrowers hold on to their existing mortgages.

Suncoast gains further risk reduction by contracts in which major Wall Street investment banks purchase mortgage-backed securities on specific dates at agreed-on interest rates and discounts. While this conservative approach is costly, the risk protection from higher interest rates is deemed worth it. The conservative operating strategy has resulted in assets more than doubling between 1987 and 1988, while net income rose from 60 cents per share in fiscal 1987 to 98 cents a share one year later. $2.7 billion was serviced in mortgage loans by December 31, 1988, versus $1.1 billion a year earlier. And the return on equity was 14 percent in 1988.[13]

The Boston Bancorp

Management consciously decided not to pursue diversification into nontraditional activities. It reasoned that the historical focus on retail deposit accounts and home mortgages could be profitable if costs were kept low.

And this Boston Bancorp has done. It limited investment in "brick and mortar," having only four branches serving middle-income communities in metropolitan Boston. A long-established bank-by-mail program eliminated the need for an extensive branch system. Use of funds primarily was in single-family mortgages, commercial mortgages in apartment buildings, and high-quality government obligations and corporate stock—conservative and

---

[13] Robert Chaut, "The Well-managed Thrift: Five Success Stories," *The Bankers Magazine*, July-August 1989, pp. 35 and 38.

far from risky. With this approach, Boston Bancrop's return-on-equity has exceeded 18 percent, and it has grown to $1.4 billion in assets.[14]

Austerity has also paid off for other S & Ls—for example, TCF Banking and Savings. New management took over during the turbulent mid-1980s. The first thing to go was a luxurious suite of executive offices, as well as 35 of the association's top brass.[15]

USA Today, in a feature story, described a number of thrifts that bucked the trend, and were success stories during a time of turmoil in the industry. The common denominator for all of these was *careful growth*, dedicated commitment to pursuing home mortgages rather than commercial deals and brokeraged deposits, and a creativity in bettering customer service.[16]

INFORMATION SIDELIGHT

THE FINE ART OF DISCIPLINE IN PLANNING AND DECISION MAKING

Planning and decision making are vulnerable to abuses—abuses in overreaching, in not prudently assessing rewards versus risks in proposals, in operating beyond reasonable means, in simply not keeping a tight rein on costs. Such abuses are especially tempting in times of wild optimism, such as was occurring in the Southwest during the oil and land boom.

Discipline needs to be imposed when the inclination is to run amuk. Discipline implies controlled behavior, careful evaluation of actions and opportunities, not growing beyond resources and management capabilities. In the quest for the fine line between disciplined and undisciplined growth, the executive faces the dual risk of being too conservative or too aggressive. The first risk may present the decision maker with missed opportunities and permit competitors to gain an advantage; the second risk may jeopardize the viability of the company. In walking this thin line, the continued viability of the company should receive priority.

CONCLUSIONS

The S & L industry in the 1980s represents the greatest industry debacle since the Great Depression of the 1930s. The pervasiveness of the disaster engulfed hundreds of savings and loans, in all types of communities, from the very small rural, to the largest cities, from areas of depressed growth to

---

[14] Ibid.

[15] Harlan Byrne, "Practicing Thrift, Austerity Pays Off for a Midwestern S & L," *Barron's*, September 21, 1987, p. 15.

[16] David Elbert and Harriet Johnson Brackey, "Slow Growth Was the Key to Survival," *USA Today* February 15, 1989, pp. B1 and B2.

those of the greatest growth. The taxpayers' bill to salvage what can be salvaged will be in the hundreds of billions of dollars.

How could this have happened? Could it have been avoided? What if anything can we learn from all this that might be transferable to other situations and other times, that in effect may lessen the probability of such happenings occurring again?

Some have attributed the blame to external circumstances that S & L executives had no control over. They were simply victims, so these would lead us to believe. Government has received much of the blame. In its desire to help the industry during a time of high and increasing interest rates, it promoted a dangerous deregulation, permitting S & Ls wide latitude to invest their funds far beyond the traditional home mortgage lending, as well as relaxing equity restraints. No one could foresee either that a wild boom in oil prices and land values would so abruptly be pricked.

Yet, such "excuses" for the debacle rest on unsubstantial foundations. While hundreds of S & Ls failed, more hundreds maintained viability and even showed strength and growth. The common denominator of uncontrollable environmental factors does not hold the valid answer of who or what to blame and how disaster could have been avoided. Furthermore, it was the height of imprudence to expect boom conditions to be everlasting.

Where then lies the blame? As with most mistakes, management cannot escape primary responsibility. In this case, the fault lies with a management that violated the integrity of the planning function. The violation occurred in two respects: (1) injudicious failure to rein in expenses during a time when the profitable spread of traditional mortgage business was narrowing and (2) a wild spree to highly risky undertakings and investments once the constraints of governmental regulation were loosened. To this one must add a good dash of outright fraud, asset-stripping, corruption—white-collar crimes. (Of course, the inability of government inspectors to monitor closely enough permitted some of the worst excesses. But we are concerned here with management mistakes, *not* government mistakes.)

WHAT CAN BE LEARNED?

We can draw significant insights from the planning blunders of the sick and dying thrifts, and the comparison with the prospering ones.

Learning Insight. *Adversity creates opportunities.*

We are left with the growing recognition that adversity—in this case, a supposedly inhospitable environment—can also create opportunities for those who would adjust, adapt, and plan creatively in this environment, even embrace it with gusto—but without reckless abandon. The S & L situation created great opportunities for firms and individuals who had the resources and skill to "rescue" the troubled thrifts, with substantial government largess. And for the healthy competitors, new growth opportunities were also created, albeit the bad image of the failures cast all S & Ls in suspicious light.

Learning Insight. *The fallacy of aggressive and conservative extremes.*

Many of the failed thrifts were victims of their own aggressiveness, carried to the extreme of recklessness. If real estate prices and a building boom had continued into the foreseeable future in the high-growth areas of the South and West, then some of the reckless speculations would have brought above-average payoffs. Unfortunately, a wild house-of-cards philosophy eventually succumbs, with the whole structure collapsing. Excesses can only be tolerated so long in the normal course of events, as has been proven time and again over many centuries. The dangers of a speculative frenzy date back at least to 1634 in Holland, when individual tulip bulbs were bid up to fantastic prices in a wild but doomed speculation.

The extremes of conservatism have dangers, too. As we examine in the next learning insight, the environment is in flux; it is constantly changing. To stand pat, not to even take minor risks regardless of potential opportunities, not to make needed adjustments to a changing business clime—these can hardly be praised. The extreme example here is the buggy whip manufacturer unwilling to adapt to the new environment of horseless carriages. In the next chapter we see the problems of an unchanging Penney Company. We will see a number of times that ultraconservatism simply invites competitors to gain advantage.

In general, a middle ground between extreme aggressiveness and risk-taking, and ultraconservatism, usually will lead to the most durable success.

Learning Insight. *Any business firm faces a dynamic environment; nothing can be expected to remain constant. This requires some degree of adaptability.*

A useful perspective of reactions to a changing environment can be gained by considering a continuum of behavior to change such as:

Degree of Responsiveness to Environmental Change

Inflexible Unchanging	*Adaptive*	*Innovative*

Thus, a firm can be viewed as occupying a certain point along this continuum: the more conservative and rigid firm toward the left, the more progressive firm that is constantly developing new ideas, toward the right.

The two terms, adaptive and innovative, are somewhat different, although related. We will consider them as different degrees of responsive behavior on the same dimension. Innovative may be defined as originating significant changes, implying improvement. Adaptive implies a better coping with changing circumstances, but a response somewhat less significant than an innovative reaction.

In a sense, the failed thrifts were adaptive to a changed environment, that of greater deregulation. They adapted by forsaking any plans of judicious expansion in favor of a freewheeling strategy of high risks and opportunism. Then they found themselves unable to cope with the suddenly menacing environment of drastically falling real estate prices and a newly concerned regulatory climate.

Learning Insight. *Austerity wins out over high living.*

Nowhere is the contrast of high living and lack of cost constraints compared with relative austerity more evident than here. Reckless spending is a trap. Admittedly, when things are going well, when prospects seem boundless, the temptation is to open the floodgates of spending, both at the corporate level as well as for personal aggrandizement.

On the one hand, many of the failed thrifts were guilty of wild spending. Conspicuous examples of this were lavish entertainment, grand facilities, fleets of airplanes, even expensive art collections.[17]

On the other hand, we have examples of firms that owe their viability to their austerity. They kept themselves lean, controlled costs, and were able to survive and prosper and even be in position to take over their extravagant competitors.

Whereas some would argue that lavish spending created a public image of great success and prosperity, thus winning new business, a more sober appraisal would be one of foolish waste. Lack of cost restraints is incompatible with effective management, and should not be tolerated by shareholders or creditors.

Learning Insight. *A government "crutch" is a destructive delusion.*

The knowledge that depositors' accounts were insured up to $100,000 by the Federal Savings and Loan Insurance Corporation undoubtedly moti-

---

[17] For example, see Martha Brannigan and Alexandra Peers, "S & L's Art Collection, Ordered to be Sold, Faces Skeptical Market," *Wall Street Journal*, October 18, 1989, pp. 1, A12.

vated some of the reckless investments and other dealings of the failed thrifts. That the government would foot the cost of any speculations that turn sour, and bail out depositors, seemed a siren call for some executives. But those who felt entirely shielded by this governmental crutch were to learn to their dismay that while depositors were protected—at great cost to the government and taxpayers—they, the management, faced ouster and even the possibility of legal prosecution.

The shifting tides of politics, and the effects on legislation and regulation, bring a threat of being "blind sided" to those who rely overmuch on government support and protection. And the government has no great history of sound legislation: witness the S & L legislation of the early 1980s, designed to save the S & Ls, but in reality presenting temptation for doom that many found impossible to resist.

Learning Insight. *What is the responsibility of management?*

Managers are well paid. Isn't responsibility for protecting assets a condition for management? Even if these assets are somewhat protected by the government? Is there not also a responsibility to the enterprise, that it continue, and not be liquidated or merged into extinction? Are not managers custodians of shareholders' trust?

These are some of the troubling questions that arise when management has been completely oblivious to the greater good of the corporation and its shareholders (and depositors). Ancillary questions also arise: Can selfish greed be tolerated in managers who should have our trust and who can hardly afford to abdicate their responsibility? Can recklessness be tolerated? What should be the penalties for fraud?

USA Today opened a "hot line" for the public's responses to the S & L mess. Here is a sampling of responses.[18]

I don't see how they could have squandered this money and not get prosecuted.

When I mishandle my money, I have nobody to go bail me out. If [S & Ls] are incapable of handling the trust that was placed in them, maybe they should go belly-up.

The guilty parties to this fraud should be paying off these banks. If a guy owns a $2 million home, it should be auctioned off, and he should be put in jail.

[18] Denise Kalette, "Callers Want S & L Cheats Punished," *USA Today*, February 15, 1989, p. B1.

Every bank that approved big loans over $100,000, when they knew they were shaky, they should be made to pay them back, even if it causes executive hardship.

They've got to take responsibility for their actions. This makes Watergate look real simple compared to what they've done our country.

In this first case, then, we see management mistakes on a grand scale. Perhaps managers guilty of gross misconduct in connection with the public trust should face stronger penalties than simply ouster from a well-paying job, with most of their assets intact. What do you think?

FOR THOUGHT AND DISCUSSION

1. Would you recommend changing an S & L's mission of the early 1980s, with most government restraints relaxed? If so, what should the mission be changed to?
2. How would you respond to an S & L executive who carefully points out to you that if land and oil prices had not collapsed without warning his portfolio of high-interest loans would have brought great profitability to the firm?
3. "S & Ls no longer serve a useful purpose and they should be phased out." Evaluate this statement from the position of an executive in a solvent S & L.

INVITATION TO ROLE PLAY

You are the controller of a medium-size S & L in the mid-1980s. Your CEO is a flamboyant individual who has just announced his intention of building a new home office on a rather lavish scale. He claims this is necessary to convey the desired image of the firm. Develop a systematic analysis to disprove this recommendation.

CHAPTER 3

J. C. Penney Company—"The Old Ways Are Best"

In contrast to the rash opportunistic planning and frenzied speculation of certain segments of the savings and loan industry, here we have errors of ultraconservatism, of unbending reluctance to change the policies and practices that once had made an enterprise successful but now are outmoded. The J. C. Penney Company, for almost two decades, could not bring itself to rise from its rut of being primarily a cash-and-carry operation in small rural towns—at a time when the general public was demanding credit and one-stop shopping, and when the shift of population was to larger cities and suburbs. Finally, with the company struggling in the dust raised by its more progressive competitors, only a critical memo by a staff executive—who, in bypassing his superior, was putting his own career on the line—brought a realization of the urgent need to reevaluate 40-year-old policies and ways of doing business. But first, let us look at the successful start and early growth of the Penney Company.

THE BEGINNING

At sunrise on a spring morning in 1902, a young man, Jim Penney, opened a tiny dry goods store in Kemmerer, a frontier town in the southwest corner of Wyoming. He called the store the Golden Rule, remembering his father's admonition to deal with people according to the biblical injunction: "Therefore all things whatsoever ye would that men should do to ye, do ye even so to them."[1] The opening day was advertised by handbills distributed throughout the town. Penney remained open that day until midnight, and his sales were $466.59. After that he opened at 7 A.M. on weekdays and 8 A.M. on Sundays and remained open as long as there was a miner or sheepherder on the street. Sales for the first year were $28,898.11.[2]

Penney faced a tough competitor in Kemmerer. The town was dominated by a mining company, and a company-owned store had practically a local monopoly with most business done on credit or with the scrip issued by the mining company. Penney did not offer any credit, nor could he accept the scrip. What he did offer was values so much better that customers were willing to pay cash and carry home their purchases. He had no fancy fixtures—all the merchandise was piled on tables where customers could see and touch, and there was one price for all. Penney also had a returned-goods policy: if customers were not satisfied, they could return the purchase and get their money back.

Jim Penney had not always been successful in his business dealings. He was born on a farm in Missouri in 1875 into the big family of a poor Baptist minister. Upon graduating from high school, he worked as a clerk in a local dry goods store. His salary was $2.27 a month. But poor health forced him to resign and move West. Not wanting to work for someone else, he scraped up enough money to open a butcher shop in Longmont, Colorado. However, he soon lost this along with all his savings. His first venture into entrepreneurship had failed. The second venture was not to fail; the little store in the small mining town in Wyoming became the seed of the J. C. Penney Company.

THE SUCCESSFUL GROWTH YEARS

Penney was not content to run just one store. As the store in Kemmerer prospered, he thought of opening other stores. By 1905 he had two stores with total sales just under $100,000. In 1910, Penney changed his company's name from the Golden Rule to the J. C. Penney Company. By this time, the chain had grown to 26 stores in six western states. He kept to the same strategy that had worked well in Kemmerer. He tried to give his customers honest values, which usually meant the lowest possible prices; he stayed with a cash-only policy, and he had no fancy fixtures or high overhead expenses. Thus, he could offer low prices and still make money. Not the least of the success factors at this time was the environment Penney had chosen for his business. He confined his stores to small towns where the Penney managers

---

[1] Tom Mahoney and Leonard Sloane, *The Great Merchants* (New York: Harper & Row, 1966), p. 259.

[2] Ibid., p. 259.

could be well-known, friendly, and respectable members of the community. The lack of strong competition that would have been encountered in larger cities helped the burgeoning growth, a growth from one store to almost 1500 in only 30 years.

Something else, another uniquely Penney policy, was also necessary for such a growth rate to be achieved. Where could Penney possibly find the trained, competent, and honest managers to run the hundreds of stores that were being opened? And almost as important, where could he find the financial resources to open so many stores in such a short period of time and stock them with sufficient merchandise?

Jim Penney both financed and created the managerial resources needed by taking in "partner associates." As each store manager was able to accumulate enough capital out of his store's earnings, he could buy a one-third partnership in a new store, *if* he had trained one of his employees to the point where he could go out and effectively manage such a new store. Here then we have the great incentive to provide the resources needed by such a growing company: motivation by each store manager to find the best qualified employees and give them the best possible training. And profits would often be plowed back into the company to pay off partnership interests or to back new outlets.

By 1924 there were 570 stores and partners. Now, to get the outside financial help needed to sustain further growth, the partnerships were formed into a corporation under which the stores became company owned. The days of managers getting one-third shares of stores were over. And the complexion of the company now underwent a major change.

Up to this time, store operations had been highly individualized, with each manager making his own decisions within rather general policies. Such looseness of organization now gave way to more centralized policies and activities, a trend that was to continue in the decades to come. Operations were made more uniform, with strict budgeting systems, improved operational methods, store arrangements, merchandise, and promotions planned by experts and followed by all stores. Central buyers had more authority over managers as to what goods and prices they would carry. And store managers were now evaluated against other store managers as to their performance; promotions to better stores or to the home office went to the better producers. The Penney Company was beginning to shape itself into a unified and efficient organization. Growth continued, despite the depression of the 1930s, as shown in Table 3.1.

EMERGING PROBLEMS

Despite the substantial growth of the Penney Company and the firm entrenchment it had achieved in middle America, by the 1950s some ques-

Table 3.1   Growth of J. C. Penney Company by Stores and Sales

Year	Number of Stores	Sales (Dollars)
1902	1	28,898
1905	2	97,653
1912	34	2,050,641
1919	197	28,783,965
1926	747	115,957,865
1933	1,466	178,773,965
1940	1,586	302,539,325

Source: Norman Beasley, *Main Street Merchant* (New York: McGraw-Hill, 1948), p. 222.

tions were beginning to be raised about the theretofore successful policies. Did they need to be changed? Were they archaic for society at that time? Was the Penney Company vulnerable to competition as perhaps never before?

General merchandise firms were customarily compared with Sears. Sears was the benchmark, the model for efficient, progressive, large-scale enterprise. Montgomery Ward and Company found itself stacking up poorly against Sears due to a nonexpansion policy after World War II. And now the J. C. Penney Company, in looking at comparative sales statistics with Sears, found itself wanting.

Significant as Penney's achievement was in leading his company through difficult years of adolescence and rapid growth, the conservatism of his associates caused a long delay in the market adaptations needed for the two decades following World War II—credit, merchandise diversification, and catering to the urban market. Table 3.2 shows the growth of credit during this period, a period in which the Penney Company stuck resolutely with its cash-and-carry philosophy. Initially, such a policy had been compatible with the needs of a population dissatisfied with the lethargic inefficiencies of many independent stores and their high prices. But four decades later a reevaluation was sorely needed.

Table 3.2   Trend in Consumer Credit, 1940–1970 (Billions)

	1940	1950	1955	1960	1965	1970
Installment: Consumer goods, other than automobiles	$1.8	$4.8	$7.6	$11.5	$18.5	$31.5
Noninstallment charge accounts	1.5	3.4	4.8	5.3	6.4	8.0
Ratio of total consumer credit to disposable personal income	10.9%	10.4%	14.1%	16.0%	19.0%	18.4%

Diversification of merchandise lines was also long delayed. J. C. Penney remained only a dry goods and clothing operation until the 1960s. Appliances, furniture and carpeting, sporting goods, auto supplies—merchandise categories long carried by other general-merchandise chains such as Sears and Ward's and by department stores—were ignored by Penney. Finally, most of the Penney stores were in the more sparsely settled smaller communities west of the Mississippi. The populous and growing East and burgeoning metropolitan areas were not Penney's domain.

A reassessment of policies was needed, indeed was long overdue. Although the viability of the firm was not yet in jeopardy, its stature as a competitive entity in the mainstream of American retailing was. But how difficult it seemed to be to combat ingrained resistance to change.

The Batten Memo

In 1957, despairing of top management's willingness to change, the assistant to the president of Penney, William M. Batten, wrote a memo to the board of directors that was to have far-reaching consequences.

It was probably one of the most influential and widely publicized memos in modern corporate history. And it clearly violated the sacrosanct management principle of *chain of command* (described in the Information Sidelight). Batten had started with the company as an extra salesman 26 years before, and had come a long way. Now he was ready to stake everything on what he saw was a desperate need to change. His memo criticized the conservatism of the company for not reacting to a changing America.

In the 1950s, population growth was centering in the metropolitan areas. Income per capita was rising, and consumer buying power was being attracted toward "want" rather than "need" type of merchandise. Fashion was consequently becoming more important, and J. C. Penney was extremely weak here. The memo bluntly stated that the world in which the Penney Company had prospered was fast disappearing and that, if Penney hoped to survive, it would have to change.

Batten suggested conducting a Merchandising Character Study to define the kinds of stores that should be operated. He suggested the study should concern three basic areas:

1. To assess Penney's immediate position in merchandising compared with chief competitors such as Sears and Ward's
2. To forecast market opportunities by examining changes in population and trends in shopping, work, and leisure
3. To spell out desired changes in goods and services and voids in the marketplace that required filling

---

INFORMATION SIDELIGHT

A RECOGNIZED MANAGEMENT PRINCIPLE: AVOID BYPASSING AND FOLLOW THE CHAIN OF COMMAND

Bypassing occurs when a subordinate goes over the head of his or her immediate supervisor to appeal a decision or request a directive from a higher authority. Sometimes the bypassing occurs in the other direction as, for example, if the vice president of sales deals directly with a sales representative instead of going through the field supervisor. Invariably the employee will give preference to the instructions of the senior executive, and the authority and influence of the immediate supervisor will be undermined.

While bypassing in general should be condemned and the chain of command (or line of authority) adhered to in communications and directives, this does not mean that all direct contacts between higher executives and employees in the lower ranks should be condemned. But, except for emergencies, they should usually be limited only to occasional contacts aimed at building morale or obtaining firsthand information. The other exception is in a grievance procedure in which the employee has a complaint that cannot satisfactorily be resolved with the supervisor. Industrial psychologists here would condone a free and open right of appeal, even though this smacks of bypassing.

The action of Batten in going over the head of his boss violated the integrity of the chain-of-command relationship, although he might claim the situation was an emergency and warranted such action.

After two years, in 1959, the Merchandising Character Study was completed. The conclusions were that Penney was selling only soft goods and limited home furnishings, and that most of the advertising appeals were to women. It was decided that Penney needed to pull in the entire family in areas having the greatest population growth. As one vice president commented in regard to the preponderance of apparel and home furnishings:

> We had no browsing areas for men while their wives shopped, like paint and hardware departments. We had nothing to attract the kids, like a toy department. We realized we needed to tend more toward the one-stop shopping idea.[3]

The year following his audacious memo, Batten was made president of Penney with the mandate to implement the changes necessary. The question was whether it was now too late to catch up with its competitors, to regain the ground lost during the years of conservative and unchanging policies.

---

[3] Alfred Law, "From Overalls to Fashion Wear," *Wall Street Journal*, October 22, 1964, p. 1.

The problems were at last defined and known to all. But could they be over-come, and quickly?

AT LAST, CHANGE

In September 1958, J. C. Penney began testing the feasibility of offering *credit.* At first, only 24 stores were the object of this experiment. More than 3 years were required for Penney to establish its credit operation chainwide. But at least the necessity of credit to keep up with changing times, and to do well with the big-ticket items such as television and washing machines, was realized.

Coming late into the consumer credit field, however, afforded the Penney Company certain advantages. An almost completely computerized system was designed, in contrast to other retailers who had started with manual systems and then were forced to computerize at an enormous cost. In order to operate its credit system manually, 37 centers would be needed to serve all the stores. However, with the use of the advanced IBM computers, only 14 regional credit offices had to be set up. At the time of Penney's installation, Sears was the only other retailer who could allow customers to shop in any store across the country and receive one bill.

By 1962, all stores offered credit. By 1964, the results were notable: 28 percent of Penney's sales volume was done on credit. Revenues in 1964 amounted to $600 million from more than 5 million active accounts. By 1966, credit sales were responsible for 35 percent of all sales; by 1973, credit sales were over 38 percent of total sales. By 1967, J. C. Penney had 12 million charge accounts, twice the number of Diners Club and American Express combined.

As intended, the establishment of credit led the way for Penney to diversify its merchandise mix. It began to follow Sears into carrying hard goods (appliances, furniture, and the like) along with its soft goods. For many years J. C. Penney had been the nation's largest seller of women's hosiery, sheets and blankets, coats and dresses, work clothes, and men's underwear. Prior to 1960, soft goods averaged 95 percent of total sales. Admittedly, soft goods, to some extent, had shielded Penney from the ups and downs in the economy, because soft goods normally are the last thing people cut down on during hard times; appliances and furniture, on the other hand, can usually be postponed or deferred until times look better. But such soft goods typically afford a low markup, and profitability rests on high turnover and sales volume. There is also a limit to how much soft goods the market can absorb, and certainly sales and profit potential is ultimately limited without diversification beyond soft goods.

First attempts at merchandise diversification came as J. C. Penney moved into higher-priced women's dresses, leather goods, and furniture. Merchan-

INFORMATION SIDELIGHT

IMPORTANCE OF CREDIT

As an extreme example of the importance of credit in enhancing consumer demand and consequent purchasing, consider the Superior, Wisconsin Penney store in 1959, one of the early stores experimenting with credit. Superior, an iron-ore shipping port at the far western end of Lake Superior, experienced wide fluctuations in business and income due to weather, strikes, and economic slowdowns. Sales at this Penney store had remained static for over 3 years. The first year that credit was offered, sales increased over 30 percent.

Admittedly, the Superior example is not a typical Penney store. The need for credit by people with irregular incomes is the greater. In place of credit, Penney had always offered the "layaway plan." Here a store held the selected goods for a customer until they were completely paid for—often by small weekly or biweekly payments— and only then released them to the customer. This plan was heavily pushed by Penney for expensive items and for merchandise sold in advance of the season. But increasingly, customers did not want deferred gratification of their wants. Not if some other store was giving credit, thereby permitting them to have the immediate pleasure of a desired product.

dise assortment was widened by adding designer dresses and youth-minded sportswear for both men and women. By 1962, Penney began to add hard goods, with the new merchandise appearing in new or enlarged stores, and to a lesser extent in other stores where space could be found. In 1963 Penney opened it first full-line department store having such new departments for Penney as appliances, televisions, sporting goods, paint, hardware, tires, batteries, and auto accessories. The new stores subsequently allocated about 25 to 30 percent of total floor space to these new lines of hard goods.

By 1965, Penney had 173 stores with radio-TV departments, 103 with major appliances, 67 with sporting goods, 58 carrying paint and hardware, and 42 centers handling tires, batteries, and auto accessories. Diversification had begun in earnest.

Penney also sought to offer hard goods in stores that were too small to stock such goods. General Merchandise Company, a small but highly automated mail- order company, was acquired in 1962. Catalog centers were then set up in many stores as a means of offering customers a much wider variety of goods. In 1971, catalog sales moved into the black, and Penney's at last had the means to compete on equal terms with the long-established businesses of Sears and Ward's.

Replacement of older, smaller soft-line stores averaging from 30,000 to 40,000 sq ft with new full-line units was also proceeding in earnest. These new stores ranged in size from 43,000 to 220,000 sq ft. averaging 165,000.

Other diversifications into discount stores (Treasure Island stores), drug stores (Thrift Drug), and supermarkets proceeded. Overseas expansion was also occurring with a controlling interest in a major Belgian retailing firm, Sarma, S.A., obtained in 1968, while in 1971 Penney entered the Italian market.

The conservative policies had been abandoned and replaced with a vigorous growth orientation. But could the sales and profits that were lost ever be completely retrieved? Perhaps the most important question was: Could the ground lost to Sears in the decade and a half of outmoded policies ever be regained?

A MISTAKE RECTIFIED

By the late 1960s and into the 1970s J. C. Penney was at times almost matching the expansion effort of Sears, a firm more than twice as large. Table 3.3 shows the capital expenditures for Sears and J. C. Penney during those years, as well as the percentage of these expenditures to sales. You can see from this table the much greater percentage of sales commitment of Penney to expansion. But has Penney been able to make up the lost ground?

Table 3.3   Capital Expenditures of Sears and Penney, 1968–1973

	Sears		Penney	
Year Ending January	Capital Expenditures (000,000)	Percentage of Sales	Capital Expenditures (000,000)	Percentage of Sales
1968	$186	2.5	$111	4.0
1969	139	1.8	127	3.8
1970	211	2.4	139	3.7
1971	259	2.8	204	4.9
1972	339	3.1	185	3.8
1973	392	3.2	210	3.4

Source: Adapted from Moody's Industrials, and respective annual reports.

Table 3.4 shows the sales volume since 1940 of Penney compared with Sears. It also shows the market share of Penney relative to Sears, that is, the percentage of Penney's sales to total Sears and Penney sales. Figure 3.1 shows the market share of Penney more graphically, as well as the trends during the long period of 1940 to 1974.

You can see from these charts that the sharp upward trend in market share (or sales relative to those of Sears) in the early and mid-1940s was reversed in the late 1940s. Penney's market share then eroded badly, reflect-

Table 3.4   Relative Sales Volumes, Penney and Sears, 1940–1974

Year	Penney (000)	Sears (000)	Market Share (Sales as a Percentage of Total Penney and Sears Sales) Penney	Sears
1942	$ 490,295	$ 915,058	35	65
1944	535,363	851,535	38	62
1946	676,570	1,045,259	39	61
1948	885,195	1,981,536	32	68
1950	949,712	2,168,928	31	69
1952	1,079,257	2,932,338	28	72
1954	1,107,157	2,981,925	27	73
1956	1,290,867	3,306,826	28	72
1958	1,409,973	3,600,882	28	72
1960	1,437,489	4,036,153	26	74
1962	1,553,503	4,267,678	27	73
1964	1,834,318	5,115,767	26	74
1966	2,289,209	6,390,000	26	74
1968	2,745,998	7,330,090	27	73
1970	3,756,092	8,862,971	30	70
1972	4,812,239	10,006,146	32	67
1974	6,243,677	12,306,229	33	67

Source: Adapted from respective annual reports.

Market share of Penney compared to Sears (i.e., Penney sales as a percentage of total Sears and Penney's sales)

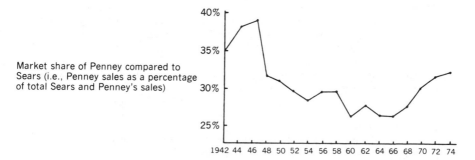

Figure 3.1

ing the outmoded policies of Penney. Not until 1970 was Penney able to improve its market share and begin a new favorable upward trend. Even though the actions in the 1960s improved the situation, the results are still far below the trend established earlier and the market share previously attained.

The recent growth efforts of Penney can hardly be faulted or even improved upon. The fact remains, however, that unless major competitors also stumble, a substantial lead built up by one firm due to less aggressive or more error-prone efforts of another firm, is not likely to be caught.

HOW COME THE LAPSE OF 1945–1958?

It is one of the anomalies of human endeavor that individuals of great accomplishment and innovativeness can be both visionary and short-sighted, inspired and blind. Henry Ford is perhaps the foremost example of such strengths and weaknesses: originating mass production of the automobile, but steadfastly refusing to budge from his original idea of a black Model T.

Jim Penney and his company fell into a similar myopia of resistance to changing times. The policies that worked so well in the early years of the Penney Company became outmoded. Still, the temptation is to stick with the historically successful and proven. There is difficulty in breaking from accepted ways of doing things.

Partly accounting for the resistance to change of the Penney Company was the leadership. For the most part, top Penney executives fought their way up through the ranks; the leadership was composed of Penney's associates who had been involved in the company's early growth. For example:

Earl Sams worked first as James Penney's clerk in Kemmerer, then managed a store for him, and in 1917 became president of the company, serving from 1917 to 1946, whereupon he became board chairman.

The successor of Sams, Albert Hughes, tutored Penney's sons in Latin but, deciding that retailing would be more exciting, started in the Penney store in Moberly, Missouri, and later managed stores in Utah and Georgia. He was named president in 1946 and served until he stepped aside for Batten (of the famous memo) in 1958.

Even William Batten, the changemaker, was thoroughly imbued with the traditional Penney philosophy. He first worked for Penney in 1926 while attending high school, and joined the company full time in 1935 as shoe salesman.

After Batten moved up to chairman in 1964, Ray Jordan became president, culminating a Penney career which began in the small town of Picher, Oklahoma, in 1930.

The Penney Company can boast of its firm policy of promotion from within, and proudly point out examples of this in the ranks of its top executives. But we might ponder whether such a policy can be carried too far. The absence of new blood can be a negative influence. Although trainees may be inspired as to their opportunities and potential attainment, policies tend to become self-perpetuating and innovation stymied without the presence of fresh ideas or even disruptive influences from outsiders.

WHAT CAN BE LEARNED?

Learning Insight. *Alertness to major changes in the environment does not require a major research commitment.*

If a firm is to gird itself for change, it must first recognize and evaluate exogenous trends, that is, those outside the firm. A research department or a long-range planning staff may help here in monitoring the environment and supplying information about changes to those executives who need to know. But most major changes in the environment should be obvious to all, simply by being alert to what is taking place in the industry and the economy. For example, data about the burgeoning popularity of credit were readily available from government statistics and industry data for many years before Penney hesitantly began to act. Similarly, the movement of people from rural areas to cities and the ever-increasing stores in suburban shopping centers were nothing arcane or mysterious, but evident to all.

Sometimes persons in responsible positions can see, but not perceive: they are blinded by their accustomed ways of doing things—until something shocks them, as Batten's memo did, or as severely deteriorating operating results finally may. Alertness to the environment, a willingness to change, and, occasionally, even a willingness to initiate changes·where the situation seems ripe—these are the attributes of the successful and aggressive firm. (The Information Sidelight box provides more discussion on *environmental scanning*, that is, being alert to what is happening outside the firm that may affect it for good or ill.)

INFORMATION SIDELIGHT

ENVIRONMENTAL SCANNING

Here we have the final step of the strategic planning process described in the "Information Sidelight" in Chapter 2: assessing environmental changes in light of opportunities and possible emerging problems.

Environmental scanning essentially is a systematic effort to monitor changes in the external environment that may affect the company and should influence its strategic planning. It stands to reason that a firm should keep itself alert to changes in customer preferences and needs, changes in competition, changes in the economy, and even changes in international aspects, such as opportunities in Europe, Japanese potential inroads in productivity and quality control, and the ever-lurking OPEC petroleum machinations.

How can a firm keep itself alert to subtle, insidious, as well as the more obvious changes? I like to use the term "sensors" here: a firm should have sensors monitoring the environment. Such sensors may be a marketing or economic research department. But such a formal organizational entity is not really necessary to provide primary monitoring. Executive alertness can be a vital part. Most changes do not occur suddenly and without warning—one exception has been the OPEC dictation regarding oil prices (and this is a looming threat in the 1990s), but even these could have had the worse scenarios appraised. By listening to feedback from customers, from sales representatives, from suppliers; by keeping abreast of the latest information and projections in business journals; and even by simple observation of what is happening in stores, in advertising, with prices, and with the introduction of new technologies, information about the environment and how it is changing should be readily available.

Environmental scanning can be organized and formal, or strictly informal and subjective. But it is disturbing that many executives overlook, disregard, or are not even aware of important changing environmental factors that threaten to affect their present and future business. The Penney executives were guilty of this myopia in the 1940s and 1950s. But they were not alone. Adidas had a serious lapse in the 1970s. In the 1980s, Nestle ignored environmental factors to its peril. And as discussed later in this section, Joel Hyatt parlayed a great untapped opportunity in the legal environment.

Learning Insight. *Major reliance on inbreeding or promotion from within perpetuates tradition at the expense of alertness to change.*

The Penney example suggests the need for fresh blood in an organization. Total reliance on inbreeding and promotion from within tends to foster a narrow and parochial perspective. The traditional way of doing things usually prevails in such a corporate environment. (The fact that Batten, in moving up through the ranks, was able to point his finger at the flaws and emerging dangers in such an eminent tradition reflects all the more on his strengths. But then he was the exception.) Added to the lack of alertness to a changing environment is great *resistance to change* (as the following Information Sidelight discusses).

We are not suggesting here that the opposite course of action—that is, heavy commitment to filling important executive positions with outsiders —is to be advocated. This approach plays havoc with morale of trainees and lower-level executives. Rather, a middle ground usually is preferable: filling many executive positions from within the organization, promoting this idea to encourage both the achievement of present executives and the recruiting of trainees, and at the same time bringing strong outsiders into the organization where their strengths and experiences can be most valuable. Moderation is more desirable than major reliance either on promotion from within or without.

INFORMATION SIDELIGHT

RESISTANCE TO CHANGE

People as well as organizations have a natural reluctance to embrace change. Change is disruptive. It can destroy accepted ways of doing things and familiar authority-responsibility relationships. It makes people uneasy, because their routines will likely be disrupted; their interpersonal relationships with subordinates, co-workers, and superiors may well be modified. Positions that were deemed important before the change may be downgraded. And persons who view themselves as highly competent in a particular job may be forced to assume unfamiliar duties amid the fear that these cannot be handled as well.

Resistance to change can be combatted by good communication with participants about forthcoming changes. Without such communication, rumors and fears can assume monumental proportions. Acceptance of change can be facilitated if employees are involved as fully as possible in planning the changes, if their participation is solicited and welcomed, and if assurance can be given that positions will not be impaired, only changed. Gradual rather than abrupt changes also make a transition smoother as participants can be initially exposed to the changes without drastic upheavals.

In the final analysis, however, needed changes should not be delayed or canceled because of their possible negative repercussions on the organization. If change is necessary, it should be initiated. Individuals and organizations can adapt to change—it just takes a bit of time.

Learning Insight. *Innovative thinking can be fostered in an organization; however, this requires top management support and encouragement.*

The lack of innovativeness of the Penney Company in the 1940s and 1950s reflects a need in many organizations to foster innovative thinking among employees and executives. In addition to fresh blood, top-management support and encouragement is needed. A willingness to change is important, because if ideas are never acted on, the creative instincts of an organization soon atrophy.

Fostering innovation can take many forms. One way is to expose personnel to fresh thinking, perhaps through some mix of sharp new people and seminars and institutes where there is exposure to people from other organizations and experiences. Stimulating creativity can also come from quickly recognizing and rewarding creative individuals.

Update

As Penney moved into the 1980s, it had 552 full-line department stores, 1130 smaller units devoted to soft goods (apparel and piece goods), a $1.54 billion catalog business, 361 Thrift drugstores, an insurance business generating $42 million, and a Brussels-based chain of 76 food and general merchandise stores under the Sarma name. It had phased out 37 discount units under the Treasure Island name at the end of 1980. In 1977, it had disposed of several other operations that were not performing satisfactorily profit-wise, including its Italian retail stores and the supermarket operation.

By 1981, emphasis turned to expanding the full-line department stores and upgrading the fashion image of the company. Although this greater commitment to fashion was a costly and lengthy strategy change, it seemed to be paying off for Penney by the end of the decade. Sales and profits for 1989 for the largest nonfood retailers were:

	1989 Sales ($ millions)	1989 Net Profits ($ millions)
Sears[a]	53,181	1,024
K mart	28,447	736
Wal-Mart	24,335	973
Penney	15,678	870

[a] Sales and profits for Sears include all operations, not just retail operations.
Source: "Annual Report on American Industry," *Forbes*, January 8, 1990, pp. 192, 196.

In the decade of the 1980s, Sears was faltering in its retail operation, despite the robust revenues that were mainly attributable to its strength in financial service operations, particularly its Allstate insurance business. During 1989, sales at Sears slipped below that of the previous year and earnings shrunk, with the result that long-term debt ratings were downgraded.[4] During the decade of the 1980s, Wal-Mart was the big success story, brushing past K mart in earnings, while nearly approaching it in sales. And the competitive jockeying continues.

FOR THOUGHT AND DISCUSSION

1. Can you think of other less drastic incentives for store managers to develop managers than that practiced by Penney Company in its early years of growth?
2. How might a good business research department have alerted Penney top management to the need for credit and merchandise diversification? Could such alerting have been accomplished without formal research?
3. Do you think the growth of the Penney Company in the last several decades could have been accomplished any quicker? If so, how?

INVITATION TO ROLE PLAY

1. Place yourself in the position of Batten in 1957. Would you have taken the risk of sending a highly critical memo to the board of directors? What do you think would be the consequences of such a memo in some firms?
2. You have been assigned the responsibility of setting up the diversification into appliances, furniture, sporting goods, hardware, and other hard-line departments new to Penney. Be as specific as you can as to how you would go about doing this. How would you go about upgrading the fashion image?

[4] Francine Schwadel, "Duff & Phelps Cuts Ratings on Sears Debt," *Wall Street Journal*, December 28, 1989, p. C11.

4

Contrasts of the Running Boom: Adidas and Nike

Adidas had been the innovator in its industry, running shoes, and later, in ancillary apparel and athletic equipment. It had set the standards that subsequently were followed by almost all its competitors.

Somehow, the innovator and standard-bearer allowed itself to be overtaken and passed by upstart foreign firms—this time U.S. firms, of whom the most notable was Nike—in its biggest and most rapidly growing market. And the wonder is that these interlopers did nothing distinctive or innovative. They simply followed the tried and tested strategy of the old master.

How could this be?

PART A   ADIDAS—OPENING THE DOOR FOR COMPETITORS

It is the early 1970s. Adidas dominates the running-shoe industry. It has done so for decades. Now it stands on the threshold of one of the biggest surges of popularity that any recreational pursuit has ever known. Tens of millions of people will take up running or jogging in the next few years; other millions of nonrunners will be buying running shoes because they are comfortable, and because they convey an aura of fitness and youth—an image most people are eager to emulate.

Does Adidas cash in on this recreational boom of the century? In one of the classic errors of miscalculation and conservative planning, Adidas underestimates the U.S. market. Even worse, it underestimates the aggressiveness of U.S. competitors. Most of these competitors are upstart firms that had not even been around at the beginning of the decade. In just a few years, Adidas will be pushed aside by one of the nation's fastest-growing firms, Nike.

HISTORICAL BACKGROUND

Rudolf and Adolf Dassler began making shoes in Herzogenaurach, in what is now West Germany, shortly after World War I. Adolf, known as Adi to his family, was the innovator, and Rudolf was the seller of his brother's creations. The brothers achieved only moderate success first, but then, in 1936, a big breakthrough came. Jesse Owens agreed to wear their shoes in the Olympics and won his gold medals in front of Hitler, the German nation, and the world. The lucrative association of shoes with a famous athlete was to trigger a marketing strategy that Adidas—and other athletic shoe manufacturers— was to practice from that point on.

In 1949, the brothers had a falling out and, indeed, never again spoke to each other outside of court. Rudolf took half the equipment and left his brother to go to the other side of town and set up the Puma Company. Adolf established the Adidas Company from the existing firm ("Adidas" was derived from his nickname and the first three letters of his surname). Rudolf and his Pumas never quite caught up with Adolf's Adidas, but they did become number two in the world.

Adolf was constantly experimenting with new materials and techniques to develop stronger, yet lighter shoes. He tested thorny sharkskin in attempts to develop abrasive leather for indoor flats. He tried kangaroo leather to toughen the sides of shoes.

The first samples of Adidas footwear were shown at the Helsinki Olympic Games of 1952. Then, in 1954, the German soccer team, equipped with Adidas footwear, won the World Cup over Hungary. The shoes were definitely a factor in the win, as Dassler had developed a special stud to screw into the shoes that allowed good footing on the muddy playing field that day; Hungary's shoes did not give the same traction.

Dassler's many innovations in the running-shoe industry included four-spiked running shoes, track shoes with a nylon sole, and injected spikes. He developed a shoe that allowed an athlete to choose from 30 different variations of interchangeable spike elements that could be adapted to an indoor or outdoor track as well as to natural or artificial surfaces.

With its great variety of superior products, Adidas dominated in the widely publicized international showcase events. For example, at the Mon-

treal games, Adidas-equipped athletes accounted for 82.8 percent of all individual medal winners.[1] This was tremendous publicity for the company, and
sales rose to $1 billion worldwide.

But competitors were emerging. Prior to 1972, Adidas and Puma had
practically the entire athletic shoe market to themselves. Although this was
changing, Adidas seemingly had built up an insurmountable lead, providing footwear for virtually every type of sporting activity as well as diversifying into other sports-related product lines: shorts, jerseys, leisure suits, and
track suits; tennis and swimwear; balls for every kind of sport; tennis rac-
quets and cross-country skis; and the popular sports bag that carried the
Adidas name as a prominently displayed status symbol.

STRATEGIC PLANNING

The strategic planning originated by the Dassler brothers became the guiding influence for the entire industry. The Dasslers had long used international athletic competition as a testing ground for their products. Many years
of feedback from these athletes led to continual design changes and improvements. Agreements were entered into with professional athletes to use their
products. However, Adidas's strength was in international and Olympic
events in which the participants were amateurs, and such endorsement contracts were more often made with national sports associations rather than
with individuals.

Following the lead of Adidas and Puma, endorsement contracts with
athletes have become commonplace. For example, every player in the
National Basketball Association is under contract to at least one manufacturer. The going rate for an endorsement contract today ranges from $500 to
$150,000. The athlete must wear a certain brand and appear in various pro-
motional activities. It has become an industry practice to spend about 80 percent of the advertising budget for endorsements and 20 percent for media
advertising. The distinctive logos that all manufacturers have developed are
key to the effectiveness of these endorsement contracts. Such logos permit
immediate identification of product; fans and potential customers can see the
product actually in use by the famous athlete. These logos also permit effective product diversification into apparel, bags, and so on.

To increase volume quickly, production facilities were sought where
shoes could be made cheaply and in great quantities, in areas such as Yugoslavia and the Far East. Medium-size firms in such countries were therefore
signed up as licensees and goods were produced to specifications. Great out-
lays for plants and equipment were thus avoided and costs could be kept low.

---

[1] Norris Willett, "How Adidas Ran Faster." *Management Today,* December 1979, p. 58.

Finally, Adidas led the running-shoe industry into offering a very wide variety of shoe styles—shoes to fit all kinds of running activities, from various kinds of races to training shoes. Shoes were also offered for every type of runner and running style. The great variety of offerings, more than a hundred different styles and models for Adidas, was to be exceeded only by Nike as it charged to capture the U.S. market.

THE 1970s RUNNING MARKET

During the late 1960s and early 1970s, the environment affecting the running-shoe industry changed dramatically and positively. Americans were increasingly concerned with physical fitness. Millions of previously unathletic people were searching for ways to exercise. The spark that ignited the booming interest may have been the 1972 Munich Olympics. Millions of television viewers watched Dave Wottle defeat Russian Evgeni Arzanov in the 800-meters and Frank Shorter win the prestigious marathon. But the groundwork for the running boom had been laid before. The idea of fitness perhaps first came to the attention of the general public in a trailblazing book by Dr. Kenneth Cooper, *Aerobics*, which sold millions of copies and gave scientific evidence of the physical benefits of a running (or jogging) regimen. A little less than 10 years later, another book with monumental impact, *The Complete Book of Running* by James Fixx, also sold millions of copies and was on the bestseller list for months.

Through the decade of the 1970s, the number of joggers increased. Estimates by the end of the decade were that 25 to 30 million Americans were joggers, while another 10 million wore running shoes around home and town.[2] The number of shoe manufacturers also increased. The original three of Adidas, Puma, and Tiger were joined by new U.S. brands: Nike, Brooks, New Balance, Etonic, and even J. C. Penney, Sears, and Converse. To sell and distribute these new shoes, specialty shoe stores such as Athlete's Foot, Athletic Attic, and Kinney's Foot Lockers sprouted up nationwide. New magazines catering to this market were starting up and showing big increases in circulation: for example, *Runner's World*, *The Runner*, and *Running Times*. These magazines provided the advertising media no wasted coverage in reaching runners.

The Loss of Dominance

In the midst of the great running boom, Adidas coasted on its past laurels. The new U.S. brands, and particularly Nike, were quick to capitalize on the diminishing aggressiveness of Adidas. Yet this was a time when foreign

---

[2] "The Jogging Shoe Race Heats Up," *Business Week*, April 9, 1978, p. 125.

products of all kinds were eagerly sought by American consumers, while American-made goods were often viewed as inferior in quality, dependability, and style and produced by a high-priced, not-too-dedicated labor force.

Table 4.1 shows the competitive positions of the top brands in the U.S. market at the beginning of 1979, with the running boom still in its ascendancy. By now, the formerly absolutely dominant Adidas had fallen far behind Nike, and was struggling to stay ahead of Brooks and New Balance. Two years later, Nike had 50 percent of the total market.

Table 4.1   U.S. Running-Shoe Competitive Positions, 1978

	Percentage of Total U.S. Market
Nike	33%
Adidas	20
Brooks	11
New Balance	10
Converse	5
Puma	5

Sources: Compiled from various published materials, including "The Jogging Shoe Race Heats Up," *Business Week*, April 9, 1978, p. 125.

Adidas's Mistakes—What Went Wrong?

Adolph Dassler died in 1978. Perhaps this was a factor in Adidas's waning aggressiveness, although the management transition after his death appeared to have gone smoothly. And actually, Nike had made its big inroads by this time. So we have to seek further to find an explanation for why a front-runner stumbled and gave the lead to someone coming from far back in the pack.

Undoubtedly, Adidas underestimated the growth of the market for running shoes. For a firm that had been in this business for four decades and had always seen the stability of slow growth during these years, a skepticism about the extent and duration of the "boom" would seem most reasonable. And Adidas was not alone in misjudging the potential and the opportunity. Some of the U.S. firms that were traditionally strong in the lower-priced athletic shoe industry, notably Converse and Uniroyal's Keds, were caught flatfooted in the race to bring new and technologically improved models to the market. These major producers of tennis shoes and sneakers (Converse made two-thirds of U.S. basketball shoes) also vastly underestimated the potential and did not direct strong efforts until they were completely outclassed by Nike and several other newer U.S. manufacturers.

In gearing an operation for rapid growth, sales forecasting becomes a vital element of the planning and preparation for dealing with the opportunity at hand. All aspects of a firm's operation are necessarily based on the sales estimates for the coming period(s): for example, production planning and facilities, inventories, and sales staff and advertising efforts. But when sales are reaching uncharted territory, the firm faces the dilemma of *optimistic versus conservative sales projections* (as the following Information Sidelight discusses).

It seems evident that Adidas, in addition to underestimating the market, also underestimated the aggressiveness of Nike and the other U.S. manufacturers. Perhaps, being the leader with seemingly an unassailable position, this was a natural consequence. After all, foreign brands in many product lines commanded a mystique and attraction that no domestic brands could. And then, how could small U.S. manufacturers, starting practically from scratch, pose any serious threat to the more than three decades of seasoned experience of Adidas? So, the perception that U.S. firms were mere weak opportunists seemed not unreasonable.

But we know that U.S. manufacturers were not weak opportunists striving for a stray bone. Nike, among others, saw an opportunity, seized it, and charged. Perhaps this happening is less a reflection of Adidas's deficiencies

INFORMATION SIDELIGHT

OPTIMISTIC VERSUS CONSERVATIVE SALES PLANNING—CONSEQUENCES OF INACCURATE SALES FORECASTS

The sales forecast—the estimate of sales for the period(s) ahead—serves a crucial role, because it is the starting point for all planning and budgeting. When the situation is volatile and rapidly growing, this presents some high-risk alternatives: Should we be optimistic or conservative?

On the one hand, if the planning is conservative, the danger that the firm faces when its market begins to boom is that it cannot keep up with demand and cannot expand its resources sufficiently to handle the potential. It simply does not have enough manufacturing capability and sales staff. The results invariably is to abdicate perhaps a good share of this growing business to competitors who are willing and able to match their capability and strategic planning efforts to the demands of the market.

On the other hand, for a firm facing burgeoning demand, the judgment should be made whether this is likely to be a short-term fad or a more permanent situation. You can see how easily a firm can permit itself to become overextended in the buoyancy of booming business, only to see the collapse of such business actually jeopardizing its viability.

When a firm is operating under extreme conditions of uncertainty, forecasted and actual results should be carefully monitored and the forecast adjusted upward or downward as indicated by empirical sales data.

than a credit to Nike. But we can still raise doubts about Adidas's role in the Nike inroads. Should not Adidas have been more alert in such an easy-to-enter industry? After all, neither the technology nor the plant investment requirements were such as to preclude other firms from entering the arena. Should not the frontrunner have recognized this ease of competitive entry and acted aggressively to discourage it—especially when demand was increasing geometrically? Strong promotional efforts, new product introductions, a step-up in research and development, sharper pricing practices, expanding the network of dealers—these actions might not have prevented competition, but, given the resources of the market leader, they should have lessened the inroads. But Adidas did not take aggressive counteractions until its dominance had been severely breached.

PART B   THE SUCCESS OF NIKE

In this case, the antithesis of Adidas, we have a remarkable success story. This success also produced one of Forbes's Four Hundred Richest Americans: Philip H. Knight, the cofounder and chairman of Nike, Inc., the athletic shoe company.

PHIL KNIGHT AND THE BEGINNING OF NIKE

Phil Knight was a miler of modest accomplishments. His best time was 4:13, hardly in the same class as the below 4:00 world-class runners. But he had trained under the renowned coach, Bill Bowerman, at the University of Oregon in the late 1950s. Bowerman had put Eugene, Oregon, on the map in the 1950s when year after year he turned out world-record-setting long-distance runners. He was constantly experimenting with shoes, because of his theory that an ounce off a running shoe might make enough difference to win a race.

In the process of completing his MBA at Stanford University, Phil wrote a research paper based on the theory that the Japanese could do for athletic shoes what they were doing for cameras. After receiving his degree in 1960, Knight went to Japan to seek an American distributorship from the Onitsuka Company for Tiger shoes. Returning home, he took samples of the shoes to Bowerman.

In 1964 Knight and Bowerman went into business. They each put up $500, and formed the Blue Ribbon Shoe Company, sole distributor in the United States for Tiger running shoes. They put the inventory in Knight's father-in-law's basement, and they sold $8000 worth of these imported shoes that first year. Knight worked by day as a Cooper & Lybrand accountant, while at night and on weekends he peddled these shoes mostly to high school athletic teams.

Knight and Bowerman finally developed their own shoe in 1972 and decided to manufacture it themselves. They contracted the work out to Asian factories where labor was cheap. They named the shoe, Nike (rhymes with psyche), after the Greek goddess of victory. At that time they also developed the "swoosh" logo, shown below, which was highly distinctive and subsequently was placed on every Nike product. The Nike shoes' first appearance in competition came during the 1972 Olympic trials in Eugene, Oregon. Marathon runners persuaded to wear the new shoes placed fourth through seventh, whereas Adidas wearers finished first, second, and third in these trials,

Nike faced severe competition in the athletic-shoe industry. This industry was absolutely dominated at that time by foreign manufacturers, particularly two German firms, Adidas and Puma, with Tiger number 3. Knight and Bowerman realized that they had no hope for capturing a large share of the market unless they could develop a product better than what was currently available. And up to then American-made running shoes just did not match most foreign shoes, particularly Adidas.

On a Sunday morning in 1975, Bowerman began tinkering with a waffle iron and some urethane rubber, and he fashioned a new type of sole, a "waffle" sole whose tiny rubber studs made it more springy than those of other shoes currently on the market. This product improvement gave Knight and Bowerman an initial impetus on their way to the heights of success. The strategic planning that propeled Nike to tops in the U.S. market was more imitative than innovative, however. It was patterned after that of the very successful Adidas. But the result was that the imitator outdid the originator.

NIKE'S CHARGE

The new "waffle sole" developed by Bowerman proved popular with runners, and this along with the favorable market brought 1976 sales to $14 million, up from $8.3 million the year before and only $2 million in 1972.

Nike stayed in the forefront of the industry with its careful research and development of new models. By the end of the decade Nike was employing almost 100 people in the research and development section of the company. Over 140 different models were offered in the product line, some of these the most innovative and technologically advanced on the market. This diversity came from models designed for different foot types, body weights, running speeds, training schedules, sexes, and different levels of skills.

Some 85 percent of Nike's shoes eventually were manufactured in 20 different overseas locations, while factories in New Hampshire, Maine, and Oregon made 15 percent of Nike's shoes. By the late 1970s and early 1980s, demand for Nikes was so great that 60 percent of its 8000 department store, sporting goods, and shoe store dealers gave advanced orders, often waiting 6 months for delivery. This gave Nike a big advantage in production scheduling and inventory costs.

Figure 4.1 shows the phenomenal growth of Nike, with sales rising from $14 million in 1976 to $694 million only 6 years later. Figure 4.2 shows the market shares in the U.S. market for the beginning of 1979. By then Nike was the market leader with 33 percent of the market; within two years it had taken an even more commanding lead, with approximately 50 percent of the total market.[3] Indicative of the great visibility and wide appeal that Nike had achieved, in 1981 *Forbes* asked 150 junior high students in a middle-class Dallas neighborhood what their favorite athletic shoe was. All 150 listed Nike first, often citing its status as an expensive "designer" shoe.[4]

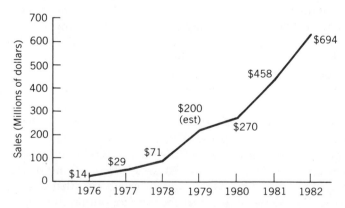

Figure 4.1 Nike sales growth, 1976–1981. (*Source:* Company annual reports.)

[3] Victor F. Zonana, "Jogging's Fade Fails to Push Nike Off Track," *Wall Street Journal,* March 5, 1981, p. 25.

[4] Reported in John Merwin, "Nike's Fast Track," *Forbes,* November 23, 1981, p. 62.

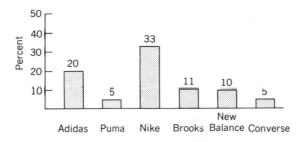

Figure 4.2 Domestic running-shoe market shares, 1978 (*Source:* Compiled from "The Jogging-Shoe Race Heats Up." *Business Week*, April 9, 1979, p. 125.)

Nike continued to stay in the forefront of technology. In early 1979 it introduced the revolutionary "Tailwind." Called the "next generation in footwear," and advertised as "air travel," the Tailwind was developed by an aerospace engineer from Rockwell International and used a sole cushioned of polyurethane-encapsulated air chambers. The three-year R&D effort involved exhaustive testing by everyone from "policemen to podiatrists." At $50, it carried the highest price tag yet in the industry. Yet, demand was so great that Nike was forced to allocate it to dealers.[5]

In 1980 Nike went public, and Knight became an instant multimillionaire, reaching the coveted *Forbes's* Richest Four Hundred Americans with a net worth estimated at just under $300 million.[6] Bowerman, age 70, had sold most of his stock earlier, and owned only 2 percent of the company, worth a mere $9.5 million.

As the running boom matured and no longer offered the growth of a few years earlier, Nike began moving into children's shoes and apparel, and athletic bags. Nonshoe products especially appeared to offer considerable potential, as Adidas derived an estimated 40 percent of its sales from such products as apparel and athletic bags, which had been of miniscule value for Nike up to 1980. Nike was also diversifying into other kinds of shoes. By the end of 1980, basketball shoes accounted for 24 percent of Nike's sales, with tennis and other racquet-sport shoes adding another 18 percent. See Table 4.2 for the approximate breakdown of U.S. sales by major product types for the three years 1978 through 1980. Plans were also readied to expand into hiking and deck shoes, and Nike was gearing up to invade the overseas markets, especially Western Europe, long the domain of Adidas.

---

[5] "The Jogging Shoe Race Heats Up," p. 125.
[6] "The Richest People in America—The *Forbes* Four Hundred," *Forbes*, Fall 1983, p. 104.

Table 4.2 Nike's Dollar and Percentage Sales by Product Categories, 1978–1980

| | Year Ended May 31 | | | | | |
| | 1978 | | 1979 | | 1980 | |
	Dollars (in thousands)	Percentage	Dollars (in thousands)	Percentage	Dollars (in thousands)	Percentage
Running	39,000	55	80,500	55	107,600	43
Basketball	14,300	20	27,800	19	61,800	24
Tennis and other racquet	12,200	17	25,500	17	46,700	18
Children's	1,600	2	5,500	4	21,400	8
Apparel	1,300	2	2,200	2	8,100	3
Field sports	900	1	1,900	1	4,300	2
Leisure	1,000	2	1,200	1	1,600	1
Other	300	1	1,000	1	1,700	1
Total	70,600	100	145,600	100	253,200	100

Source: Company prospectus.

In the January 4, 1982, edition of *Forbes*, in the "Annual Report on American Industry," Nike was rated number 1 in profitability over the previous five years, ahead of all other firms in all other industries.[7]

INGREDIENTS OF SUCCESS

Unquestionably, Nike faced an extraordinarily favorable primary demand in the decade of the 1970s. Jogging and keeping fit were sweeping the nation as few sports or activities had ever. Nike was positioned to take advantage of this trend, and indeed most of the running-shoe manufacturers had impressive gains during these years. But we know that Nike's success went far beyond simple coasting with a favorable primary demand. Nike outstripped all its competitors, including the heretofore dominant Adidas. Nike was able to overcome whatever aura or mystique such foreign producers as Adidas, Puma, and Tiger had.

Nike as it began to reach its potential offered an even broader product line than Adidas, which had pioneered with a great variety of shoe styles. A broad product line can have its problems; it can be overdone, hurt efficiency, and greatly add to costs. Most firms are better advised to pare their product line, to prune their weak products so that adequate attention and resources can be directed to the winners. Here we see the disavowal of such a policy, and yet, this is one of the great successes of the decade. What is a prudent product mix?

Although Nike may have violated some product mix concepts, let us recognize what they accomplished and at what cost. By offering a great variety of styles, prices, and uses, Nike was able to appeal to all kinds of runners; it was able to convey the image of the most complete running-shoe manufacturer of all. In a rapidly evolving industry in which millions of runners of all kinds and abilities were embracing the idea, such an image became very attractive. The image was conveyed of a company that could provide shoes to fit every runner's needs, running styles, and special problems. And no other shoe manufacturer, not even the vaunted Adidas, could offer as much. Furthermore, in a rapidly expanding market, Nike found that it could tap the widest possible distribution with its breadth of product line. It could sell its shoes to conventional retailers, such as department stores and shoe stores; it could continue to do business with the specialized running-shoe stores. It could even be not too concerned about discounters getting some Nike shoes since there were certainly enough styles and models to go around—different models for different types of retail outlets, and everyone could be happy.

---

[7] *Forbes*, January 4, 1982, p. 246.

Short production runs and many styles generally add to production costs, but perhaps in Nike's case this was less of a factor. Most of the shoe production was contracted out—some 85 percent to foreign, mostly Far Eastern, factories. Short production runs were less of an economic deterrent where many foreign plants were contracting for part of the production.

Nike early on placed a heavy emphasis on research and technological improvement. It sought ever more flexible and lighter weight running shoes that would be protective but also give the athlete, world-class or slowest amateur, the utmost advantage that running-shoe technology could provide. Nike's commitment to research and development is tangibly evident in the approximately 100 employees working in this area, many holding degrees in biomechanics, exercise physiology, engineering, industrial design, chemistry, and other related fields. The firm also engaged research committees and advisory boards, including coaches, athletes, athletic trainers and equipment managers, podiatrists, and orthopedists, who met periodically with the firm to review designs, materials, and concepts for improved athletic shoes. Activities included high-speed photographic analyses of the human body in motion, the use of athletes on force plates and treadmills, wear testing using over 300 athletes in an organized program, and continual testing and study of new and modified shoes and materials. Some $2.5 million was spent in 1980 on product research, development, and evaluation, and the 1981 budget was approximately $4 million. For such an apparently simple thing as a shoe, this is a major commitment to research and development.

As a final point-of-sale testing, Nike maintained seven retail outlets, called "Athletic Departments." The goals of these were to bring product information to the consumer as well as provide feedback to Nike's research and development teams. These outlets served as sensors and helped Nike monitor the market and provided an additional distribution channel.

Nike attempted no major deviation from the accepted and successful marketing strategy norm of the industry. This norm was established several decades before by Adidas. It primarily involved testing and development of better running shoes, a broad product line to appeal to all segments of the market, a readily identifiable trademark or motif prominently displayed on all products, and the use of well-known athletes and prestigious athletic events to show off the products in use. Even the contracting out of much of the production to low-cost foreign factories was not unique to Nike. But Nike used these proven techniques better and more aggressively than any of its competitors, even Adidas.

For example, let us consider how Nike used athletes to promote its brand. Knight had made a rather well-publicized statement that one can pay $50,000 for a full-page advertisement in *Sports Illustrated* but it is impossible to buy the front cover. But by getting top athletes who would make the cover of *Sports Illustrated* to wear Nike shoes, Knight essentially "makes" the front cover. When such athletes are seen on television, in person, or on the cover of *Sports Illustrated* wearing the familiar Nike logo, the publicity gained for Nike is almost inestimable. Viewers will readily emulate the famous athlete by also choosing Nike for their own use. An impressive list of athletes have been under contract to wear Nike products: John McEnroe, Nolan Ryan, Alberto Salazar, Sebastian Coe, Henry Rono, half a dozen LA Dodgers, and the defensive line of the Dallas Cowboys, among others. In 1979, Coe was the first individual to hold the world records for the 800 meter, 1500 meter, and 1-mile runs. Rono was the first individual to hold world records in the 3000 meter steeplechase, and the 3000, 5000, and 10,000 meter runs.

This use of athletes was certainly followed by all such manufacturers; however, Nike was able to gain the best in many cases, partly through its R&D efforts, which placed it in the forefront of technological improvements, and also because of the momentum it had built up as the fastest growing and soon the biggest firm in the industry. "The secret to the business," explained Knight, "is to build the kind of shoes professional athletes will wear, then put them on the pros. The rest of the market will follow."[8]

Perhaps some of the accolades for the aggressive success of Nike should be tempered by the deficiencies of its competitors. Adidas began to slip in its aggressiveness; it began to coast on its laurels and certainly did not recognize the formidable inroads of Nike until rather late. Furthermore, although it had been innovative in developing improved versions of running and racing shoes, it slipped a bit in the 1970s. For a time, Nike's shoes were lighter, more cushioned, and more flexible than Adidas. Even after Adidas recognized the serious threat of Nike, its efforts were weak both in its introduction of new and advanced-design products and in its promotional efforts.

Some of the U.S. companies that were traditionally strong in the lower priced athletic shoe industry, notably Converse and Uniroyal's Keds, were caught flatfooted in the race to bring new and technologically improved models to the market. These major producers of tennis shoes and sneakers (Converse made two-thirds of U.S. basketball shoes) vastly underestimated the strength and the longevity of the "running boom" and did not direct strong efforts towards this market until they were completely outclassed by Nike and several other U.S. manufacturers.

And not all the U.S. manufacturers had sufficient production savvy to take advantage of the heated market. For example, Brooks, a U.S. firm that had attracted initial market success, dissipated its strength with poor quality control. Defective shoes and shoe returns destroyed its momentum both with consumers and with dealers.

---

[8] Merwin, "Nike's Fast Track," pp. 59–60.

Finally, a key factor in the continued success of Nike as the running market matured and began to ease slightly was its strong commitment to diversification. Children's shoes, apparel, leisure shoes, and field sport shoes exemplified the expanded product diversity. This product line expansion got underway at the peak of the running boom (about 1978–1979) and helped ensure future growth. Also, Nike began strenuous efforts to expand geographically. It began marketing shoes in Europe in 1981 and in Japan by January 1982.

NIKE POSTSCRIPT—THE PENDULUM SWINGS

It is difficult for firms to maintain a pattern of success. A few firms have done so year after year, even decade after decade—McDonald's most readily comes to mind here, but even this stalwart has shown signs of slipping in recent years. Most firms have their time of success, find success slipping away, and become ordinary enterprises. With Nike, the pendulum began swinging back in 1983, and in 1984 one notable business periodical headlined an article: "Nike Loses Its Footing on the Fast Track: Earnings Are Dismal, Management Is Shuffling, and Many Wonder if Founder Philip Knight Has Run Out of Breath."[9]

The running-shoe industry peaked in 1983, with sales of about 19 million pairs of shoes, a significant jump over the nine million sold in 1977. In 1984, the number of pairs sold rose only 2 percent, and the next year the bottom fell out. Nike was no longer a successful company.

Nike supposedly had recognized years before that the running boom could not possibly continue forever, and it had planned to diversify into apparel in 1979 and push overseas in 1981. By 1984, apparel accounted for 21 percent of U.S. revenues, up from 3 percent in 1980, while foreign sales were 18 percent of total sales. But profits proved disappointing in both these areas of diversification.

In view of the tapering of demand, Nike was still surprised and overextended. The decline in running-shoe demand was not so much a result of fewer people running but was more a consequence of less use of running shoes for casual dress. In addition, the market began to fragment, with shoes for aerobics, basketball, and tennis competing with running shoes for shelf space. As it turned out, Nike made the same planning mistake Adidas had a decade earlier: underestimating an opportunity. Nike was late into the fast-growing market for shoes worn for the aerobic dancing that was sweeping the country, fueled by best-selling books by Jane Fonda and others.

---

[9] "Nike Loses Its Footing on the Fast Track . . . " *Fortune,* November 12, 1984, p. 78.

Nike's management style came under attack. Phil Knight had recruited many athletes for his executive positions, so much so that the company resembled a fraternity according to some critics. In the summer of 1983, Knight turned over the presidency to Robert Woodell, a former long-jump champion. Fifteen months later, Knight took back his job. The loose, paternalistic management structure developed by the company in its early entrepreneurial days appeared inadequate for Nike now that it was almost a billion-dollar firm.

Upon resuming the presidency and direct involvement with day-to-day operations, Knight began tightening the organizational structure and aggressively cutting costs. About 400 people were laid off, some 10 percent of the work force. He planned to change the image from that of a running-shoe company to a total-fitness orientation, while maintaining its 50-percent share of the running-shoe market. In late 1985, he achieved a major coup. In shifting promotional emphasis from many to only a few well-known athletes, Knight signed Chicago Bulls basketball player, Michael Jordan, for a reputed $2.5 million to promote "Air Jordan" shoes. This shoe, introduced in July 1985, was a runaway success, with orders exceeding $90 million during the balance of the year.

By fiscal 1988, revenues were $1.7 billion, a 40 percent gain over 1987; net income was $167 million, a 60 percent increase over 1987. But new competitors, such as Reebok, were also capitalizing on the expanded fitness market. In 1989, Reebok's sales were $2.3 billion, close on the heels of Nike's $2.4 billion. Adidas had slipped to $320 million, behind Avia, Keds, Converse, and L.A. Gear. The summit can be precarious as others jockey to become "king of the hill."

ADIDAS AND NIKE: WHAT CAN BE LEARNED?

Usually we attribute the success of a firm to one or more of the following: doing things differently from competitors and in such a way as to meet customers' needs better; recognizing opportunities previously unrecognized; or plowing more resources into the effort than hapless competitors are able to muster. But the source of Nike's success was different.

Learning Insight. *Effective imitation without innovation or greater resources can still lead to success.*

Of course, imitation must be judicious. A strategy worth imitating should be historically successful. In the case of the running-shoe industry, the strategy of Adidas in offering many models, associating its brand with major athletic events and athletes themselves, and constantly seeking new products was proven successful over a long period. All running-shoe manufacturers followed the same strategy, but Nike did it better.

While being imitative, a firm must develop its own identity. Successful imitation is not a slavish effort to be identical. Only the successful policies, standards, and actions are imitated. It would have been rank absurdity, and even illegal, for Nike to have closely copied the logo and name of Adidas. With effective imitation, there is still room to develop a distinctive image, trademark, or logo and to establish an organization and management alert to new opportunities.

Learning Insight. *The front-runner is vulnerable, particularly in easy-entry industries with rapidly expanding markets.*

The front-runner is much more vulnerable in a rapidly growing industry. If the investment in technological know-how and financial resources to enter the industry is not great, the vulnerability of the front-runner increases. This situation characterized the running-shoe industry in the 1970s.

The long-term industry leader tends to be complacent. It is a natural reaction, this lulling of competitive wariness. Sharply rising demand is reassuring. Sales will be increasing robustly for the industry leader during such a time, but increasing sales may mask a declining market position in which competitors are gaining at the expense of the dominant firm.

Learning Insight. *In an expanding market, beware of judging performance on increases in sales rather than market share.*

Market share refers to the percentage of total industry sales accounted for by an individual firm. A market share analysis evaluates company performance by measuring revenues relative to those of competitors. Changes in market share from preceding periods, especially when these changes show a worsening competitive position, should induce strenuous efforts to ascertain the cause and take corrective action. When a market is expanding, such as the running-shoe market, market share changes should be most carefully monitored.

The critical lapse of Adidas, faced with the growing strength of Nike and its U.S. contemporaries, and the greatly increasing industry potential, suggests a need for better monitoring demand and competitive factors. Alert executives should be able to detect nascent changes by encouraging systematic feedback from those closest to the market—sales representatives, dealers, and suppliers alike—by keeping abreast of latest trade journal statistics and commentaries, as well as other sources including the popular press. There must also be a willingness to act on significant changes in industry conditions, but such willingness is often difficult for veteran firms since it requires disassociating themselves from perspectives and practices of a different past.

Cautions in the Use of Market-Share Data. Although market-share information is a valuable management tool, it should not be used as the primary or only measure of operating performance. It ignores profitability and this is a major flaw. Too much emphasis on increasing competitive position often leads to rash sales growth at the expense of profits. Executives can be motivated in this direction because their prestige is bound up with company size and growth relative to other firms in the industry. Heavy advertising or concentration on short-term sales at the expense of more satisfied customers and dealers will increase market share, but profitability may be adversely affected.

The great value of market-share measurements is that they identify possible problem areas that need further investigation. Perhaps there is a satisfactory explanation for an initial decline in market share. For example, it might be caused by a large sale occurring in an adjacent period or due to a temporary production slowdown for a model change. However, a declining market share may indicate a serious problem that needs prompt corrective action in order to prevent a loss in competitive position that can never be regained.

Learning Insight. *In coping with product-life uncertainties, be flexible in order to avoid taking unacceptable risks.*

Every firm needs to react with its environment and the subtle and not-so-subtle changes taking place. This is especially important when the product life cycle is uncertain in scope and duration. (The boxed information discusses *product life-cycle uncertainties.*)

The uncertainties about the extent and durability of the life cycle led Converse and Keds, the two biggest makers of low-priced athletic shoes, to move far too slowly into the running-shoe market, and they never gained much ground. Had the bubble burst, had the running boom been a short-lived phenomenon, would Nike have been able to maintain its viability in a greatly diminished market? We think so. Several years before the leveling-off and maturing of the market, Nike diversified into related but different products. It had kept production flexible by contracting the greater portion of its manufacturing to foreign factories. Consequently, it did not establish a large infrastructure with high fixed costs and vulnerability to falling demand.

INFORMATION SIDELIGHT

PRODUCT LIFE-CYCLES UNCERTAINTIES

Just as do people or animals, products have stages of growth and maturity—that is, life cycles. There are four stages in a product's life cycle: introduction, growth, maturity, and decline.

Below are representative life cycles for a typical consumer-goods product, and for one that is more of a fashion or fad item. Notice how abruptly sales peak and decline for a fad item in comparison with a more standard one. Once the decline begins for a fad or fashion product, it is usually impossible to reverse or even slow.

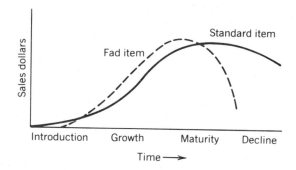

The life cycle for running shoes was influenced by the population of runners and the transference of running-shoe use from dedicated joggers and runners to others who bought them as a symbol of fitness or because they found them comfortable for casual use.

A major question confronting the industry was whether the purchase of running shoes was a fad or a longer-lasting phenomenon representing a change in the lifestyle of many Americans. No one could doubt that the growth stage would level out and reach maturity. Less certain, however, was how many millions of runners and others would eventually comprise the market—and how rapid the decline would be. Such uncertainties plagued running-shoe manufacturers. On the one hand, if a firm geared up for continued growth and a maintenance of high-level demand, the results would be devastating when demand fell drastically. Unless flexibility could be built into the production, and unless alternative markets were identified and targeted, a firm could find itself with so much excess capacity that its viability might be jeopardized. On the other hand, if it did not gear its production to a sufficiently high level, the door was open for competitors to carve out great chunks of market share. The product life cycle, its estimate and realization, was a crucial consideration.

Learning Insight. *No one is immune from mistakes; success does not guarantee continued success.*

Many executives fool themselves into thinking success begets continued success. It is not so. No firm, industry leader or otherwise, can afford to rest on its laurels, to disregard a changing environment and aggressive but smaller competitors. Adidas had a commanding lead, but it was overtaken and surpassed by Nike, a rank newcomer, and a domestic firm with few resources. In an era when foreign brands (of beer, watches, cars, etc.) had a mystique and attraction for affluent Americans that few domestic brands could achieve, Adidas let down its guard at a crucial point. In the same way, Nike lagged in its underestimation or unawareness of the strategic opportunity in aerobic dancing.

Would Nike have achieved its success if Adidas had been more aggressive? Was a major part of the Nike success due not to its own efforts but to the deficiencies of Adidas? Perhaps this is a realistic assessment. On the one hand, we would have to answer this hypothetical question by conceding that Nike probably would not have been nearly as successful if Adidas had not dropped its guard. On the other hand, with a rapidly expanding market and easy entry, Nike could have entered successfully and become a viable and profitable operation.

Learning Insight. *The reward of entrepreneurship can be great indeed.*

The Nike case illustrates the great payoff possible for the entrepreneur of a successful and popularly exciting firm who takes his or her company public and sells shares to general investors. In this book we will examine other such examples of the fantastic rewards possible in taking a private enterprise public. Entrepreneurship can have the greatest monetary payoff possible of any endeavors in our society.

FOR THOUGHT AND DISCUSSION

1. Do you think Adidas could have successfully blunted the charge of Nike? Why or why not?
2. In what ways does the age and experience of a firm tend to induce myopia and resistance to change?
3. "The success of Nike was strictly fortuitous and had little to do with powerful strategic planning." Evaluate this statement.
4. Discuss the pros and cons of optimistic versus conservative sales forecasts for a hot new product.

INVITATION TO ROLE PLAY

1. As an Adidas executive, how would you propose to counter the initial thrusts at your market share by Nike and other U.S. running-shoe producers?

2. As an executive for a medium-size U.S. running-shoe manufacturer, you recognize that the popularity of running is beginning to lessen. What planning recommendations would you make now that the product demand-curve is moving down?

5

Coca-Cola's Classic Planning Blunder

On April 23, 1985, Roberto C. Goizueta, chairman of Coca-Cola, made a momentous announcement. It was to lead to more discussion, debate, and intense feelings than perhaps ever before encountered from one business decision.

"The best has been made even better," he proclaimed. After 99 years, the Coca-Cola Company had decided to abandon its original formula in favor of a sweeter variation, presumably an improved taste, which was named "New Coke."

Not even three months later, public pressure brought the company to admit that it had made a mistake, and that it was bringing back the old Coke under the name "Coca-Cola Classic." It was July 11, 1985. Despite $4 million and two years of research, the company had made a major planning miscalculation, in its estimate of customer acceptance of a product change. How could this have happened with such an astute and successful firm? The story is intriguing and provides a number of sobering insights as well as a happy ending for Coca-Cola.

THE HISTORY OF COCA-COLA

Early Days

Coca-Cola was invented by a pharmacist who rose to cavalry general for the Confederates during the Civil War. John Styth Pemberton settled in Atlanta after the war and began putting out patent medicines such as Triplex Liver

Pills and Globe of Flower Cough Syrup. In 1885, he registered a trademark for French Wine Coca, "an Ideal Nerve and Tonic Stimulant." In 1886, Pemberton unveiled a modification of French Wine Coca which he called Coca-Cola, and began distributing this to soda fountains in used beer bottles. He looked on the concoction less as a refreshment than as a headache cure, especially for people who had overindulged in food or drink. By chance, one druggist discovered that the syrup tasted better when mixed with carbonated water.

As his health failed and Coca-Cola failed to bring in sufficient money to meet his financial obligations, Pemberton sold the rights to Coca-Cola to a 39-year-old pharmacist, Asa Griggs Candler, for a paltry $2300. The destitute Pemberton died in 1888 and was buried in a grave that went unmarked for the next 70 years.

Candler, a small-town Georgia boy born in 1851 (and hence too young to be a hero in the Civil War), had planned to become a physician but changed his mind after observing that druggists made more money than doctors. He struggled for almost 40 years until he bought Coca-Cola, but then his fortunes changed profoundly. In 1892, he organized the Coca-Cola Company, and a few years later downgraded the therapeutic qualities of the beverage and began emphasizing the pleasure-giving qualities. At the same time, he developed the bottling system that still exists, and for 25 years he almost singlehandedly guided the drink's destiny.

Robert Woodruff and the Maturing of the Coca-Cola Company

In 1916, Candler left Coca-Cola to run for mayor of Atlanta. The company was left in the hands of his relatives who, after only three years, sold it to a group of Atlanta businessmen for $25 million. Asa was not consulted, and he was deeply distraught. The company was then netting $5 million. By the time of his death in 1929, annual profits were approaching the $25 million sale price. The group who bought Coca-Cola was headed by Ernest Woodruff, an Atlanta banker. Coke today still remains in the hands of the Woodruff family. Under the direction of the son, Robert Winship Woodruff, Coca-Cola became not only a household word within the United States, but one of the most recognized symbols the world over.

Robert Woodruff grew up in affluence, but believed in the virtues of personal achievement and effort. As a young man, he ignored his father's orders to return to Emory College to complete the remaining years of his education. He wanted to earn his keep in the real world, and not "waste" three years in school. Eventually, in 1911 he joined one of his father's firms, the newly organized Atlantic Ice & Coal Company, as a salesman and a buyer. But he and his father violently disagreed again, this time over the purchase by Robert of trucks from White Motors, to replace the horse-drawn carts and drays of the day. Ernest fired his son and told him never to return home again. So Robert promptly joined White Motors. At the age of 33, he had become the nation's top truck salesman and was earning $85,000 a year. But then he heeded the call to come home.

By 1920, the Coca-Cola Company was threatened by bankruptcy. An untimely purchase of sugar just before prices plummeted had resulted in a staggering amount of borrowing to keep the company afloat. Bottler relations were at an all-time low because the company had wanted to raise the price of syrup, thus violating the original franchise contracts in which the price had been permanently fixed. In April of 1923, Robert was named president, and he cemented dealer relationships, stressing his conviction that he wanted everyone connected with Coca-Cola to make money. A quality control program was instituted and distribution was greatly expanded: by 1930, there were 64 bottlers in 28 countries.

During World War II, Coke went with the GIs. Woodruff saw to it that every man in uniform could get a bottle of Coca-Cola for five cents whenever he wanted, no matter what the cost to the company. Throughout the 1950s, 1960s, and early 1970s, Coca-Cola ruled the soft drink market, despite strong challenges by Pepsi. It outsold Pepsi by two to one. But this was to change.

BACKGROUND OF THE DECISION

Inroads of Pepsi, 1970s and 1980s

By the mid-1970s, the Coca-Cola Company was a lumbering giant. Performance reflected this. Between 1976 and 1979, the growth rate of Coca-Cola soft drinks dropped from 13 percent annually to a meager 2 percent. As the giant stumbled, Pepsi Cola was finding heady triumphs. First came the "Pepsi Generation." This advertising campaign captured the imagination of the baby boomers with its idealism and youth. This association with youth and vitality greatly enhanced the image of Pepsi and firmly associated it with the largest consumer market for soft drinks.

Then came another management coup, the "Pepsi Challenge," in which comparative taste tests with consumers showed a clear preference for Pepsi. This campaign led to a rapid increase in Pepsi's market share, from 6 to 14 percent of total U.S. soft-drink sales.

Coca-Cola, in reaction, conducted its own taste tests. Alas, these tests had the same result—people liked the taste of Pepsi better, and market share changes reflected this. As Table 5.1 shows, by 1979 Pepsi had closed the gap on Coca-Cola, having 17.9 percent of the soft-drink market, to Coke's 23.9 percent. By the end of 1984, Coke had only a 2.9 percent lead, while in the grocery store market it was now trailing 1.7 percent. Further indication of the diminishing position of Coke relative to Pepsi was a study done by Coca-Cola's own marketing research department. This showed that in 1972 18 percent of soft- drink users drank Coke exclusively, while only 4 percent drank only Pepsi. In 10 years, the picture had changed greatly: only 12 percent now claimed loyalty to Coke, while the number of exclusive Pepsi drinkers almost matched, with 11 percent. Figure 5.1 shows this graphically.

Table 5.1   Coke and Pepsi Shares of Total Soft-Drink Market 1950s–1984

	Mid-1950s Lead	1975		1979		1984	
		% of Market	Lead	% of Market	Lead	% of Market	Lead
Coke	Better than 2 to 1	24.2	6.8	23.9	6.0	21.7	2.9
Pepsi		17.4		17.9		18.8	

Sources: Thomas Oliver, *The Real Coke, the Real Story* (New York: Random House, 1986), pp. 21, 50; "Two Cokes Really Are Better Than One—For Now," *Business Week*, September 9, 1985, p. 38.

What made the deteriorating competitive performance of Coke all the more worrisome and frustrating to Coca-Cola was that it was outspending Pepsi in advertising by $100 million. It had twice as many vending machines, dominated fountains, had more shelf space, and was competitively priced. Why was it still losing market share?

The Changing of the Guard

J. Paul Austin, the chairman of Coca-Cola, was nearing retirement in 1980. Donald Keough, the president for Coca-Cola's American group, was expected to succeed him. But a new name, Roberto Goizueta, suddenly emerged.

Goizueta's background was far different from that of the typical Coca-Cola executive. He was not from Georgia, was not even Southern. Rather, he was the son of a wealthy Havana sugar plantation owner. He came to the United States at 16 to enter an exclusive Connecticut preparatory school, Cheshire Academy. He spoke virtually no English when he arrived, but by using the dictionary and watching movies, he quickly learned the language—and became the class valedictorian.

He graduated from Yale in 1955 with a degree in chemical engineering, and returned to Cuba. Spurning his father's business, he went to work in Coke's Cuban research labs.

Goizueta's complacent life was to change in 1959 when Fidel Castro seized power and expropriated foreign facilities. With his wife and their three children, he fled to the United States, arriving with $20. With Coca-Cola, he

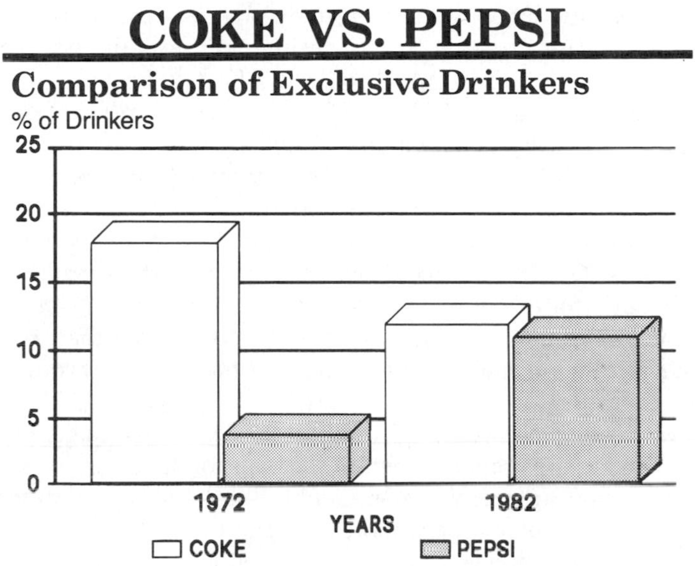

COKE VS. PEPSI

Comparison of Exclusive Drinkers

% of Drinkers

Figure 5.1. Coke versus Pepsi: Comparison of exclusive drinkers.

soon became known as a brilliant administrator, and in 1968 was brought to company headquarters. In 1980, Goizueta and six other executives were made vice chairmen, and began battling for top spot in the company.

Chief executive officer J. Paul Austin, soon to retire because of Alzheimer's disease, favored an operations man to become the next CEO. But he was overruled by Robert Woodruff, the 90-year-old patriarch. In April 1980, the board of directors approved Austin's and Woodruff's recommendation of Goizueta for the president. When Goizueta became chairman of the board in March 1981, Donald Keough succeeded him as president.

Shortly after, Goizueta called a worldwide manager's conference in which he announced that nothing was sacred to the company anymore, that change was imminent, and that they had to accept that. He also announced ambitious plans to diversify beyond the soft-drink industry.

In a new era of change announced by a new administration, the sacredness of the commitment to the original Coke formula became tenuous, and the ground was laid for the first flavor change in 99 years.

Marketing Research

With the market share erosion of the late 1970s and early 1980s, despite strong advertising and superior distribution, the company began to look at the product itself. Evidence was increasingly suggesting that taste was the single most important cause of Coke's decline. Perhaps the original secret formula needed to be scrapped. And so Project Kansas began.

Under Project Kansas in 1982 some 2000 interviews in 10 major markets were conducted to investigate customers' willingness to accept a different Coke. People were shown storyboards, comic strip-style mock commercials, and asked series of questions. One storyboard, for example, said that Coke had added a new ingredient and it tasted smoother, while another said the same about Pepsi. Then consumers were asked about their reactions to the "change concept" (for example, "Would you be upset?" and "Would you try the new drink?") Researchers estimated from the responses that 10 to 12 percent of Coke drinkers would be upset, and that half of these would get over it, but half would not.

While interviews showed a willingness to try a new Coke, other tests disclosed the opposite. Small consumer panels or focus groups revealed strong favorable and unfavorable sentiments. But the technical division persisted in trying to develop a new, more pleasing flavor. By September 1984, they thought they had done so. It was a sweeter, less fizzy cola with a soft, sticky taste due to a higher sugar content from the exclusive use of corn syrup sweetener that is sweeter than sucrose. This was introduced in blind taste tests, where consumers were not told what brand they were drinking. These tests were highly encouraging, with the new flavor substantially beating Pepsi, whereas in previous blind taste tests Pepsi had always beaten Coke.

As a result, researchers estimated that the new formula would boost Coke's share of the soft-drink market by one percentage point. This would be worth $200 million in sales.

Before adopting the new flavor, Coca-Cola invested $4 million in the biggest taste test ever. Some 191,000 people in more than 13 cities were asked to participate in a comparison of unmarked various Coke formulations. The use of unmarked colas was intended to eliminate any bias toward brand names. Fifty-five percent of the participants favored New Coke over the original formula, and it also beat out Pepsi. The research results seemed to be conclusive in favor of the new formula.

The Go Decision

While the decision was made to introduce the new flavor, a number of ancillary decisions had to be reconciled. For example, should the new flavor be added to the product line, or should it replace the old Coke? It was felt that bottlers generally would be opposed to adding another cola. After considerable soul-searching, top executives unanimously decided to change the taste of Coke and take the old Coke off the market.

In January 1985, the task of introducing the new Coke was given to the McCann-Erickson advertising agency. Bill Cosby was to be the spokesman for the nationwide introduction of the new Coke scheduled for April. All departments of this company were gearing their efforts for a coordinated introduction.

On April 23, 1985, Goizueta and Keough held a press conference at Lincoln Center in New York City in order to introduce the new Coke. Invitations had been sent to the media from all over the United States, and some 200 newspaper, magazine, and TV reporters attended the press conference. However, many of them came away unconvinced of the merits of the new Coke, and their stories were generally negative. In the days ahead, the news media's skepticism was to exacerbate the public nonacceptance of the new Coke.

The word spread quickly. Within 24 hours, 81 percent of the U.S. population knew of the change, and this was more people than were aware in July 1969 that Neil Armstrong had walked on the moon.[1] Early results looked good; 150 million people tried the new Coke, and this was more people than had ever before tried a new product. Most comments were favorable. Shipments to bottlers rose to the highest percent in five years. The decision looked unassailable. But not for long.

AFTERMATH OF THE DECISION

The situation changed rapidly. While some protests were expected, these quickly mushroomed. In the first four hours, the company received about 650 calls. By mid-May, calls were coming in at a rate of 5000 a day, in addition to a barrage of angry letters. The company added 83 WATS lines, and hired new staff to handle the responses. People were speaking of Coke as an American symbol and as a longtime friend that had suddenly betrayed them. Some threatened to switch to tea or water. Here is a sampling of the responses.[2]

> The sorrow I feel knowing not only won't I ever enjoy real Coke, but my children and grandchildren won't either. . . . I guess my children will have to take my word for it.

> It is absolutely TERRIBLE! You should be ashamed to put the Coke label on it. . . . This new stuff tastes worse than Pepsi.

[1] John S. Demott, "Fiddling with the Real Thing," *Time*, May 6, 1985, p. 55.
[2] Thomas Oliver, *The Real Coke, the Real Story* (New York: Random House, 1986), pp. 155–156.

It was nice knowing you. You were a friend for most of my 35 years. Yesterday I had my first taste of new Coke, and to tell the truth, if I would have wanted Pepsi, I would have ordered a Pepsi not a Coke.

In all, more than 40,000 such letters were received that spring and summer. In Seattle, strident loyalists calling themselves Old Coke Drinkers of America laid plans to file a class action suit against Coca-Cola. People began stockpiling the old Coke. Some sold it at scalper's prices. When sales in June did not pick up as the company had expected, bottlers demanded the return of old Coke.

The company's research also confirmed an increasing negative sentiment. Before May 30, 53 percent of consumers said they liked the new Coke. In June, the vote began to change, with more than half of all people surveyed saying they did not like the new Coke. By July, only 30 percent of the people surveyed each week said that they liked the new Coke.

Anger spread across the country, fueled by media publicity. Fiddling with the formula for the 99-year-old beverage became an affront to patriotic pride. Robert Antonio, a University of Kansas sociologist, stated, "Some felt that a sacred symbol had been tampered with."[3] Even Goizueta's father spoke out against the switch when it was announced. He told his son the move was a bad one and jokingly threatened to disown him. By now company executives began to worry about a consumer boycott against the product.

Coca-Cola Cries "Uncle"

Company executives now began seriously thinking about how to recoup the fading prospects of Coke. In an executive meeting, the decision was made to take no action until after the Fourth of July weekend, when the sales results for this holiday weekend would be in. Results were unimpressive. The decision was then made to reintroduce Coca-Cola under the trademark of Coca-Cola Classic. The company would keep the new flavor and call it New Coke. The decision was announced to the public on July 11th, as top executives walked onto the stage in front of the Coca-Cola logo to make an apology to the public, without admitting that New Coke had been a total mistake.

Two messages were delivered to the American consumer. First, to those who were drinking the new Coke and enjoying it, the company conveyed its thanks. The message to those who wanted the original Coke was that "we heard you," and the original taste of Coke is back.

The news spread fast. ABC interrupted its soap opera, *General Hospital*, on Wednesday afternoon to break the news. In the kind of saturation cover-

---

[3] John Greenwald, "Coca-Cola's Big Fizzle," *Time*, July 22, 1985, p. 48.

age normally reserved for disasters or diplomatic crises, the decision to bring back old Coke was prominently reported on every evening network news broadcast. The general feeling of soft-drink fans was joy. Democratic Senator David Pryor of Arkansas expressed his jubilation on the Senate floor: "A very meaningful moment in the history of America, this shows that some national institutions cannot be changed."[4] Even Wall Street was happy. Old Coke's comeback drove Coca-Cola stock to its highest level in 12 years.

On the other hand, Roger Enrico, president of Pepsi-Cola USA, said: "Clearly this is the Edsel of the '80s. This was a terrible mistake. Coke's got a lemon on its hands and now they're trying to make lemonade."[5] Other critics labeled this the blunder of the decade."[6]

WHAT WENT WRONG?

The most convenient scapegoat, according to consensus opinion, was the marketing research that preceded the decision. Yet, Coca-Cola spent about $4 million and devoted two years to the marketing research. About 200,000 consumers were contacted during this time. The error in judgment was surely not from want of trying. But when we dig deeper into the research efforts, some flaws become apparent.

Flawed Marketing Research

The major design of the marketing research involved taste tests by representative consumers. After all, the decision point involved a different-flavored Coke, so what could be more logical than to conduct blind taste tests to determine the acceptability of the new flavor, not only versus the old Coke but also versus Pepsi? And these results were significantly positive for the new formula, even among Pepsi drinkers. A clear "go" signal seemed indicated.

But with the benefit of hindsight some deficiencies in the research design were more apparent—and should have caused concern at the time. The research participants were not told that by picking one cola, they would lose the other. This turned out to be a significant distortion: any addition to the product line would naturally be far more acceptable to a loyal Coke user than would be a complete substitution, which meant the elimination of the traditional product.

---

[4] Ibid.
[5] Ibid., p. 49.
[6] James E. Ellis and Paul B. Brown, "Coke's Man on the Spot," *Business Week*, July 29, 1985, p. 56.

While three to four new tastes were tested with almost 200,000 people, only 30,000 to 40,000 of these tests involved the specific formula for the new Coke. The research was geared more to the idea of a new, sweeter cola than the final formula. In general, a sweeter flavor tends to be preferred in blind taste tests. This is particularly true with youth, the largest drinkers of sugared colas, and the group that had been drinking more Pepsi in recent years. Furthermore, preferences for sweeter-tasting products tend to diminish with use.[7]

Consumers were asked whether they favored change as a concept, and whether they would likely drink more, less, or the same amount of Coke if there were a change. But such questions could hardly probe the depth of feelings and emotional ties to the product. And the decisions and plans based on the flawed research were themselves vulnerable.

Symbolic Value

The symbolic value of Coke was the sleeper. Perhaps this should have been foreseen. Perhaps the marketing research should have considered this possibility and designed the research to map it and determine the strength and durability of these values—that is, would they have a major effect on any substitution of a new flavor?

Admittedly, when we get into symbolic value and emotional involvement, any researcher is dealing with vague and nebulous attitudes. But various attitudinal measures have been developed to measure the strength or degree of emotional involvement, such as the *semantic differential*, described on the next page.

Herd Instinct

A natural human phenomenon asserted itself in this case—the herd instinct, the tendency of people to follow an idea, a slogan, a concept, to "jump on the bandwagon." At first, acceptance of the new Coke appeared to be reasonably satisfactory. But as more and more outcries were raised—fanned by the press—about the betrayal of the old tradition (somehow this became identified with motherhood, apple pie, and the flag), public attitudes shifted vigorously against this perceived unworthy substitute. And the bandwagon syndrome was fully activated. It is doubtful that by July 1985 Coca-Cola could have done anything to reverse the unfavorable tide. To wait for it to die down was fraught with danger—for who would be brave enough to predict the durability and possible heights of such a protest movement?

_____

[7] "New Coke Wins Round 1, But Can It Go the Distance?" *Business Week*, June 24, 1985, p. 48.

INFORMATION SIDELIGHT

MEASURING ATTITUDES—THE SEMANTIC DIFFERENTIAL

An important tool in attitudinal research, image studies, and planning decisions is the *semantic differential*. It was originally developed to measure the meaning that a concept—perhaps a political issue, a person, a work of art, or in marketing, a brand, product, or company—might have for people in terms of various dimensions. As first presented, the instrument consisted of pairs of polar adjectives with a seven-interval scale separating the opposite members of each pair. For example:

Good —— —— —— —— —— —— —— Bad

The various intervals from left to right would then represent degrees of feeling or belief ranging from extremely good to neither good nor bad, to extremely bad.

This instrument has been refined to obtain greater sensitivity through the use of descriptive phrases. Examples of such bipolar phrases for determining the image of a particular brand of beer are:

Something
special —— —— —— —— —— —— —— Just another
drink

American
flavor —— —— —— —— —— —— —— Foreign
flavor

Really peps
you up —— —— —— —— —— —— —— Somehow doesn't
pep you up

The number of word pairs varies considerably, but may be as many as 50 or more. Flexibility and appropriateness to a particular study are achieved by constructing tailor-made word and phrase lists.

Semantic differential scales have been used to compare images of particular products, brands, firms, and stores against competing ones. The answers of all respondents can be averaged and then plotted to provide a "profile," as shown below for three competing beers on four scales (actually, a firm would probably use twenty or more scales in such a study).

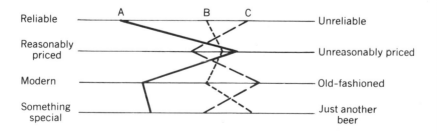

> In this profile, brand A shows the dominant image over its competing brands in three of the four categories; however, the negative reaction to its price should alert the company to review pricing practices. Brand C shows a negative image, especially regarding the reliability of its product. The old- fashioned image may or may not be desirable, depending on the type of customer being sought; at least the profile indicates that brand C is perceived as being distinctive from the other two brands. Probably the weakest image of all is that of brand B; respondents viewed this brand as having no distinctive image, neither good nor bad. A serious image-building campaign is desperately needed if brand B is to compete successfully; otherwise, the price may have to be dropped to gain some advantage.
>
> Simple, easy to administer and analyze, the semantic differential is useful not only in identifying where there might be opportunities because these are presently not well covered by competitors, but it is also useful to a well- established firm—such as Coca-Cola—to determine the strength and the various dimensions of attitudes toward its product. Semantic differential scales are also useful in evaluating the effectiveness of planning changes, such as a change in advertising theme. Here the semantic differential could be administered before the campaign and again after the campaign, and any changes in perceptions pinpointed.

Could, or should, such a tide have been predicted? Perhaps not, at least as to the full strength of the movement. Coca-Cola expected some resentment. But perhaps it should have been more cautious, and have considered a "worst case" scenario in addition to what seemed the more probable, and been prepared to react to such a *contingency.*

INFORMATION SIDELIGHT

CONTINGENCY PLANS

Planning involves resource deployment through the use of budgets. Resources to be deployed include both work force and facilities: the number of people to be involved in the particular aspect of the operation and the amount of money and facilities required to meet planned goals and expectations. Such resource deployment depends on certain assumptions made about both the external and internal environment. When plans are made for major projects, such as new Coke, and resources committed, the success of the commitment depends greatly on the accuracy of the assumptions that are made. When, as events unfold, it can be seen that certain assumptions were either overly optimistic or overly pessimistic, then plans and resource deployments need to be revised.

Contingency plans are well used when dealing with a new product or project and an uncertain future. Different plans may thereby be developed for the different contingencies or sets of conditions that may occur. For example, Plan A may assume a certain level of acceptance; Plan B may be developed for better-than-expected circumstances; Plan C may be ready to put to use if early results are discouraging. When such plans are drawn up in advance, a firm is better able to cope with varied outcomes and can either marshal additional resources or cut back to more realistic expectations.

With such contingency plans developed, Coca-Cola would have been better prepared to react to the surprising resistance to its new product. For example, it could have developed plans for different levels of customer acceptance, including the worst scenario that was actually encountered: nonacceptance and public agitation. While in this case, the decision-making under crisis conditions apparently worked out satisfactorily, in another instance it might not have. Carefully thought-out alternative actions generally have a better payoff than decisions made quickly in a crisis situation.

WHAT CAN BE LEARNED?

Learning Insight. *Taste is an unreliable preference factor.*

Taste tests are commonly used in marketing research, but I have always been skeptical of their validity. Take beer, for example. Do you know of anybody—despite strenuous claims—who can in blind taste tests unerringly identify which is which among three or four disguised brands of beer? We know that people tend to favor the sweeter in taste tests. But does this mean that such a sweeter flavor will always win out? Hardly. Something else is operating with consumer preference other than the fleeting essence of a taste—unless the flavor difference is extreme. Research and decisions that rely primarily on taste tests tend to be more vulnerable to mistakes.

Brand image usually is a more powerful sales stimulant. Advertisers consistently have been more successful in cultivating a desirable image or personality for their brands or the types of people who use them, than by such vague statements as "better tasting."

Learning Insight. *Beware of tampering with the traditional image.*

Not many firms have a 100-year-old tradition to be concerned with, or even 25, or even 10. Most products have much shorter life cycles. No other product has been so widely used and so deeply entrenched in societal values and culture as Coke.

The psychological components of the great Coke protest make interesting speculation. Perhaps, in an era of rapid change, many people wish to hang on to the one symbol of security or constancy in their lives—even if this is only the traditional Coke flavor. Perhaps many people found this protest to be an interesting way to escape the humdrum, by "making waves" in a rather harmless fashion, and in so doing see if a big corporation might be forced to cry "uncle."

One wonders how many consumers would even have been aware of any change in flavor had the new formula been quietly introduced. But, of course, the advertising siren call of "New!" would have been muted.

So, do we dare tamper with tradition? In Coke's case the answer is probably not, unless it is done very quietly; but then Coke is unique.

Learning Insight. *Tampering with a major product still in high demand may be risky indeed.*

Conventional wisdom advocates that changes are best made in response to problems, that when things are going smoothly the success pattern or strategy should not be tampered with. Perhaps. But perhaps not.

Actually, things were not going all that well for Coke by early 1985. Competitive position had steadily been declining to Pepsi for some years. Vigorous promotional efforts by Pepsi featuring star Michael Jackson had increased market share of regular Pepsi by 1.5 percent in 1984, while regular Coke was dropping 1 percent. Moreover, regular Coke had steadily been losing competitive position in supermarkets, dropping almost 4 percent between 1981 and 1985. And foreign business, accounting for 62 percent of total soft-drink volume for Coca-Cola, was showing a disappointing growth rate.[8]

---

[8] "Pepsi's High-Priced Sell is Payoff Off," *Business Week*, March 4, 1985, pp. 34–35; "Is Coke Fixing a Coke That Isn't Broken?" *Business Week*, May 6, 1985, p. 47.

So there was certainly motivation for considering a change. And the obvious change was to introduce a somewhat different flavor, one more congruent with the preference of younger people who were the prime market for soft drinks. We do not subscribe to the philosophy of "don't rock the boat" or "don't change anything until forced to." However, Coca-Cola had another option.

Learning Insight. *Major changes often are better introduced without immediately discarding the present.*

The obvious alternative was to introduce the new Coke, but still keep the old one. The lesson here is "don't burn your bridges." Of course, in July Roberto Goizueta brought back the old Coke after some months of turmoil and considerable corporate embarrassment and competitive glee—which was soon to turn to dismay. The obvious drawback for having two Cokes was dealer resentment at having to stock an additional product in the same limited space, and bottler concern at having a more complicated production run. Furthermore, there was the real possibility that Pepsi would emerge as the number 1 soft drink due to two competing Cokes—and this would be an acute embarrassment for Coca-Cola.

Learning Insight. *Sheer advertising expenditures does not guarantee effectiveness.*

Coca-Cola was outspending Pepsi for advertising by $100 million, but its competitive position in the 1970s and early 1980s continued to erode in comparison to Pepsi's. Pepsi's campaign featured the theme of the "Pepsi Generation" and the "Pepsi Challenge." The use of a superstar such as Michael Jackson also proved to be more effective with the youth market for soft drinks than Bill Cosby for Coca-Cola. Any executive has to be left with the sobering realization that the sheer number of dollars spent on advertising does not guarantee competitive success. A smaller firm can still outdo a larger rival.

Learning Insight. *The power of the media needs to be considered in decisions that are likely to generate widespread interest.*

The press and broadcast media can be powerful influencers of public opinion. With the new Coke, the media undoubtedly exacerbated the herd instinct by publicizing the protests to the fullest. After all, this was news. And news seems to be spiciest when an institution or person can be criticized or found wanting. The power of the press should also be sobering to an executive and ought to be one of the factors considered with certain decisions that may affect the public image of the organization.

Update

Forced by public opinion into a two-cola strategy, the company found the results to be reassuring. By October 1985, estimates were that Coke Classic was outselling New Coke by better than 2 to 1 nationwide, but by 9 to 1 in some markets; restaurant chains, such as McDonald's, Hardee's, Roy Rogers, and Red Lobster had switched back to Coke Classic.

For the full year of 1985, sales from all operations rose 10 percent and profits 9 percent. In the United States Coca-Cola soft-drink volume increased 9 percent, and internationally 10 percent. Profitability from soft drinks decreased slightly, representing heavier advertising expenses for introducing New Coke and then reintroducing old Coke.

Coca-Cola's fortunes continued to improve steadily if not spectacularly. By 1988, it was producing five of the 10 top-selling soft drinks in the country, and now had a total 40 percent of the domestic market to 31 percent for Pepsi.[9]

Because the soft-drink business was generating about $1 billion in cash each year, Roberto Goizueta had made a number of major acquisitions, such as Columbia Pictures and the Taylor Wine Company. However, these had not met his expectations and were disposed of. Still, by 1988 there was a hoard of $5 billion in new cash and debt capacity, and the enticing problem now was how to spend it.

Table 5.2   1986 Family of Cokes

Kinds	Millions of Cases
Total of one cola in 1980	1,310.5
1986	
Coca-Cola Classic	1,294.3
Diet Coke	490.8
Coke	185.1
Cherry Coke	115.6
Caffeine-Free Diet Coke	85.6
Caffeine-Free Coke	19.0
Diet Cherry Coke	15.0

Source: "He Put the Kick Back into Coke," *Fortune*, October 26, 1987, p. 48.

[9] John H. Taylor, "Some Things Don't go Better with Coke," *Forbes*, March 21, 1988, pp. 34–35.

The most successful diversifications were in the soft-drink area. As recently as 1981 there had been only one Coke, and not too many years before, only one container—the 6½-oz glass bottle. Today, only one-tenth of 1 percent of all Coke is sold in that bottle.[10] Now Classic is the best-selling soft drink in the United States, and Diet Coke is the third largest selling. New Coke is being outsold by Classic about seven to one. Table 5.2 shows the total sales volume, expressed as millions of cases, of the Family of Coke.

The future for Coca-Cola looks bright. Per capita soft-drink consumption in the United States has been rising significantly in the 1980s:[11]

	Per Capita Consumption	Percent Increase
1980	34.5 gal.	
1986	42 gal.	22%

The international potential is great. The per capita consumption outside the United States is four gallons. Yet 95 percent of the world's population lives outside the United States.

In Closing

Some called new Coke a misstep, others a blink. At the time there were those who called it a monumental blunder, even the mistake of the century. But it hardly turned out to be that. As sales surged, some competitors accused Coca-Cola of engineering the whole scenario, in order to get tons of free publicity. Coke executives stoutly denied this, and admitted their error in judgment. For who could foresee, as *Fortune* noted, that the episode would "reawaken deep-seated American loyalty to Coca-Cola."[12]

FOR THOUGHT AND DISCUSSION

1. How could Coca-Cola's marketing research have been improved? Be as specific as you can.
2. When a firm is facing a negative press, as Coca-Cola was with the new Coke, what recourse does the firm have? Support your conclusions.

---

[10] Thomas Moore, "He Put the Kick Back into Coke," *Fortune*, October 26, 1987, pp. 47–56.
[11] *Pepsico 1986 Annual Report*, p. 13.
[12] Thomas Moore, "He Put the Kick . . . p. 48.

3. Do you think Coca-Cola would have been as successful if they had introduced the new Coke as an addition to the line, and not as a substitute for
   the old Coke? Why or why not?

INVITATION TO ROLE PLAY

1. Assume that you are Roberto Goizueta, and are facing increasing pressure in early July 1985 to abandon the new Coke, and bring back the old
   formula. However, your latest marketing research suggests that only a
   small group of agitators are making all the fuss about the new cola. Evaluate your options and support your recommendations to the board.
2. You are the public relations director of Coca-Cola. It is early June 1985,
   and you have been ordered to "do something" to blunt the negative publicity. What ideas can you offer that might counter or replace the negatives
   with positive publicity?

6

Contrast—A Success In Strategic Planning: Hyatt Legal Services

In 1970, there were 355,000 lawyers in the United States. By 1984, there were 622,000. By 1995, at the present growth rate there will be over one million. The United States already has over twice as many lawyers per thousand people as England, about 5 times as many as West Germany, and over 25 times as many as Japan.[1] Each year over 30,000 new lawyers are admitted to the bar, but openings exist for only 20,000 new lawyers a year. The surplus of lawyers has brought about a whole new environment in the legal profession, one in which there is vastly more competition than formerly, and this arouses pressures to increase efficiency, lower prices (although most of the big legal firms resist this), and tap a wider customer base. A new look at long-range or strategic planning appears needed in such costly expertise. In the vanguard of nontraditional planning and a new breed of lawyers is Joel Hyatt.

THE LEGAL ENVIRONMENT OF THE 1970s

Despite an ever-increasing number of lawyers and availability of legal services, many people have not availed themselves of legal help. The American Bar Association commissioned a survey in 1971 to determine if an unmet need existed for legal services. Over 2000 households across the country

---

[1] Richard Greene, "Lawyers Versus the Marketplace," *Forbes*, January 16, 1984, p. 74.

were interviewed, and the ABA was forced to conclude that "lawyers are consulted for slightly less than one-third of all the problems that reasonably could be called legal problems."[2] The implications were unmistakable: despite legal problems and an abundance of lawyers to service such problems, many people were not contacting lawyers.

The reason behind this situation was not difficult to ascertain. For years the legal profession had been charging premium prices for lawyers' services, even for routine procedures such as wills, uncontested divorces, and bankruptcy proceedings. It was acknowledged that "if you're rich, you can afford a good lawyer and if you're poor, there's free legal aid, but if you're in the middle, you're stuck."[3]

A few lawyers attempted to remedy this situation. Steve Meyers and Len Jacoby are credited with opening the first legal clinic in Los Angeles in 1972. By 1983, they were the nation's second largest legal clinic chain, with 75 offices in New York, New Jersey, and California. Annual revenues were more than $14 million in 1981.[4] Only Hyatt Legal Services had more offices.

While clinics such as Jacoby and Meyers, and certain smaller local affiliations of lawyers, were attempting to cater to the middle-income market, local bar associations in many communities were arrayed to thwart this growth by challenging those lawyers who advertised and insisting that all members of the bar maintain minimum fee schedules at rather high levels for various legal services. A major setback for the old guard of the legal profession, however, occurred in 1975 when the United States Supreme Court ruled that lawyers should no longer be permitted to fix prices or maintain minimum fee schedules.

The monumental Supreme Court case that paved the way for the marketing of the legal profession involved a Virginia couple who wanted to purchase a house. The couple had checked with 19 lawyers only to find that none would charge less than $522.50 to handle the closing transaction, this being the minimum fee set by the Fairfax County Bar Association. The couple sued the bar association, alleging that this practice was in violation of the Sherman Anti-Trust Act. And the Supreme Court agreed.

Another Supreme Court case in 1977 further paved the way for aggressive marketing practices and legal clinics. In *Bates* v. *State Bar of Arizona*, the Court struck down the Arizona State Bar Association rules against lawyers advertising. The Court held that such rules were in violation of the Constitution's protection of free speech, and lawyers were thus given the right to advertise.

---

[2] "Paying Less for a Lawyer," *Consumer Reports*, Sept. 1979, p. 522.
[3] Craig Waters, "The Selling of the Law," *Inc.*, March 1982, p. 58.
[4] Ibid.

With the Supreme Court decision, the year was not yet over when Joel Hyatt opened his first legal clinic office.

JOEL HYATT

Joel Hyatt, formerly known as Joel Hyatt Zylberberg, is from Cleveland, Ohio. He graduated from Yale Law School and then worked for a prestigious corporate law firm of Paul, Weiss, Rifkind, Wharton, & Carson in New York City. He left the firm to manage his father-in-law's successful campaign for the U.S. Senate. A few months after the Supreme Court ruling for the right to advertise, Joel and his wife Susan, daughter of Senator Howard M. Metzenbaum (Democrat of Ohio), returned to Cleveland to open the first Hyatt legal clinic.

By May of 1978, Hyatt had four clinics located around metropolitan Cleveland and was becoming a familiar figure to thousands living in the Cleveland area. Early on, Joel realized the importance of television advertising in promoting a low-cost clinic that could survive only if it had a high client volume. He himself appeared in these commercials, and his low-key, personable, and sincere manner was a powerful inducement to hundreds of viewers who had previously viewed all lawyers with suspicion.

Investment in new outlets and the advertising necessary to promote the concept of legal clinics requires substantial capital. Not every young practicing attorney has the resources needed for this. As he opened his first clinics, Joel estimated that the initial investment needed before the clinics would start to turn a profit would be in the middle to upper six figures. A large portion of this investment came from his wealthy wife.[5] By contrast, Jacoby and Meyers started small and financed most of its expansion through internally generated funds.

By the end of 1979 Hyatt had nine clinics around northern Ohio and wanted to continue expanding. In order to achieve his expansion goals, large amounts of investment capital would be needed—far more than he had used before or had readily available. The clinics were not yet generating the levels of internal funds needed for a large expansion. Some outside source of funding was needed.

COMPONENTS OF THE STRATEGIC PLAN

The Target Customer

The main thrust of Hyatt, and most other legal clinics, is to provide rather routine legal services for low- and middle-income people who either need

---

[5] Steven Brill, "T.V. Pitchman for Cut-rate Legal Advice," *Esquire*, May 9, 1978, p. 87.

legal services but cannot afford them or who have tried to solve legal problems without the effective assistance of counsel. This market is large, estimated at some 70 percent of the total population.[6] In the past, such customers had been relatively untapped except for such extreme cases as criminal charges or lawsuits. Consequently, all of Hyatt's marketing efforts were directed to winning this large body of potential customers, a *strategic window* as described in the box.

INFORMATION SIDELIGHT

STRATEGIC WINDOW

A *strategic window* is an opportunity in the market not presently well tapped by competitors that fits well with the firm's competencies. Strategic windows often exist for only a short time, before they are filled by alert competitors. Strategic windows are usually found in the strategic planning process by a systematic analysis of the environment, looking at the threats and opportunities it holds, and analyzing the competency of the firm and its managerial values as to what is or is not appropriate to that particular enterprise and its orientation. The process of identifying such opportunities may be a key part of a formal strategic planning process, or it may come about more subjectively and even intuitively, as was perhaps the way of Joel Hyatt.

However he arrived at the identification of a strategic window in the legal profession, it was quickly to be recognized as a wide and durable "window," one that the legal profession had long disdained. As we shall soon see, it was to become a glorious opportunity for Hyatt, and one that may even springboard him to national political prominence.

We have to recognize that the clinic-type market was intentionally shunned by most large law firms as simply not being sufficiently profitable compared with other areas of law, especially corporate clientele. Until the emergence of legal clinics, this middle-income market was primarily serviced by sole practitioners or small partnership firms, but these were too small to compete with the legal clinics that used assembly-line office procedures or generated volume through advertising.

As Hyatt continued to expand, an offshoot of this middle-income market began to look attractive—prepaid legal services. Legal insurance could be purchased in the same manner as hospital and medical insurance, with such services paid for by the employer where this could be negotiated through collective bargaining agreements. It was estimated that 20 percent of union members would have use for these services.[7]

---

[6] Ibid., p. 90.

[7] "Legal Services Plan Emerges," *Wall Street Journal*, April 26, 1983, pp. 1, 5.

Joel Hyatt had significant assets for reaching this market. His father-in-law had strong union support. This, and a geographical location in the heavily unionized midwest, helped propel the firm to three contracts with labor unions by 1983, including the large 160,000-member Sheet Metal Workers' International Association. Hyatt envisioned such prepaid legal insurance as the next big fringe benefit that unions would negotiate:

> It's a benefit most employers can afford to add. It represents about two to seven cents out of the hourly wage, which is a lot less than most medical benefits, and the services offered are really important to the workers' lives. If we do succeed in making prepaid legal services the next major fringe benefit, that will be terribly important. It would mean access to lawyers for hundreds of thousands of workers. And, of course, it would be financially important for us.[8]

The Product or Service

The product provided by the Hyatt Legal Clinics is a very simple one: providing low-priced consultation on routine legal matters with minimum frills. Clients enter the waiting room and await consultation from one of the lawyers at the clinic site. The accoutrements of most legal offices are lacking: no fancy artwork on the walls, no elaborate decor, not even names on the office doors.

Instead of using an extensive law library, the Hyatt lawyers use pre-printed forms. These forms are titled, for example, "simple will" or "uncontested divorce."

Each Hyatt legal clinic has from one to three lawyers, and each lawyer sees about 60 clients per month. The clinics have adopted the extended hours popularized by the discount-store retailers who remained open at night and on Sundays at a time when conventional retailers were open no more than one night a week and never on Sunday. The Hyatt offices are open nights and weekends, times shunned by traditional law firms. The clinic hours offer their target customers the important convenience of not needing to take time off from work. Initial consultations usually last 20 to 30 minutes and one-fourth to one-third of the problems typically are solved in the initial consultation.

Pricing

To win the desired target market, pricing of the legal services is all-important. Low prices and high volume of business are key elements of the strategy. But another aspect of the pricing strategy, leader pricing, provided

---

[8] Tamar Lewin. "Leader in Legal Clinic Field." *New York Times*, May 9, 1983, p. D.10.

an extra impetus. (See the following Information Sidelight for a more thorough discussion of leader pricing.)

The widely promoted leader pricing of only $15 was used for the initial consultation fee.

INFORMATION SIDELIGHT

LEADER PRICING

Retailers in particular have long used "leaders" to attract customers to their stores. Leaders are items intentionally offered at very low prices in order to stimulate store traffic. The expectation is that people induced to come to the store because of the advertised leaders will buy other merchandise priced more profitably. Sometimes retailers will even price certain leader merchandise at or below cost—these are commonly referred to as "loss leaders"—to make such goods particularly attractive to customers.

All items or services typically do not make good leaders. The most effective price leader should

1. Be well known and widely used.
2. Be priced low enough to attract numerous buyers.
3. Not usually be bought in large quantities and stored.
4. Enjoy a high price elasticity of demand (i.e., demand should sharply increase as prices are lowered).
5. Not closely compete with other goods in the firm's merchandise or service offerings.[9]

Hyatt used leader pricing very effectively and essentially met these desired characteristics. By strongly promoting a very low price for the initial consultation, he accomplished two objectives: (1) to induce prospective clients to visit Hyatt facilities at low risk, thereby being exposed to the friendly and nonintimidating environment, and (2) to cater to their specific legal needs with services that could yield a reasonable profit.

In a sense, then, Hyatt used leader pricing as a come-on—a promotional device to attract prospective clients in the best retailer tradition. The low leader price that was heavily promoted in turn gave the whole operation an aura of reasonably priced legal services, so contrary to the general perceptions of lawyers, and this was exactly what this target market was most interested in and most in need of.

The other fees were fixed in advance so that clients knew exactly what they would be paying for the various services. Any additional court costs were borne by the client.

[9] Donald V. Harper, *Price Policy and Procedure* (New York: Harcourt, Brace and World, 1966). p. 253.

A simple will usually cost between $45 and $65 for both husband and wife. An uncontested divorce was about $275; filing for bankruptcy about $350. Most traditional law firms handle such cases as these by the hour, and total charges would usually be much more. On more complicated matters, the Hyatt lawyers charged $40 an hour, this also being significantly lower than the $100 plus hourly fees charged by most attorneys.

The low fee structure, of course, was partly possible because of the sheer volume of business. But the operation also was kept lean, especially compared with most legal firms. Hyatt lawyers were paid from $17,000 to somewhat over $40,000, depending on their experience and managerial ability. This was much less than the compensation paid by most legal firms where even beginning lawyers can be paid over $30,000. An endemic surplus of lawyers today makes the Hyatt compensation sufficiently attractive to obtain good personnel.

The high-volume/low-profit caseload necessitates efficient office procedures. The newest computer and word-processing equipment aids this. For example, a sophisticated system allows the clinics' lawyers to prepare in a matter of minutes simple wills, dissolution agreements, trust agreements, and other standard documents geared to meet most clients' needs. For a particular type of document, the lawyers will spell out special requirements of the client into a dictaphone and then a paralegal or computer specialist will feed this information into a computer. The computer is instructed to choose, from various legal paragraphs stored in the memory, the particular phrases necessary. The computer then integrates this material along with the names and specific details supplied by the client, and produces a personalized, professionally typed document. An ordinary will, for example, can be completed in 30 minutes, including the client interview time.

Promotion

Intensive television advertising has been important in the success of Hyatt. Joel himself stars in the commercials. This personal touch enhances the ads' effectiveness because he is very photogenic and able to project sincerity. All the commercials have had the same theme: Hyatt Legal Services with their capable and qualified lawyers can handle a variety of legal problems, and initial consultations only cost $15 or $20.

Hyatt reportedly spent $2,281,800 for advertising in 1982, double the amount spent in 1981.[10] The TV commercials have been particularly effective in reaching the target market, the working-class consumer, which is the largest TV-watching group.

[10] Christopher C. Gilson, "How to Market Your Law Practice," *Journal of Advertising Research*, Dec. 1981, p. 36.

THE MERGER WITH H & R BLOCK

In order to finance his expansion goals, Joel Hyatt needed an outside source of funding, and he found it in H & R Block, the highly profitable tax preparation firm. Block has tax offices in every city in the United States with a population of more than 5000. The company prepares one out of every ten federal income tax returns. Although Block was highly profitable and had liquid assets of over $150 million in 1980, its founder, Henry Block, was concerned because the company's annual growth rate was down from the previous years. In addition, the new IRS short form was being used by many taxpayers without any assistance, thus eliminating some of the market for Block services. It was only natural that Henry Block should look for some diversions, especially through acquiring other service-oriented firms with high growth.

The match with Hyatt Legal Services seemed perfect. Block and Hyatt operations appealed to the same type of customer. These middle-income people could be easily drawn both to the tax offices and the legal clinics through mass television advertising. Hyatt certainly represented a desirable growth potential. And Block could provide Hyatt with office space, management and advertising expertise, and expansion capital.

Because of laws forbidding ownership of law firms by nonlawyers, Hyatt and Block worked out a unique format whereby Block could purchase in 1980 the tangible assets of Hyatt (i.e., the computers, office furniture, leaseholds, etc.) for $2 million under a subsidiary, Block Management Company. But Hyatt and his lawyer partners maintain the ownership of Hyatt Legal Services, Block Management provides secretarial, computer, and paralegal services, as well as advertising, marketing support, and office space, and in return receives a stipulated management fee. Basically, Block provides everything but the actual legal services.[11]

The merger with Block resulted in rapid expansion. From 10 offices in northern Ohio in 1980, by the end of 1983 Hyatt had expanded to well over 100 offices in about 20 states. It employed some 300 lawyers, thus ranking among the nation's 15 largest law firms. At the present rate of growth, Hyatt expected to be the largest law firm in America by mid-1985.[12] Statistics on revenue and profitably of these operations are kept confidential and not available because Hyatt is still a privately owned law firm.

The nation's second largest clinic, Jacoby and Meyers, presents an interesting comparison with Hyatt. Jacoby and Meyers started in California and by 1983 had 75 offices, employing about 150 lawyers. Receipts per attorney

---

[11] "H & R Block: Expanding Beyond Taxes for Faster Growth," *Business Week*, December 8, 1980, pp. 76–78.
[12] Greene, "Lawyers Versus the Marketplace," p. 76.

in their operation have yielded profits in the range of 15 to 20 percent.[13] Despite more years of experience and proven profitably. Jacoby and Meyers have not been able to raise the capital to match Hyatt's expansion rate. The relationship with H & R Block was a powerful spur to Hyatt's growth and potential, although in 1987, an impatient Joel Hyatt bought out the Block interest.

INGREDIENTS OF SUCCESS

The Hyatt success exemplifies the effectiveness of good strategic planning. The key factors are:

1. Finding a strategic window, an untapped target market.
2. Planning a strategy strictly directed to this target market.

There is nothing mysterious or arcane about this. But what makes Hyatt unique is that it does not deal with a tangible product such as toothpaste, apparel, or machinery, nor a facility such as a retail store, but with a non-product, a service. And we find that the same planning and strategy principles apply to both the tangible and the intangible.

Joel Hyatt found (or really, simply recognized) a huge strategic window, a vast untapped target market, consisting of an estimated 70 percent of the total population, that was turned off by traditional law firms and attorneys who were justifiably seen as catering to the rich, not only in prices but also in demeanor and opulence. Indeed, the large law firms shunned this lower income market. Joel set about changing the image of lawyers, at least as far as his firm was concerned, to one easily approachable, common in touch, and bargain priced. He then had to persuade this vast potential market that they needed lawyers, perhaps almost as much as they needed dentists or physicians.

The success of the initial Hyatt efforts paved the way for a more organized tapping of the target market, the market of organized labor. It was not difficult to persuade union leaders that their members needed legal services as well as the more traditional medical services long negotiated in union contracts. The vast and relatively amorphous target market was assuming identifiable and very reachable customer segments.

Specifically, the planning strategy that Joel used to tap his strategic window consisted of the following:

1. Mass TV advertising was used, geared to the consumer group that tends to be the heaviest user of TV. Money was budgeted for TV advertising in amounts never dreamed of before by such a service

---

[13] Waters. "The Selling of the Law," pp. 58–60.

sector. And the judicial ruling of 1977 legitimatizing advertising by the legal profession created a rare opportunity for people like Hyatt who had the "audacity" to grasp such an opportunity aggressively. Certainly no traditional legal firms could be expected to compete vigorously with this new media tool, wedded as they were to the traditional and viewing such techniques as still anathema and incompatible with their conservative image and clientele. The attractively photogenic Joel Hyatt was a big factor in the success of this advertising. No hired actor could have engendered the same sincerity and personal interest to the audience as the young founder of such as upstart firm.

2. Instead of locating in awe-inspiring suites in prestigious office buildings, as most law firms are wont to do, Hyatt opened his legal clinics in areas convenient to the masses he was seeking to woo—in shopping centers and walk-in sites on neighborhood commercial streets. The offices themselves were simply furnished and unintimidating, where an unsophisticated client could feel comfortable and not awed. Many offices were opened as quickly as could reasonably be done and were open nights and weekends. The merger with Block which made available many of the already operating Block tax outlets, spurred the opening of additional convenient clinics.

3. To be effective, any strategy should be coordinated so that all elements are harmonious and correctly geared to the needs and wants of the target customer. Hyatt's pricing strategy was fully harmonious. Very low prices compared to those of the established competitors were offered for the routine legal transactions that could almost be mass-produced. A very low "leader" initial consultation fee was used to attract clients who normally would be reluctant to go to a lawyer because of the cost. Most of the general public has seen enough publicity about fabulous lawyers' fees in well-publicized court cases to fear even initial contacts as being far beyond their means. But Hyatt clearly designates prices and offers services for modest fees.

The early success of the strategy of Joel Hyatt made this an attractive merger candidate. An apparently ideal suitor appeared with H & R Block, the income tax preparation people whose clientele were virtually the same as Hyatt's target market. The merger with Block brought Hyatt over the threshold to great growth. Block supplied the needed financing. Block had thousands of outlets, at least some of which could accommodate legal clinics as well as income tax preparation services. And Block had the management expertise needed to effectively control hundreds and thousands of far-flung operations although Hyatt chafed at Block's slow response to expansion opportunities.

THE CONTRASTS: PLANNING BLUNDERS AND BULL'S-EYES— WHAT CAN BE LEARNED?

The success of Hyatt contrasts sharply with the plannning blunders we have seen in Part I.

A Strategic Window or Folly?

Perhaps some of the S & L executives thought they saw a strategic window with the lifting of most federal regulations in the early 1980s. We know that the market opportunities they thought they saw—for example, freedom to speculate wildly on a land and oil boom—were the heights of folly. And yet, Joel Hyatt saw an incredible strategic window that had never been tapped by the establishment. And his strategic window of opportunity proved to be a starting point toward the country's largest law firm and a possible political career. What was the difference between these opportunities? And what insights can we draw from them?

> **Learning Insight.** *A strategic window is an opportunity, not a conduit for recklessness.*

> While new ventures usually involve some risk, there is a point at which the risk becomes unacceptable. This is all the more true when other persons' monies are at stake, especially those who cannot afford major losses. The gambler who wants to risk his stash on a highly risky venture can be tolerated: only he (but perhaps also his family) suffers from his reckless abandon. But the company executive who embraces wild schemes with shareholders, depositors, or both, becomes a far more sinister and unacceptable presence in the business environment. We need have little sympathy for the S & L executives who perpetrated their schemes without concern for their depositors, even if fraud were not an issue—and we know it was in some instances.

> Does Hyatt's strategic window endeavor resemble these S & L debacles? Hardly. The strategic window was genuine—it met a real need of a large body of the population. Ordinary people and their savings were not at stake; indeed, they could only be benefited if Joel Hyatt's ideas were in target.

A Strategic Window is not Forevermore

Most strategic windows are short-term opportunities in the competitive environment. Yet the one Hyatt pursued was hardly short term. The window that Adidas successfully capitalized on was long lasting, although at the height of its opportunistic attractiveness, competitors, (most notably Nike) were rushing to fill it. But it was not everlasting.

> **Learning Insight.** *A firm that finds a strategic window must be prepared to defend its position, as vigorously as possible.*

Letting down its guard will permit other firms to gain the competitive advantage. While Hyatt has strongly built on its opportunity with aggressive expansion, competitors are intruding on the window also. Smaller law firms, especially, are finding this target market to be attractive and well within their capabilities.

Unchanging Policies and Strategies—a Myopia?

In these cases we have seen contradictions regarding the desirability of unchanging policies and practices. I had long believed that not to change was the height of folly, a handmaiden of ultraconservatism. The Penney example certainly confirms this, and the Adidas case supports it in the sense that aggressiveness must not be diminished regarding successful policies. But we see a major contradiction in comparing the successful S & Ls to the failures: the successful ones almost all stayed with their traditional and conservative lending policies. And Coca-Cola's surprising confrontation with its customers who wanted nothing changed repudiates the desirability of change without most careful evaluation. Perhaps Hyatt gives us more balanced insights.

> **Learning Insight.** *Where all customers' needs are not being fully met, traditional policies ought to be changed, modified, or expanded. Where customers' needs are completely met, change may be folly.*

Of course, alertness to the environment and creativity are involved in assessing present customer satisfaction and any unfulfilled or emerging needs.

The Spirit of Entrepreneurship

We have to, rather gladly, come to the conclusion that innovative opportunities are far from past in our mature economy. They exist and will continue to exist for those who are unwilling to accept the accustomed and the ordinary. The creative mind, not in tune with stereotypical ways of doing things, should give vitality to entrepreneurship and to our society.

> **Learning Insight.** *Great success in entrepreneurship comes from questioning the traditional, coupled with the willingness to take a calculated risk.*

FOR THOUGHT AND DISCUSSION

1. Discuss the conditions favoring legal clinics in the 1970s.
2. In numbers the low- and middle-income consumer segment suggests enormous potential for legal services. But what are some factors that may make this potential less than it seems?

INVITATION TO ROLE PLAY

As a young lawyer who has just passed the bar exam, you have been approached by a Hyatt representative to join this growing organization. You are undecided whether to join Hyatt, to join an old traditional law firm, or to hang up your own shingle. What are some of the considerations that would guide your decision?

TWO

ORGANIZATIONAL MISHANDLING

7

From Monumental Failure To Outstanding Success: The Edsel And The Mustang

In the annals of business history perhaps no greater turnaround was ever achieved by one company in the space of a few years than that of the Ford Motor Company in the late 1950s and early 1960s. In the late 1950s, Ford hatched the blunder that to this day has become synonymous with fiascos of monumental proportions—the Edsel. A few years later, in 1962, it developed the most successful new car model ever introduced up to that time—the Mustang.

Did the Edsel mistake result in a tremendous learning experience at Ford? Or did the Mustang success come from simple luck? Or could the success of the Mustang reflect more the genius of one man, a man not involved with the Edsel but the key force behind the Mustang, a man we know today more for his success with another automaker than with Ford—Lee Iacocca?

PART A   THE EDSEL—ORGANIZATIONAL INCOMPATIBILITY WITH POTENTIAL

The factors behind the Edsel demise were more than strictly organizational, although an expensive and separate dealer organization was a major contributor. The Edsel case could also have been placed in the section on Planning, since the product itself, the name, how it was introduced, quality control problems—all contributed to the demise. But without the separate and expensive dealer organization, might there still be an Edsel today?

AN EARLIER BLUNDER

Henry Ford introduced the Model T in 1909. It sold initially for $850 and was available in only one color, black. The Model T quickly became a way of life. Ford conducted mass production on a scale never before seen, introducing and perfecting the moving assembly line so that the work moved to the worker. Ford sold half the new cars made in this country up to 1926 and had more than double the output of his nearest competitor, General Motors (GM). Prices by 1926 had fallen to as low as $263. For 17 years, the Model T had neither model changes nor significant improvements, except for a lowering selling price as more production economies were realized.

But, by the mid-1920s, millions of Americans wanted something fancier, and GM brought out Chevrolet, featuring color, comfort, styling, safety, modernity, and—most of all—a showy appearance. And the Model T was doomed.

In desperation, Henry Ford had the Model T painted attractive colors; fenders were rounded, the body lengthened and lowered, the windshield slanted. But still sales declined. Finally, in May 1927, Ford stopped production altogether for nearly a year while 60,000 workers in Detroit were laid off, and a new car, the Model A, slowly took shape, with a changeover estimated to have cost Ford $100 million. Although the Model A was successful, the lead lost to GM was never to be regained.[1]

In the 1920s, a failure in market assessment was devastating. To some extent, the failure of the Edsel was also due to bad market assessment. This led to overly ambitious expectations and organizational planning.

THE EDSEL

The Edsel, Ford's entry into the medium-price field, was introduced for the 1958 model year in early September of 1957. This gave it a jump on competitors, who traditionally introduce new models in October and November of the previous years. Ernest Breech, the board chairman of the Ford Motor Company, set the 1958 goal for the Edsel Division at 3.3 to 3.5 percent of the total auto market. In a 6-million-car year, this would be about 200,000 cars. However, the company executives considered this a very conservative estimate and expected to do much better. Ten years of planning, preparation, and research had gone into the Edsel. The need for such a car in the Ford product line appeared conclusive. Approximately $50 million was spent for advertising and promotion in the pre-introduction and introduction of the

---

[1] Adapted from Jonathan Hughes, *The Vital Few* (Boston: Houghton Mifflin, 1966), pp. 274–358.

car. And, in the late summer of 1957, the success of the massive venture seemed assured. The company did not expect to recover the $250 million of development costs until the third year, but the car was expected to be operationally profitable in 1958.

Rationale

The rationale for the Edsel seemed inescapable. For some years, there had been a growing trend toward medium-priced cars. Such cars as Pontiac, Oldsmobile, Buick, Dodge, DeSoto, and Mercury were accounting for one-third of all car sales by the middle 1950s, whereas they had formerly contributed only one-fifth.

Economic projections confirmed this shift in emphasis from low-priced cars and suggested a continuing demand for higher-priced models in the decade of the 1960s. Disposable personal income (expressed in 1956 dollars) had increased from about $138 billion in 1939 to $287 billion in 1956, with forecasts of $400 billion by 1965. Furthermore, the percentage of this income spent for automobiles had increased from around 3.5 percent in 1939 to 5.5 or 6.0 percent in the middle 1950s. Clearly, the economic climate seemed to favor a medium-priced car such as the Edsel.

The Ford Motor Company had been weakest in this very sector, where all economic forecasts indicated the greatest opportunity lay. GM had three makes, Pontiac, Oldsmobile, and Buick, in the medium-price class; Chrysler had Dodge and DeSoto appealing to this market; but Ford had only Mercury to compete for this business, and Mercury accounted for a puny 20 percent of the company's business.

Studies had revealed that every year one out of five people who bought a new car traded up to a medium-priced model from a low-priced car. As Chevrolet owners traded up, 87 percent stayed with GM and one of its three makes of medium-priced cars. As Plymouth owners traded up, 47 percent bought a Dodge or DeSoto. But as Ford owners traded up, only 26 percent stayed with the Ford Motor Company and the Mercury, its one entry in this price line. Ford executives were describing this phenomenon as "one of the greatest philanthropies of modern business," the fact that Ford uptraders contributed almost as much to GM's medium-price penetration as Chevrolet had been able to generate for GM.[2]

So the entry of the Edsel seemed necessary, if not overdue.

---

[2] Henry G. Baker, "Sales and Marketing Planning of the Edsel," in *Marketing's Role in Scientific Management,* Proceedings of the 39th National Conference of the American Marketing Association, June 1957, pp. 128–9.

Research Efforts

Marketing research studies on the Edsel covered a period of almost 10 years. The conclusions were that the personality of the new car (called the "E-car" initially, before the Edsel name had been selected) should be one that would be regarded as the smart car for the young executive or professional family on its way up. Advertising and promotion, accordingly, would stress this theme. And the appointments of the car would offer status to the owner.

The name for the E-car should also fit the car's image and personality. Accordingly, some 2000 names were gathered, and several research firms sent interviewers with the list to canvass sidewalk crowds in New York City, Chicago, Willow Run, and Ann Arbor, Michigan. The interviewers asked what free associations each name brought to mind. But the results wee inconclusive.

Edsel, the name of Henry Ford's only son, had been suggested for the E-car. However, the three Ford brothers in active management of the company, Henry II, Benson, and William Clay, were lukewarm to this idea of their father's name spinning "on a million hubcaps." And the free associations with the name Edsel were on the negative side, being "pretzel," "diesel," and "hard sell."

At last ten names were sent to the executive committee, but none of them aroused any enthusiasm. The name Edsel was finally selected, although it was not one of the recommended names. Four of the ten names submitted were selected for the different series of Edsel: Corsair, Citation, Pacer, and Ranger.

Search for a Distinctive Style

Styling of the Edsel began in 1954. Stylists were asked to be both distinctive and discreet, in itself a rather tall order. The stylists studied existing cars and even scanned the tops of cars from the roof of a 10–story building to determine any distinguishing characteristics that might be used for the Edsel. Consumer research could provide some information as to image and personality desired, but furnished little guidance for the actual features and shape of the car. Groups of stylists considered various "themes" and boiled down hundreds of sketches to two dozen to show top management. Clay and plaster mock-ups were prepared so that three-dimensional highlights and flair could be observed. The final concept was satisfying to all 800 stylists.

The result was a unique vertical front grille—a horse-collar shape, set vertically in the center of a conventionally low, wide front end—push-button transmission, and luxury appointments. The vertical grille of the Edsel was compared by some executives to the classic cars of the 1930s, the LaSalle and

Pierce Arrow. Push buttons were stressed as the epitome of engineering advancement and convenience. The hood and trunk lid were push button; the parking brake lever was push button; the transmission was push button. Edsel salespersons could demonstrate the ease of operation by depressing the transmission buttons with a toothpick.

The Edsel was not a small car. The two largest series, the Corsair and the Citation, were 2 in. longer than the biggest Oldsmobile. It was a powerful car, one of the most powerful made, with a 345 horsepower engine. The high performance possible from such horsepower was thought to be a key element in the sporty, youthful image that was to be projected.

A Separate Division for Edsel

Instead of distributing the new Edsel through established Ford, Mercury, and Lincoln dealers, a separate dealer organization was decided upon, to be controlled by a separate headquarters division. These new dealers were carefully selected from over 4600 inquiries for dealer franchises in every part of the United States. Most of the 1200 dealers chosen were to handle only Edsel, with dual dealerships restricted to small towns. Consequently, there were now five separate divisions for the Ford Motor Company: Ford, Mercury, Lincoln, Continental, and Edsel.

Although establishing Edsel as a separate division added to the fixed costs of operation, this was thought to be desirable in the long run. An independent division could stand alone as a profit center, and this should encourage more aggressive performance than if Edsel were merely a second entry in some other division.

The dealer appointments were made after intensive study to learn where to place each dealer in the nation's 60 major metropolitan areas. Population shifts and trends were carefully considered, and the planned dealer points were matched with the 4600 inquiries for franchises. The Edsel was to have the best-located dealer body in the automobile industry. Applicants for dealerships were carefully screened, of course. Guides used in selection included: reputation, adequate finances, adequate facilities, demonstrated management ability, the ability to attract and direct good people, sales ability, proper attitude toward ethical and competitive matters, and type of person to give proper consideration to customers in sales and services.[3] The average dealer had at least $100,000 committed to this agency. Edsel Division was prepared to supply skilled assistance to dealers so that each could operate as effectively and profitably as possible and also provide good service to customers.

---

[3] Baker, "Sales and Marketing Planning," p. 143.

Promotional Efforts

July 22, 1957, was the kickoff date for the first consumer advertising. It was a two-page spread in *Life* magazine in plain black and white, and showed a car whooshing down a country highway at such speed it was a blur. The copy read: "Lately some mysterious automobiles have been seen on the roads." It went on to say that the blur was an Edsel and was on its way. Other "pre-announcement" ads showed only photographs of covered cars. Not until late August were pictures of the actual cars released.

The company looked beyond their regular advertising agencies to find a separate one for the Edsel. Foote, Cone and Belding was selected, this being 1 of the 2 in the top 10 who did not have any other automobile clients. The campaign designed was a quiet, self-assured one that avoided as much as possible the use of the adjective "new," because this was seen as common-place and not distinctive enough. The advertising was intended to be calm, not to overshadow the car.

The General Sales and Marketing Manager, J. C. Doyle, insisted on keeping Edsel's appearance one of the best-kept secrets of the auto industry. Never before had an auto manufacturer gone to so much trouble to keep the appearance hidden. Advertising commercials were filmed behind closed doors; the cars were shipped with covers, and no press people were given photographs of the car before its introduction. The intent was to build up an overwhelming public interest in the Edsel, causing its arrival to be antici-pated and the car itself to be the object of great curiosity. Some $50 million was allocated for this introductory period.

THE RESULTS

Introduction Day was September 4, 1957, and 1200 Edsel dealers eagerly opened their doors. And most found potential customers streaming in, out of curiosity, if nothing else. On the first day, more than 6500 orders were taken. This was considered reasonably satisfying. But there were isolated signs of resistance. One dealer selling Edsels in one showroom and Buicks in an adjacent showroom reported that some prospects walked into the Edsel showroom, looked at the Edsel, and placed orders for Buicks on the spot.

In the next few days, sales dropped sharply. For the first 10 days of Octo-ber there were only 2751 sales, an average of just over 300 cars a day. To sell 200,000 cars per year (the minimum expectation), between 600 and 700 would need to be sold each day.

On Sunday night, October 13th, the Ford Motor Company put on a mammoth television spectacular for Edsel. The show cost $400,000 and starred Bing Crosby and Frank Sinatra, two of the hottest names in show business at that time. Even this failed to cause any sharp spurt in sales. Things were not going well.

For all of 1958, only 34,481 Edsels were sold and registered with the motor vehicle bureaus, less than one-fifth the target sales. The picture looked a little brighter in November 1958 with the introduction of the second year models. These Edsels were shorter, lighter, less powerful, and had a price range from $500 to $800 less than their predecessors.

Eventually, the Edsel Division was merged into a Lincoln-Mercury-Edsel Division. In mid-October 1959, a third series of annual models of Edsels was brought out. They aroused no particular excitement either, and on November 19, 1959, production was discontinued. The Edsel was dead.

Between 1957 and 1960, 109,466 Edsels were sold. Ford was able to recover $150 million of its investment by using Edsel plants and tools in other Ford divisions, leaving a nonrecoverable loss of more than $100 million on the original investment plus an estimated $100 million in operating losses.

WHAT WENT WRONG?

So carefully planned and organized. Such a major commitment of work force and financial resources, supported by decades of experience in producing and marketing automobiles. How could this have happened? Where were the mistakes? Could they have been prevented? As with most problems, there is no one simple answer. The marketplace is complex. Many things contributed to the demise of the Edsel: among them, poor judgment by people who should have known better (except that they were so confident because of the abundance of planning) and economic conditions outside the company's control. We will examine some of the factors that have been blamed for the Edsel's failure. None of them alone would have been sufficient to destroy the Edsel; in combination, the car didn't have a chance.

Exogenous Factors

One article, in discussing the failure of the Edsel, said, "In addition to mistakes, real and alleged, the Edsel encountered incredibly bad luck. Unfortunately, it was introduced at the beginning of the 1958 recession. Few cars sold well in 1958; few middle-priced cars sold, even fewer Edsels."[4] A dealer in San Francisco summed it up this way: "The medium-priced market is extremely healthy in good times, but it is also the first market to be hurt when we tighten our belts during depression . . . when they dreamed up the

---

[4] William H. Reynolds, "The Edsel Ten Years Later," *Business Horizons*, Fall 1967, p. 44.

Edsel, medium-priced cars were a big market, but by the time the baby was born, that market had gone "helter-skelter."[5]

The stock market collapsed in 1957, marking the beginning of the recession of 1958. By early August of 1957, sales of medium-priced cars of all makes were declining. Dealers were ending their season with the second-largest number of unsold cars in history up to that time. Table 7.1 shows total U.S. car sales from 1948 (as the country was beginning production after World War II) until 1960. You can see from this table that 1958 sales were the lowest since 1948.

Table 7.1   U.S. Motor Vehicle Sales, 1948–1960

Year	Units Sold
1948	3,909,270
1949	5,119,466
1950	6,665,863
1951	5,338,436
1952	4,320,794
1953	6,116,948
1954	5,558,897
1955	7,920,186
1956	5,816,109
1957	6,113,344
1958	4,257,812
1959	5,591,243
1960	6,674,796

Source: 1973 Ward's Automotive Yearbook (Detroit: Ward's Communications), p. 86.

Table 7.2 shows the production of the major makes of medium-priced cars from 1955 to 1960. Note the drastic drop-off of all makes of cars in 1958, but the trend had been downward since 1955.

The trend was changing from bigger cars to economy cars. American Motors had been pushing the compact Rambler, and, in the year the Edsel came on the market, sales of foreign cars more than doubled. This change in consumer preferences was not solely a product of the 1958 recession, which indicated that it would not reverse once the economy improved. Sales of small foreign cars continued to be very strong in the following years, reflecting public disillusionment with big cars and a desire for more economy and less showy transportation. Table 7.3 shows the phenomenal increase in import car sales during this period, a trend that should have alerted the Edsel planners.

[5] "Edsel Gets a Frantic Push," *Business Week*, December 7, 1957, p. 35.

Table 7.2   U.S. Medium-Priced Car Production, 1955–1959 (units)

	1955	1956	1957	1958	1959
Mercury	434,911	246,629	274,820	128,428	156,765
Edsel			54,607	26,563	29,667
Pontiac	581,860	332,268	343,298	219,823	388,856
Oldsmobile	643,460	432,903	390,091	310,795	366,305
Buick	781,296	535,364	407,283	257,124	232,579
Dodge	313,038	205,727	292,386	114,206	192,798
DeSoto	129,767	104,090	117,747	36,556	41,423

Source: 1973 Ward's, pp. 112, 113.

Table 7.3   U.S. Sales of Import Cars, 1948–1960

Year	Units Sold
1948	28,047
1949	7,543
1950	21,287
1951	23,701
1952	33,312
1953	29,505
1954	34,555
1955	57,115
1956	107,675
1957	259,343
1958	430,808
1959	668,070
1960	444,474

Source: Automobile Facts and Figures, 1961 Edition (Detroit: Automobile Manufacturers Association), p. 5, compiled from U.S. Department of Commerce statistics.

Other exogenous factors were also coming into play at the time of the Edsel's introduction. The National Safety Council had become increasingly concerned with the "horsepower race" and the way speed and power were translating into highway accidents. In 1957, the Automobile Manufacturing Association, in deference to the criticisms of the National Safety Council, signed an agreement against advertising power and performance. But the Edsel had been designed with these two features uppermost: a big engine with 345 horsepower to support a high-performance, powerful car on the highways. Designed to handle well at high speeds, its speed, horsepower, and high-performance equipment could not even be advertised.

Consumer Reports was not overly thrilled about the Edsel. Its 800,000 subscribers found this as the first sentence in the magazine's evaluation of the Edsel: "The Edsel has no important basic advantage over the other brands." Negative articles and books regarding the "power merchants" of Detroit were also appearing about this time. John Keats published his *Insolent Chariots,* and the poet Robert Lowell condemned our "tailfin culture."[6]

Marketing Research

The failure of the Edsel cannot be attributed to a lack of marketing research. Indeed, large expenditures were devoted to this. However, these efforts can be faulted in three respects.

First, the research efforts directed to establishing a desirable image or "personality" for the new car were not all that helpful. Although they were of some value in determining how consumers viewed the owners of Chevrolets, Fords, Mercurys, and other brands and led the Edsel executives into selecting the particular image for their car, in reality there was an inability to translate this desired image into tangible product features. For example, although upwardly mobile young executives and professionals seemed a desirable segment of consumers for Edsel to appeal to, was this best done through heavy horsepower and high-speed performance features, or might other characteristics have been more attractive to these consumers? (Many of these consumers were shifting their sentiments to the European compacts about this time, repudiating the "horsepower race" and the chrome-bedecked theme of bigness.)

Second, much of the research was conducted several years before the introduction of the Edsel in 1957. Although demand for medium-priced cars seemed strong at that time, the assumption that such attitudes would be static and unchanging was unwise. A strong shift in consumer preferences was undetected—and should have been noticed. The increasing demand for imported cars should have warranted further investigation and even a reexamination of plans in light of changing market conditions. At the very least, this should have led to some toning down of optimistic expectations for the Edsel and more conservative sales forecasts and budgets.

The last area where the marketing research efforts can be criticized is in the name itself, Edsel. Here the blame lies not so much with the marketing research, which never recommended the name in the first place, as with a Ford management that disregarded marketing research conclusions and opted for the name, regardless.

Much has been written about the negative impact of the name. Most of this may be unjustified. Many successful cars on the market today do not

---

[6] As reported in John Brooks, *The Fate of the Edsel and Other Business Adventures* (New York: Harper & Row, 1967), p. 57.

have what we would call winning names. For example, Buick, Oldsmobile, Chrysler, even Ford itself are hardly exciting names. A better name could have been chosen—and was, a few years later, with the Mustang, and also the Maverick—but it is doubtful that the Edsel's demise can justifiably be laid to the name.

The Product

Changing consumer preferences for smaller cars came about the time of the introduction of the Edsel. Disillusionment was setting in regarding large-sized, powerful cars. However, other characteristics of the car also hurt. The styling, especially the vertical grille, aroused both positive and negative impressions. Some liked its distinctiveness, seeing it as a restrained classic look without extremes. But the horse-collar shaped grille turned other people off.

The biggest product error had to do with quality control. There was a failure to adhere to quality standards: cars were released that should not have been. Production was rushed to get the Edsel to market on schedule and also to get as many Edsels as possible on the road so that people could see the car. But many bugs had not been cleared up. The array of models increased the production difficulties, with 18 models in the four series of Ranger, Pacer, Corsair, and Citation.

As a result, the first Edsels had brakes that failed, leaked oil, were besieged with rattles, and sometimes the dealers could not even start them. Before these problems could be cleared up, the car had gained the reputation of being a lemon, and this was a tough image to overcome. The car quickly became the butt of jokes.

The Separate Edsel Organization

A major mistake that can be singled out was the decision to go with a separate division and separate dealerships for Edsel. Although this separation was supposed to lead to greater dealer motivation and consequently stronger selling push than when such efforts are diluted among several makes of cars, the cost factors of such separation were disregarded. Having a separate division was expensive and raised breakeven points very high because of the additional personnel and facilities needed. Furthermore, Ford did not have ample management personnel to staff all its divisions adequately.

Despite the care used in selecting the new Edsel dealers, some of them were underfinanced, and many were underskilled in running automobile dealerships compared to the existing dealers selling regular Ford products. Other Edsel dealers were "dropouts" or the less successful dealers of other car makers.

An additional source of difficulty for the viability of the Edsel dealers was that they had nothing else to offer but Edsel sales and service. Dealers usually rely on the shop and maintenance sections of their businesses to cover some expenses. Edsel dealers not only did not have any other cars besides the Edsel to work on, but the work on the Edsel was usually a result of factory deficiencies; dealers could not charge for this work. Dealers quickly faced financial difficulties with sales not up to expectations and service business yielding little revenue.

Promotional Efforts

Contrary to what could be reasonably expected, the heavy promotional efforts before the Edsel was finally unveiled may have produced a negative effect. The general public had been built up to expect the Edsel to be a major step forward, a significant innovation. And many were disillusioned. They saw instead a new-styled luxury Ford, uselessly overpowered, gadget- and chrome-bedecked, but nothing really so very different; this car was not worth the buildup.

Another problem was that the Edsel came out too early in the new car model year—in early September—and had to suffer the consequences of competing with 1957 cars that were going through clearance sales. Not only did people shy away from the price of the Edsel, but in many instances they did not know if it was a 1957 or 1958 model. *Business Week* reported dealer complaints: "We've been selling against the clean-up of 1957 models. We were too far ahead of the 1958 market. Our big job is getting the original lookers back in the showrooms."[7]

Some dealers had complained about overadvertising too early, but now they were complaining of lack of promotion and advertising in October and November, when the other cars were being introduced. At the time when the Edsel was competing against other new models, advertising was cut back; Edsel executives saw little point in trying to steal attention normally focused on new models.

Finally, one of the more interesting explanations for the failure of the Edsel was:

> oral symbolism . . . responsible for the failure of the Edsel. The physical appearance was displeasing from a psychological and emotional point of view because the front grille looked like a high open mouth . . . Men do not want to associate oral qualities with their cars, for it does not fit their self-image of being strong and virile.[8]

---

[7] "Edsel Gets a Frantic Push," p. 35.
[8] Gene Rosenblum, *Is Your VW a Sex Symbol?* (New York: Hawthorn, 1972, p. 39.

PART B THE MUSTANG—SIMPLICITY FOR THE GREAT REVERSAL

The Mustang was introduced April 17, 1964, a little over four years after the Edsel was discontinued. In the first four months that the Mustang was on the market, more Mustangs were sold than Edsels had been sold in its twenty-six-month history. The Mustang ranks as one of the automotive industry's most successful new model introductions and demand continued to flourish.

LEE IACOCCA

Lee Iacocca played a primary role in the success of the Mustang, becoming Ford Division general manager in 1960. He embodied the great American success story. The son of an Italian immigrant, he saw education as the route to success. He went to Lehigh University and later to Princeton for a master's degree in engineering. "In my day you went to college, not to go into government or to be a lawyer, but to embark on a career that paid you more money than the guy who didn't go. For 32 years I was motivated by money," Iacocca was to say some years later.[9]

He started with the Ford Motor Company as an engineer trainee in 1946 at $125 a week. As he moved upward through the Ford organization, he transferred to sales, later becoming sales manager then vice president and general manager of the Ford Division. By 1977 he was president of the entire Ford Motor Company, earning $978,000. But in July 1978, Henry Ford abruptly fired him. The falling out was attributed to basic disagreement between Ford and Iacocca over the pace of downsizing cars: Iacocca wanted to move fast, whereas Ford was worried about the impact of such additional investment on short-term profits and wanted to move more slowly. Today, Iacocca is better known for being the savior of Chrysler.

In addition to being a natural salesman, Iacocca has a genius for assessing the general public's desires for cars. While still a sales manager he noticed that many people were pleading for Ford to bring back the old two-seat Thunderbird. The youth market appeared to Iacocca to show increasing potential, and as his voice began to be heard more in the organization he was able to push his ideas of a personal car directed to the youth market. He wanted such a car to be inexpensive, but peppy and sporty-looking.

---

[9] "Off to the Races Again," *Fortune*, December 4, 1978, p. 15.

THE ENVIRONMENT FOR THE AUTOMOBILE IN 1964

The decade 1954 to 1964 brought big changes to the auto industry. In 1954, Nash and Kelvinator merged with Hudson Motor Car Company to form American Motors, and Studebaker merged with Packard to form the Studebaker Corporation. The Packard line was discontinued in 1958, and Hudson was dropped in 1959. The Edsel was introduced in late 1957 and dropped in 1959. Import cars were trickling into the United States around 1955 and gaining popularity. By the late 1950s, both Studebaker and American Motors were successfully producing small cars.

In 1960, Kennedy was elected president. His popularity brought with it a new emphasis on youth. Kennedy also inherited a sluggish economy, and this he tried to remedy with tax cuts that increased disposable income. In 1963, he dropped the excise tax on automobiles. The ground was now laid for a greatly stimulated demand for cars.

In 1961, some 23 automakers were fighting for a market that had been 7,920,000 cars in 1955 (1955 is used as a base comparison year since it was the industry's best year, not exceeded until 1964). The number of makes of cars had been steadily declining since 1921, when 61 competitors were vying for a much smaller market. Some of the well-known makes that failed were:

- Packard, after 59 years;
- Hudson, after 49 years;
- Nash, after 40 years;
- Auburn, after 38 years;
- Pierce Arrow, after 37 years;
- Franklin, after 33 years;
- Hupmobile, after 32 years;
- Reo, after 32 years; and
- Stutz, after 24 years.

In the early 1960s, the remaining car makers began introducing many new models: some 350 different ones were brought to market in 1961 and another 400 in 1962. Consumer preferences appeared to be changing, and the automakers were offering a great assortment trying to find which would gain acceptance. But the sheer number of choices was leading to customer confusion. Adding to the confusion was the introduction of luxury series of Chevrolets, Fords, and Plymouths, while additional models of Pontiacs, Buicks, and Dodges were being brought out at both the high- and low-end of their markets. There was severe price overlapping. The top three automakers were also now producing compacts to counter the inroads being made by imports as well as by the American Motors' Rambler compact.

The economy was sluggish in 1961, and economic uncertainties about the Kennedy administration appeared to throttle demand. Many consumers delayed their purchases during the 1961 and 1962 model years, but confidence began building. Dealer stocks at the beginning of the 1963 model year were the lowest since 1957. The year 1963 proved to be a good sales year, with about 7 million cars sold.

The overall economy looked good in 1964. Disposable income was increasing about 5 percent over 1962. Consumer use of credit was burgeoning, and this always augured well for car sales. The growth of two-car families was a particularly optimistic factor, with well over 700,000 expected in 1964. More sobering was the gain made by imports to about 8 percent of the U.S. market. Other lower-priced sports cars were also gaining in popularity.

For the most part, car makers virtually ignored the fascination of youth with autos. Cars play an important role both as a symbol and as an instrument of maturity, although such insights had only begun to be recognized in the early 1960s. But now the realization was growing that the 15- to 24-year-old group constituted a vibrant and growing market segment. Demographic studies showed that the number of 20- to 24-year-olds would increase by 54 percent by 1970. In the same period, the 15- to 19-year-old group would grow 41 percent. Both increases were far greater than anticipated gains in total population.

THE MUSTANG

Marketing Research Efforts

After the prodigious marketing research efforts that preceded the Edsel disaster, it would not have been surprising for Ford to give short shrift to marketing research in the succeeding years. But research was used, though on a smaller scale than in the 1950s.

The statistics on demographics, and particularly on the growing youth market, were widely circulated throughout the company. The company received strong indications that older Americans were acquiring more youthful tastes and becoming involved in activities considered youthful for the time, such as golf and tennis. Thus it seemed that the right car might appeal not only to youth but to older people looking for symbols of youth. Additional research revealed that more people were buying sports cars and their accounterments: bucket seats, zippy engines, and four-speed stick shifts.

It was decided to make the Mustang a sports car. Since many of the individuals in the youth market were just getting started in their careers, the new car had to be versatile. It needed to be priced low enough to meet the needs of the young, low-income earner in addition to middle-income groups; it had to have a back seat and a trunk to accommodate small families, and, if possible, it should appeal to the growing number of two-car families. Thus it should be a family car. In sum, the Mustang ought to be all things to all people. These were the conclusions of the research studies. Now these had to be turned into specifications for the styling and engineering departments.

After designs were drawn up, the results from showing the designs to panels of consumers were fed back to product planning where reevaluations were made of the designated desirable and undesirable design features. After a model of the car was developed, there was further research into how well the design met consumer preferences. An interesting situation developed. In trying to determine the best price for the Mustang, Ford invited 52 couples to view a model of the car. When they thought it was to be priced at $3500 they found a lot of things wrong with the car, but when they were given a price less than $2500, the consumers thought it had great styling and plenty of back seat room.

At this point, with the car now developed and favorable consumer research feedback at hand, Mustang sales were projected at 200,000 units for 1964. Before the official launch date, Ford test marketed the car with strongly positive results.

The Product

The Edsel fiasco was still a sharp and painful memory: The $200 million loss and 9 years of "wasted" research soured upper management on any similarly ambitious undertaking. Recognizing managerial prejudices, Iacocca developed the Mustang for only $65 million dollars, and did so in 3 years. The car was pieced together from the Falcon, a compact car, and the Fairlane, a midsize car. It was "cross-sourced," that is, built from existing stock. The six-cylinder engine and transmission to power the car were taken from the Falcon. Beyond the costs of new body styling, the only other major expense was in designing a suspension system. Iacocca in an interview described the people involved with it as basically "lunching off the rest of the corporation."[10]

The long hood/short deck style of the Mustang was to fascinate buyers through the 1960s and early 1970s. In fact the styling hardly changed during those years. The car came in three basic forms: a hardtop, a convertible, and a semifastback coupe. Convertible sales started at the 100,000 unit annual level but dropped to 15,000 a year by 1969. The notchback hardtop was the sales leader. The coupe, also known as the 2 + 2, soon overtook the convertible in sales and averaged about 50,000 units annually through 1970.

The standard Mustang engines during the first six months of production were the 170 cubic inch, six-cylinder and the 260 cubic inch, V-8 small

---

[10] "Ford's Mustang: The Edsel Avenged," *Forbes*, September 1, 1964, pp. 13–14.

block. By Fall of 1964, these engines had been bored and stroked to 200 CID and 289 CID respectively. More powerful engines were added, including large block V-8s by 1970.

Part of the Mustang's appeal lay in its many options, which enabled a customer to personalize the car. Careful use of the order form could result in anything from a cute economy car to a thundering fast drag racer or a deceptively nimble sports car. Transmission choices included automatics, four-speeds, three-speeds, and stick-overdrive units. Handling packages, power steering, disc brakes, air conditioning, tachometer and clock packages were also available. A special GT package offered front disc brakes, a full gauge instrument panel, and special gadgets. A variety of interiors were available, along with accent stripes and special exterior moldings.

To position the Mustang in the marketplace and to make it affordable by youth, the base sticker price was set at $2,368 for a six-cylinder hardtop. The price was advertised nationally in virtually all announcement material.

Choosing a name for this new car presented the expected problems: " . . . the name is often the toughest part of a car to get right. It's easier to design doors and roofs than to come up with a name," as Iacocca reminisced in his autobiography.[11] Finalists from thousands of suggestions were: Bronco, Puma, Cheetah, Colt, Mustang, and Cougar. Finally, Mustang was chosen, not named for the horse but for the famous World War II fighter plane. But it was thought to have "the excitement of wide-open spaces and was American as all hell."

The Promotional Blitz

Ford launched a massive campaign in print and television to promote the Mustang. The intent was to cover as many potential markets as possible in a short period of time. Families, women, and youth were target audiences for Ford's bold introduction of the new model.

On April 2, 1964, barely two weeks before Mustang's debut, Ford began the TV onslaught. Simultaneous programs were purchased on all three networks. During the next month, Mustang commercials were run on 25 different programs on all three networks. The TV coverage placed Mustang commercials in 95 percent of all homes with TV, with an average frequency of 11 messages per home. Color pages were bought in 191 newspapers in 63 markets. Black and white ads were placed in other newspapers, for a total of 2,612 newspapers in 2,200 markets. Four-page color inserts appeared in *Life, Look, Reader's Digest, Saturday Evening Post,* and 20 other national magazines.

There were also additional promotional efforts that were more innovative. Ford joined with Alberto-Culver to run a national contest for Command

---

[11] Lee Iacocca, *Iacocca* (New York: Bantam, 1984), p. 69.

hair dressing: the Command Sports Car Sweepstakes. This brought mention of Mustang on radio in 60 to 70 commercials per week in 31 major markets for almost two months. Mustang was also pictured on display material, on two million Command packages, and in Alberto-Culver national advertisements.

Ford worked out similar arrangements with other companies, such as AMT Toy Company, Holiday Inn, Sea & Ski Company, Jantzen, and the Indianapolis Motor Speedway. A model Mustang could be purchased for one dollar from AMT Toys. Mustangs were displayed in lobbies of 200 Holiday Inn motels and were featured in their directories and in their national advertising. They were displayed in 15 of the country's busiest airports. At University of Michigan football games several acres of space were rented, with huge signs proclaiming, "Mustang Corral." Sea & Ski introduced a new style of sunglasses called Mustang, and the company's national advertising featured the sports car with the glasses. Major department stores used actual Mustangs as props for some of their displays. Jantzen conducted a Miss Smile contest with the Mustang as its grand prize. The Indianapolis 500-mile race had a Mustang convertible as its pace car for 1964.

Among other things, Ford set up a traffic-building registration contest that offered 1,000 prizes, including 25 Mustangs. A 3-million-piece mailing inaugurated the contest.

Four days before the official launching, a hundred reporters participated in a 70-car Mustang rally from New York City to Dearborn, Michigan, some 700 miles. Enthusiastic commentaries in hundreds of magazines and newspapers added to the growing excitement about this new car. A coup of no small moment was the simultaneous featuring of the Mustang on the covers of both *Time* and *Newsweek.*

Results

The Mustang took off. On April 17, Ford dealers were mobbed with customers; one dealer even had to lock his doors against a huge crowd outside. During the first weekend it was on sale, four million people visited dealer showrooms.

Initial expectations were that 75,000 Mustangs would sell during its first year. But optimism was growing, and by the introduction sales projections were 200,000. A second plant was converted to Mustang production, bringing annual capacity up to 360,000. And still it was not enough; a third plant had to be converted. While people were buying Mustangs in record numbers, most were also ordering from a long list of profitable options, spending an additional $1000. And in the first two years alone, the Mustang generated net profits of $1.1 billion.

The first 100,000 units sold in only 92 days. Over four hundred thousand were sold in the first 12 months. The success of the Mustang brought some production economies. There was no complete assembly-line shutdown for model changes between 1964 and 1965; the 1964 models were still rolling off the line while the 1965 models were being tooled for the next production run.

How long would it last? Ford expected General Motors and Chrysler to enter the market with competitive models, although it was thought it would take several years to develop a new model. It was not until Fall, 1966 that Chevrolet introduced a competitor, the Camaro, with styling similar to the Mustang: long hood, short deck, and same length wheelbase. Chrysler followed soon after with the Barracuda. But the Mustang more than held its own, maintaining more than half of the market for lower-priced sports cars.

KEYS TO SUCCESS

External

The economic cards were better stacked for the Mustang than for the Edsel. Productivity was increasing by 1964 and, as a result, so was the standard of living. Since wage increases did not outpace changes in productivity, inflation was not a problem. By the mid-1960s there was a build-up of demand for new cars. Table 7.4 shows total U.S. car sales for the period between 1960 and 1970. Up to that time, 1965 was the largest sales year in automotive history. With the luck of perfect timing, the Spring introduction in April 1964

Table 7.4   U.S. Motor Vehicle Sales, 1960–1970

Year	Units Sold
1960	7,905,117
1961	6,652,938
1962	8,197,311
1963	9,108,776
1964	9,307,860
1965	11,137,830
1966	10,396,299
1967	9,023,736
1968	10,820,410
1969	10,205,911
1970	8,283,949

Source: Automotive News 1978 Market Data Book Issues, p. 10.

enabled the Mustang to take full advantage of the situation. There was less competition from new model introductions since these had taken place in the Fall.

There were also social changes taking place that benefited the Mustang. A national preoccupation with youth and physical fitness, just beginning to emerge, accelerated by the late 1960s. The Mustang was a car that portrayed youth and vitality, even in its name. A sports car or a sporty car was a natural product for this changing environment.

Marketing Research

In contrast to the Edsel experience, marketing research was kept current. Several methods were used by the company to monitor the youth market, including hot rod shows and sponsorship of college campus activities. The hot rod shows gave Ford ideas about car styling, handling, and performance. The youth market was creating its own type of automobiles, which the researchers saw as supporting the need for a personal car. By being on college campuses, Ford could see that students bought foreign cars as a display of independence, individualism, and personal taste. Ford researchers concluded that this was the age when buyer preferences form. Consequently, Ford made a major effort to capture this growing market.

The Product

The unique body style—long hood/short deck—appealed to many. Quality control was high. This emphasis on quality became a company-wide policy for all models (although quality never seemed to match that of foreign cars in many person's minds). The Mustang also filled a need in the market for a personal car: It could be tailored to the individual through the wide choices of models and options. The more options a customer bought, the greater the profit margin since options typically carry higher markups than basic cars. Furthermore, since production costs were low, there was a large profit margin on the basic car. Therefore, record sales were accompanied with above-average profit margins.

Promotion

Virtually every medium was used effectively. The various creative promotional contests helped gain additional attention as well as to convey desirable image associations, particularly that of the youthful sports car. Drawings or raffles helped increase traffic flow through dealer showrooms. Promotional efforts had continuity and timing. Information flowed constantly from television to radio, to print, and finally to personal selling. Before long, almost everywhere one looked, the Mustang could be seen. Knowledge of the Mustang was pervasive throughout the country.

Distribution

This time Ford decided to use its regular dealers to sell Mustangs. By using its existing 6400 dealers, the substantial added costs of a new division were avoided, and the breakeven point for reaching profitability was kept moderate. (See the boxed information on *The Breakeven Point* for a more specific discussion of these issues.)

INFORMATION SIDELIGHT

THE BREAKEVEN POINT

A breakeven analysis is a vital tool in making go/no go decisions about new ventures. This can be shown graphically as follows: Below the breakeven point, the venture suffers losses (as Edsel did); above it, the venture becomes profitable.

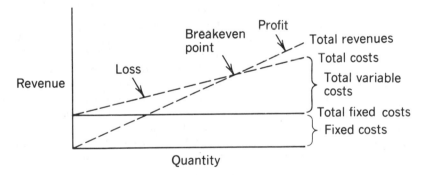

Hypothetical comparison of Edsel (with separate dealer organization) and Mustang (without separate dealer organization):

For this example, let us assume that promotional expenses and other basic operating expenses for the first year are $50,000,000 for both cars. These are fixed costs or overhead that the two ventures will incur regardless of sales. Assume that the average profit contribution beyond production costs and the other variable costs is $400 per car (actually for the Mustang the profit contribution was considerably higher because of lower production costs and increased sales of more profitable optional equipment). The sales needed to breakeven are:

$$\text{Breakeven} = \frac{\text{Total fixed costs}}{\text{Contribution to overhead}}$$

$$= \frac{\$50,000,000}{\$400} = 125,000 \text{ units}$$

But the Edsel had substantial additional fixed costs because of its separate dealer organization. We can estimate these additional costs as:

Salary and expenses for 100 field representatives for liaison with 1,200 dealers	$ 6,000,000
Salary and expenses for Edsel organizational staff—management and back-up personnel and facilities	4,000,000
Additional operating expenses—overhead, telephone, postage, etc.	2,000,000
Total Additional Costs	12,000,000

Therefore, the Edsel breakeven is:

$$\frac{\$12,000,000 + \$50,000,000}{\$400} = 155,000 \text{ units}$$

But the actual sales of Edsel were 54,607 units the first year, 26,563 the second year, and 29,667 the last year, far below the breakeven point. The higher fixed costs of the separate dealer organization only exacerbated the situation.

In making go/no go decisions, these costs can be estimated quite closely. What cannot be determined as surely are the sales figures. Certain things can be done to affect the breakeven point. Obviously it can be lowered if the overhead is reduced, say from $50,000,000 to $30,000,000. Higher selling prices also result in a lower breakeven because of higher per unit profit (but would probably affect total sales quite adversely). Promotional expenses can be either increased or decreased and affect the breakeven point; but they probably also have an impact on sales. But the drain of a costly separate dealer organization had a major negative impact on the breakeven point, and does not appear to have made any positive contribution to sales.

In addition, the increased traffic that Mustang created brought potential buyers for other Ford models. Many of the operational expenses normally incurred by a new model can be spread over the older models. Dealer reputations were already established with adequate financing and sales and service-center staffing. With a product in great demand, there is no concern about having a sufficiently motivated sales force. Once the sales potential of the Mustang could be seen, any sales force would be highly motivated and enthusiastic. Success feeds on success.

THE EDSEL AND THE MUSTANG—WHAT CAN BE LEARNED?

Few pairs of successes and failures can match the range of learning insights provided by analysis of the Edsel and the Mustang.

Learning Insight. *The prudent way of dealing with product demand uncertainties is to maintain flexibility during product introduction, and to have contingency plans prepared.*

A major contributor to the Edsel disaster was a sales expectation way too high. Sales forecasting for a new product is hazardous at best. Sometimes sales greatly exceed expectations, as with the Mustang; at other times they may not even come close to achieving expectations. This is one of the calculated risks of decision making in an uncertain environment. If one is too optimistic, production and other resource allocations will be too high, and heavy costs will be incurred. Yet, as we have seen in the case of Adidas, sales expectation that are too low play into the hands of more aggressive competitors.

In dealing with an uncertain future for a new product, the greatest possible flexibility should be sought. The organization should be prepared for expansion, while not allowing the commitment of resources to bring on disaster if expectations are not realized. This suggests going easy on such things as heavy plant expansion and the accompanying fixed costs until demand is more assured. Contingency plans (discussed in Chapter 5) should be developed for different resource allocations and decisions at varying levels of demand.

Learning Insight. *The breakeven point should be kept as low as possible, especially on new and untried ventures.*

Edsel's separate dealer organization had a devastating effect on profitability because of the high breakeven point it required. The Edsel could have been sold through existing Ford and Mercury dealers without greatly increasing distribution costs of the new car and without subjecting the dealers to high risks, because they would have had their other makes of cars on which to fall back. The 18 models of Edsel further increased the breakeven point. While the optimistic sales forecast led to decisions that increased the breakeven point, this need not have been the case, as was shown by the Mustang. Less ambitious organizational and product planning would have lowered the breakeven point.

What can be learned? Optimistic forecasting is bad? Confidently going ahead with an ambitious project is folly? No, not at all. But the decision maker must weigh carefully the risk/reward factors of costly and ambitious decisions. Mistakes *will* be made. The future is never certain, despite research and careful planning. The environment is always changing, whether we consider customer attitudes and preferences, competitive efforts, or such unpredictable factors as foreign-created petroleum shortages and skyrocketing energy prices, or the reverse—petroleum gluts and plummeting prices.

When a decision involves high stakes and an uncertain future—which translates into high risks—is it not wiser to approach the venture somewhat conservatively, not spurning the opportunity, but also not committing all resources and efforts until success appears more certain?

It can be argued that with a new model of car—whether the Edsel, or K-cars, or X-cars—the huge start-up investment militates against halfway measures. But separate dealerships need not be established; an array of models can be reduced; even advertising can be more conservatively placed. And the compelling example of the Mustang shows that not all new model introductions need involve gigantic tooling and production costs.

Learning Insight. *The external economic and social environment is important, and so is luck.*

Some maintain that luck confounds careful planning and analysis and rewards the intuitive and impulsive. Some even rail against the injustice of raw luck and its rewarding of the unworthy. But let's face it. Luck, opportunism, providential timing—these can be powerful factors in the success of firms and individual careers; and they can also be handmaidens of disaster.

The Edsel could hardly have been introduced at a worse economic time, with a recession in full force and demand for all cars dropping. The Mustang caught the other swing of the pendulum, with an upward looking economy and pent-up demand leading to the largest sales volume year in automotive history in 1965. This raises the intriguing question: Would the Edsel have been a success if it had been introduced later, say in the early 1960s? We would still have to answer in the negative, however. Despite a more favorable economy, something else in the environment was against the Edsel. Consumer tastes and interests had shifted from the type of car the Edsel represented to smaller, sportier models that the Mustang heralded.

Learning Insight. *Marketing research does not guarantee successful decisions.*

Despite being regarded as the mark of sophisticated management, marketing research by no means guarantees a correct decision. Marketing research provided the Mustang planners with insights that aided the success of the car with respect to design acceptability and optimal pricing. But marketing research is no panacea. Consumer statements regarding preferences often can be difficult to interpret and translate into design characteristics of a finished product. And when research is done incorrectly, or research conclusions are biased or self-serving, it may be worse than useless since it may allay reasonable cautions by prudent executives. The millions of dollars spent on marketing research for the Edsel was wasted since research efforts were terminated two years before the car was introduced, at a time when consumer preferences were changing. Dated research is worse than stale news, since it may lead to costly decisions that are far off the mark.

Learning Insight. *Planning and long lead-time preparation do not assure success.*

This caveat flies in the face of the common belief—even the gut feeling—that better planning is the key to personal and all other kinds of success. The stark reality, we are forced to concede, is that heavy planning efforts have the same relationship to success as heavy marketing research efforts: They should help improve the decision-making process, but they by no means guarantee correct decisions. Circumstances and opportunities can drastically change between the planning and the realization.

The Edsel case brings reality to the rosy veneer associated with exacting planning. The planning of the Mustang, on the other hand, was done with far less specificity, with years less lead time, and while it erred on the side of conservatism, there was sufficient flexibility built into the production planning to cope with success. Does this excoriate extensive planning? Have executives deluded themselves about the benefits of finely honed planning? We hardly want to condemn planning as worthless and a waste of time. Rather, planning ought to be relegated to a more realistic role—along with other popular tools of "sophisticated" management—and concede that it can err. Perhaps moderation in relying on planning and other sophisticated managerial tools is best—even though in some circles this smacks of heresy.

Learning Insight. *Poor quality control has a lasting stigma.*

The first Edsels had many defects, worse than most new car introductions. The reputation for poorly constructed cars soon spread and became pervasive—long after the worst flaws had been corrected. Any firm flirts with danger when it allows lax quality control to permit many defectives to reach the market. Reputations are long lasting. And this can be a significant impediment, or a powerful advantage. For example, consider Maytag.

The Maytag Company is located in a small town, Newton, Iowa. Compared to its competitors, General Electric and Whirlpool, it is a small company. But Maytag makes what many people, including *Consumer Reports*, consider to be the best equipment. The company has not directed its efforts to the new-home market and builders who demand price concessions. Instead, it has chosen as its major market the customer seeking a replacement for a cheaper washing machine that has given trouble. Such a customer often is willing to pay a premium for a trouble-free machine. And this Maytag achieves. Unlike other companies in the industry, Maytag makes no periodic model changes. Instead, it seeks to simplify its products and make them reliable. And Maytag's advertising of the "lonesome repairman" effectively reinforces the deserved reputation for trouble-free quality.

Learning Insight. *There is no assured correlation between expenditures for advertising and promotion and sales success.*

As we saw in the Coca-Cola case, much greater expenditures for advertising than Pepsi did not produce a competitive advantage, so we see here as with the Edsel that massive amounts of advertising did not produce the desired results. Ford spent millions of dollars to promote both the Edsel and the Mustang. We might surmise that the Mustang promotional efforts were more effective than the Edsel, especially in attracting a particular segment of consumers, the youth market. In fact, neither promotional campaign can be seriously criticized. There was, however, one key difference. While Edsel advertising brought people into dealer showrooms, what they saw there did not meet their expectations as the Edsel car itself had little appeal when seen close up. The Mustang, on the other hand, was appealing both in ads and in physical presence.

Creative advertising, if backed with sufficient expenditures, can induce people to try the product—or at least to examine it more closely. But if the product does not meet expectations, there will be no repeat buying or, in the case of cars, no purchase.

FOR THOUGHT AND DISCUSSION

1. How would you have instituted environmental sensors to provide up-to-date information to Ford executives about changing exogenous conditions?

2. How would you respond to the comment that the failure of the Edsel, despite extensive planning (starting 10 years before the product finally was introduced), means that planning too far in advance is futile?

3. List as many pros and cons as possible for having Edsel as a separate division (with separate dealers) rather than as part of an existing division (and dealer organization) such as Lincoln-Mercury. Which of your pros and cons do you consider to be most important (which means that they deserve a higher weighting in the overall analytical process)?

4. How could the Edsel have been a more innovative entry into the medium-price market? What features might have made it successful?

5. Was the success of the Mustang more attributable to lucky timing than to any inspired organizational and resource planning?

INVITATION TO ROLE PLAY

1. Assume the role of the Ford executive responsible for the Edsel operation. What strategy would you have used both in the introductory period and in the subsequent several years to enable it to attain both viability and success? Be as specific and complete as you can and be prepared to defend your proposals against other alternatives. Be sure your recommendations are reasonable and practical.

2. As a staff planner for Ford, you have been asked to evaluate the desirability of a luxury addition of the Mustang line. What factors do you think ought to be considered in this $100 million decision, and how would you research and evaluate them?

8

Three Discounters and Their Organizational Confusion: Korvette, Woolworth, W. T. Grant

In this chapter we examine three different retail organizations competing to become the dominant firm in the discounting or lower-price sector. All three of these firms had a run at it, and then faltered, primarily because of organizational deficiencies in coping with growth. One of these, W. T. Grant Company, so aggressively went after the trophy of "biggest" that it overextended itself fatally. Korvette was first on the scene, with the most experience—but the head-start advantage went for naught. Woolworth had the resources and the great name acceptance, but it could not cash in on them. The most unlikely firm was to make it to the top, becoming the world's largest discounter, second only to Sears in total retail sales. S. S. Kresge Company, with its K mart stores, triumphed in one of the great success stories (described in the next chapter). What were the secrets—the magic ingredients—that spelled success for K mart and failure for its major competitors? The answer is an intriguing story with sad overtones: the unfulfilled promise of Korvette and the extinction of the 70-year steady growth of Grant.

PART A   THE DREAM THAT WAS KORVETTE

Gene Ferkauf was the classic American success story. He began his retail career in his father's luggage store. Visionary and eager to grasp opportunities, he disagreed with his father's traditional philosophy of merchandising, which was to sell goods at prices to maximize per-unit profits. He believed that pricing that achieved a small profit per unit of sale would yield greater total profits, *if sales volume could be greatly increased by so doing.* Accordingly, Ferkauf struck out on his own, opening a luggage shop in a second-floor loft on an offstreet in Manhattan. The name of the business he chose arbitrarily: E. J. Korvette.

While the basic stock was luggage, as an accommodation to his customers Ferkauf began selling appliances at close to cost. Soon he branched out into fountain pens and photography equipment. In the early days, Ferkauf sold all appliances for $10 over the wholesale cost. And people began lining up on the sidewalk outside and down the block to get into the store to purchase such bargains. Ferkauf found he was making money with the appliance sales and was operating at a $1 million a year rate. By the end of 1951 he had moved his store to street level and opened a branch in Westchester. Sales climbed to $9.7 million in 1953.

Gene Ferkauf was a quiet man who shunned public limelight. At stockholder meetings he liked to sit mute. He believed in casual clothes, was contemptuous of formality, and spurned an office and other executive amenities. But he believed in friends.

In the early 1950s, a group of 38 men, almost all Brooklyn high school pals of Ferkauf, ran the company. They were called the "open-shirt crowd" or "the boys." Korvette's management operated from a dingy old building with Ferkauf presiding at a beat-up desk in one corner. The company grew, incredibly, from $55 million to $750 million in sales within 10 years, thereby becoming one of the fastest growing companies in the history of retailing. In the early 1960s, the company was opening huge new stores on the average of one every 7 weeks.

In the 1950s and early 1960s Korvette led the discount revolution sweeping the country. The American consumer relished the idea of low prices, some of which were 40 percent less than department store prices. Korvette profits and stock seemed headed for the stratosphere. To achieve profitability with low markup requires low overhead. To achieve the latter, Korvette and the other discounters operated in austere surroundings. Stores and fixtures were simple, even pipe racks were used for hanging garments; no credit or delivery were offered at first; and self-service was the rule in order to cut down on salary expense. Just as important as paring costs, lean stocks of merchandise were offered—a narrow selection of best-selling sizes and styles—to maximize merchandise turnover and thereby increase the *return on investment.* (See the following boxed information.)

As the company continued its discounting policies, it encountered state fair-trade laws, which permitted manufacturers to set the minimum prices for which their goods could be sold by retailers. Some of the major manufacturers, including General Electric, wanted to maintain an image of quality and protect their regular dealers from price cutting. Korvette, by selling below the fair-trade prices, was vulnerable to lawsuits by such manufactur-

INFORMATION SIDELIGHT

IMPORTANCE OF TURNOVER ON PROFITABILITY

For an example of the effect of higher turnover on profitability, compare the operations of a department store and a similar size discount store.

Department store sales	$12,000,000
Net profit percent	5
Net profit dollars	$600,000
Stock turnover	4

$$\text{Average stock} = \frac{12,000,000}{4} \qquad \$3,000,000$$

Return on investment (without considering investment in store and fixtures) =

$$\frac{600,000}{3,000,000} = 20\%$$

A similar size discount store might have turnover of 8 with a net profit percentage of only 3%:

Discount store	
Sales	$12,000,000
Net profit percent	3
Net profit dollars	$360,000
Stock turnover	8

$$\text{Average stock} = \frac{12,000,000}{8} \qquad \$1,500,000^a$$

Return on investment =

$$\frac{360,000}{1,500,000} = 24\%$$

Thus, the discount store can be more profitable than the comparable department store (as measured by the true measure of profitability, the return on investment), even though the net profit is less. Furthermore, the discount store not only has a lower investment in inventory to produce the same amount of sales, but also has less invested in store and fixtures.

[a] To simplify this example, inventory investment is figured at retail price, rather than cost, which would technically be more correct. However, the significance of increasing turnover is more easily seen here.

ers. At the time the company went public in 1955, 34 fair-trade lawsuits were pending against it. This was not as bad as it might seem, however. Enforcement of fair trade rested with the manufacturer who wanted it for his products. In 1956, Korvette received a legal boost when a New York court threw out a suit brought by the Parker Pen Company on the grounds that Parker was not sufficiently enforcing its fair-trade program. Many manufacturers found enforcement difficult amid the spate of discount stores, and the lack of severe penalties limited its effectiveness as a deterrent. Actually, fair trade and list prices aided discount stores since customers could readily see the base price from which the item was discounted.

TROUBLE!

In the four years between 1962 and 1966, store space and sales volume more than tripled. But "genius though Ferkauf might be at minding the store, he had neither the temperament nor the desire to mind the office."[1] With no more than a dozen outlets, Ferkauf, on "foot patrol," could give on-the-scene guidance. But his organization failed to provide any serious substitute for the diminishing face-to-face supervision of Ferkauf and his home-office executives. The constant addition of stores placed enormous pressures on management: *the span of control* was becoming too wide (see the following box for a discussion of span of control). There was enough work and problems in running existing stores without having simultaneously to bring on the additional operations. Buyers, busy filling the needs of the old stores, somehow had to provide for the new stores as well. Advancement, of course, was fast. Section and department managers moved quickly into jobs as store managers, and less experienced people took their places. But there was little time either to develop top-notch management people or to screen for the best.

Along with the sheer number of new stores opening, the doubling and tripling of floor space, and merchandise and management problems, several other factors created trouble by the mid-1960s. One was geographical. As long as new stores were added in the East, and particularly around metropolitan New York City, close contact by the home office was maintained. But this close personal guidance and control was lost with the expansion to Detroit, Chicago, and St. Louis.

It was hard to line up good management people to run operations out of New York City, and profits were lower. Invading a new market area often brought strong competitive reactions from established merchants. In Chicago, for example, Sears and other retailers reacted to Korvette's entry with

---

[1] Lawrence A. Mayer, "How Confusion Caught Up with Korvette," *Fortune*, February 1966, p. 154.

INFORMATION SIDELIGHT

SPAN OF CONTROL

One of the major principles of organizational theory is that the span of control—the number of subordinates reporting to an executive—should be small enough so that they can be properly supervised. A number of factors can affect this optimum span. Obviously, the more experienced and able the executive is, as well as the subordinates, and the more stable and similar the operations are, the wider the span that can be adequately handled. But there is a limit to how many subordinates one person can supervise effectively. Many experts have studied organizations and concluded that higher management can supervise from 4 to 8 subordinates, whereas the span can reach 8 to 15 or occasionally more at the lower management levels.

Intimately related to span of control is another aspect of organizational theory: levels of supervision. A span that is too wide can be narrowed by adding one or more supervisory levels, as shown below:

Wide span, one supervisory level:

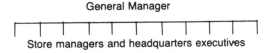

Moderate span, two supervisory levels:

Moderate span, three supervisory levels:

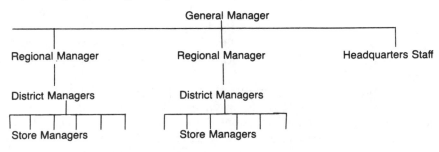

As you can see, the narrower the span—that is, the fewer subordinates supervised by or reporting to one executive—the more supervisory levels and the more executives (and their secretaries and staffs) are required.

Although a span can be unmanageably wide, as Ferkauf's was, there are some drawbacks to establishing additional levels of supervision. The wide span is advantageous in terms of cost, because fewer executives and their staffs must be paid. Also, the more executive levels involved, the more difficult and the less accurate becomes communication up and down the levels. Decision making will be less flexible and slower because more executives will be involved. Morale may also be adversely affected in an organization with many levels, simply because the senior executives are further removed and have less direct personal influence with rank and file employees and lower-level executives. Therefore, span of control decisions need to be balanced with the desirability of keeping supervisory levels to a minimum.

heavy price reductions and promotions, making it difficult for Korvette to gain a solid market position.

Further strains were caused by Korvette's switch to soft goods and fashion merchandising. Ferkauf, as most discounters, started with hard goods: refrigerators; washing machines; TV and stereo equipment; small appliances, such as irons, toasters, and blenders; and photo equipment. The route to a general merchandising operation brought Korvette into clothing and other soft goods, which offered higher profit margins. But risks were higher from markdowns and unsalable inventories brought about by fashion and seasonal obsolescence, and the demands on management were greater than for the more stable hard goods.

Food merchandising presented Ferkauf with new difficulties. There was a good rationale for expanding with supermarkets—consumers generally stock up with groceries weekly; by building supermarkets adjacent to discount stores, heavier and more constant customer traffic can be realized. In 1961 Korvette had two supermarkets. Then the firm started adding supermarkets, winding up with 22, six of these in Detroit and Chicago, unfamiliar territory to an Eastern retailer inexperienced in the local purchase of meat and produce.

Unfortunately, the basic tenet of discount merchandising—high turnover—was disregarded with the food operation. The food stores were opened without warehousing, which meant they had to stock more goods to minimize out-of-stocks. But a heavy inventory is not compatible with lean, fast-moving stocks and high turnover. Furthermore, competition in the supermarket industry was increasing about this time.

Losses from food operations reached $12 million by 1964, and Ferkauf was forced to turn to the outside for help. A merger with Hill Supermarkets, a 42-store chain on Long Island, seemed the answer. But the merger did not solve the problems, and in 1968, after several years of frustration, the food division was finally abandoned.

The final problem plaguing Korvette was its furniture department which was, in fact, a leased operation. The lessee's operations were undercapitalized, and serious management and inventory problems were emerging by 1963, the time of Korvette's greatest expansion efforts. Since customers were not aware that the furniture operation was leased, Korvette bore the brunt of complaints about service and deliveries, and its reputation was being badly affected. Finally, Korvette took over the operation, but it continued to be a profit drain.

1966, The Year of Decision

The strains on Korvette were beginning to show clearly by 1966. Although net sales for the last six months of fiscal 1965 were more than 10 percent higher than for the same period the year before, earnings declined from $16.6 million to $13.9 million. Then, for the generally unprofitable first quarter of the year, Korvette saw the deficit grow from $1.12 million in 1965 to $4.45 million in 1966. There were other indications of trouble. Inventory turnover was down by one-third from 1961; sales per square foot also fell by one-third. And Korvette stock had dropped from a peak of 50½ in May 1965 to 13 by the beginning of 1966.

Finally, the expansion policies were toned down. Only three new stores were opened in 1966, and attention was turned to the existing stores and efforts to increase customer traffic.

Rather unexpectedly, on September 25, 1966, Korvette was merged with Spartans Industries, a smaller discount chain with only $375 million in sales in 1965 compared with $719 million for Korvette. Ferkauf, eased out of active management, left Spartans in 1968 to develop his own boutique chain and faded from the limelight. Charles Bassine, the chairman, turned his attention to developing tighter controls for the Korvette operation: controls over merchandise, costs, markups, markdowns, shrinkage, and expenses.

After 1966

Despite the stronger management that Spartans provided, the Korvette operation could not regain its previous strength. An attempt was made to raise Korvette's profit margins by upgrading the merchandise with higher-price lines, but this served to drive away many of the old bargain-hunting customers. While sales of Spartans Industries were now over a billion dollars, there was a continual fight to generate profits. Bassine tried to unload the unprofitable parts of his operation, such as the supermarkets, but profits were little improved. In 1970, the apparel business was hit by a flood of cheaper foreign imports, and a recession hurt retail sales. In 1970, the Korvette division lost $3.7 million.

In 1971, Spartans merged with Arlen Realty & Development Corporation, a big real estate developer, and younger blood was brought into top management. To no avail—Korvette continued either to lose money or barely break even. In early 1979, Korvette experienced a third transfer of control. Arlen was able to sell a majority 51 percent interest in the Korvette 50-unit chain to a French retail and manufacturing group, Agache-Willot, for $30 million.

Continued losses and cash crises plagued the retailer, and bankruptcy was threatened in 1980 before the French parent agreed to restructure $55 million of debt to institutional lenders. The decision was made to liquidate the company gradually, and by the middle of 1981 the remaining 12 stores were in the process of being sold. Korvette, the pioneer discounter, is little more than a memory.

PART B WOOLWORTH'S WOOLCO: DISCOUNTING PROVES INCOMPATIBLE

Woolworth has a long and successful history. It was the first variety store chain, and it became the largest—with Kresge a distant second. With the growing popularity of discount stores by the early 1960s, the decision to move into discounting with a Woolco subsidiary seemed unquestionably right. Kresge was attempting this with its K mart venture, and Woolworth had greater size and resources than Kresge. But by 1982 Woolworth had had enough and called quits to the money-draining discount operation. How could Woolworth have failed so mightily—when K mart's success was so great that the venerable name of Kresge was changed to K mart?

THE BEGINNINGS OF WOOLWORTH

Frank W. Woolworth conceived an exciting idea during the 1870s when the country was still recovering from the Civil War: a one-price retail store. He conceived the idea while working as a clerk in a retail store in Watertown, New York where he helped introduce the "5¢ counter." The success of this counter convinced him that a five-cent store would also thrive.

He opened his pioneering store in 1879 in Utica, New York. His first sale was a five-cent fire shovel. However, the location proved to be bad, and the enterprise failed in less than four months. Not deterred, Frank Woolworth opened another store in Lancaster, Pennsylvania, and by the end of the first day knew he had a success and began thinking of other stores.

The five-cent price proved somewhat limiting, and a year later he added a ten-cent line. The ten-cent limit held for 52 years. The idea of offering a great variety of merchandise at one low fixed price, and of keeping goods on open display was adopted by other pioneer merchants including Sebastian Kresge in the late 1800s and W. T. Grant in 1906. The concept was revolutionary for the time since in most retail outlets counters were kept bare, with merchandise on high shelves or under the counter and brought out only at the customer's request.

Woolworth continued opening new stores and acquiring other smaller chain operations. In 1909 Woolworth opened his first dime store in Liverpool, England, and within five years had 44 stores in England. By 1955, at the threshold of the discount movement, Woolworth had 2064 stores with sales of almost $800 million; Kresge had 673 stores and sales of $354 million; and W. T. Grant had 572 stores and sales of $350 million.

WOOLWORTH MOVES INTO DISCOUNTING

By 1962 discounting was at its height. Traditional retailers were running scared, and the movement was attracting dozens of brash interlopers. Many of these firms failed in the next decade as competition became keener and retailers with greater resources and merchandising acumen began to diversify into discounting.

Discounting seemed a natural diversification for such major variety chains as Woolworth and Kresge. Larger stores and a wider range of merchandise would be needed, but the customers would be the same and the merchandising strategy would not be that different. Both Kresge and Woolworth opened their first discount stores in the same year, 1962.

While Kresge dedicated itself to discounting, Woolworth moved far more slowly. Resources for expansion were divided among development of the Woolco stores, upgrading and enlarging the regular variety stores, and expansion of certain specialty operations, notably the Kinney shoe stores and Richman clothing outlets. In 1970, Kresge overtook Woolworth in sales, and by 1973 Kresge was the country's largest discounter.

Some Worrisome Portents

By 1974 the Woolworth Company was a giant complex of 2058 variety stores, 283 Woolco stores, 1481 Kinney shoe stores, and 266 Richman outlets. In 1973, sales were $3.7 billion, more than twice the volume of 10 years before, but profits were only half the level of 10 years before. Woolworth's position was particularly worrisome because it compared poorly with that of other leading retailers as shown in Table 8.1.

The retail environment had become tougher than ever, and while the discounting field had grown to a $30 billion annual business, it was going through a massive shakeout. Woolworth's profit margins were too low to generate the capital needed for expansion, and even with borrowing,

Table 8.1   Profit Margins of Major
Retailers, 1973

Company	Net Profit Percent of Sales
Sears	5.5%
Penney	3.0
Kresge	2.9
Woolworth	1.8

Source: Company public records.

start-up plans had to be scaled down. To reduce short-term debt, Woolworth floated a $125 million issue of debentures in 1974, the second time in three years that the company had to resort to debt financing.

Still, the outlook did not appear too bad for Woolworth in the mid-1970s. Chief executive officer Lester A. Burcham could tell shareholders that 1974 sales had comfortably passed the $4 billion milestone, just two years after breaking the $3 billion level. However, in a more somber note, company executives worried: "We can get the sales. But we have to get the profitability."[2]

But even sales of individual Woolco stores did not meet expectations. Sales for the large units were conservatively expected to be at least 5 million a year, and such sales were achieved by a disappointingly few stores. Meanwhile, foreign operations, especially in the British subsidiary, showed a similar pattern—increasing sales and languishing profits. All the while K mart was achieving new heights of sales and profits.

Edward Gibbons Faces a Worsening Situation

Edward G. Gibbons joined Woolworth in 1973 as vice president for finance. At the time, Gibbons worked hard to improve the company's serious debt problems. In 1975 he was made president, and later became the company's first outside chief executive officer (CEO). It had been traditional for all the top executives to have *come up through the ranks* of the Woolworth organization. (This policy or practice has certain advantages and limitations as discussed in the boxed material.) Gibbons was respected by both the retailing and financial communities as a sound and objective analyst and corporate executive. He was a deeply private man, a no-nonsense type of manager.

---

[2] "The Problems That are Upsetting Woolworth," *Business Week,* June 28, 1974, p. 72.

INFORMATION SIDELIGHT

THE ISSUE OF PROMOTION FROM WITHIN

When it comes to promoting its personnel, an organization has two options: it can promote from within, or it can fill important management positions from outside the organization.

Promotion from within was the policy traditionally followed by a number of major retailers, including Woolworth, Penney, and Kresge, for virtually all their line management positions. For some specialized staff jobs, such as law and research, outsiders were sought if such expertise could not be found in the existing organization.

A rigid policy of promoting from within—some call this inbreeding—has several advantages. It develops intense motivation, loyalty, and dedication to the traditions of the company. The rungs upward in the ladder can be seen by many aspiring trainees and executives as entirely possible and within reach, and this can be a powerful spur.

But the policy of promoting from within can be carried too far. Policies can become self-perpetuating. Innovation can be stymied without the fresh ideas— even disruptive influences—of outsiders. In such an environment a narrow perspective and traditional ways of doing things almost invariably prevail.

A middle ground usually is more desirable: filling many executive positions from within the organization in order to motivate present executives and help in recruiting trainees, while at the same time bringing strong outsiders into the organization where their strengths and particular experiences can be most valuable. As with most things, moderation is more desirable than relying predominantly on either promotion from within or from without.

And his performance as president seemed impressive as he took the company from sales of \$4.7 billion in 1975 to \$7.2 billion in 1981.

But the Woolco operation continued to bedevil Gibbons and Woolworth. It was not profitable and, worse than that, was a serious drain on financial resources. In December 1981 both Standard & Poor's and Moody's downgraded the company's senior debt. Belatedly, Gibbons tried shrinking the stores' size by renting space to outside retailers. But more drastic measures appeared needed if Woolco was to be salvaged. Gibbons recruited Bruce G. Allbright, a discounting expert, to engineer Woolco's recovery. Gibbons noted, "We feel that the discount-store business has a very bright future but only for those who do it very well. Anyone else won't survive."[3]

Allbright had impressive credentials. He was president of the Target Stores discount division of Dayton-Hudson Corporation. Target was one of the most successful discount chains, with sales of \$2.4 billion and profits of

---

[3] "Finally, Woolworth Wields the Ax," *Business Week*, October 11, 1982, p. 119.

$150 million from 167 stores in 1982. Gibbons gave Allbright virtually a free hand to solve Woolco's problems.

But the woes intensified during 1982. In the first six months Woolco lost more money than in all of 1981, and it was now losing in excess of $1 million a week. Standard & Poor's placed the company on credit watch, and major lenders were pressuring Woolworth to do something about its short-term debt, which had reached $788 million by October 31.

In August, Allbright persuaded Harold Smith to leave his post as executive vice president of the Magic Mart discount store chain to help him revive Woolco. Meantime, Woolworth's other businesses were not doing well enough to help Woolco's cash position, and even though Gibbons had confidence in Allbright, there seemed little doubt that it would take at least three years before Woolco could hope to turn a profit.

The Decision

On September 24, 1982, Chairman Gibbons announced at a board meeting the termination of the company's largest division, Woolco. Pressure had been building throughout the year to shutter all 336 of the Woolco stores, despite their contributing $2.1 billion or almost 30 percent of all Woolworth sales. Jobs of 35,000 to 40,000 people were eliminated, and a $325 million after-tax write-off was taken.

Two days after this announcement, Gibbons, a troubled man at age 63, entered the hospital for a routine operation. Thirty days later he was dead from kidney failure. Allbright was the hoped-for-savior but in his nine months with the company, he did not have enough time to resurrect the division. Apparently not informed beforehand of the closing, Allbright was publicly outlining his plans for reviving Woolco less than two weeks before the closing announcement. He was asked to stay on with the company but declined to do so.

POSTMORTEM

Problems of Growth

Vigorous expansion creates problems and stresses for any organization. In Korvette's case, the expansion came from a small base of 9 stores; suddenly there were 25. Supervision and control formerly handled on a face-to-face basis proved insufficient. The company did not have enough trained executives at all levels. While promotion was necessarily fast, ill-trained and marginal people were thrust into responsible positions. Recruiting top-notch people was a problem, partly because discount stores lacked the prestige of more conventional retailers. Organizational policies did not help either, since

Korvette was highly centralized with all merchandising and other policies dictated from the home office. If rapid growth was to be achieved in an absence of tight controls, decentralization, giving more authority and responsibility to store executives, would have helped, but decentralization would have been possible only with higher-paid and more carefully selected store executives.

Korvette started from a hard goods base. Before Ferkauf and his associates could gain experience in merchandising the riskier soft lines and fashion goods or recruit people with this experience, the go-ahead was given for rapid expansion. A delay until soft goods merchandising was better understood would have helped.

With Woolworth, the problem was not one of too rapid and unassimilated expansion, but rather too conservative growth. Kresge was opening an average of 45 to 50 K mart stores a year up to the 1970s when it began opening much larger numbers, but Woolworth was not opening even 30 stores in one year until 1980. Furthermore, these openings were scattered rather than geographically concentrated: "Woolco would open one store in Columbus, Ohio and move on to another market, while K mart opened up three, four, and five stores in Columbus and got economies of distribution and, more important, advertising."[4]

A crucial flaw in the Woolco venture dated back to the beginning in 1962. Woolworth management was ambivalent about the move to discounting, not committing itself fully to either variety stores or discounting—at a time when Kresge shifted its whole emphasis to discounting. The ingrained variety store management just could not let go and give priority to the discount operation.

Woolworth management believed that their cautious attitudes were fully justified. They felt that the "Woolworth Company was too valuable an asset to just go in one direction."[5] Although a conservative approach and a multifaceted strategy may be prudent under many circumstances, it made Woolworth vulnerable to aggressive competitors.

Image Problems

Image was a troublesome factor for both Korvette and Woolworth. At first, in the golden days of Korvette, the discount image—bare-bones prices—had great customer appeal. However, as Korvette expanded with more stores and into soft goods and fashion lines, Ferkauf's conception of the company changed. He saw it no longer as a discount store, but rather as a promotional department store. He opened a store on Fifth Avenue of Manhattan, only a

[4] Geoffrey Smith, "We're Moving! We're; Alive!" *Forbes*, November 21, 1983, pp. 66–71.
[5] "How Kresge Became the Top Discounter," *Business Week*, October 24, 1970, p. 63.

few blocks from some of the most fashionable stores in the world, such as Bonwit Teller and Lord & Taylor. A massive chandelier was placed in the lobby; the discount image was disavowed. "We have Cadillacs that pull up to the store, and women get out and enjoy, as everybody enjoys, being able to buy something a little bit cheaper than they normally would. We have some of the most famous people come into our stores."[6]

But with upgrading of the merchandise, markups rose from less than 8 percent in 1950 to 33 percent in 1965. If Korvette was to escape the discount image, how could it do so and keep its old customers? Korvette became similar to the basement operations of department stores—it carried standard markup items supplemented by loss leaders used for promotional purposes. As merchandise was upgraded, as new stores became more elaborate, as services such as credit were offered, there was an increase in overhead. The uniqueness was lost. Gradually, Korvette acquired the expense structure of traditional retailers, but without the level of expertise of department and specialty stores in the way of quality and fashion merchandising.

A hazy or imprecise image plagued Woolco right from the beginning. Woolworth management could not decide what they wanted Woolco to be—an expanded variety store, a discount store, or a medium-priced department store. Advertising featured Woolco stores as "promotional department stores," implying something of a cross between a discount and a department store. The company failed to establish a clear identity, either for its variety or discount outlets. Indeed, the variety stores and the Woolco stores tended to blur together. The bigger variety stores began to rival the Woolco stores in size, while the Woolco discount prices were often no lower than those of the variety stores.

Organizationally, confusion existed also. Initially, the Woolco division was established as an autonomous unit, completely independent of the variety store division. While this seemed to signify a major commitment to discounting, it increased fixed costs, fragmented the efforts of the total company, and certainly involved less total commitment to discounting than that of Kresge where the whole organization, and not just a separate division, was geared to discounting. More than this, Woolworth faced inherent problems with inexperienced managers and the plodding efforts of a new organizational structure.

By 1971, faced with a heavy overhead that seemed to destroy any hope of profits, the buying and distribution for both Woolco and the variety stores were consolidated. While this lowered the breakeven point, it led to further blurring of the Woolco and Woolworth images. Despite efforts to vary brands and merchandise selections between the two, there was considerable

[6] Robert Drew-Bear, *Mass Merchandise: Revolution and Evolution* (New York: Fairchild Publications, 1970), p. 124.

overlap, and prices continued to run higher than those of discount-store rivals. Consolidation did not bring the needed profits.

External Factors

With Korvette leading the way, the onslaught of discounters in the 1950s and early 1960s was traumatic; some called it the revolution in retailing. However, by the mid-1960s, other retailers were beginning to act aggressively against discounters. Department stores and appliance retailers blunted the initial competitive advantage of discounters either by matching them price for price on identical goods, or else by stocking their own private brand appliances and other items that prevented price comparisons. Many retailers shifted parts of their operations to self-service and eliminated some of the frills that made their operations high cost. And the major advantage discounters got from using high merchandise turnover to yield a good return on investment despite low markups was copied by other retailers. Meanwhile, average costs and markups were rising for all discounters. The result, predictably, was that customers no longer streamed in to just any discount store. Those stores that expanded too rapidly or those less efficient than competitors were ousted from the market.

With the maturing of the discount-store industry in the 1960s, other kinds of discounters came on the scene; they were well-financed, well-managed, and they swept away marginal competitors. K mart was one of these. Major department-store corporations, such as Dayton-Hudson, L. S. Ayres, and Allied Stores, opened discount subsidiaries, carefully run with well-trained, high-caliber personnel, and with definitive policies. These latter discount stores had the advantage of drawing on years of experience with fashion merchandising of their mother firms.

Woolco seemingly should have been one of these survivors. Instead, it found itself beset on all sides. In the middle of the road, it faced the vigorously expanding K mart with more attractive prices and a much more efficient operation. Away from the middle of the road it faced other discounters moving in two directions: (1) toward plusher atmospheres while still keeping low prices (such as the Target Stores of Dayton-Hudson), and (2) toward specialization in limited merchandise areas (such as Toys "Я" Us) offering tremendous assortments in narrow lines at low prices. Despite its huge stores and heavy quantities of goods, Woolco compared poorly with many of its competitors, while its prices were turning off bargain-conscious consumers.

UPDATE

Did getting rid of Woolco improve the operating results of Woolworth? The answer is yes, but one wonders what might have been achieved several years down the road if Woolworth had persevered with Woolco and brought it into the black. The immediate result was that sales dropped from over $7 billion in fiscal 1981 to $5 billion the next year while profits remained virtually the same at $82 million. In the following years, sales gradually rose toward the $6 billion level, although not achieving this level by 1986, while profits showed a nice rise, reaching $177 million for fiscal 1985.

By 1988, Woolworth operated 6799 stores worldwide, 5127 of these being specialty stores in 30 different formats. It still had 1140 five-and-dimes, and these had their loyal shoppers and continued to make money. But the specialty stores in regional malls were expected to account for 46 percent of total sales and 65 percent of operating income worldwide by 1991. (Specialty stores are those carrying a limited range of merchandise, such as Foot Locker athletic-shoe stores.) Among the specialty stores by 1989 were Kinney, Foot Locker, Susie's, Lady Foot Locker, Athletic Shoe X-Press, Richman, Anderson-Little, Kids Mart, Little Folk Shop, Tennis Lady, and Woolworth Express. These specialty stores produce sales of about $250 to $300 a square foot versus $112 a square foot at a Woolworth five-and-ten.[7]

Incidentally, Woolco in Canada was continued, and is thriving.

PART C   W. T. GRANT COMPANY: THE FATAL EXPANSION

In June of 1975, James Kendrick, 62-year-old chief executive of W. T. Grant Company, had his back to the wall. He was in charge of a retail giant of almost 1200 stores with sales of nearly $2 billion. But the company was on the verge of bankruptcy. Grant owed $600 million in short-term loans and $100 million in long-term debt to 143 banks. It had incurred a staggering $175 million loss for 1974. And the losses were continuing: $54 million in the first quarter of 1975. Dividends, which had been paid for 69 years, were suspended. On June 1, Grant was to pay $57 million to retire its debt to 116 of the banks. Failure to do so might well induce some of the creditors to push Grant into bankruptcy.

PRELUDE

The blame for this situation was not Kendrick's. The previous management had been deposed in a director's revolt in August 1974. Kendrick was a long-time Grant employee who had been running a subsidiary, Zeller's, Ltd., in Canada. Seven years before, he had been a candidate for president of Grant. But he had been passed over and exiled to Canada because he had ques-

---

[7] "Specialty Stores Spruce Up Bottom Line," *USA Today,* February 26, 1988, pp. 19, 28.

tioned policies of the Board. Now Edward Staley, chairman of the board, and the other top executives had been ousted and Kendrick had been tapped for the company's greatest trial.

Staley was founder William T. Grant's brother-in-law. As the aged Grant became less active, he turned increasingly to Staley to run the company. Staley was president from 1952 to 1959, but he remained in active control under various titles until 1974. He supported Richard C. Mayer, the president of Grant from 1968 to 1974, who led Grant into an expansion course that was both heady and disastrous.

Before Richard Mayer became Grant's president in 1968, he had set up the company's credit operation so successfully that it contributed 25 percent of sales in 1972. Mayer was interested in vigorous expansion. Shortly after he assumed the presidency, the company broke out of a three-year earnings rut and joined the ranks of $1 billion plus retail firms. Encouraged by this progress, Mayer set a goal of $2 billion in sales by 1972, one of the most ambitious expansion programs ever plotted by a retailer.

HISTORY

"Looking back to the earliest days I can remember, it seems to me that I always wanted a store," wrote William T. Grant. He sold shoes in his hometown of Malden, Massachusetts, and headed the shoe department of a Boston department store when he was only 19. In 1906, taking his life savings of $1000, he opened his first store in Lynn, Massachusetts. A second store was opened within two years, and the firm continued its steady growth.

While his stores were similar to the five-and-tens of Woolworth and Kresge, William Grant saw an opportunity for stores with prices above those of the five-and-tens and below the more expensive department stores. His first stores carried the 25-cent price theme. As the company expanded through the years, it was thought of primarily as a variety store. In the late 1960s, W. T. Grant went heavily into high-ticket durables such as TV sets, furniture, and appliances.

Grant retired from active management of the company at age 48, but continued as chairman of the board until his ninetieth birthday in 1966. On his fiftieth anniversary with the company in 1956, Grant reiterated his childhood conviction about the thrill of retailing:

> I know of no other business which could give a man so much action, so much challenge, so much satisfaction and so rich a reward for good service to the community than this wonderful business of ours. I have enjoyed every minute of it.[8]

---

[8] Adapted from a publication of the W. T. Grant Company commemorating the decease of William T. Grant.

THE GO-GO EXPANSION YEARS

As 1972 drew to a close, Richard Mayer looked back with satisfaction at the company's growth in the previous 10 years, and he ordered the record of this growth distributed to the financial community, company employees, interested vendors, and stockholders. The statistics were indeed impressive. Some of the more important ones are shown here:

	1962	1972	Percentage Increase in Ten Years
Total number of stores	1,032	1,208	17
Total sales	$686,263,000	$1,644,747,000	140
Credit sales	$ 97,478,000	$ 406,763,000	317
Net earnings	$ 9,004,000	$ 37,787,000	320
Net worth	$141,381,000	$ 334,339,000	137
Percentage earned on net worth	6.4	11.3	
Dividends paid on common stock	$ 6,997,000	$ 20,807,000	197

Mayer was particularly proud of the statistics on store growth since he had assumed the presidency in 1968:

	1963–1967	1968	1969	1970	1971	1972
New stores opened	202	41	52	65	83	92
Stores enlarged	55	11	3	8	5	5
Stores closed	148	35	49	44	31	52
Store space in thousands of square feet:						
Opened during period	10,933	3,205	3,950	5,360	7,254	7,070
Closed during period	(2,962)	(759)	(1,277)	(1,058)	(693)	(1,198)
At end of period	28,736	31,182	33,855	38,157	44,718	50,618

Source: W. T. Grant Company, *Facts and Highlights, Ten Fiscal Years Ended January 31, 1973.* p. 5.

These statistics made Grant look like a winner, a growth company attractive both to investor and creditor. However, one aspect of the operational performance nagged Mayer a bit and gained some attention from the investment community. Earnings were in a three-year decline from a high of

$41,809,000 in 1969, despite sales increases of over $500 million. However, Mayer had a ready explanation. He figured three to five years were necessary for a new store to mature before customer acceptance allowed a store's sales and profits to reach an acceptable level. Mayer assured his critics that he expected a couple of years of flat earnings as multiple openings caused start-up expenses to balloon while recently opened stores were still in the maturing period.

There were other statistics that should have given him concern. Long-term debt had risen from $35 million to $126 million in the 10-year period, an increase of 377 percent. The stock-to-sales ratio had risen sharply. Sales per square foot between 1968 and 1972 dropped from $35.13 to $32.50. At this level it was less than half those of its major competitors. During this same period the company had closed over six million of its least productive square feet. This, along with the worsening ratios, suggested that the new stores were not generating strong sales.

The expansion efforts of Grant during 1971 and 1972, as measured by square feet of space added, were a close second to Penney in 1971 and third in 1972 behind Penney and Kresge. The expansion policies are the more amazing considering how much bigger Penney and Kresge were than Grant:

| | Sales | |
	1971	1972
Penney	$4,812,000,000	$5,530,000,000
Kresge	3,140,000,000	3,875,000,000
Grant	1,375,000,000	1,645,000,000

Furthermore, Grant far exceeded the expansion efforts of Sears, the largest retailer, with sales about ten times greater than Grant's.

The new stores Grant opened were more than twice the size of the average store of 1964, and some 75 percent were in suburban shopping centers. (The smaller stores that were being phased out were often located in deteriorating downtown locations.) Average sales per store had risen to about $1 million compared to $646,000 in 1964.

Grant's expansion was highlighted by their superstores, stores of 180,000 square feet, although the size of other new stores ranged down to 60,000 square feet. There were two separate location strategies. The big stores, 120,000 to 180,000 square feet, were placed in medium-size enclosed malls, with a Sears, Ward, or even a major discounter as a co-anchor. On the other hand, smaller stores being built in neighborhood and convenience centers were aimed at dominating a small market where there was no nearby competition from major general merchandisers.

The larger stores were required by Grant's effort to expand and upgrade the product lines to include big-ticket items such as television sets, major appliances, power tools, automobile accessories, sporting goods, and camera equipment. The superstores even carried garden equipment, furniture, and auto servicing. By 1971 the product line was made up of about 25 percent family fashions, 50 percent hard goods, and 25 percent small wares and services. This was a distinct change from the product line of a variety chain that once had 50 percent of its products in family fashions and very little in hard goods. The average store now stocked over 21,000 items in all price ranges. About 70 percent of the merchandise carried the Grant private label, permitting Grant to offer somewhat lower prices than if nationally advertised brands were handled.

A program to facilitate all-out expansion was implemented that cut down the development time for new stores from 90 days to 60 days. The developer's architect was no longer required to submit working drawings to the chain for final approval provided he would certify that the plans conformed to Grant's specifications. Under the old method, plans were submitted to Grant and usually many changes were made before final approval. Eliminating the review procedure resulted in widely fluctuating costs. But with an objective of pell-mell expansion, shortcuts had to be taken.

Approaching Disaster, 1973 and 1974

Mayer's expansion plans continued unabated for most of 1973. Only Kresge's K mart added more square feet of space. Operations were deep in the red for the first nine months of 1973. But since the last quarter of the year is the most crucial one for retail operations because of the peak Christmas business, management waited until December to make any further decisions regarding the expansion program. In December, Grant had gains of 3.7 percent, the smallest of any major retailer. The expansion program was a disaster. Management belatedly became aware that more stores do not necessarily mean profitable sales. While remaining chief executive, Richard Mayer gave up the presidency to operations man Harry Pierson. The expansion program was over.

For the full year of 1973 sales rose to $1.8 billion. But profits dropped 78 percent to $8.4 million, the lowest profits since 1967 when sales were only $575 million. And 1973 was a year in which Sears, Penney, Kresge, and Woolworth all showed record earnings. Grant's return on equity, once 15 percent, dropped to less than 5 percent. More ominous, however, long-term debt increased to $222 million from only 35 million in 1970, and short-term debt increased to $450 million.

Grant's troubles were only beginning. In 1974, sales fell to $1.7 billion, and the firm suffered a gargantuan loss of $175 million. Dividends were suspended for the first time in Grant's 69-year history. And James Kendrick was engaged in an eleventh-hour effort to save the nation's seventeenth-largest retailer from extinction.

To cut costs, Kendrick planned to close 126 stores in 1975, trim the payroll from 82,500 to 69,000, and pare the company's credit unit, which accounted for 62 percent of the 1974 losses. Contributing to the problems facing Kendrick was a loss of $24 million for store closing costs, heavy interest charges, and massive markdowns of slow-moving goods.

June 1975

Finally, Kendrick was sweating out the June 2, 1975 payment of $57 million required to retire the company's debt to 116 of the 143 banks that provided the financing for the ill-fated expansion. Failure to pay these smaller creditors might well force bankruptcy. The bigger banks had more at stake and would not be inclined to sink the company in an effort to get a faster settlement. The financial and investment community waited. The news finally hit the press and the market tape that Grant had somehow managed to come up with the $57 million. Kendrick now had a little breathing room.

Causes of the Dilemma

Ill-conceived and too-vigorous expansion certainly must take the blame for many of the Grant problems. Kendrick said:

> The expansion program placed a great strain on the physical and human capability of the company to cope with the program. These were all large stores we were opening, and the expansion of our management organization just did not match the expansion of our stores.[8]

A former operations executive noted: "Our training program couldn't keep up with the explosion of stores, and it didn't take long for the mediocrity to begin to show."

There was another underlying factor that played a major role in the Grant dilemma. After all, other firms have expanded rapidly in the past, such as the Penney Company and most of the other major chains in the 1920s. Kresge and their K mart stores vigorously expanded for over a decade, and were the epitome of success. But Grant's expansion was hindered by a lack of a definable and distinctive image. Was Grant a variety chain? A discounter? A general merchandise chain? What should Grant be? Or more realistically, what should it strive to be?

[9] "How W. T. Grant Lost $175 Million Last Year," *Business Week*, February 24, 1975, p. 75.

The company assumed a mid-position between a discounter and a general merchandise firm—neither fowl nor ass. As merchandise lines were expanded and prices upgraded, Grant veered strongly away from the variety-store image, but in some ways still retained it. (For example, certain typical variety-store departments, such as candy, were still kept near the front of stores.) On the other hand, Grant did not try to keep up with K mart in discounting prices although its prices were competitive enough to be called promotional. Mayer coined the phrase "one-stop family shopping stores," suggesting a general merchandiser such as Sears and Penney. However, Grant lacked the punch of either of these and was unable to offer the service or the established brands of Sears or Penney. For example, Grant's major brand, Bradford, was practically unknown, and many people were reluctant to buy appliances and similar goods where quality and service were questionable. Given time, Grant could have established acceptance of its own brand, but problems were emerging too fast under its expansion policies.

The vigorous expansion, which led to inefficiencies and mediocre performance, added to an uncertain and murky image, and resulted in inventory problems as some merchandise from the broadened product line—especially appliances—did not sell. Store buyers, in their eagerness to stock huge stores, often bought larger quantities than could be moved as seasons, styles, and tastes changed. But there was a reluctance to mark down and clear out this inventory. One merchandising executive recalled "mounds of goods that just sat year to year collecting dust; they had so much stuff just sitting there they couldn't free up the dollars to do a good seasonal merchandising job."[10]

Many of the new stores were not living up to expectations and with some merchandise categories stagnant, Grant began a heavy credit promotion in an effort to move these goods. But too much leniency in granting credit led to disastrous uncollectible accounts and credit write-offs.

The mix of stores added to Grant's difficulties. The new stores were never really standardized. They came in sizes from 54,000 square feet to 180,000, with different interiors and exteriors and different merchandise assortments. Some stores were free-standing, without other stores nearby; others were in malls; still others in strip centers.

Since many Grant stores had low sales productivity, developers often refused to give them choice locations. Consequently, many of the new stores were in poor sites. On top of these problems, Grant filed a suit in February 1975 against three former employees charged with taking "hundreds of thousands of dollars in bribes in connection with store leases," which relegated Grant to many poor store locations. Lawsuits were pressed against the former real estate vice president, the Southern real estate manager, and the

[10] Ibid., pp. 75–76.

Midwest real estate manager, alleging kickbacks and bribery: "some store sites and rental terms may not have been in our best interest and may have contributed to some of our problems."[11]

Climax, 1975

The $57 million payment toward the debt reduction was made. Slender breathing room was gained, but could Kendrick bring the company back to viability? Kendrick sought to undo the damages and move ahead. He proposed going after the same mass market as K mart and Woolco and to be competitive in price. He decided to deemphasize big-ticket items, and strengthen infants' and children's wear, white goods, and curtains and draperies. He planned to spend $6 million on television spots in 35 major markets. Mayer had been a credit man, little versed in merchandising and operations. Now Kendrick proposed to stress basic merchandising, such as keeping stocks fresh and clean and taking prompt markdowns. "We failed to stock *staples*, which in turn led to an overabundance of slow-selling items," Kendrick pointed out. He also recognized that Grant's merchandising program may have been too promotional-minded, and that not enough reliance was placed on national brands.[12]

In the next few years, Kendrick hoped to pare the system to a core group of 900 stores, and stabilize sales volume at about $1.5 billion. He intended to increase the use of brand-name goods and increase the dollar volume per square foot. Complicating the problem of streamlining, however, were the many long-term leases running anywhere from 10 to 20 years for some stores due to be closed because of poor locations. Unless these could be subleased, their expense drain would continue for some time.

As a further merchandising tool, Grant planned to accept BankAmericard and MasterCharge sales, thereby playing down its own dismal credit operation. While recognizing the expenses involved in these bank cards, the company hoped to attract more customers.

Despite the efforts of Kendrick and the sharp reversal of previous policies, the picture steadily worsened during 1975. For the six months ended July 31, 1975, the chain lost $111.3 million. Landlords were asked to roll their store rents back 25 percent; some complied. Loan agreements were renegotiated with 27 banks headed by Morgan Guaranty, in which $300 million of the $640 million owed to the banks was subordinated (that is, given lower priority for repayment) to bills owing suppliers, and, in general, the loan provisions were moderated. Subordinating the bank loans was vital, since Grant had some $500 million worth of goods on order, but many suppliers were holding up deliveries for fear they would not be paid.

---

[11] Ibid.

[12] "It's Get Tough Time at W. T. Grant," *Business Week*, October 19, 1974, p. 46.

INFORMATION SIDELIGHT

IMPORTANCE OF MAINTAINING STAPLE GOODS

Staple items sell day by day in steady, if unspectacular, amounts. In many departments, such as stationery, notions, hoisery, housewares, hardware, sporting goods, candy, toilet goods, and domestics and linens, staples account for most of the total sales. But because such goods sell steadily without fanfare, there is the temptation to pay little attention to them. Special purchases, new items, interesting styles—these tend to get the attention and enthusiasm.

But a serious error is made in minimizing the importance of staple goods. Out-of-stocks here result not only in a lost sale, but, since many staple items do not have ready substitutes, customers are forced to go to competitors to purchase the items. Sending a customer away may have these undesirable consequences:

The store loses customer goodwill because of the extra shopping effort required.

A customer perceives the store as inefficient and poorly merchandised, and decides to shift business permanently.

A customer may decide to satisfy other buying needs in the competing store where the staple item is available.

Grant was losing money faster than anticipated and was forced to announce that it was operating with a negative net worth; that is, its debts exceeded its assets. This was the beginning of the end. On October 2, 1975, Grant entered bankruptcy proceedings, filing a petition under Chapter 11 of the federal Bankruptcy Act. W. T. Grant Company thus became the second biggest U.S. company to enter bankruptcy proceedings (the biggest was Penn Central Transportation Company in 1970), and the largest retailer ever to do so.

Under Chapter 11 bankruptcy, a company continues to operate, but has court protection against creditors' lawsuits while working out a plan for paying its debts. Some shareholders, in a separate action, filed to have the proceedings converted to Chapter 10 bankruptcy. This is a more drastic move in which control of the company passes to a court-appointed trustee whose interests are more with the creditors and who will try for a complete financial reorganization and, if necessary, may liquidate some or all of the company's assets to raise money to pay creditors.

In the fall of 1975, the company squeaked past the threat of complete liquidation, retrenching with hundreds of store closings, including most of those west of the Mississippi. If there was to be any chance for survival and eventual payment of creditors, strong Christmas sales were needed. However, with suppliers fearful of providing goods because of the bankruptcy proceedings, the chance of the company's being adequately stocked for Christmas business was jeopardized.

UPDATE

W. T. Grant Company did not make it. On February 9, 1976, six banks and one vendor on the creditors' committee that had been formed after Grant went into Chapter 11 bankruptcy proceedings voted for liquidation (four other creditors on the committee voted against liquidation). On February 11, the federal Bankruptcy Court in New York ordered the liquidation to begin. Some 1073 retail stores were closed and 80,000 persons put out of work. Furthermore, Grant's banks had to write off approximately $234 million in bad loans, and its suppliers some $110 million in unpaid bills.

FOR THOUGHT AND DISCUSSION

1. We have noted that one of the serious problems Korvette faced during its rapid growth was lack of adequate systems and procedures, particularly regarding feedback and controls from the stores. What controls or performance measures would you want to have established in this situation?
2. Personal supervision by Ferkauf was possible when he had only a small number of stores in a limited area. With steady expansion, such personal supervision was no longer possible. What might have been done at this point to assure adequate supervision of stores?
3. Was the major mistake of Woolworth that it did not put sufficient stake into the Woolco operation, that it was reluctant to go all out as Kresge did? Discuss, considerating any trade-offs.
4. How do you think it might have been possible for Grant to expand as vigorously as it did and to do so successfully?

INVITATION TO ROLE PLAY

1. Place yourself in the role of Eugene Ferkauf, a tremendous innovator and leader of the discount movement with Korvette. You have just been proclaimed by famed educator Malcolm McNair as one of the six greatest merchants in U.S. history. You are humble, yet ecstatic at this honor. Now how do you prove it? Be as specific as possible.
2. As the CEO of Woolworth at the time of the Woolco abandonment, how would you support your decision to the board of directors? Be as persuasive as possible—your job as CEO may depend on this.
3. You are a staff assistant to James Kendrick of Grant. He has just assumed leadership of the company. You have been asked by him to develop plans for a course of action to keep the company viable. Be as specific as you can, and be prepared to defend your recommendations.

9

Contrast—Organizational Simplicity, A Key to Success: K Mart

And now we come to K mart, the winner in the monumental struggle to be the biggest factor in discount retailing, and even the biggest factor in the total retail competitive environment.

K mart was a latecomer to the discount scene. Kresge brought to its K mart operation proven management and merchandising techniques and resources, with which it was able to convert the operations of a neighborhood variety store to that of a giant discount store. Yet, other retailers, such as Woolworth and W. T. Grant, had tried to do likewise and were to fail. Why?

One man brought about the change for Kresge.

HARRY B. CUNNINGHAM

In 1957, Harry Cunningham left a meeting with Frank Williams, the president. Cunningham was in a state of shock, tinged with euphoria. He had just been informed of his appointment as a vice president of the Kresge Company. This did not completely surprise him, since he had had a feeling a promotion was imminent. But his assignment—that was the surprise, and what a wonderful challenge—perhaps.

Harry's thoughts went back to his early years with Kresge, the only firm for which he had ever worked. He remembered his beginnings—a stockroom trainee in the Lynchburg, Virginia, store back in 1928, almost 30 years before. After attending Miami University (Ohio) for two years, his money

ran out and he could not return to school. The stockroom job was uninterest-
ing and unchallenging compared to the intellectual stimulation of college,
but he stuck it out and gradually worked up in the ranks of store management. In 1953, he was promoted to the home office as sales director of the
company. There, top management was impressed with his ideas; he was
even invited to some of the board meetings. And now this.

His thoughts swung from his career path to the company and its deteriorating prospects. The S. S. Kresge Company, founded as a five-and-dime in
1897 by Sebastian Spring Kresge and second only to Woolworth among variety store chains, now faced greatly worsening prospects. Part of the problem
appeared social: the company's traditional customers' needs and wants were
changing. At the same time, discounters were invading the market with a
strong price appeal. Part of the problem, Kresge management admitted, was
that Kresge had moved away from the founding philosophy of "quality at
the lowest possible price" to a larger concentration on specialty items with
low turnover rates and higher prices. But regardless of the causes, the situation seemed clear: Kresge had a serious long-term problem, and the solution
was uncertain.

Back in his office, with an effort Harry focused his mind on the present
and the promise or disappointments lurking in the future. His new assignment as vice president was bewilderingly different and completely unstruc-
tured. He was freed of operating responsibilities for two years to study the
changing competitive environment, with particular attention to the discount
stores threatening the variety stores. At the end of the two years, Frank Williams told him, he was to return with his recommendations for the Kresge
Company, and to prepare himself for the presidency of the company.

The Turning Point

In those two years, Harry Cunningham logged more than 200,000 air miles
studying competition all over the country. In Garden City, Long Island, he
observed in great detail a major unit of Korvette. He concluded that the concept was great, with the key element being the tremendous rate of turnover.
But he also recognized shortcomings in the Korvette operation, namely that
Ferkauf was running the business singlehandedly and that it lacked the
organizational expertise to handle the growth Cunningham hoped to
achieve. He came to believe that Kresge was "overstored" with variety
stores, and was competing with itself in the shopping centers, whereas other
units were tied to long-term leases in deteriorating neighborhoods. Meanwhile, the discounters were cutting deeper into sales; only a minuscule sales
gain was recorded from 1955 to 1960, and profits were slipping.

Cunningham came back convinced that discounting was the way to go.
In May 1959 he was made president and chairman of the executive commit-

tee and began laying the groundwork for the expansion he saw ahead. He was determined that Kresge would build the needed organization within the company. His executives were instructed to study intently the discount industry. He wanted to take Kresge into discounting full scale, with no room for second thoughts, but he had to sell the idea to his organization:

> Discounting at the time had a terrible odor. . . . If I had announced my intentions ahead of time I never would have made president. . . . I had the authority, but if you haven't sold the people in your organization, you'll fall flat on your face. I had to convince them that they were an important part of an exciting venture.[1]

He first had to sell the board, and this was not easy. His initial presentation was met by reservations such as "We have been in the variety business for sixty years—we know everything there is to know about it, and we're not doing very well in that; and you want to get us into a business we don't know anything about."[2]

Part of the persuasive argument that Cunningham used to convince the board was that the basic concepts of discounting—low gross margin, high turnover, concentration on return on investment—merely represented a return to the basics of the original variety-store concept, except that the discount format meant much broader merchandise assortments. Looked at this way, the proposed venture into discounting was less daunting, a less extreme diversification than appeared at first glance.

In March 1961, the official decision was made to move into discounting. But Cunningham found that some of the older executives at all levels were incapable of making the adjustment and had to be replaced. By the fall of 1961, every operating vice president, regional manager, assistant regional manager, and regional merchandise manager was fresh on the job. But these new executives were all insiders who had proven themselves in various aspects of Kresge management, were receptive to new ideas, and eager for the challenges Cunningham envisioned.

A vice president, C. Lloyd Yohe, was sent out in the field to study exactly how Kresge should enter this market; Yohe was subsequently made general manager of the discount operation. On his return, he set up guidelines for the new operation, including facilities and layout, siting, salaries, operating ratios, and productivity.

In October 1961, Cunningham ordered his real estate department to obtain signed leases for no less than 60 stores, with 40 to be opened in 1963.

---

[1] Eleanore Carrath, "K mart Has to Open Some New Doors on the Future," *Fortune*, July 1977, p. 144.

[2] Robert E. Dewar, "Kresge Company and the Retail Revolution," *University of Michigan Business Review*, July 1975, p. 2.

This was a rental commitment of $30 million—and certainly millions more in fixtures, merchandise, and other needs—before the first prototype store even opened. It was an audacious move, but it was supported by the firm confidence of Cunningham in the viability of the discount concept and the strength of his organization.

To staff the stores, the vice president of personnel was assigned the job of working out a work-force formula for recruiting, training, and executive development. One of the big questions at that time was whether or not the present Kresge buyers were competent to buy for the new discount operation. The buyers were emphatic in declaring that they were, and the decision was made not to establish a separate buying staff.

Staffing such a vast expansion program was challenging; but it was also highly motivating for the rank and file management personnel, who could readily see the vastly expanded promotional opportunities in the months and years ahead. Over 400 new employees were hired after recruiting teams visited more than 100 colleges and universities. Work-force development was considered indispensable to a rapidly growing, far-flung operation.

In the beginning, certain of the new departments—cameras, sporting goods, jewelry, men's and boy's furnishing, and food—were so unfamiliar it was decided to lease them to experienced operators. Gradually, as the organization gained more experience with the diverse lines, these departments were taken over by K mart people. By 1980, of the nonfood departments only footwear was still leased.

Action

In the first two years of his presidency, Cunningham was faced with the problem that an increasing number of variety stores were in poorer, decaying neighborhoods where Kresge had long-term leases. Instead of closing these stores, even though their rent would continue, it was decided to experiment and convert some of them to small discount stores called Jupiter Stores. These were a far cry from the much larger K marts, but they were successful enough that many were again able to turn a profit. The Jupiter Stores sold basic staple products at low prices in austere surroundings. But they were profitable, gave the company an additional taste of discount strategy, and provided a training ground for future K mart managers.

In March 1962, in Garden City, Michigan, the first K mart was opened. It was an immediate success, as customers thronged to the attractive store with the low prices. Cunningham's bold gamble appeared vindicated. Company executives observing the milling crowds and the many busy checkout stands had to believe this was the way of the future for Kresge.

At the time, the company had 803 variety stores and a few Jupiter Stores. The company had experienced a 34 percent decrease in profits between 1958 and 1962. Before the end of the decade, S. S. Kresge Company owned the nation's largest discount store chain. Table 9.1 shows the rapid growth of K mart during the 11 years from 1968 to 1978. The number of new stores added each year is almost incredible, particularly in 1976. In that year, Kresge took over 145 former W T Grant stores and in addition established 126 new units for a total of 271 new stores. To do so, K mart promoted 310 assistant store managers to store managers and hired 27,000 people to support one of the greatest yearly expansions ever achieved by a retailer— one that experts believed could never be topped.

The growth of Kresge's sales volume is compared to its major competitors in Table 9.2. Starting from a much lower base, in 1976 Kresge became the second largest general merchandise retailer, passing J. C. Penney Company and trailing only Sears, with almost twice the sales volume of Woolworth.

Table 9.1   The Growth of K mart, 1968–1978

Year (as of January 31)	Number of K marts in Operation	Stores Added Each Year
1968	216	54
1969	273	57
1970	338	65
1971	411	73
1972	486	75
1973	580	94
1974	673	93
1975	803	130
1976	935	132
1977	1206	271
1978	1366	160

Source: S. S. Kresge published reports.

Table 9.2   Sales Volume and Percentage Change for K mart and Major Competitors, 1961–1976 (Millions of Dollars)

	Kresge		Sears		Penney		Woolworth	
Year	Sales Volume	Percent Change	Sales Volume	Percent Change	Sales Volume	Percent Change	Sales Volume	Percent Change
1961	$ 450		$ 4,267		$1,554		$1,061	
1966	1,090	142	6,805	59	2,549	64	1,574	48
1971	3,100	184	10,006	47	4,812	89	2,801	78
1976	8,380	170	14,900	49	8,354	74	5,152	84

Source: Moody's Industrial Manual and company annual reports.

With such rapid expansion, was Kresge in danger of overcommitment and even bankruptcy with its bold expansion? The answer is a resounding "No!" If we examine the long-term debt as a percentage of sales of Kresge and its major competitors, we find Kresge's is the lowest. For example, in 1974 long-term debt of Kresge was 3.8 percent of sales; Sears was 8.4 percent; Penney 5.3 percent; Woolworth, 9.9; and (soon-to-be-bankrupt) Grant at 12.1 percent. Kresge financed its expansion for the most part with internally generated funds.

During the early and mid-1970s, nearly a dozen discount chains were in bankruptcy, reorganization, or receivership. In addition to Grant, some of the better-known firms with severe problems were Arlan's (which had acquired the faltering Korvette in 1971), Mammoth Stores, and Spartan. Penney's Treasure Island stores and Woolworth's Woolco followed a few years later. K mart, however, emerged strong, profitable, and dominant in most metropolitan areas. Indeed, up to 1980 only one K mart store was ever closed, and five new K marts were opened in the same market area at the same time.

On March 17, 1977, shareholders of S. S. Kresge Company voted to change the corporate name to K mart Corporation in recognition of the success of the discount operation, which by 1976 was producing 94 percent of the corporation's annual domestic sales.

INGREDIENTS OF SUCCESS

Observers have cited a number of factors behind the success of K mart:

- Emphasis on high turnover
- Emphasis on low markups, low prices, and heavy sales volume
- Emphasis on first-quality goods and national brands—no seconds or distress goods
- Across the board discounting rather than selected specials
- One-stop shopping format
- Clustering

What these observers fail to appreciate is that these factors are not unique to K mart: these same policies and practices are common to almost all discount operations.

High turnover is the key ingredient of discounting strategy for all discounters. It is the kingpin that enables firms to emphasize low prices and yet prosper on low markups. (Review the boxed information in the Korvette case, which demonstrates with numbers that impact of turnover on profitability.) High turnover is achieved by carrying only the most popular sizes and items—there is no room for slow sellers or fringe sizes.

The policy of carrying only first-quality goods with an emphasis on national brands was a policy of the early discounters. This was in contrast with the policy of bargain basements of department stores and some promotional-type stores that sought closeouts, distress goods, and seconds that could be sold at low prices and still yield a good markup. Discounters believed the only way they could gain customer acceptance was to offer regular quality merchandise, preferably well-known national brands that were presold by the manufacturer's advertising.

The one-stop shopping format adopted in the early planning for K mart was a practice followed by Korvette and many of the early discounters. A wide range of departments, including food and furniture, was common. Actually, K mart not not go as far with the one-stop format as stores like Korvette, since it did not try to maintain a full furniture and carpeting department.

The idea of clustering—opening a number of stores in a metropolitan area at the same or nearly the same time—was also a strategy practiced by Korvette. The advertising impact of a number of stores sharing the expense was more powerful than that of competing firms with fewer units to share the advertising burden, and the technique also increased the effectiveness of management and control.

Consequently, we have to look further to identify the factors unique to K mart's success at a time when many discount firms were faltering and some areas were becoming oversaturated with stores. The following are characteristics we can identify as the unique ingredients of the success of K mart:

- *Rapid but controlled growth.* The line is thin between overly ambitious expansion and overconservative caution. The first can leave a firm vulnerable to financial overextension, and the latter can result in lost opportunity and competitive inroads.

  Kresge may have walked the thin line in its ambitious expansion plans. But it had several trumps. Most of the organizational requirements were already in place. Management personnel and training programs were well established and tested. Store location and planning research and analyses were also well seasoned. Controls for far-flung units had been operational for decades. All of these important factors for a mighty expansion drive already existed.

- *Organizational simplicity.* Unlike other established firms, such as Penney and Woolworth who ventured into discounting with a separate subsidiary, K mart kept its variety store organization—the same buyers, store planners, and management personnel. And this worked. Their skills were transferable and could be shared. In return, there is organizational simplicity. And this brought the advantages of better communication, coordination, and cooperation by all sectors of the corporation than normally could be expected when such functions and activities are divided. It also brought lower overhead.

- *Simplicity of store planning and layout.* According to the size of the market area, five different sizes and models of K marts were constructed:

  1. 40,000 sq ft (for cities 8000 to 15,000 in population)
  2. 65,000 sq ft (for up to about 50,000 in population)
  3. 70,000 sq ft (for the 75,000 population target)
  4. 84,000 sq ft (for the large metropolitan markets)
  5. 95,000 sq ft (for still larger metropolitan markets)

  Thus, K mart was able to enter a market with the most effective competitive size for the market. Stores and layouts were standardized to maximize the effectiveness and speed of planning, stocking, and opening.

- *High-quality store management.* The key factor of high-grade management differentiated K mart from most of its competitors, including the ill-fated Korvette. Kresge had long had one of the strongest college recruiting and management development programs of any chain, and this commitment was intensified with the heavy labor requirements brought about by the K mart expansion. Each manager was given considerable autonomy—far more than is customarily given to chain store managers—and responsibilities, including hiring and training personnel, ordering merchandise, and controlling expenditures and inventory. To ensure their preparation for such responsibilities, store managers were given top salaries and intensive training. A 21-week orientation program began their training, followed by on-the-job experience as a manager of either a Jupiter or Kresge variety store. The next step was comanager of a K mart unit. After approximately nine years of management experience, the successful candidates were given a K mart to manage. Compensation and further promotion were based on how well the manager handled the profit-center responsibilities and his or her ability to generate a proper return on investment.

- *Adaptability.* K mart exhibited an adaptability to changing circumstances unusual in a large organization that had been successful following a different strategy. At least four strategy modifications can be identified:

  1. The early strategy of all discounters was a bare minimum of service, to keep costs and prices rock-bottom. Consequently, they offered no credit, nor did K mart in its early years. However, by

1970 the company sensed the need for credit service and began accepting bank credit cards as well as issuing its own credit card. The latter was dropped four years later because of costs, but the bank credit cards are still accepted.

2. Early discounters were located in free-standing sites or abandoned warehouses and the like, and K mart found great success in building its own free-standing stores isolated from other stores and from the restrictions of shopping centers. But the company was flexible enough to enter its first regional mall in 1978 and now uses both types of locations.

3. By the mid-1970s Kresge determined that stores could be located much closer together than had earlier been thought. This strategy change paved the way for greater expansion and more density of market coverage.

4. When the first K mart store was opened, leased departments accounted for half of total sales volume. But K mart began taking over the leased departments as it acquired more experience with the unfamiliar lines of merchandise, allowing it to exercise greater control and to obtain greater profits over a wide-ranging array of products.

K MART AND THE FAILURES: WHAT CAN BE LEARNED?

The success of K mart contrasts sharply with the failures of other what-should-have-been major forces in the discount arena. Intuitively we know that powerful learning experiences exist here for all firms faced with powerful competitors—and this includes most firms.

Learning Insight. *Success can come simply, merely by doing the ordinary better than competitors.*

K mart in many ways followed the traditional discount store format, the same format and policies followed by Korvette, Woolco, Topps, Spartan, Zayre's, and a host of others. But it did it better: a better job of planning operations and selecting locations; a better job of setting up the organization; a better job of training and developing people, both managerial and nonmanagerial.

Not surprisingly, we will find a similar situation with McDonald's in a later section of the book: McDonald's, in its great growth years toward market dominance of the fast-food industry, simply did things better and more consistently than its competitors.

Learning Insight. *One individual can exert a profound influence—for good or bad—on an organization's fortunes.*

In less than a decade, Harry Cunningham transformed the slipping and mediocre Kresge into an industry leader. At about the same time, another chief executive, Richard Mayer of W. T. Grant Company, led his firm to disaster and liquidation. And Eugene Ferkauf, the pioneer, the one with the vision and head-start, saw Korvette crumbling around him.

Suppose Harry Cunningham had been mistaken in his assessment of the opportunity for Kresge in discounting. The Kresge Company might have become another Grant if it had attempted uncontrolled expansion. The line can be thin between aggressiveness and rashness. Vigorous growth can lead a firm to great success or total failure.

Learning Insight. *Rapid growth is possible without jeopardizing viability, but it must be controlled growth. Beware of a growth-at-any-cost mentality.*

K mart showed that rapid growth is possible without jeopardizing viability, whereas Korvette and Grant show the perils of overextension. But rapid growth should only be attempted when it can be controlled, when it does not outstrip the work force, research and planning, and financial resources. Objectives, policies, and management and financial controls should be well defined, and lines of authority and performance measures should be specified. It must be clear who is responsible for what, and how performance is to be measured.

Only when growth is controlled is it likely that a seasoned and strong management team can be available so that merchandising, operating, and staff departments can function smoothly. (The boxed information discusses the important role of *management development* for an organization aspiring to rapid growth.) In building the most effective operation, testing is necessary in order to make adjustments and modifications where needed. Without time to sit back and analyze past successes and failures, faults are undetected and uncorrected, and strengths are not pinpointed and acted upon. For example, a well-run discount operation needs strong and well-designated policies regarding store security (since with self-service and fewer employees per customer than in traditional stores, shoplifting and employee theft are more tempting) and the control of waste and shrinkage.

Perhaps the major point to be learned from the experience of Grant is the fallacy of growth at any cost. Stores were opened without regard either for sound location or for an adequately trained organization. Adding millions of square feet of selling space each year may increase sales, but at what

---

INFORMATION SIDELIGHT

MANAGEMENT DEVELOPMENT

Any growing firm needs competent executives and staff professionals to step into new opening slots. Managerial expansion can come in two ways:

1. From internal management development
2. By recruiting from outside the organization

Internal management development presumes a body of trainees who have the potential competence and motivation to fill important executive slots in the future. But time is needed to give such trainees the experience, coaching, and perhaps formal training to fulfill such expectations. For example, the S. S. Kresge Company at one time planned a five-year program to develop new college graduates—to whom they paid very competitive salaries to recruit—to become small variety-store managers.

The alternative is to conduct a vigorous recruiting campaign and obtain experienced executives from outside the organization. Unfortunately, such an approach, if relied upon primarily, can play havoc with the morale of present employees who see little chance for their advancement. (You may want to review "The Issue of Promotion from Within," in the last chapter.) Furthermore, the firm's compensation package and reputation must be attractive enough to woo outsiders. This may mean that the pay scale must be higher than that of competing firms, and this can place an organization at a cost disadvantage. Generally, a commitment to hiring from outside is not prudent on a scale large enough to support vigorous expansion.

Of course, there is another alternative to developing from within or bringing from without. People can be promoted quickly to fill slots, with the hope that they can develop on the job and not make too many mistakes in the process. This is akin to filling responsible positions with "bodies" and characterizes much of the expansion efforts of Korvette and W. T. Grant. The consequences of ignoring management development or of outpacing it can be dire indeed.

---

cost? In the extreme case of Grant, the cost was the destruction of the company.

The dilemma that confronted Korvette was by no means unique among the discounters of the day. Riding a wave of consumer enchantment with lower prices (and the self-service and convenience of parking and store hours), many discount store entrepreneurs found themselves with a few successful stores and developed grandiose plans for expansion. It was natural to bring their friends and relatives in to the good thing as Ferkauf did. (See the following discussion of the perils of nepotism and cronyism.) Many thus overextended themselves, both financially and managerially, and were in trouble. The difference with Korvette was that its attained size was much greater than most of its contemporaries before problems began to overwhelm it. Largely this is a credit to the work load of a peripatetic Ferkauf, who was able to supervise directly a large number of stores before it became too much for him.

And then there was K mart. Despite the almost unbelievable growth in number of stores—opening as many as 271 huge stores in a single year—K mart had the trained employees to staff them effectively, and most of the funds needed were generated internally without the need for heavy outside financing.

Learning Insight. *Simplicity is important for smooth growth.*

Simplicity may well be one of the keys to controlled growth. K mart's organization was kept simple; it was hardly more complex than when Kresge had only variety stores. No separate organization was created for the discount operation. And the existing organization found the challenge and opportunity of developing the new venture to be highly motivating, beckoning it to greater responsibilities and advancement. Similarly, the store facilities were geared to simplicity in planning and operating, with standardized sizes of stores, layouts, displays, and so on. The control and the merchandise assortment plans—all were simply adaptations and modifications of those developed over decades of variety store operations.

Learning Insight. *It is important to maintain a stable and clear-cut image and undeviating objectives.*

As growth and success came to K mart, it resisted the temptation to try to be something it was not, such as upgrading to a department store, thereby confusing its customers and blurring its image. Korvette was not able to resist this temptation, and it succeeded in alienating many of its former customers. Grant was not sure what it should be, nor were its customers. Even Woolworth was confused as to what Woolco should be—a full-fledged discount store or a promotional department store—and developed a fuzzy image.

To be successful, a retailer needs to build a distinctive image. Many years ago the problems of an image deficiency were cited:

> What happens to the retail store that lacks a sharp character, that does not stand for something special to any class of shoppers? It ends up as an alternative store in the customer's mind. The shopper does not head for such a store as the primary place to find what she wants. Without certain outstanding departments and

---

INFORMATION SIDELIGHT

PROS AND CONS OF CRONYISM AND NEPOTISM

Cronyism is the selection of friends for high executive positions. In general, cronyism offers these advantages to an organization:

1. The loyalty of these executives is ensured, because they are already close friends and presumed confidants of the chief executive.
2. Communication and a close working relationship is enhanced.
3. Strengths and weaknesses of each individual should be known factors and not come as unpleasant surprises, as they can be when outsiders are brought into the organization.

The major drawbacks of selecting most or all of the top cadre of executives from close personal friends are:

1. Such a small body of executive candidates may bring very limited expertise and ability to the organization.
2. A narrow organizational perspective is promulgated, because most of these people will have come from similar backgrounds and probably have similar views on most matters.
3. Morale and motivation of the rest of the organization may atrophy because of the perceived lack of advancement opportunities.
4. Because people have been selected more on a basis of friendship than ability, there may be a real reluctance to pressure them for performance and to discipline or discharge those who are performing poorly.
5. As a result of the above factors, such organizations tend toward complacency and conservatism.

On balance, the drawbacks and dangers of cronyism far outweigh the benefits.

Related to cronyism and a phenomenon of many small and medium-size family-owned businesses is the reserving of important managerial positions for family members and relatives—*nepotism*. The pros and cons are similar to those of cronyism.

---

lines of merchandise, without clear attraction for some group, it is like a dull person.[3]

Grant had not really established a desired image when its vigorous expansion effort began. Prices and quality were sometimes competitive and sometimes not. The guiding force of a unified image needed for coordination and expansion was not there.

---

[3] Pierre Martineau, "The Personality of the Retail Store," *Harvard Business Review*, January—February 1958, p. 50.

Learning Insight. *It is very difficult to upgrade an image.*

To upgrade customers' perceptions of a firm is never easy, but that is what Korvette tried. Eugene Ferkauf made his initial entry into the market by gaining a reputation as an aggressive discounter of appliances. But as he expanded he tried to upgrade. These attempts to redefine Korvette as a promotional department store aimed at a higher-income clientele were made for over a decade without any conspicuous success. To attempt to upgrade an image is difficult and can cost a firm its old bargain-conscious customers without gaining a significant number of other customers.

Learning Insight. *For an organization desiring rapid expansion, there are strong arguments for a decentralized management.*

Most discounters, such as Zayre's, Spartans, and Korvette, were centralized with home office executives having major authority for most policies and decisions regarding store operation and merchandise. In the most extreme cases, the store manager only "carries the keys"; that is, he was responsible for opening and closing the store, seeing that adequate workers were on hand, store maintenance, and displays and other dictates of the home office. There was little opportunity to exert initiative, and accordingly such jobs were neither well paid nor of very high caliber.

A few discount firms, notably K mart, decentralized and gave their store managers much more authority over operations and merchandising. These managers were well trained (seven to ten years before becoming K mart managers, versus one to two years for some other discount chains), and well paid.

The combination of high-caliber field executives (store managers) and decentralized authority to encourage their initiative and motivation is in sharp contrast with the centralized organization, which fosters low-level field executives. Home office supervision under a decentralized organization becomes, with expansion, somewhat uneven because an inordinate amount of attention is necessarily focused on opening new outlets. Older stores tend to be neglected, and the growth is not completely digested. With high-level field executives under a decentralized organization such a situation tends to be minimized.

Learning Insight. *Basic merchandising principles must not be neglected in the pursuit of growth through additional outlets.*

Grant violated basic merchandising principles in its rush toward expanding square footage of selling space. Markdowns were not taken when needed; as a result merchandise was no longer fresh, clean, and attractive. Staple or basic merchandise should have been carefully maintained to avoid out-of-stocks, but was not. New merchandise lines should have been tested and planned, rather than being abruptly placed on sale. Signs of deteriorating conditions should have been watched for and corrective actions taken quickly. With Grant, the burgeoning debt, lessening merchandise turnover, the low sales per-square-foot ratios—all these should have alerted management to something seriously amiss. For example, the creeping problem of high inventories should have been detected and prompt action taken; inventory as a percent of sales rose from 18.3 percent in 1969 to 24.3 percent in 1972. In the six years before 1969, this stock-to-sales ratio had never been higher than 19.0 percent. When it reached 20.8 percent in 1970, and certainly when it reached 21.7 percent in 1971, action should have been taken.

Finally, a major issue is raised in these cases. Should we concentrate our efforts, or should we spread them over more alternatives? When we consider the laggard performance of Woolco, the desirability of concentrating rather than diffusing efforts seems confirmed. This strategy is not unlike that facing military commanders: do we concentrate our forces to secure a breakthrough, or do we spread our efforts to cover all sectors?

No sweeping generalization is possible for this dilemma. In the case of K mart versus Woolco, the concentration of efforts worked to perfection. But if the K mart venture had failed . . . ? At what point should you commit your full resources to a new and unproven venture? And if there is misjudgment, a full commitment may mean disaster. Perhaps the prudent approach to discounting was that of Woolworth. But a conservative and prudent approach is bound to fail against the aggressively successful approach. Risks cannot be avoided in decision making.

UPDATE

During the early and mid-1980s, K mart continued to grow. By 1985 it had 2178 K mart stores and 227 old Kresge and Jupiter outlets. It began diversifying, particularly into discount specialty stores, with a Designer Depot off-price apparel chain and Builders Square home improvement centers. However, these were not yet contributing much to earnings. A major acquisition was the 898-unit Waldenbooks chain.

While the growth of K mart continued, it was beginning to be eclipsed by another discounter, Wal-Mart. For 1989, K mart still led in total sales, with $28.4 billion to Wal-Mart's $24.3. But Wal-Mart had surpassed K mart in net income, with $973 million to K mart's $736 million. In rate of growth, Wal-Mart was now the big winner with a five-year average sales gain of 34.3

percent to K mart's 7.8%, while the average return on equity was 36.0 percent to K mart's 16.1 percent over this five-year period of the late 1980s.

FOR THOUGHT AND DISCUSSION

1. The success of K mart, the imitator not the innovator, suggests that being first to the market may be less advantageous than coming later. Evaluate this reasoning.
2. Discuss how K mart was able to make itself so attractive to capable managerial people and trainees, while Korvette and Grant could not? What were the keys?
3. Wal-Mart, especially in the latter 1980s, has decisively outclassed K mart. What accounts for outstanding success being so difficult to maintain?

INVITATION TO ROLE PLAY

1. You are the personnel director of the Kresge Company. The decision has just been made that the firm will shift as rapidly as possible into discounting. You face a major challenge to provide a sufficient number of trained executives at all levels. How would you propose to do this? In particular, address the issue of recruiting experienced executives from other organizations.

10

Campeau Corporation—
A Raider Finds
Indigestion

The 1980s was a time of frenzied takeovers and leveraged buyouts (LBOs). Sometimes the buyers were friendly; more often they were hostile raiders, making their powerful challenges with heavily borrowed funds, usually so-called junk bonds. These provided the lender with high interest, but also with greater risk of default than many other investments.

A major player in the latter 1980s was Robert Campeau, a French Canadian real-estate developer. Campeau, in May 1988, scored a major victory over R.H. Macy & Co. in a bitter battle for Federated Department Store Corporation, and its prestigious division, Bloomingdale's. Less than two years earlier, he had acquired another major department store corporation, Allied Stores. A retailing empire was his.

He was soon to find these acquisitions too big to swallow.

ROBERT CAMPEAU

Campeau's is an intriguing rags to riches story. He grew up as the 8th of 13 children of a devout Catholic family in the mining town of Sudbury, Ontario. His father was an auto mechanic. Robert left school at 14 to help support the family. He swept garage floors at a local mining company.

By 1949, he was a factory supervisor. During his free time, he built a house in Ottawa for his wife and young child. However, instead of moving them in, he sold the place for $3,000 profit, doubling his money. Thus, encouraged, he went on to build 40 more houses that year. And this was the beginning of his road to great wealth.

In the 1950s and 1960s he gained not only his fortune but a reputation as a master builder. He put up 20,000 houses around Ottawa; he was the first to build on Toronto's lakefront, now one of the city's priciest areas; he went on to be a major builder for the Canadian government. He became good friends with Pierre Trudeau, the Prime Minister of Canada, and they frequently went on ski trips.

His ambition led him to attempt several corporate takeovers in Canada, including that of Royal Trustco Ltd., one of Canada's oldest and richest trust companies. All these attempts failed, and he blamed prejudice of British-descent financiers against a French Canadian. So he turned his sights south.

With the acquisition of Federated, his empire consisted of 382 department stores. But his personal life was in shambles. He was suing his eldest son in a corporate power struggle. He divorced his wife to marry his mistress, with whom he already had sired two children his first family did not even know about.

What kind of boss is Robert Campeau? He has been widely characterized as eccentric, emotional, ego driven—some call his a mercurial temperament—hardly an easy man to work for. One talented executive, Robert H. Morsky, former vice chairman of the successful Limited Stores, could only stand Campeau for two months before leaving after a clash of egos. Campeau has been known to call employees at 3 A.M. He berates executives publicly, even shrieking at them. He is even accused by former associates of cheating them at golf. One former executive who worked briefly for Campeau characterized him as having an "Ivan the Terrible management style."[1]

Naturally, in such a managerial clime, Campeau had trouble keeping competent executives.

The Acquisition Binge

After failing in takeover attempts in Canada, Campeau turned his attention to the United States in 1986, with a vengeance. In his quest for major acquisitions, he found an expensive takeover expert and investment banker in Bruce Wasserstein and First Boston Corporation. Allen Finkelson, a partner of a New York law firm, was another key player. They found Campeau eager to take risks with little concern for debt accumulation or liquidity constraints.

Although he knew nothing about retailing, Campeau bought Allied Stores Corporation, an operator of such department stores as Jordan Marsh, for $3.4 billion in December 1986. Then, in May 1988, he won the highly publicized 10- week battle to gain Federated and its Bloomingdale's upscale

---

[1] Kate Ballen, "Campeau Is on a Shopper's High," *Fortune*, August 15, 1988, pp. 70–74.

department stores—and paid a premium price of $6.6 billion to do so—in a bidding war with Macy's. In the process he incurred hefty expenses: $167 million in golden parachutes and other stock buyouts for former Federated executives; over $200 million in investment banking, legal, and other fees; and $150.5 million for bridge-loan fees and interest to First Boston Corp., and two other investment bankers.

The classic strategy of raiders who are willing to incur mountainous debt to gain the takeover has been to sell off some of the assets, some of the divisions they acquire, and thus pay off a portion of the debt. Thereby, they supposedly should be able to handle the interest payments on the remainder of the debt. Campeau was no different.

By late 1988, he had cut over $6 billion from his debt load by selling certain divisions of Allied and Federated. He raised $1.2 billion by selling Allied's Brooks Brothers and Ann Taylor divisions, and Federated's Gold Circle, Main Street, and Children's Place Stores. He wanted to keep the Jordan Marsh and Maas Brothers chains that had produced almost two-thirds of Allied's profits in 1986 before he bought it. Table 10.1 shows his "empire" after his initial pruning of assets. Campeau wanted to retain some of Federated's best stores: Bloomingdale's, Lazarus, Abraham & Straus, Burdines, and Rich's/Goldsmiths. He slashed expenses by $125 million a year at Allied, and $250 million at Federated—mostly by eliminating employees. For example, 5000 jobs were eliminated at Federated alone. By early 1989, further sales of Federated's specialty and discount stores were expected to bring total debt down to $5.6 billion. It appeared that the combined cash flow of Allied and Federated should amount to about twice the $600 million needed for interest payments, a comfortable margin.

Table 10.1 Campeau's Holdings, Summer 1989, after Initial Asset Sales

Allied Stores Corp.:
> Jordan Marsh, 26 stores—Connecticut, Maine, Massachusetts, New Hampshire, New York, Rhode Island
> Maas Brothers-Jordan Marsh, 28—Florida, Georgia
> Stern's, 24—Pennsylvania, New Jersey, New York
> The Bon, 39—Idaho, Montana, Oregon, Utah, Washington, Wyoming

Federated Department Stores:
> Abraham & Straus, 15—New Jersey, New York
> Bloomingdale's, 17—Connecticut, Florida, Massachusetts, Maryland, New Jersey, New York, Pennsylvania, Texas, Virginia
> Burdines, 30—Florida
> Lazarus, 43—Indiana, Kentucky, Michigan, Ohio, West Virginia
> Ralphs Supermarkets, 132—California
> Rich's-Goldsmith's, 26—Alabama, Georgia, South Carolina, Tennessee

Campeau had other plans. He believed that both Allied and Federated could be streamlined by consolidating their backroom operations, and by motivating executives through stock options. And he saw the possibility of *a real synergy of real estate and retailing.*

In capitalizing on the possible synergy of real estate and retailing, Campeau planned to open three to five shopping centers annually, in partnership with Edward DeBartolo, the shopping center czar, who had loaned Campeau $480 million originally. With Campeau's prestigious stores anchoring such shopping malls, there would be no difficulty attracting other retail tenants. Campeau also planned to expand the Bloomingdale's chain by 17 stores over the coming five years.

Trouble!

Just 18 months after scoring the major victory over Macy's and obtaining Federated, the dream became a nightmare. By September 1989, Campeau needed cash, a lot of it, and quickly. By now the company was carrying almost $11 billion in short- and long-term debt, and the annual interest bur-

---

INFORMATION SIDELIGHT

SYNERGY

Synergy is the creation of a whole that is greater than the sum of its parts. Thus, the whole can accomplish more than the total of the individual contributions. In an acquisition, synergy occurs if the two or more entities, when combined, are more efficient, productive, and profitable than they were as individual operations before the merger.

How can such synergy occur? If duplication of efforts can be eliminated, if operations can be streamlined, if economies of scale are possible, if specialization can be enhanced, if greater financial and managerial resources can be tapped—then a synergistic situation is likely to occur. Such an expanded operation, then, should be stronger than anything that was before.

In theory, the concept of synergism is a mighty stimulus for acquisitions and for the investors who make them possible. But instead of some combination of efforts being strongly reinforcing, sometimes the reverse happens: that is, negative synergy, where the combined effort is worse than the sum of individual efforts. If friction arises between the entities, if there is an incompatibility of organizational missions, if an organizational climate is fostered that is fearful, resentful, and frustrated, then synergy is not likely to be achieved. And if greater managerial and financial resources are not realized—if indeed financial resources are depleted because of the credit demands due to the acquisition—then synergy becomes negative. The whole, then, is less than the sum of its parts. Until such a situation can be corrected, an organizational blunder on a grand scale has been accomplished. Unfortunately, this would prove to be the case with Campeau.

den was more than $1 billion. By December 1, $401 million in notes were due First Boston Corporation.

The first inklings of trouble were encountered the year before, in November 1988. This was the Christmas season with its heavy short-term borrowing needs. And Campeau's ability to tap previous lenders was petering out. Underwriters at First Boston had failed to sell a $1.5 billion offering of junk bonds for the Federated unit. They scaled back the offering to $750 million, but still could not find sufficient investors, and had to keep a large portion of the bonds themselves. And they were "burned," as Federated bonds soon dropped 20 percent, while bonds of Allied Stores declined 45 percent. Other financing by bonds fell through as well, with the public becoming skittish about junk bonds.

But working capital was rapidly depleting at both Allied and Federated stores. At the same time, costs were not dropping significantly, despite Campeau's efforts to reduce overhead. While Campeau was able to weather the Christmas 1988 borrowing needs, now another Christmas season was looming, with most of this merchandise payable in October. And the situation was critical if his stores were to have merchandise to sell during the peak selling season. With apparently nowhere else to turn, Campeau finally approached Olympia & York, owned by the wealthy Reichmann family of Toronto, with whom he had already borrowed substantially in his acquisition drives.

The Climax

On September 11, 1989, *USA Today* reported in a cover story that Bloomingdale's, the "jewel" of Campeau's "retail empire," was on the block, up for sale.[2] Indeed, only Bloomingdale's with its high-fashion image, would return, in one shot, the kind of cash Campeau needed to meet interest payment deadlines. It was estimated by analysts as likely to sell for $1 to $1.5 billion. None of the other divisions would individually bring in nearly as much. And Bloomingdale's, of all his acquisitions, was the asset he was most proud of, had the highest expectations for.

By the end of the week, the headlines trumpeted that Campeau had saved his retail kingdom, that he had convinced the Reichmann's to give him a crucial $250 million loan to keep the corporation afloat. However, to do this he had to give up control of the company. An Olympia & York executive, Lionel G. Dodd, was named chairman of a four-man committee formed to oversee the restructuring, and Campeau was conspicuously left off the panel.

---

[2] Patricia Gallagher, "Bloomie's On Block in Bid to Buy Time," *USA Today*, September 11, 1989, pp. 1B and 2B.

Expectations were widespread that several more divisions, in addition to Bloomingdale's, would be put up for sale.

Analysis

While precariously extended, Campeau had expected to meet his financial obligations. What went wrong? Part of the trouble was that cash flow from these big retailers was considerably less than Campeau had expected. Part of the trouble was sagging apparel sales nationally. But the day-to-day operations of the stores were also faltering. The layoffs may have cut into muscle as well as fat. Perhaps the pruning of thousands of jobs in order to cut overhead had severely strained management and staff operations. Such upheavals would demoralize any organization: instead of tending to business, the natural reaction of employees would be fear when and on whom the ax would fall next, and résumés would be readied and other job opportunities explored. Even at that, the cost-reduction plans were up to $200 million too optimistic.

Campeau paid far too much for the Federated purchase. A *Wall Street Journal* article claimed that he paid $500 million too much, and that this was key to the financial problems. Actually, Campeau had initially offered $4.2 billion for Federated, but finally won at $6.6 billion.

The first asset sales went smoothly. In the spring and summer of 1988, Bullock's, I. Magnin, Foley's, and Filene's were sold for $2.75 billion, and Ralphs was spun off and refinanced to generate $800 million in cash. But the remaining asset sales fell far short of expectations. Campeau expected to sell Gold Circle, MainStreet, The Children's Place, and assorted real estate for $727 million; instead, these brought only $562 million.

With inadequate asset sales, incomplete cost-cutting, and a grim look for apparel sales, this was a bad time to bring out Federated's $1.5 billion issue of junk bonds, and only $750 million of these were sold at exorbitant costs and interest rates. The stage was set for disaster for Campeau. Obviously, imprudent borrowing was at the heart of Campeau's troubles. But times were turning against all corporate raiders who had amassed vast fortunes earlier in the 1980s. Many such acquired businesses were deeply in the red, and their huge debt payments were contributing to defaults that were beginning to play havoc on the junk bond market, the major source of marauder financing. The raider strategy of "using somebody else's money to leverage and strip a company to get rich . . . the days of the free ride" were nearing an end.[4]

---

[3] Jeffrey A. Trachtenberg, Robert Melnbardis and David B. Hilder, "An Extra $500 Million Paid for Federated Got Campeau in Trouble," *Wall Street Journal*, January 11, 1990, pp. A1, A6.

[4] John Greenwald, "The Big Comeuppance," *Time*, December 11, 1989, pp. 74–76.

Retailing presents a rather unique situation for working capital requirements, which makes highly leveraged operations more risky. The Christmas season accounts for one-third of the year's sales and about one-half of the year's profits. But to achieve this, a heavy inventory buildup is needed, and this requires substantial short-term funds. In addition, Federated and Allied divisions needed money for a number of longer-term projects, such as developing private-label goods (which carry a higher profit margin), and normal remodeling and refurbishing of stores. The heavy leverage used left little cushion for such financial needs. Already, earlier in 1989, another department-store takeover of Bonwit Teller and B. Altman stores by Australia's Hooker Corporation had gone into Chapter 11 bankruptcy.

INFORMATION SIDELIGHT

TRANSFERABILITY OF MANAGEMENT SKILLS

Are management skills transferable to other companies and other industries? The common belief is that they are, that the successful manager or administrator in one situation will be able to effectively use these skills and talents in other endeavors, even those completely unrelated to the particular industry experience. Perhaps.

But we see a paradox with Campeau. A hugely successful real estate magnate and developer, he acted more like a babe in the woods in his retail empire building. He vastly overestimated his sales and cash flow projections, he greatly underestimated his ability to pare expenses and sell off assets. He completely miscalculated the substantial financial needs of major retail stores in their buildup of inventories for the peak Christmas selling season. And he practically destroyed a smooth-functioning organization and its morale.

Can it be that there is a limit to the transferability of management skills? Could it be that at least with retailing the outsider has a considerable period of adjustment and learning before being able to effectively take the reins? Or could it be that skill as a raider and as a financial manipulator does not prepare one for operational management? Although we can hardly generalize to all individuals and all situations, the Campeau debacle casts some doubts on the cherished notion of complete and easy transferability of managerial skills. And other raiders, such as T. Boone Pickens and Carl Icahn have not proven notably successful in operating their conquests.

CONTRAST: A & W—A HIGHLY LEVERAGED BUYOUT THAT SUCCEEDED

Lest we conclude that all takeovers involving heavy borrowing are ill-advised, reckless, and imprudent, let us look at a positive justification. A & W root beer is part of America's motorized culture, with roadside stands dating back to 1919. But the draft root beer was not sold by the bottle until 1971, when it quickly became the top-selling root beer in the country, surpassing brands such as Hires and Dad's. Still, root beer was not nearly as popular as cola in the competition for shelf space.

In 1983, A & W's root beer syrup business was sold to a group of investors. Along with the concentrate business, the new owners also got Lou Lowenkron, who had come to A & W in 1980 after some 25 years experience in the soft-drink industry. He quickly found that new ownership did not mean money for expansion, and he thought a golden opportunity was being wasted by not capitalizing on the potentially powerful A & W name.

In 1986, Lowenkron engineered a leveraged buyout for $74 million, with $35 million in junk bonds. The buyout raised A & W's long-term debt to a dangerous 90 percent. But Lowenkron at last had full control of the company. Unlike Campeau and most of the other raiders, he had an intimate knowledge both of the company and of the industry. He quickly made some major moves. First, he introduced a cream soda, A & W's first line expansion in 70 years. Today, A & W holds half of the $350 million U.S. cream soda market. Then he bought the rights to three other brands: Squirt, a grapefruit soda; Country Time Lemonade; and Vernors, a spicy ginger drink. Together, these three brands by 1989 accounted for more than a third of A & W's revenues and about 40 percent of operating profit. Along with its soda pop, A & W has emerged as the clear leader in niche soft drinks. For 1989, the company's sales surpassed $110 million, more than triple what they were before the buyout, while profits reached $10 million, as against a small loss in 1986.[5]

What was the difference with Campeau? We see at least three major differences in the A & W experience, and that of Campeau and most other raiders:

1. The leader of the buyout was highly experienced in that particular industry.
2. He had a personal interest, and had developed a real commitment to overcome the deficiencies of the present operation and ownership.
3. He brought innovation and fresh growth to a staid and conservative organization.

So, we must conclude that although highly leveraged buyouts are risky because of the heavy debt burden, they represent the means for good management to replace ineffective or highly conservative management.

---

[5] For more details, see Edward Giltenan, "Root Beer Gloat," *Forbes*, December 11, 1989, pp. 156–160.

WHAT CAN BE LEARNED?

The Campeau situation is by no means unique. It represents the great infatuation that raiders and investors had with leveraged buyouts, and the ready acceptance of junk bond financing that made them possible. That this acceptance of junk bond financing was to sour dramatically by 1989—hastened in large part by the highly publicized excesses of Campeau—brought the collapse of such high risk financing sooner than even the most pessimistic experts predicted.

Learning Insight. *Highly leveraged situations are extremely vulnerable, and this vulnerability does not need worsening economic conditions.*

During most of the 1980s, many managers, and not just raiders like Campeau, pursued a strategy of debt financing in contrast to equity (stock ownership) financing. Funds for such borrowing were usually readily available, heavy debt had income tax advantages, and profits could be distributed among fewer shares so that return on equity was enhanced. During this time a few voices decried the overleveraged situations of many companies. They predicted that when the eventual economic downturn came many such firms would find themselves unable to meet the heavy interest burden. Most lenders paid little heed to such lonesome voices, and encouraged greater borrowing.

The widely publicized problems of Campeau, and the earlier problems of Hooker and other raiders, suddenly changed the expansionist lending sentiments. The hard reality dawned that some of these boycotts were fragile indeed. Especially when they rested on optimistic projections for asset sales, for revenues, for cost savings—or else the interest payments could not be met. An economic slowdown proved unnecessary to bring some of these ill-advised speculations to their knees.

We have to conclude that, in deciding on a heavy commitment to borrowed funds, a worst-case scenario must be used in estimating cash-flow sufficiency. Commitments that depend on optimistic projections and allow no room for more sobering developments should be shunned.

Learning Insight. *The synergy of mergers and acquisitions is suspect.*

As we discussed in an "Information Sidelight" earlier this chapter, the concept of synergy is that a new whole is better than the sum of its parts. Theoretically, this would seem possible since operations can be streamlined for more efficiency and since greater management and staff competence can be brought to bear, as greater financial and other resources can be tapped. Yet, we saw no synergy in Campeau's case, and none in Hooker's acquisitions; such synergy is not readily apparent in many other acquisitions as well. More often, such concentrations incur severe digestive problems— problems with people, systems, and procedures—that take time to resolve. Furthermore, greater size does not always beget economies of scale. The opposite may in fact occur: An unwieldy organization, slow to act, and vulnerable to more aggressive, innovative, and agile smaller competitors. The siren call of synergy is often an illusion.

Learning Insight. *Retailing presents unique working capital problems.*

These increase the risk of highly margined undertakings.

As noted earlier, because of the great seasonality and the substantial buildup of inventory necessary for the Christmas season, working capital requirements just for ordinary operations present serious problems to highly leveraged situations. Campeau carelessly overlooked this.

Further adding to the seriousness of the liquidity needs, vendors become reluctant to ship needed goods at the first hints that they might not get paid. Any publicity about financial problems can play havoc with getting sufficient merchandise to meet Christmas selling needs—this was proving true even for the prestigious Allied and Federated stores. Despite the cash transfusion of the Reichmann brothers, vendors were still concerned about Christmas shipments. A Dun & Bradstreet cautionary note, reported in the December 7, 1989 *Wall Street Journal*, exacerbated the problem. And a week later, one of the largest factoring companies in the country, Heller Financial, told its clients to stop shipping merchandise to Campeau's retailing operations.[6]

Learning Insight. *The concept of organizational restructuring for acquisitions is becoming a myth.*

The idea of restructuring generally means "downsizing," in raider parlance that is. Some assets or corporate divisions consequently are sold off, and the remaining organization is streamlined, which usually means layoffs. Thereby, the raider can pay off some of the huge debt burden and generate more cash flow to cover the remaining interest payments.

---

[6] Jeffrey A. Trachtenberg, "Campeau Assails Dun & Bradstreet's Advice to Clients Not to Ship It Goods," *Wall Street Journal*, December 7, 1989, p. A4; Jeffrey A. Trachtenberg, "Heller Financial Tells Clients to Halt Shipping Their Goods to Campeau Units," *Wall Street Journal*, December 15, 1989, p. A3.

The assumption is that the parts are worth more if sold than the corporation as a whole is valued by investors, as reflected in stock prices. The other assumption is that the organization has gotten fat and inefficient, and people and operations can readily be pruned.

For some years, this strategy of restructuring or downsizing seemed to work fairly well, as eager investors bid up the prices of spun-off assets. But the investment mood changed, with disillusionment setting in. Campeau did not anticipate this change, and could not sell some of his divisions for the expected prices. Another raider, L. J. Hooker Corp., was not even able to sell its B. Altman department-store chain, and had to liquidate it.[7] By late 1989, many raiders in addition to Campeau, were mired in debt, saddled with bankrupt companies, and finding that they could not run companies as efficiently as the bosses they had ousted. Such well-known corporate raiders as Merv Griffin and T. Boone Pickens were among those having a rude awakening.[8]

Not the least of the emerging problems coming from the organizational restructuring of the LBOs was the demoralization of the organizations involved. Massive layoffs and forced retirements, complete reassigning of people, traumatic personnel and policy changes, destruction of accustomed lines of communication and authority —these were hardly the inputs needed to preserve stability and motivation. Worse, in many instances the raiders, such as Campeau, in their rush to try to free up working capital to meet hefty interest charges, began their restructuring and streamlining without sufficient assessment and preparation. The operational deficiencies of Federated stores after the Campeau takeover illustrate the negative consequences of hasty major "restructuring."

Learning Insight.   *Great success tends to be ephemeral.*

So many times, we find that great successes are not lasting, they have no staying power. Already in these early chapters, we have seen how Adidas did not maintain its success pattern; K mart, the great success of the 1960s and 1970s, is faltering now to Wal-Mart. Somehow, the success pattern gets lost, or forgotten, or was not well rounded. Other times, an operation grows beyond the capability of the originator. And hungry competitors are always lying in the wings, waiting to take advantage of any lapse. An agglomeration of factors beset the corporate raiders of the late 1980s. At least in some instances, the key delimiting factor was this: They could not manage.

---

[7] Barbara Rudolph, "Debacle on 34th Street," *Time*, December 11, 1989, p. 77.
[8] Greenwald, "The Big Comeuppance."

INFORMATION SIDELIGHT

THE ROLE OF EGO

Reporters in the national press were quick to label Campeau's acquisitive thrust as an ego trip, intimating that an inflated ego was behind a reckless expansion binge. Perhaps they were right. Coming from humble beginnings, Campeau—like many other highly successful people—felt an overwhelming drive to be successful, to the extreme. Ego drive, or profound ambition, may be a good thing. It can be the major fuel for hard work, personal advancement, and entrepreneurship. But ego needs to be harnessed. The drive can exceed the bounds of what is prudent (just as we saw with some of the S & L excesses). Ego getting out of hand can lead to excesses of spending—for example, the desire for flamboyance, both personal and in corporate spending. At this point, ego is no longer a positive factor but becomes a negative and even destructive influence. As with so many things, moderation appears key to most successes, and is much more desirable than either extreme.

They were able to amass the financial strength for their acquisitions, but they could not handle the operational consequences. Staying power is the name of the game for lasting success. The comet that flares through the sky and dies brilliantly is hardly the material of lasting success. Yet, this describes many corporate buccaneers in the decade of the 80s, albeit they were a colorful and awesome presence—and they frightened many boardrooms. And they had awesome *egos*, which could be a strength but also a crucial weakness.

UPDATE

By early 1990, the Campeau Corporation was on the verge of bankruptcy. Reputations and fortunes were being wrecked in the process. Robert Campeau was removed from active participation, and relegated only to real estate operations. He had lost wealth it took a lifetime to accumulate: nearly $500 million. Most of this represented the paper losses on some 27.7 million shares of rapidly depreciating stock in his company. A good part of this had already been seized by creditors for nonpayment of loans. Perhaps as bad as his financial losses was the humiliation of falling from stardom.

The troubles also were enveloping the wealthy Reichmanns, who had badly misjudged the extent of the Campeau problems. Altogether, they are estimated to have put more than $700 million into Campeau, with this stake largely depreciated.

The First Boston Corporation that masterminded both Campeau takeovers and lent its own money to help complete the deals, now found itself with a soured reputation for imprudence, as well as hundreds of millions in losses, so much so that its debt rating was downgraded by Moody's. Also hurt was Bruce Wasserstein, one of the guiding lights of Campeau's efforts, who now faces a loss of personal prestige and attractiveness as a consultant.

On January 15, 1990, the Campeau Corporation filed for Chapter 11 bankruptcy protection from its creditors.

FOR THOUGHT AND DISCUSSION

1. Campeau bought good, even the best, properties. How could he have gone so wrong?
2. Discuss the organizational mistakes in this case, and how they might have been avoided.
3. Why did not the concept of synergy appear to work in this case?
4. Are management skills not transferable to retailing institutions? Discuss.
5. What are the key differences between successful and unsuccessful LBOs in the present environment?

INVITATION TO ROLE PLAY

As a management consultant, how would you advise Campeau on organizational restructuring after his initial acquisitions of Allied and Federated? Do you think these moves would have made any difference? Why or why not?

Three

FLAWED LEADERSHIP AND STRATEGY EXECUTION

11

Coors—"We Are Immune To Competition"

A tragedy occurred in the winter of 1960 that was to have an impact on the fortunes of the Adolph Coors Company, brewers, some 15 years later. On the morning of February 9, Adolph Coors III, 44-year-old chairman of the board of the brewing empire, kissed his wife and four children good-bye and drove off for the plant 12 miles away. He was never seen alive again.

For months, one of the most intensive manhunts in Colorado history took place. Finally, on September 26, more than 7 months later, tattered clothing and scattered bones were accidentally discovered in a desolate, heavily wooded area of aspen and pine about 40 miles southeast of Denver. Apparently, after the body had been dumped, the remains were scattered by coyotes or hogs. Dental charts confirmed the identification of Coors.

THE GOLDEN YEARS

Adolph Coors III had been sharing leadership responsibilities with his father, Adolph Coors II. After the murder, the father again assumed the sole leadership mantle, even though his official title was treasurer, until he died in 1970 at the age of 86. The elder of the two surviving sons, William H. Coors, became the chairman and chief executive; the other son, Joseph, was president. There were no formal lines of authority, although Bill generally handled the technical side of brewing and Joe the financial and administrative functions.

Both Bill and Joe (employees called them by their first names) were lean, tall, and rugged outdoorsmen. In fact, they regarded physical fitness and athletic recreation as so important for their employees that executives and workers were sent to outdoor-survival schools. Golf was subsidized for employees. Ski trips were underwritten. But Bill and Joe were concerned with more than the therapeutic benefits of fresh air for their employees; they encouraged them not only to participate in these programs, but also to compete. "If you can't fight competition, you don't need to survive," Bill Coors asserted.[1]

Sensational Growth

By 1970, Coors's accomplishments in the brewing industry were awesome— all the more so in light of Coors's nonconformity to existing industry practices. The company produced only one kind of beer, and this in a single brewery, albeit the largest in the world. It sold its beer in only 11 Western states, most of them the most sparsely populated areas of the United States. It refused to build branch plants and had not expanded its territory in 22 years. The one brewery in Golden, Colorado, was not even close to its biggest market, California—indeed, the average barrel of Coors traveled over 900 miles. Finally, its ads featuring rushing mountains streams, and the slogan "Brewed with pure Rocky Mountain Spring Water" had not been changed in 33 years.

Yet, Bill and Joe Coors's little regional brewery had moved up to the big time. With a 19 percent increase in production in 1969 over 1968, it moved into fourth place in the national beer rankings, the only regional brewer to come close to the national brewers. In 1969, the production of the top four breweries was as follows:

Anheuser-Busch	18.8 million barrels
Joseph Schlitz	13.7 million barrels
Pabst	10.2 million barrels
Coors	6.4 million barrels

Furthermore, in 9 of the 11 states where it had distribution, Coors topped all other brands in sales. Among the full 11 states, Coors's market share was 30 percent. In California, it had 41 percent of the market by 1973, compared with only 18 percent for the industry leader, Anheuser-Busch; in Oklahoma, almost 70 percent of all beer sold was Coors. Overall demand was so out-

---

[1] William M. Bulkeley, "Colorado's Coors Family Has Built an Empire on One Brand of Beer," *Wall Street Journal*, October 26, 1973, p. 1.

stripping supply that the company was forced to ration its product among distributors.

In compiling this performance record, the brothers eschewed a marketing orientation. Bill Coors stated this succinctly: "Our top management thrust is on engineering and production . . . we're production-oriented. Nobody knows more about production than I do."[2] Emphasis was on making a quality beer in terms of processing and raw materials. The product was a mild, light-bodied beer, scientifically tested and brewed, using hops, rice, Rocky Mountain spring water, and a specially developed strain of barley grown by contract farmers.

Great pains were taken to preserve the flavor. Pasteurization, which would add to the ease of preserving, was shunned, because it would slightly affect the taste. To give the best quality assurance, the beer was canned at near-freezing temperatures and shipped under refrigeration to refrigerated warehouses. To ensure perfection of taste further, distributors were required to pull Coors cans off the shelves in 60 days, lest there be some fading of the flavor.

Coors had become the beer of celebrities, from President Ford, who packed Coors on Air Force One, to Henry Kissinger, as well as such actors as Paul Newman (who, in an *Esquire* interview, claimed, "The best domestic beer, bar none, is Coors") and Clint Eastwood. In these years, the famous, as well as the rank and file, were all contributing to the Coors "mystique." Some 300,000 Coors fans a year toured the brewery; others made "pilgrimages" to a waterfall near Grand Lake, Colorado, which was supposed to be the one pictured on Coors bottles and cans. T-shirts and sweatshirts emblazoned with "Coors—Breakfast of Champions" were being sold by entrepreneurs hoping to cash in on the Coors mystique. And in the East, where Coors was not directly distributed, it could sell for three times the regular price.

Besides the product, the company was unique from the rest of the industry in certain other respects. In the heady years of the 1960s and early 1970s, Bill and Joe shunned outside expertise. Advertising and promotion were handled by inside staff, and total expenditures averaged only one-quarter those of major competitors. Construction at the brewery was done by Coors's own construction crews. Company engineers designed machinery for the can plant. Management talent was developed and promoted from within the organization, rather than brought in from outside.

The guiding philosophy of the company since it was founded by a German orphan who stowed away on a U.S.–bound ship to avoid conscription into the German army—the first Adolph Coors, in 1873—was to refuse to go to a bank for a loan. Such fiscal conservatism led the company to reject some

---

[2] "The Brewery That Breaks All the Rules," *Business Week*, August 22, 1970, p. 60.

seemingly attractive expansion possibilities. For example, the company's can-manufacturing subsidiary, Coors Container Company, was instrumental in developing the technical process for making a two-piece aluminum can. Coors, however, sold the process to Continental Can Company and American Can Company: "We could have dominated the industry, but we would have had to borrow from the banks, and Coors doesn't do that."[3] Between 1970 and 1974, to keep up with the burgeoning demand for Coors beer, some $276 million was spent on plant expansion. And how was this financed? All of it from cash flow.

How Come The Mystique?

What was the magic of Coors? How durable was this magic or mystique likely to be? Perhaps part of the mystique was accidental and fortuitous: being a Western-made brew at a time when the freedom and environmental purity of the West—emphasized by Coors's slogan, "Pure Rocky Mountain Spring Water"—was seen by many consumers as contrasting sharply with the degradation of the industrial centers of population. But was it a better beer—better tasting, higher quality? There were many who said it was. Whether real or imagined, Coors offered a "unique selling proposition" that distinguished it from other beers. One could claim that coming from a single brewery ensured better quality control and uniformity of ingredients and flavor. The company liked to boast that Coors was the most expensively brewed beer in the world. A plant geneticist was employed full-time to develop improved strains of barley for malting. Most hops were imported from Germany. And, as noted before, great pains were taken to prevent any deterioration of the flavor in shipping and handling.

Undoubtedly, part of the mystique came from the contagion generated by the aficionados, those famous and not so famous. A Western image conveying the out-of-doors and environmental purity, a light-tasting beer . . . perhaps the timing could not have been better in the 1960s and the early 1970s. (In the cigarette industry, Marlboro rose to become the top seller on a somewhat similar advertising and image thrust: The Marlboro man.)

It hardly seemed to Bill and Joe that the golden image of their beer could in the span of just a few years fade drastically. How could it help but be enduring?

Going Public

For 103 years, ever since the first Adolph Coors opened his brewery on the trail to the Colorado gold camps, the company stayed private—talks of hav-

---

[3] Bulkeley, "Colorado's Coors Family," p. 27.

ing public or outside shareholders were anathema to the Coors family. And it seemed that the company could indeed finance large-scale capital expenditures internally. Throughout the decade of the 1960s, its average rate of growth was over 10 percent, all this without turning to outside stock ownership or borrowing. In 1975, Coors had only $2 million in long-term debt on its books, against $375 million in equity.

But, in 1975, the proud family tradition had to be abandoned. With the death of Bill and Joe's parents, the Internal Revenue Service presented a bill for $50 million in inheritance taxes. Many companies would have solved such a problem by going into debt, but Bill and Joe decided to go public as the lesser of two evils. To avoid the risk of relinquishing control of the company to outsiders, they would offer only nonvoting shares. Furthermore, to avoid diluting the equity, no more than five percent of net income would be paid as dividends.

The time for such a stock offering was not very propitious. The Dow Jones Industrial Average was then moving between 620 and 690, and many were the investors who thought it would go still lower. Added to a sick stock market, the restrictions placed on this new stock venture were hardly likely to appeal to many investors. Because the shares would be nonvoting, this precluded listing on the New York Stock Exchange, as well as being offered for sale in many states, including California, where Coors's stock could otherwise have had a warm reception. The nonvoting feature would also make the stock offering unattractive to many large institutional investors.

In the end, Coors lucked out. When the offering finally reached the market, the stock market was beginning to rebound. Coors's investment bankers found so much interest in the stock in the last days before the offering that they raised the price to $31 a share. And it was a sellout the first afternoon. Not only was $50 million raised to pay off the inheritance taxes, but an additional $77 million went into company coffers. This $127 million offering was the first major new stock issue to come to market since 1973 and the fourth largest offering by industrial companies in the previous 10 years. The mystique of the company and its beer mitigated all the negative factors impinging on demand.

Geographical Expansion

Bill Coors now turned his attention to geographical expansion. The first target was eastern and southern Texas. Prior to this, the only Texas inroads were in the northern part of the state around Dallas, and the western part.

Eager to jump on a lucrative bandwagon, potential distributors lined up like beauty queen candidates, vying for selection by Coors. The contest, however, was hardly for the weak or poorly financed, because Coors's distributors had to build refrigerated warehouses to keep the beer under 40 degrees until opened by customers. From 4000 "panting" contestants, Coors selected 29 distributors for the eastern Texas expansion.

By 1976, Coors was also invading Montana and looking closely at expansion into Washington State, Arkansas, Nebraska, and Missouri, the latter state being the home base of Anheuser-Busch, the largest brewer. Bill Coors was also laying plans for expanding to the heavily populated Eastern market: "I think we've got a good enough beer—the beer that won the West—to assure ourselves 20 percent to 25 percent of the nationwide market," he told *Forbes's* reporters in the summer of 1976.[4] A bold statement this, with Anheuser holding 24 percent of the total market, while Coors had only 8.2 percent—although admittedly on far less than national distribution, (in fact, on only 20 percent of the total national distribution).

The question of whether expansion could still be handled out of the one brewery in Golden seemed not particularly troublesome to Bill. The Golden brewery was already at an annual capacity of 12.3 million barrels, and about 1 million barrels of capacity was being added a year; Bill was aiming for a total of 25 million. "Eventually we might build other breweries," he said. "But if you take a circle up around from where we already ship to in Northern California, you hit Atlanta, Georgia."[5]

The growth and profitability picture—and the highly successful public stock offering—should have been cause for heady optimism and great satisfaction for the Coors brothers. Sales for 1975 were $520 million, up from $350 million just 4 years before. Operating margin on net sales had reached 28 percent, the highest in the industry. Profit per barrel averaged almost $9, about double that of Anheuser. But there were some ominous portents on the horizon.

STORM SIGNALS FOR COORS, 1975–1976

Although the successful public stock float spurred new ambitions, trouble was brewing in the California market—a key market that accounted for almost 40 percent of all Coors's sales. In a bitter dispute with Coors's Oakland distributor, the California Teamsters called for a statewide boycott of the beer. At the same time, Anheuser was bringing on line a new 3.75 million barrel brewery in northern California. As a result, in this key market, Coors's sales dropped about 10 percent in 1975, while market share fell 4 percent to 36 percent. Anheuser picked up most of this, gaining 3 percent to a 23.2 percent share of the California market. Perhaps another contributor to the market share losses in California was a hefty price hike made in 1974 without first warning retailers.

---

[4] "Off Coors," *Forbes*, June 1, 1976, p. 60.
[5] Ibid., p. 61.

Several other aggravations were also being encountered. In January 1975, the Federal Trade Commission was upheld by the Supreme Court in its efforts to loosen the tight grip Coors had held on its 167 distributors. Then, the Equal Opportunities Commission filed a suit against Coors alleging discrimination against minorities in hiring and in promotion. And the Colorado Health Department charged Coors with polluting Clear Creek, in the very same valley where the "Rocky Mountain Spring Water" rises.

Finally, brother Joe was embarrassed as the Senate Commerce Committee vetoed his nomination to the board of the Corporation for Public Broadcasting, citing Coors' ownership of a right-wing television news service as a conflict of interest. Joe had long been known locally as an archconservative, but his political views came to national attention in 1975 when the *Washington Post* ran four lengthy stories about his right-wing efforts in allegedly using Television News, Inc., a broadcast news agency subsidiary of the Coors Company, to further his own political views. This publicity, as well as the fact that the news subsidiary was losing money, induced the company to close down the TV news service. Whatever negative effect might have emanated from the unfavorable publicity could not be gauged.

Some dangers could be seen in the decision to push East, even though such a move, if successful, would greatly increase Coors's sales as well as lessen the risks inherent in relying on only a few markets—such as the California one—for maintenance of growth and even viability. To attempt to enter the Eastern markets would bring Coors face to face with entrenched major brewers: Schlitz, Pabst, and Philip Morris's Miller, in addition to Anheuser-Busch. Miller, in particular, looked like a most formidable competitor; it had become the nation's fastest-growing major beer company and by the beginning of 1976, had moved to third place in the U.S. beer market, moving ahead of Coors in the process. Undoubtedly, Coors's move to the East would necessitate massive additional advertising expenditures. Although sales might be increased by such expansion efforts, more questionable was what effect such expansion would have on profits. Furthermore, despite optimism by Bill Coors about their one brewery being adequate to supply their entire national market, rather serious logistical problems could be expected.

THE BREWING INDUSTRY

Concentration has increasingly characterized the brewing industry. In the last several decades, the number of beer firms dropped from 900 to 50. The smaller local and regional brewers just could not match the economies of scale of the big brewers, nor could they match their aggressive marketing efforts. In the span of only 8 years, from 1970 to 1978, the combined market share of the five largest brewers increased from 49 percent to 74 percent of total industry sales.

The hottest product in the brewing industry by the mid-1970s had become light beer, or low-calorie beer. About 10 percent of industry sales were accounted for by lights, and 30 percent of Miller's, with the trend rising rapidly. Initial introductions of low-calorie beers had failed because they were marketed as diet drinks to consumers who did not drink much beer in the first place. Miller changed the thrust by positioning its Lite to heavy drinkers, with the theme that they could drink as much beer as before without feeling so filled (a subtle inference was that they could thereby consume more beer). Profitably speaking, the lights are good business: they sell for more than premium beers, and they cost less to make.

The other growth area is super-premium beers, so called because they sell for higher prices. For years, Anheuser's Michelob had the market almost to itself, with its only real competition coming from imported beers. Miller was the first to intrude on Michelob's market niche by arranging first to import Lowenbrau from Germany, and then to produce a domestic version of Lowenbrau.

Table 11.1 shows the relative sales of the big five of the brewing industry from 1973 to 1977; Table 11.2 shows the relative profit performance for this period. Notice particularly the major burst of Miller both in sales and profits.

Anheuser-Busch, the industry leader, makes Budweiser, Budweiser malt liquor, Michelob, and Busch Bavarian. As Tables 11.1 and 11.2 show, its business was booming. It had 10 breweries operating full blast, yet could hardly keep up with demand. The meteoric rise of Miller had to cause concern, but Anheuser, it seems, had the marketing muscle and financial resources to more than match Miller's marketing efforts and building plans.

Miller Brewing Company makes Miller High Life, Miller malt liquor, Miller Lite, and Lowenbrau, Miller was a sickly company run by an aging management when it was acquired by Philip Morris, the tobacco company, in 1969. Philip Morris moved its tobacco executives in to run the brewing operations and found that beer and cigarettes have a great deal in common, both being low-priced, pleasurable products processed and packaged on high-speed machinery; they can be advertised and distributed similarly to many of the same end-use customers. With aggressive marketing efforts, Miller moved up from eighth to second place among U.S. brewers by 1977, and was trying hard to catch Anheuser. Its Lite beer, introduced in January 1975 with a blitz advertising campaign, was a marketing coup, and, by 1978, Miller was selling 10 million barrels of Lite, equal to its entire beer sales only four years before.

Joseph Schlitz Brewing Company—maker of Schlitz, Schlitz malt liquor, Old Milwaukee, Promo, and Schlitz Light—had staggered badly, both in sales and especially in profits, as Table 11.2 shows. After 15 years of unin-

Table 11.1   Relative Sales of Top Five U.S. Brewers, 1973–1977

	Sales (millions of dollars)				
	1973	1974	1975	1976	1977
Anheuser-Busch	1109.7	1413.1	1645.0	1441.2	1838.0
Miller	275.9	403.6	658.3	982.8	1327.6
Schlitz	703.0	814.5	923.0	1000.0	937.4
Pabst	355.4	431.3	525.0	600.5	582.9
Coors	378.8	467.8	520.0	593.6	593.1

Source: Company annual reports.

Table 11.2   Relative Profits of Top Five U.S. Brewers, 1973–1977

	Net Profits (millions of dollars)				
	1973	1974	1975	1976	1977
Anheuser-Busch	65.6	64.0	84.7	55.4	91.9
Miller	(2.4)	6.3	28.6	76.1	106.5
Schlitz	55.2	49.0	30.9	50.0	17.8
Pabst	23.8	18.3	20.7	32.4	21.8
Coors	47.5	41.1	59.5	76.5	67.7

Source: Company annual reports.

terrupted growth, it lost second place to Miller in 1977. The product mix had proven weak, with sales of premium and light beers—the more profitable items in the line—falling off more than its lower-priced beers. In addition, Schlitz had problems coming up with a superpremium beer to compete with Michelob and Lowenbrau.

Pabst makes Pabst Blue Ribbon, Pabst Extra Light, and Andeker of America. It found it impossible to keep pace with Anheuser-Busch and Miller. Because of intense competition, it was forced to spend more and more for advertising, but volume continued to slide. Pabst Blue Ribbon lost considerable ground in certain major Midwestern markets; Pabst's light beer and Andeker, its super-premium beer, were both weak contenders.

TARNISH ON THE GOLDEN PROSPECTS, 1977–1978

In 1977, the boom lowered. Although Tables 11.1 and 11.2 show Coors as faltering considerably less than Schlitz and Pabst in sales and profits, 1977 marked a serious trend reversal after the heady years of growth. Furthermore, the reversal did not appear to be short lived, but rather symptomatic of serious underlying problems.

In 1977, Coors earned $1.92 a share, down 12 percent from 1976. It shipped 12.8 million barrels of beer, down 5 percent from 1976. It lost market share in many of the 16 Western states where it had the bulk of its distribution. The problems continued into 1978. For the first half of 1978, barrelage was down another 12 percent; per-sharing earnings were down from $1.02 the year before to $0.56. In California, which had accounted for 39 percent of its sales, it had been surpassed by Anheuser-Busch. Coors's stock, which had been subscribed for $31 in 1975, was now hovering around $16, a loss of about 50 percent for the first public stockholders. Only a few years before, Coors had been selling its beer by allocation only; now, suddenly, it had to cut back production. Bill Coors was forced to admit: "Making the best beer we can make is no longer enough."[6]

The Eastern markets no longer beckoned, either. They were heavily saturated with strong, well-entrenched competitors. In fact, the big Eastern brewers were moving West because of this. Anheuser had built a new plant in California. Miller was building one. Schlitz had expanded its capacity in the West. Coors, with its single plant in the mountains of Colorado, faced exorbitant transportation costs in trying to reach the Eastern markets, all the more so because it wanted to ship its beer under refrigeration to preserve its quality. Unfortunately, the quality image of the beer had suffered from bootleggers bringing it into the East with careless handling and selling it at black-market prices. Coors had even been forced to take out newspaper ads in some Eastern cities advising beer drinkers not to drink Coors. But a negative image had been created in the minds of many Eastern beer drinkers.

Labor Problems

Labor problems exacerbated a deteriorating situation. On April 5, 1977, the brewery workers at the Golden, Colorado, plant walked out. A week after the walkout, the AFL-CIO approved a nationwide boycott of the company's beer.

The company was unyielding and now raised the issue that all prospective employees take lie-detector tests. The idea of polygraph testing hearkens back to the kidnapping of Adolph Coors III and the family fears that this could happen again. Eventually, more than 1000 of the 1472 workers who walked out returned, and the rest were replaced. The strike lasted 15 months, and eventually the union was rejected by the employees. But the wrath of labor was incurred in the process, and Coors now ranked with J.P. Stevens Company on union hate lists.

Opinions differ as to the effects the union boycott had on Coors's sales and profits: how much of the decline was due to labor boycotting, and how

---

[6] "A Test for the Coors Dynasty," *Business Week*, May 8, 1978, p. 69.

much was due to intensified competition? Bill Coors blamed most on the boycott: "It was a shock for us to find that, as far as the union is concerned, anything goes. No lie is too great to tell if it accomplishes their boycott objectives. We view the boycott as a monument to immorality and dishonesty."[7]

The mystique of Coors, the image it had glorified in what seemed to give it a competitive edge over all other brews, was gone, abruptly, bewilderingly.

Competition

As evident from Table 11.1, the aggressive efforts of Anheuser and Miller were hurting the other members of the big five, not to mention the smaller regional brewers. The erosion of Coors's share of California, its biggest market, where previously it had 40 percent of the beer business, was particularly worrisome, especially as it hinted at a greater erosion to come. In the first 6 months of 1978, Anheuser took over first place with a 35 percent share, with Coors dropping to 25 percent. Even more threatening was the surging Miller. Although number 2 nationally, Miller was still a poor third in California, with less than 10 percent of the market. But Miller was building a brewery there, and Coors certainly had to expect that once its production facilities were established at a sufficiently high level, Miller's aggressive thrust would be leveled at California. Coors would then be placed in the vulnerable position of trying to match the expenditures and the expertise of both Miller and Anheuser in a hotly contested market.

DEFENSIVE REACTIONS

The company turned to market research to determine where it had gone wrong. The answer was definitive. The beer industry was growing at only 3 percent a year, but almost all the growth was coming from two products: light or low-calorie beer, and superpremium beer. Coors offered neither of these, relying on its traditional one kind of beer. Furthermore, research revealed that 4 out of every 10 new light beer drinkers had switched from Coors. In addition to the lack of a responsive and aggressive product mix vis-à-vis competitors, Coors also had a hard-to-open press-tab can that hardly met consumers' desire for convenience and ease of operation.

Coors finally moved to rectify the product deficiencies of a single-beer strategy and, in the spring of 1978, introduced its first new product in 20 years, Coors Light. The company also began developing a superpremium beer, planning market tests in early 1980. It was considering naming this

---

[7] "Coors Beer: What Hit Us?" *Forbes*, October 16, 1978, p. 71.

Herman Joseph's, after Coors founder Adolph Herman Joseph Coors, thereby emphasizing family name and tradition. Coors's reluctance in expanding the product line is understandable, if not recommended: producing different kinds of beer in the same brewery poses serious production problems and results in sharply higher costs than if there is one long and unchanging production line.

Coors now began directing its geographical expansion to the Central states and those parts of the West it had not previously served. In 1978, it began distribution in Missouri, Iowa, and in parts of Washington State. In early 1978, it announced plans to begin distribution in Arkansas, which would bring to 17 the number of states in which it was now marketing its beer. The Coors brothers were reaching some painful conclusions, among them that the company must abandon its comfortable role as a regional brewer and emerge as a national power. "There'll be fewer than 10 breweries left in the United States in 10 years," predicted Bill Coors. "I don't say we have to be number one, but we do have to stay in the top five to survive."[9]

Coors's promotional expenditures had been lagging far behind those of its major competitors, and even of some of the much smaller regional brewers. See Table 11.3. Accordingly, in 1976, Coors had hired the J. Walter Thompson agency to enhance its corporate image, and, in 1978, budgeted a whopping increase in the advertising budget to $15 million.

Table 11.3   Relative Advertising Expenditures for Top Eight Brewers, 1973–1976[a]

	Expenditures (millions of dollars)			
	1973	1974	1975	1976
Anheuser-Busch	20.5	17.8	27.4	28.5
Jos. Schlitz	19.7	20.9	26.5	34.1
Miller	10.9	13.6	21.3	29.1
Pabst	7.2	8.4	9.6	9.7
Coors	1.4	1.6	1.2	2.0
Olympia	3.3	3.9	5.8	5.7
Stroh	4.5	4.4	4.0	5.0
F. & M. Schaefer	4.4	4.3	2.7	2.5

[a] These expenditures are understated, because they do not include the large sums typically spent by brewers on point of purchase materials and other nonmeasured media.
Source: Advertising Age, September 26, 1977, p. 112.

[8] "New Coors Brand Nears Test Stage," *Advertising Age*, December 10, 1979, pp. 2 and 86.
[9] As quoted in John Huey, "Men at Coors Beer Find the Old Ways Don't Work Anymore," *Wall Street Journal*, January 19, 1979, pp. 1 and 24.

For the full year of 1978, Coors registered a small sales gain to $624.8 million. However, profits again declined to 454.8 million, almost 20 percent below 1977 profits and almost 29 percent under the peak year of 1976. Even back in 1975, profits had been higher. And Coors's stock had now declined to less than $14 a share by early 1978.

The question at this point was whether Coors waited far too long to awaken to a changing and much more aggressive marketplace. Deeply embedded policies of conservatism, misplaced confidence in the everlasting appeal of a beer and of an image that dispelled the need for aggressive or even conventional marketing efforts, and finally, a confrontation philosophy with union employees—all these factors may have brought the venerable Coors brewery to a point of no return. Not that the viability of the company was in jeopardy, but perhaps the golden, glory years were over for all time.

WHAT CAN BE LEARNED?

The Coors case evinces a classical disregard for *external factors*, especially present and potential competitive inroads, at least until great damage had been done to its positions in its markets and to its future promise. In particular, its marketing function was atrophied.

Learning Insight. *An internal, production orientation is passé in today's competitive environment.*

Coors's problem was not that the company was not growth-minded; it was—if increasing the productive capacity of the single brewery and venturing into other geographical regions can be construed as growth-minded. However, this philosophy of growth gave no recognition to changes in the environment, especially in the competitive picture—changes that necessitated adjustments and modification in business and marketing strategy. But alas, it is tempting when things are going well, when a product is receiving accolades from ordinary people as well as the famous, to be lulled into a sense of unrelieved complacency, to envision nothing going wrong, to see a favorable image as insulating the company and its brand from all competition and adversity. Such a perception of the environment tends to provoke less than desirable consequences (we will see this again in the Harley Davidson case). It tends to make a firm arbitrary and dictatorial in its relation with dealers, employees, and even customers—in other words, it promotes a "take it or leave it" attitude.

INFORMATION SIDELIGHT

AN INTERNAL VERSUS AN EXTERNAL ORIENTATION TO STRATEGY PLANNING AND EXECUTION[10]

A firm, in its strategy planning and execution, can primarily focus on internal factors, such as technology and cost cutting. The key to attracting customers is thereby seen in improving production and distribution efficiency and lowering costs if possible. Henry Ford pioneered this philosophy in the early 1900s with his Model T. Texas Instruments is a modern-day example, becoming dominant in pocket calculators and digital watches by improving its efficiency and bringing down prices.[11] Coors was certainly successful with such a management orientation up to about 1976. But then, conditions changed; the competitive environment became more hotly contested in Coors's markets, and consumers started switching their preferences to different types of beer, notably, light beers and premium beers. The internal or production orientation is most appropriate in two situations.[12]

1. Where demand for a product exceeds supply, such as in new technologies and in developing countries.
2. Where the product cost is high and the market can only be expanded if costs can be brought down as (Texas Instruments faced).

An external orientation recognizes the fallacy of the assumption that products will forever sell themselves, "if we can only maintain our production and technological superiority." Looking outside the firm to the business environment results in major priority given to determining customers' needs and wants, how these may be changing as evidenced by shifts in buying patterns, and adapting products and services accordingly. The external focus also permits more responsiveness to other external forces that may be factors, such as major competitive thrusts, changing governmental laws and regulations, economic conditions, trade union forces, and the like. With such an external orientation, attention will more likely be directed to locating new opportunities brought about by changing environmental conditions, rather than being engrossed with internal production and technological advances. Such an orientation is more geared to meeting and even anticipating change, and—like it or not—the environment for doing business is more and more dynamic today. Externally oriented firms usually have the advantage.

---

[10] Sometimes they are referred to as a production orientation (the internal focus) and a marketing orientation (the external emphasis).

[11] "Texas Instruments Shows U.S. Business How to Survive in the 1980s," *Business Week*, September 18, 1978, pp. 66 ff.

[12] Philip Kotler, *Marketing Management*, 4th Ed. (Englewood Cliffs, N.J.: Prentice-Hall, 1980), p. 27.

Learning Insight. *A "cash cow" philosophy is dangerous for a major product vulnerable to competitive inroads.*

Coors apparently regarded its situation as a "cash cow" from which the profits can be fully milked, while investments in advertising, in new product planning, and other expenditures were kept at a minimum. Certainly, as Table 11.3 reveals, Coors's expenditures for advertising were woefully below those of other brewers, even those much smaller than Coors. The following Information Sidelight shows the *cash cow strategy in relating to alternatives.* Unfortunately, a cash cow implementation strategy can leave a firm vulnerable to competition, especially when the total market is large, as the beer market was.

INFORMATION SIDELIGHT

BOSTON CONSULTING GROUP'S APPROACH TO STRATEGY IMPLEMENTATION

The Boston Consulting Group, a leading management consulting firm, has boiled down the major strategy decisions a firm faces to only four, depending on a firm's competitive position in a particular industry and the growth of that industry. Accordingly, a firm's major business categories can be classified as: Stars, Question Marks, Cash Cows, and Dogs. Figure 11.1 presents a matrix of this concept.

A different strategy implementation is recommended for each of these business categories, as follows:

Category	Strategy Implementation
Stars	*Build.* In a dominant market position and a rapidly growing industry, more investment and long-term profit goals are recommended, even if they come at the expense of short-term profitability.
Question Marks	*Build or Divest.* The decision as to whether to commit more resources to trying to build such products into leaders or whether to divest and use company resources elsewhere is not clear cut and easily made. It may depend on the strength of major competitors and how well heeled the company is: for example, it may decide it cannot provide sufficient financing to achieve the growth needed vis-à-vis competition.
Cash Cows	*Harvest.* When in a dominant position in a low-growth industry, the recommended strategy implementation is to reap the harvest of a strong cash flow. Only enough resources should be reinvested to maintain competitive position.
Dogs	*Divest.* There is no use wasting resources on poor competitive positions in low-growth industries. The recommended strategy is to sell or liquidate this business.

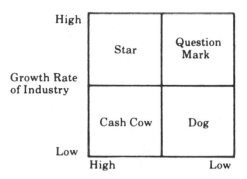

High

Growth Rate
of Industry

Low

| Star | Question Mark |
| Cash Cow | Dog |

High   Low

Relative Market Dominance Compared to Largest Competitor
(Market Share)

Figure 11.1. Matrix of a firm's major business categories

Star = Dominant market position in a high-growth industry
Question Mark = Weak market position in a high-growth industry
Cash Cow = Dominant market position in a low-growth industry
Dog = Weak market position in a low-growth industry

Coors, at the time of this mistake, was obviously in a cash flow situation, with high profits but minimum growth prospects facing the industry. It did not want to disrupt the harvesting of this business. But it became greedy in the sense of being reluctant to invest resources that might have resulted in diluting the beautiful cash flow.

Learning Insight. *It is difficult to build up a good image, but easy to lose it.*

Here we see the sad but nonetheless to-be-recognized impermanence of a good image. It is difficult to develop an image of quality and great desirability; even more difficult and time-consuming is the cultivation of a mystique. Although such an image can be a company's biggest asset while it lasts, it can be a fleeting thing. Coors's image of quality and great taste was lost in the Eastern markets because of bootleggers carrying the beer into these markets illegally and selling it at greatly inflated prices, while maintaining no quality care such as product rotation and adequate refrigeration. But we also see that consumer wants can be fickle and can change drastically: today's sought-after image may not necessarily be that of next year. The new sought-after image became light or low-calorie beer, and super-premium beer. Coors's brand image was dimmed.

Learning Insight. *Never underestimate competitors' potential for major inroads.*

A firm should not beguile itself into minimizing the threat of competition, both present and potential. Coors was guilty of this, under the illusion of the invincibility of its product vis-à-vis competing brands. (We saw a similar flaw in the thinking of Adidas, and will soon with Harley Davidson: such illusions are tempting indeed.) Yet, we can see how easily such an entrapment could occur: during the heady days of the early 1970s, Coors dominated every market it was in. But the reality was soon to impose itself. Without greatly increased marketing expenditures and, probably, the establishment of additional breweries closer to the market, there could be little chance of cracking the Eastern market against entrenched and powerful competitors. Furthermore, even Coors' captive and cherished Western markets—particularly the important California market—were vulnerable to the aggressive efforts of major competitors. A firm cannot expect the status quo to endure.

UPDATE

By 1981, Coors was budgeting some $87 million for advertising and promotion. This was nearly double what the company had spent two years before, and compares with a bare $1.2 million spent in 1975. Coors Light was running neck and neck with Miller's nationally dominant Lite in the 20 states in which Coors was now selling. But its problems were hardly solved.

Both barrelage and income were down. Coors's share of the California market had dropped to 20 percent in 1981. Anheuser was invading the Coors's stronghold of Texas, and its Bud Light gained 3 percent of the total market in one month. And Coors was still undecided whether to begin total distribution of its Herman Joseph's of 1868, which it had been test marketing for a year without making inroads against Anheuser's Michelob.

In 1984, however, Coors appeared to have honed its strategy. It moved aggressively into the Southeast in 1983 and captured some 11 percent of the market, with a good coordination of advertising and dealer incentives. But Coors was still struggling to combat competitive erosion in its original Western markets. In California, its competitive position had fallen to 16.1 percent by 1983; here, in the state with the highest beer consumption in the nation, it had a 37.8 percent share of the market in 1972.

By 1984, Coors was in 26 states with its Coors Premium and Light brands. But it was still testing Herman Joseph's of 1868, which had been in and out of test since May 1980; it was also experimenting with another potential premium beer, Golden Lager, with the results not suggesting a strong "go." Coors was still clinging to its fifth place among all brewers and had a 7.6 percent share of the market, exactly the same as it had had in 1978 with a much smaller geographic distribution.

Then, on August 19, 1987, the AFL-CIO ended its 10-year boycott against the company, satisfied that the major complaints had been addressed. In the next two months Coors gained more than 1800 new accounts, and this spurred optimism. Advertising expenditures for 1987 were expected to total $200 million, with an increase planned for 1988. A massive campaign—television, radio, print, and outdoor advertising—was primarily aimed at young adults. Coors Light, dubbed the "Silver Bullet," was also being promoted to the large Hispanic market, with the beer described as part of the *pura vida*, the good life. For 1988, a major nationwide rollout of six products was planned: Coors, Coors Light, Coors Extra Gold, George Killian's Irish Red, Herman Joseph's Original Draft, and Herman Joseph's Light. Expansion into Delaware, Pennsylvania, and Indiana would give Coors entry into all 50 states.

In 1989, a proposed purchase of Stroh Brewery fell apart when Coors discovered that the Detroit brewer was in worse shape than expected. Still, as Coors moved into the 1990s, it had taken third place among U.S. brewers, thanks largely to strength in Coors Light and in a new popular-priced beer introduced in 1989, Keystone. And the firm was in strong financial shape.

FOR THOUGHT AND DISCUSSION

1. How do you account for the fact that Coors beer achieved such a success despite the company's lack of advertising, new product development, and national distribution?
2. Discuss why an internal orientation is particularly unsuited for the brewing industry.
3. Do you think the company's fortunes would have remained strong and growing if advertising expenditures had been doubled or tripled during the late 1960s and early 1970s?
4. Is it likely that Coors's labor disputes had any serious effect on its fortunes? Why or why not?
5. At this time, 1986, should Coors plan to go national? Examine as many pros and cons as possible.

INVITATION TO ROLE PLAY

1. Place yourself in the role of Peter Coors, the young senior vice president for sales and marketing. How would you attempt now (as of 1986) to

reverse the company's fading performance? Be as specific as you can; also consider and identify any constraints to a corporate strategy that should be recognized. You might also want to consider how a mystique might again be built up for the Coors brand.

2. Place yourself in the role of a staff analyst. You have been asked to evaluate the desirability of opening another brewery in the East—perhaps in Virginia. Consider as many pros and cons as you can (you will, of course, have to make some assumptions, especially regarding construction costs). Develop a recommendation for a go/no-go decision, and be prepared to defend it before a top management committee.

12

Chrysler Corporation— "Can We Even Survive?"

On May 11, 1982, a headline in the business section of the Cleveland *Plain Dealer* stated, "Steel Imports Surge Aids Port." The article noted that a shipment of foreign steel was being unloaded on Cleveland docks the same day that domestic steel mills were reporting their lowest operating rate within recent memory. As many as 20 more ships carrying steel imports were expected to arrive in the next 30 days. The article further observed that the scene of imports unloading was nettling a domestic steel industry with 100,000 workers on layoffs and more than 30,000 on short workweeks.

In industry after industry, U.S. firms were finding it difficult to compete successfully against foreign competitors, not only in our own domestic market but in foreign markets as well. Business publications were calling for a reindustrialization of America,[1] which no one saw as being easily or quickly accomplished. No industry was more beset by foreign competition and by an inability to match foreign productivity and attractiveness of foreign-made products than the auto industry. And Chrysler was the most grievously beset.

IACOCCA TO THE RESCUE?

In November 1978, Lee A. Iacocca became president of the ailing Chrysler Corporation, at one time the fourth-largest industrial corporation in the

---

[1] For example, *Business Week*, June 30, 1980, entire issue.

United States. Iacocca brought to the enterprise and its hopes for survival his proven abilities of salesmanship, image-building, and cost-cutting. But many doubted that this would be enough to save the company—indeed, whether anything could. There was doubt that the entire U.S. auto industry could be saved—short of governmental subsidization, that is.

Iacocca embodied the great American success story. In an earlier era, this would have been dubbed a Horatio Alger tale, after the prominent fiction writer of rags-to-riches stories early in this century. Iacocca was the son of an Italian immigrant. He saw education as the route to success, and he went to Lehigh University and then on to Princeton for a master's degree in engineering. "In my day you went to college, not to go into government or to be a lawyer, but to embark on a career that paid you more money than the guy who didn't go. For 32 years I was motivated by money," said Iacocca.[2]

He started with the Ford Motor Company as a trainee in 1946 at $125 a week. As he moved upward through the Ford organization, Iacocca was responsible for introducing the trend-setting Mustang in 1964 (only a few years after the Edsel debacle), and followed up with the Maverick, Pinto, and Fiesta. By 1977, he was president of Ford, earning $978,000 that year. Then, in July 1978, Henry Ford abruptly fired him. The falling out has been attributed to basic disagreement between Ford and Iacocca over the pace of downsizing cars: Iacocca wanted to move fast, whereas Ford was worried about the impact of such additional investment on short-term profits and wanted to move more slowly.

After Iacocca left Ford, John J. Riccardo, chief executive of Chrysler, offered him the presidency. In accepting this, Iacocca turned down a dozen jobs that offered more money. But he was after a place in automotive history: "I might not only save a blue-chip company and 200,000 jobs, but also help the Big Three become an honest Big Three."[3]

THE CHRYSLER DILEMMA

Chrysler had long been the weak sister of the Big Three automakers. Although a multibillion-dollar firm, it was smaller, less well financed, and less talented than General Motors (GM) and Ford. It had suffered major reversals in the early 1960s, in 1970, and in 1974–1975. The monumental problems affecting the very viability of the company in the later 1970s and early 1980s had their roots in the recession of 1974–1975. At that time, a severe drop in sales forced the company to make massive cuts in capital spending and, perhaps more serious, in engineers and designers. Delays in introducing new models and quality problems resulted. For example, Chrys-

---

[2] "Off to the Races Again," *Fortune*, December 4, 1978, p. 15.
[3] Ibid.

ler compacts, Volare and Aspen, were introduced in 1976, and subsequently went through eight recalls for defects. Many Chrysler fans who had been loyal through generations turned to other makes.

In 1978, Chrysler lost $205 million. By 1979, problems worsened as gasoline prices rose sharply and the public began demanding small fuel efficient cars. Although Chrysler had some success with its subcompact Omnis and Horizons, losses were over $1 billion, and the future of the company was in doubt.

Lobbying In Washington

Iacocca turned to Washington to bail out the company. He sought Federal loan guarantees of $1.2 billion. Chrysler's lobbying had irresistible bipartisan appeal in a coming election because of the concentration of Chrysler workers and parts suppliers in such key states as Michigan, Ohio, Indiana, as well as five other states. The Carter administration strongly supported the loan-guarantee legislation, and Congress finally authorized not $1.2 billion, but $1.5 billion. Chrysler immediately drew on $800 million to help it weather the coming months.

But Chrysler's problems continued, and its actual sales for 1980 were far worse than had been predicted, with the deficit an unbelievable $1.7 billion. Although the blame could be laid on such externals as a recession and mushrooming interest rates that affected consumers and dealers alike, the failure of the widely touted K-car was crucial.

The K-Cars

The Dodge Aries and the Plymouth Reliant were introduced in September 1980 with great fanfare. These were front-wheel drive compacts, somewhat roomier and a bit more fuel efficient than GM's X-cars, introduced 18 months before. It was expected that sales would be about 70,000 for the introductory months of October and November 1980, and 492,000 for all of 1981. Instead, only 34,273 units were sold the first 2 months, and by the end of November, dealers had a 98-day supply of K-cars. GM, in contrast, had a 54-day supply of its older and virtually unchanged X-cars. Ford's new subcompacts, the Lynx and Escort, had also done considerably better than the K-cars during this period.

Thus, the poor showing of the K-cars could not be blamed solely on external factors. Chrysler had tried to price the K-car close to the X-car; it also loaded most cars with every conceivable option, consequently bringing the price from the basic $6100 car to about $8000.

The disappointment of the K-car introduction did not end Iacocca's troubles. By 1980, even the Omnis and Horizons that had done well the year before began to lose their luster. Chrysler had estimated sales of these cars at 394,000 for all of 1980; by the end of November, only 222, 814 had been sold, and dealers' inventories had risen to a 134-day supply. Even Iacocca's hopes to reenter the luxury-car market were facing disappointment. The Imperial was again introduced for the first time since 1976 with heavy advertising, even using Frank Sinatra to plug it. But sales of 1885 cars in October and November were less than half the forecast.

Iacocca's Defensive Moves

Iacocca's reaction to these disasters was to offer rebates of $380 to $1200 a car in December 1980 and in early 1981. An ambitious cost-cutting program was also announced that would save the company $1 billion in 1981. This involved four things:

1. A wage freeze for blue-collar workers.
2. A 5-percent reduction in prices charged by suppliers for 90 days and a freeze for the rest of 1981.
3. A $575-million cut in investment in new-plant capacity and new-product development.
4. Asking lenders to convert $572 million in debt to preferred stock, thereby reducing interest payments by $100 million a year.

And Chrysler went back to the loan-guarantee board for $400 million.

Although the Chrysler dilemma was unique and more serious than for other U.S. automakers, it was nonetheless symptomatic of the sorry straits confronting a major U.S. industry that had not adequately coped with foreign competition.

The U.S. Auto Industry—1970–1980

In the decade of the 1970s, U.S. automakers' share of the domestic U.S. market fell from 85 percent to 70 percent; in other words, by 1980, imports had captured almost 30 percent of the market, double that of a decade earlier. Import inroads intensified in the latter part of the 1970s. Table 12.1 shows the market share of all imports, as well as the units sold of the five leading ones from 1977 through 1980.

The vulnerability to imports came partly from Detroit's failure to build sufficient small-car capacity. American companies ignored the fact that many customers were returning to the idea of simple and efficient transportation. (This was the very idea that Henry Ford had pioneered with his Model T seven decades earlier.) When oil price increases made big cars all but obsolete, the foreign firms were ready and able to step in. Japan alone had a 22 percent share of the U.S. auto market by 1981. Only three years before, Japanese imports were 12 percent. As we can see from Table 12.1, sales volumes in 1980 were below a recession-level 9 million cars, and this included the major share carved out by imports. U.S. automakers incurred some $5.5 billion in red ink in 1980 and 1981. About 2400 dealerships folded in these two years. The president of the 20,000-member National Automobile Dealers Association asserted that "dealers are holding on by their used-car departments."[4]

Table 12.1   Import Inroads in the U.S. Auto Market—1977–1980

	1980	1979	1978	1977
Total units sold—all makes	8,760,937	10,356,695	10,946,104	10,825,235
Total imports units sold	2,469,180	2,351,053	1,946,094	1,976,512
Market share of imports (%)	28.2%	22.7%	17.8%	18.3%
Leading imports (units sold):				
Toyota	582,204	507,816	441,800	493,048
Datsun	516,890	472,252	338,096	388,378
Honda	375,388	353,291	274,876	223,633
VW	90,923	125,100	216,709	260,704
Mazda	161,623	156,533	75,309	50,609

Source: Automotive News, 1981 Market Data Book Issue.

Another aspect contributing to Detroit's problems was a growing perception by the U.S. consumer that American-made cars were inferior in quality and workmanship to foreign-made, especially to Japanese-made cars. This perception was most difficult to overcome. In particular, Ford and Chrysler heavily advertised the improved quality of their cars. But consumers remained skeptical. Some experts predicted that three years of good word-of-mouth endorsements from happy owners would be needed to overcome the prejudices against the quality of U.S. cars.[5]

Sticker Shock

Detroit was blaming all its problems on high interest rates and the discouraging effect they were having on consumer willingness to buy high-ticket items. But a consumer survey by the Survey Research Center of the University of Michigan revealed that high car prices, not interest rates, were the biggest reasons for not planning to buy a new car.

---

[4] "Detroit's Struggle to Survive," *Business Week,* January 11, 1982, pp. 62–63.
[5] "Why Detroit Still Can't Get Going," *Business Week,* November 9, 1981, p. 110.

Figures compiled by the National Automobile Dealers Association put the average selling price of a U.S.–made new car at $8900 by late 1981. Ten years before, the average price had been $3730. In the single year from 1980 to 1981, prices rose more than $1000. Even GM's Vice Chairman, Howard Kehrl, conceded, "If there's any sales problem, it's getting people to recog nize that a very high-quality small car is not cheap."[6] The term "sticker shock" began to be heard in the land. And when a potential customer saw car prices 70 percent or more higher than the last car he bought, disinclina tion to buy a new car could readily set in.

Detroit's eagerness to embrace high prices was nothing new. Neither should there have been surprise at consumer reluctance to purchase at prices that were significantly higher than a few months before. The same thing happened earlier in the 1970s. For 15 months, from 1973 to late 1974, Detroit automakers repeatedly increased the selling prices of their cars. This was a time of burgeoning inflation, with material and labor costs rising sharply. New government standards for safety and pollution control added other costs, and the automakers themselves were incorporating more expensive equipment, such as radial tires.

In this period, the average price of a new car increased by $1000. And suddenly, sales plummeted 25 percent. Automakers now began offering cash rebates for a limited time to reduce massive inventories of unsold cars. But the damage had been done, and the auto industry led the rest of the nation into a severe recession.

Did the U.S. automakers learn from this? Apparently not. Much the same thing was happening in late 1980 and 1981, when new economy-efficient cars were introduced to compete with foreign imports, but at prices that were far from "economy." By June 1981, used car sales were running 19 percent above the previous year, but domestic new car sales continued to plummet.

Detroit tried to ease buyers from their sticker shock by *rebates,* offering lower than market interest rates on new car purchases, and by some roll-backs of prices. But these were only temporary incentives, and they tended to borrow sales from future months when the rebates and other concessions ended. Even worse, the on-again, off-again bargains appeared to confuse some buyers, whereas others were convinced that special deals were a routine part of car purchasing: demand dried up drastically during those periods when no concessions were in effect.

In defense of their higher sticker prices, Detroit maintained that the front-wheel drive they had adopted for most cars produced high retooling costs. And, with sales volume down, it became essential to squeeze as much profit from every car as possible. But the elasticity of demand could not

[6] Ibid., p. 107.

INFORMATION SIDELIGHT

REBATES

A rebate is a promise by a manufacturer to return part of the purchase price directly to the purchaser. Usually, the rebate is given to consumers, although it can be offered to dealers instead in the expectation that they will pass some or all of the savings along to consumers.

Obviously, the objective of a rebate is to increase sales by giving purchasers essentially a lower price. But why not simply reduce prices? The rebate is used instead of a regular markdown or price reduction because it is less permanent than cutting the list price. Rebates can be quite effective in generating short-term business. But they may affect business negatively once the rebate has been lifted.

---

accept higher prices, whatever the rationale, and demand dried up as sticker prices increased.

OPTIONS FOR CHRYSLER

By the end of 1980, the situation for Chrysler seemed bleak indeed, with sales declining badly and losses becoming astronomical, as shown below:

	1978	1979	1980
Sales (millions)	$13,618.3	$12,001.9	$9,225.3
Losses (millions)	$ 204.6	$ 1,097.3	$1,709.7

Source: Chrysler annual reports.

At this point, several options seemed available to Chrysler if it were to survive:

1. It could greatly pare its product line, and limit itself only to the small cars that seemed to comprise most of the market demand. By so doing, the full-size and intermediate car lines would be discontinued, and their factories either permanently closed or converted so that they could produce front-wheel-drive subcompacts.
2. Large chunks of the company could be sold off, such as the parts-making operation, which had been running in the red because of underutilization. Some or all of its profitable units, such as the military tank business, Chrysler Financial Corporation, and its electronics division might also be sold to provide needed funds to support the remaining auto operation.

3. The various lines of cars might be merged into a single nameplate. Thus, Chrysler-Plymouth and Dodge lines could be pared, thereby simplifying assembly, reducing inventory of duplicate parts, and concentrating selling efforts.

4. Augmenting its lines with "niche" cars that would be so distinctive they could command a high price and yield a good profit, even on low sales volume. This was a strategy that had revived BMW, the German sports car manufacturer.[7]

5. An affiliation might be established with another auto maker, such as Volkswagen. This might provide Chrysler with needed cash, as well as a product line expanded with foreign-designed cars. Unfortunately, Chrysler was hardly an attractive property for a foreign suitor. Although it had about $2 billion in tax losses that would shield future profits from taxes, it had a colossal drawback in its debt burden: $1.2 billion in guaranteed loans, almost $1 billion in other debts, in addition to $1.2 billion in unfunded pension liabilities.

6. Chapter 11 bankruptcy was the ultimate option. This would not necessarily lead to the company's demise and liquidation. Under Chapter 11, a company continues to operate, but has court protection against creditors' lawsuits while working out a plan for paying its debts. However, Iacocca was convinced that such a reorganization under the Federal bankruptcy code would quickly lead to total collapse, with car sales screeching to a halt as a result of what is termed the *orphan syndrome*. When potential customers fear that a firm may collapse, they see warranties as worthless; they suspect that dealers might not be around to handle problems, that resale value of cars will drastically decline, and that parts may become harder to find as years go by. Consequently, only a few die-hard loyalists might still be induced to buy. To some extent, the orphan syndrome was already affecting Chrysler because of its widely publicized difficulties.

Most of the preceding options were deemed by company executives to be hardly workable. Paring down to a profitable core, as American Motors had attempted to do, was ruled out, because it was thought that Chrysler dealers needed a full line of cars if they were to compete effectively with Ford and GM. In early 1982, however, Chrysler did sell its subsidiary, Chrysler Defense Corporation, to General Dynamics for about $350 million. This division produced the main tank for the U.S. Army, the M-1, and the sale provided a cash cushion against further operating losses.

---

[7] "Could Bankruptcy Save Chrysler?" *Business Week,* December 24, 1979, p. 70.

So Iacocca and Chrysler were determined to maintain their role as a full-line auto manufacturer and to hang on doggedly until better times. One analyst critized: "The problem is not that there aren't any alternatives, but rather the man at the helm . . . Lee's in a race to show Henry (Ford) what he can do. And in the process, he's likely to become a General Custer."[8]

WHAT WENT WRONG AT CHRYSLER?

Chrysler's basic problem had long been inadequate capital. This was aggravated by an acquisitions binge in the 1960s and early 1970s. Many of these acquisitions turned out to be lemons and had to be sold at losses to raise cash in the late 1970s. For example, European car companies were acquired as Chrysler attempted to build a foreign operation that could provide a sales cushion for the periodic downturns of the U.S. market. However, only failing companies were acquired: Simca in France, and Rootes Motor Ltd. in Britain. These companies turned into cash drains, siphoning off funds needed at home.

Lacking the capital and some of the creative talents of Ford and GM, Chrysler's products tended to be not innovative, but imitative, that is, "me-too" types of cars. Such cars, lacking in prestige and advanced styling, often had to be sold at lower prices than competing cars, and Chrysler had to be satisfied with lower profit margins. This situation was hardly likely to improve soon. For example, GM spent $8 billion in 1981 on plant and equipment; this was more than Chrysler planned to spend in six years.

The current problems stem more directly from 1970 when Lynn Townsend, then chairman, decided to squeeze the most out of existing plants and product lines rather than build for the future. Although the strategy seemed sound at the time for a cash-poor company, unforeseen world events sabotaged it. Notably, the Arab oil embargo brought a new emphasis on economy and high mileage, and Federal legislation even made increased mileage standards mandatory. In 1970, subcompact cars accounted for only 3 percent of the U.S. market. And Townsend opted not to compete with the Vega and Pinto compact cars introduced in 1970 by GM and Ford. Instead, he chose to concentrate on restyling the more profitable big cars, in a $250 million model change. Just a few months later, the oil embargo destroyed the market for gas-guzzling big cars. And Chrysler did not have the smaller cars desperately sought by consumers. The two losing years of 1974 and 1975 brought the severe cutbacks in capital spending and in talented personnel that were to affect future operations.

John Riccardo, Townsend's successor, made another decision in 1975 that was to redound to the company's disadvantage. Facing the prospect of

[8] Ibid., p. 72.

costly new Federal braking and noise rules, and recognizing—again—the limited cash resources,. Riccardo decided to drop the profitable, heavy-duty truck business, and instead focus on vans and pickups. And sales of these products were the first to soften at the threat of fuel disruption and higher prices.

Can we fault Chrysler's management for failing to anticipate an oil embargo that was to bring gas lines and burgeoning prices, so that demand for big cars, vans, and the like all but dried up? Could any reasonable person have predicted such a situation? And can we fault Chrysler management for not having the same options available as the larger competitors with vastly superior financial resources? Where do we draw the line between prudent decisions and myopic ones?

The issue is complicated. And perhaps Chrysler's management was more the victim of circumstances. Perhaps the same can be said for GM and Ford management, and for that of the steel companies and the other industries vulnerable to foreign competition. Yet, some of the blame was simply an unwavering embracing of short-term profit objectives. Such objectives induce a firm to postpone plant modernization, to emphasize the most profitable products (in the case of U.S. automakers, and especially Chrysler, this meant big uneconomical cars, or small cars so loaded with expensive options that they cost as much as big cars), to cut back on research and development expenditures, and to seek maximum per unit profit, even if this meant increased inflation, not fully meeting the needs of consumers, and not even being competitive with foreign firms.

Chrysler blamed a lot of its troubles on *costly government regulations* imposed in the 1970s. For example, auto emission standards, fuel economy goals, passive seat belt or air-bag systems—these were estimated to have cost Chrysler $1 billion extra in 1979 and 1980. Being the smallest of the major automakers, it had fewer units to spread such costs over, and was thus more seriously affected than GM and Ford. The Reagan administration brought a loosening of some of the regulations. As the Information Sidelight indicates, many regulations are extremely controversial, with different points of view creating almost irreconcilable issues.

INFORMATION SIDELIGHT

SCRAPPING AUTO BUMPER STANDARDS

On May 14, 1982, the Federal government scrapped requirements that automobile bumpers must withstand a 5 mph crash without causing damage to the vehicle. Automobiles hereafter will be required to have bumpers that protect the vehicle only in crashes of up to 2.5 mph, and this may later be reduced to below 2.5 mph for some type of autos.

The bumper requirement had been highly criticized by the automobile industry as being unnecessary and adding $35 to $50 to the cost of a vehicle. On the other hand, consumer advocate Ralph Nader called the decision a "surrender to General Motors" that he claimed would cost motorists $400 million a year in added insurance premiums and repair costs. Industry experts confirmed this, estimating that insurance premiums could rise by 10 to 20 percent with the permission of weaker bumpers.[9]

In a pluralistic society in which many different interest groups are vying for legislation and regulations favorable to their position, it is impossible to satisfy all interests. However, in the early 1980s, the pendulum seemed to be swinging back to the side of management as it attempted to overcome foreign inroads.

WHAT CAN BE LEARNED?

We can draw some generalizations from the Chrysler problems that apply to the whole U.S. auto industry as well as such U.S. industries as steel, rubber, machine tools, and consumer electronics. The problems of Chrysler and the other Detroit automakers were symptomatic of problems facing other American industries as the decade of the 70s was ending: a substantial part of American industry was just not able to compete effectively against aggressive foreign competition, particularly the Japanese. A new assessment of American management philosophies seemed indicated. And a painful reevaluation of traditional ways of doing things and criteria for decisionmaking seemed essential if America were to regain its industrial dominance and if American jobs were to be saved.

Perhaps the major thing to be learned is that we in this country are not insulated from competition although we invented mass production and were in the vanguard of sophisticated management techniques. Nothing is guaranteed forever. The environment changes. Traditional ways of doing things can be vulnerable to fresh ideas. They need to be constantly appraised. We can learn from foreign competitors, just as they, for decades, have learned from us.

[9] "U.S. Auto Bumper Standard Scrapped," *Cleveland Plain Dealer,* May 15, 1982, p. 4-A.

Table 12.2 shows the key industries hardest hit in the U.S. market by foreign competitors. This table shows the extent of foreign inroads in certain key industries from 1960 to 1980 (as we saw earlier, by 1981 the auto industry was in even worse shape, with imports in one year jumping from 22.7 percent to 28.2 percent of total U.S. auto sales). Although foreign inroads in the auto industry have received the most publicity, certain other industries have suffered even more—the trend over the last several decades has been disturbing indeed.

Table 12.2   Foreign Inroads in Key Industries in the U.S. Market, 1960–1980

	Percentage of Total Industry Sales by Imports	
Industry	1960	1979
Autos	4.1%	22.7%
Steel	4.2	14.0
Electrical components	.5	20.1
Farm machinery	7.2	15.3
Consumer electronics	5.6	50.6
Footwear	2.3	37.3
Metal-cutting machine tools	3.3	26.4
Textile machinery	6.6	45.5
Calculating and adding machines	5.0	43.1

Source: Commerce Department.

U.S. Disadvantage In Productivity

Productivity in the United States has been a nagging concern. It has been slipping relative to foreign industries, and by so doing has made many foreign products more attractive costwise and qualitywise than U.S. goods. The usual measure of productivity is output per hour, that is, how much an American worker produces in an hour compared, say, to a Japanese or West German worker. The calculation is made by dividing total output of goods and services by the number of hours or number of workers used to produce them. From 1966 to 1976, the United States had the lowest growth rate in productivity of the top 11 Western industrial nations.[10]

Productivity directly affects cost. In 1978, Japanese car companies had a $700 cost advantage per car over their U.S. counterparts. In other words, because of their greater productivity, Japanese car makers could manufac-

[10] Thomas W. Gerdel, "America's Dilemma of Poor Production," *Cleveland Plain Dealer*, January 19, 1981, p. 1-D.

ture an equivalent car for $700 less than could be achieved in the U.S. Serious as this competitive disadvantage was to American firms, the difference had widened by 1981 to $1500 per car.[11]

Strong pressures began building to make American cars more competitive by reducing labor costs; with U.S. car makers facing billion-dollar deficits and with worker layoffs increasing, unions began making some concessions. But such efforts only chipped away at Japan's big manufacturing-cost advantage. Limiting Japan's imports through q;uotas was another often-mentioned recourse. But some feared that quotas might prompt Japan to shift efforts toward larger, more expensive models, an area where U.S. car makers were not as severely challenged as with small cars. The prospect that Japan might soon be competing against Detroit's entire product line struck fear in the industry.

Factors In U.S. Productivity Problems

Fingers of blame for U.S. productivity problems pointed in all directions. Although some of these factors were interrelated and due to multiple causes, for the sake of simplicity we will examine them under: lack of sufficient investment in productive facilities; short-term profit-maximizing managerial goals; and adversarial (rather than cooperative) relationship of business with labor and with government.

Lack of Adequate Investment in Productive Facilities. Outdated plants typify some U.S. industries. A major example is the steel industry. U.S. firms were still building open-hearth furnaces in the late 1950s, whereas the Japanese were building more modern plants that used the basic oxygen process, a process that ironically was a U.S. invention. The U.S. agricultural machinery industry in all practicality excluded itself from growing markets in developing countries by concentrating on making big and expensive machinery appropriate only for the U.S. market. For example, no American firm still makes a farm tractor under 35 horsepower. The failure of the U.S. machine tool industry to meet domestic market needs, because of a reluctance to build enough capacity to serve the needs of the market in periods of peak demand, simply invited foreign competition. And in consumer electronics, as we all know, most TVs, radios, stereos, and the like are now made by the Japanese; in 1960, about 95 percent of these products were supplied by domestic manufacturers. The Japanese secret: not so much lower labor costs, but superior technology and management.

---

[11] "Why Detroit Still Can't Get Going," p. 109.

Along with the sag in investment in modern plant and equipment, compared especially to Germany and Japan, has been a decline in research and development spending since the mid-1960s. This has resulted in the United States lagging behind in applying technology to commercial products. For example, robots were an American invention, but now Japan has taken the lead in applying robots to a variety of manufacturing processes.

Government regulations and a punitive tax system that penalized savings have also been blamed for a reluctance to invest in capital equipment. And, undeniably, our society in recent decades has been more oriented to spending than to savings, with interest payments on loans being fully tax deductible, whereas interest on savings is taxed as ordinary income. The last 15 years have seen a heavy imposition of regulations dealing with environmental protection, safety, health, equal employment, energy efficiency, and the like. Such regulations and the bureaucracy that interprets and enforces them have sometimes placed major obstacles in the way of investing in new plants and even in maintaining present ones. For example, the Environmental Protection Agency has forced some industries, such as steel, to invest millions of dollars—which might have gone to modernizing facilities—into pollution control devices.

Faltering investment in productive facilities has also been blamed on the huge increases in the service industries, such as health and social services, which have absorbed resources that might have gone into productive areas. Others have blamed the deteriorating rate of productivity on a shortage of engineers and too many bureaucrats, staff people, and lawyers. Even the introduction of computer technology and sophisticated office systems has been blamed. These accouterments of modern business management have been seen by some as soaking up resources that might have been better used in more directly productive facilities, and also in providing more information to management than is really needed: that is, they have placed more people in paper-shuffling roles rather than in more productive activities, and in the process added greatly to the overhead burden.

Short-sighted Management. Major reasons for the decline of U.S. industry must point more directly to management deficiencies. A major orientation of American managers has been and continues to be maximizing profits. Performance is measured by reaching profit objectives, and promotion and compensation are tied to it. The executive who does not achieve profit goals is unlikely to advance very far. Is it any wonder that all levels of executives are thinking about profits and how to get more of them? And what, really, is wrong with this? The answer lies in what kind of profits we are talking about: short-term immediate profits, or profits over the longer run. Long-range goals have tended to be sacrificed for short-run profits—in Chrysler, the rest of the U.S. auto industry, the steel industry, and in many other industries as well. Consequently, if heavy investment is needed in research, retooling, and other efforts to reach long-term goals, they tend to be postponed because such programs hurt profits in the short run.

And the fallacy of such short-sighted strategies can be clearly seen. The auto industry's postponement of the need to develop high-quality, fuel-efficient vehicles the car-buying market really wanted gave a big chunk of this business to the imports. Likewise, the steel industry postponed for decades the shifting of production from outmoded facilities, and now lacks the capital to do so. (There are exceptions to this. Standard Oil of Ohio [Sohio] made huge investments in Alaskan oil development, even to the point of facing formidable debts a decade before any returns from the investment could be expected. Eventually, the payoff came, and Sohio was flooded with profits: it earned $1.2 billion on sales of $7.9 billion in 1979.)

Adversarial Relationships of Business. Some of the blame for poor productivity is laid at labor's door. Some people maintain that lazy workers who take too many coffee breaks and who have lost their forebears' zeal for work are to blame—not only for poor productivity with its high costs, but also for an uncaring and careless attitude toward quality. Sometimes this is seen as resulting from the growth of unions with their emphasis on seniority at the expense of capability. Unions have been criticized as too greedy, too uncaring, too rigid in adhering to old ways that curb efficiency and protect the status quo. Usually, collective bargaining has taken place in an adversarial rather than a cooperative environment. This contrasts sharply with the labor-management situation in Japan, where most workers stay with the same firm for life and enjoy almost a family relationship and certainly one of teamwork and cooperation toward common objectives. *Quality circles,* as described in the Information Sidelight that follows, are a major component of the close and cooperative management and labor relations of Japanese firms.

Management is certainly far from blameless in its labor relations, in the acceptance of inflationary wage settlements, and in the tolerance of mediocre quality. It has often been the easier course of action to make contract concessions and pass the inflationary costs on to customers by raising prices, rather than suffer a lengthy strike. Eventually, the productivity and competitiveness of domestic industries have been diminished. Now, the challenge is to develop a framework within which labor and management can work together toward a common objective. Both have a stake in the competitive productivity of U.S. industries, because not only profits but jobs are truly at stake. Management has the challenge to offer new incentives to motivate workers to higher levels of productivity.

Government has also tended to take an adversarial stance toward U.S.

business. As we have noted before, regulation has tended to be obstructive, even though some regulation is clearly needed. But an explosion of regulations placed on business to achieve social goals, such as equal employment, a cleaner environment, and a safer workplace, have undeniably diverted vast amounts of capital from more productive avenues. A teamwork approach, a spirit of more cooperation and a less adversarial and litigious relationship may be essential if U.S. productivity is to be competitive. Japan and West Germany certainly have, for the most part, a harmonious and supportive relationship of government and business.

UPDATE

Of course, we know what happened to Chrysler. It became perhaps the most notable success of the half century. Even supplier firms attempted to participate in the glory, as an ad by Control Data in the *Wall Street Journal* of February 8, 1985 (page 8) headlined: "Chrysler Shaped the Greatest Turnaround in Automotive History . . . with Help from Proven Technologies of Control Data." And Iacocca's autobiography became the number 1 nonfiction best seller for many weeks.

As we come into the decade of the 1990s, the U.S. auto industry is not doing particularly well. The Japanese are steadily winning more market share, with Japanese plants in the United States increasing production whereas GM, Ford, and Chrysler have closed plants and laid off tens of thousands of white-collar employees in extensive cost-cutting efforts. As the smallest auto manufacturer, Chrysler is more vulnerable. Yet, survival is not an issue. All three are still earning substantial profits from their reduced overheads. And Chrysler has two big profit lines—minivan and Jeep—which should keep the company going until better days arrive.

FOR THOUGHT AND DISCUSSION

1. What incentives would you propose to motivate workers to higher productivity?
2. Discuss in what ways the Japanese worker differs from the typical U.S. worker. (You may need to do some research on this.) How do these dissimilarities affect labor-management relations in the two countries?
3. Quality circles have been praised by some experts as a breakthrough in management-labor relations and in improving productivity and quality. Do you see any problems with these quality circles?
4. Discuss the pros and cons of rebates versus reductions of list prices for stimulating demand.

INFORMATION SIDELIGHT

QUALITY CIRCLES

Quality circles were adopted by Japan in an effort to rid its industries of poor quality control and junkiness after World War II. Quality circles are worker-manager committees that meet regularly, usually weekly, to talk about production problems, plan ways to improve productivity and quality, and resolve job-related gripes on both sides. They have been described as "the single most significant explanation for the truly outstanding quality of goods and services produced in Japan."[12] For example, Mazda has 2147 circles with over 16,000 employees involved. They usually consist of seven to eight volunteer members who meet on their own time to discuss and solve the issues they are concerned with. In addition to making major contributions to increased productivity and quality, they have provided employees with an opportunity to participate and gain a sense of accomplishment.[13]

The idea—like so many ideas adopted by the Japanese—did not originate with them: it came from two American personnel consultants. The Japanese refined the idea and ran with it. Now, American industry is rediscovering quality circles and finding them a desirable way to promote teamwork, good feelings, and to avoid at least some of the adversarial relations stemming from collective bargaining matters or union grievances that must be negotiated.

INVITATION TO ROLE PLAY

1. How would you recommend to the executive committee a commitment to long-range profitability objectives, rather than short-term profit goals, in your organization? Discuss any difficulties you see in getting such a commitment from top management and in fostering it throughout the organization? How would you reconcile these?

2. Place yourself in the position of Iacocca. You have weathered the initial financial crunch and now have some breathing room. Your task, as you see it, is to bring Chrysler now to at least a strong third position behind GM and Ford in the next ten years. Ideally, you would like to wrest second place in the industry from Ford—you would like nothing better. Discuss how you would plan to achieve this growth objective, recognizing Chrysler's resource constraints.

[12] "A Partnership; to Build the New Workplace," *Business Week*, June 30, 1980, p. 101.
[13] As described in a Mazda ad in *Forbes*, May 24, 1982, p. 5.

13

A. C. Gilbert—Frenetic Reactions to Emerging Problems

The A.C. Gilbert Company was not a youngster, having had some 58 years of toy-making experience at the time it failed. For years its name had been respected and well known, and it signified quality.

In a mere 5 years, all this was to end. Almost incredibly, bad judgment replaced the solid achievements of the past. Changing environmental conditions were ignored for too long. Rash, frantic decisions were then substituted for a well-planned, corrective strategy that could have built on the strengths of the company.

BACKGROUND

The A. C. Gilbert Company was the product of one imaginative man's inventiveness and willingness to back his ideas himself rather than selling out. Alfred Carlton Gilbert, after graduation from Yale, established the Mysto Manufacturing Company in 1909 to make the Erector set, which he had perfected. In 1916, this company became the A. C. Gilbert Company. In time, the son, A. C., Jr., joined the company as assistant to his father and became president in 1954. In 1961, the senior Gilbert died, and the son became chairman of the board. Gilbert, Jr., was a respected figure in the toy industry, serving as president of the Toys Manufacturers of the U.S.A. in 1962–1963.

Although the company never became a large firm, it was solidly in the top 10 of toy manufacturers in the 1950s, with sales reaching over $17 million. It was strong in science toys—chemistry sets, microscopes, and Erector "engineering" sets—at a time when science was becoming important as a national priority. Gilbert had the reputation of a quality toy maker, and its American Flyer trains and Erector sets were known by generations of boys and their parents.

This was the situation as the company entered the 1960s. However, the environment for selling toys was changing. The 1960s, with their attendant prosperity, brought a booming toy market. But it was different from what Gilbert was familiar with. A new promotional medium, television, had become important for toy marketing and was superseding catalogs and window displays. But television was expensive and made the break-even point on toy sales much higher. It also enabled many items, from hula hoops to Batmobiles, to attain quick popularity. The market was changing rapidly, and a firm had to be nimble to tap the sales potential and not be caught with too heavy an inventory when demand was superseded by another fad item.

The toy market was also changing in that traditional toy stores, hobby shops, and department stores were being bypassed for self-service, high-volume supermarkets and discount stores. These new dealers were mainly interested in low-priced, heavily advertised toys with attractive packages that could act as selling tools.

So the old, successful, well-entrenched company entered the 1960s rather complacent and content with the status quo.

PROBLEMS

Anson Isaacson, president of Gilbert, had a desperate task before him. In April of 1966 he was searching frantically among financial circles to raise the money needed to operate another year, after suffering losses of $2.9 million in 1965.

Mr. Isaacson had assumed the presidency in June 1964, after A. C. Gilbert, Jr., died. He was a former vice president of Ideal Toy Company, a larger toy maker, and had been brought into the company to straighten out serious sales and profit problems that had been getting worse since 1961.

After 3 weeks of scouting for financial aid, Anson Isaacson was successful. Pledging most of the remaining unpledged assets of the company, he was able to obtain a loan of $6.250 million, of which he himself put up $250,000 to show creditors his faith in the company and his confidence in his ability to straighten out the problems. There was one frightening stipulation in the loan agreement, however. The loan was contingent on the company's making a profit in 1966. If Gilbert failed to do so, the loan would be called and the assets liquidated to satisfy the indebtedness. Isaacson was not bargaining from a position of strength and had to accept the condition. Although he did feel that, under his management, the condition would not pose a particular problem, still it lurked in the background, ominous and threatening.

PRELUDE

Now let us examine how Gilbert got into this mess. The company did not really recognize a problem until the end of 1961, at which time sales dropped from $12.6 million in 1960 to $11.6 million. In 1961, the company counted a mere $20,011 in profits. The company was obviously facing serious problems, and a program was hastily devised to correct the situation.

In early 1962, with stock prices down, the company became attractive to Jack Wrather, president of a West Coast holding company that owned the "Lassie" and "Lone Ranger" television programs, the Disneyland Hotel, Muzak Corporation (piped-in music), and a boatyard. He acquired a 52 percent interest in the Gilbert Company for some $4 million. He then replaced Gilbert top executives with his own people. Although A. C. Gilbert, Jr., remained as board chairman, his power was substantially lessened.

The 1961 sales drop was attributed to two factors: insufficient new products and insufficient advertising. Plans were formulated to boost sales to $20 million with the addition of new "hot items." The sales staff was increased 50 percent, because more aggressive selling and more frequent contacts with retailers were assumed to be directly correlated with increasing sales. After expanding the sales staff, a new general sales manager and a new director of international sales were appointed.

But this strategy proved of no avail. In 1962, sales dropped to $10.9 million, with a $281,000 loss. This loss was attributed to the cost of preparing the new, greatly expanded 1963 line and the scrapping of obsolete materials. The company was pinning its great expectations on the 1963 selling season. A major effort had been made to expand the line. For the first time, the company was offering toys for preschool children, and for girls in the 6- to 14-year-old bracket in addition to boys, who had been the traditional market segment. More than 50 new items boosted the line to 307 items, by far the largest in the company's history. The ambitious expansion program seemed fully justified and badly needed; now the market was 35 million boys and girls, instead of just 9 million boys.

Modern Packaging magazine hailed the package revitalization program in 1963.[1] Upward of $1 million was spent to repackage the entire line. Packages for Erector sets and other long-established toys had been virtually unchanged for many years; now they were given an "exciting" new full-color pictorial treatment illustrating the models in action.

---

[1] "Saving a $500,000 Investment," *Modern Packaging,* August 1963, pp. 97–98.

The future looked bright at this time, and such an aggressive approach was viewed badly overdue in an old, conservatively managed family business. Officials confidently predicted record sales and earnings.

It must have been a bitter pill when sales results finally came in (in the toy business, the Christmas selling season is crucial for the year's performance; until the results of this business season are tabulated late in the year, no one really knows how successful a year has been). Incredibly, sales continued to slide in 1963, to $10.7 million; worse, instead of a profit, there was a whopping $5.7 million loss, stemming mostly from huge returns of low-priced toys shipped on a guaranteed sale basis to supermarkets. After Christmas, Gilbert had an inventory of almost $3.5 million in unsold toys.

Corrective Efforts

At this point, Jack Wrather decided that a toymaking company needed more expert toymaking experience. He fired most of the top management he had brought in nearly 2 years before. A. C. Gilbert, Jr., reassumed the presidency, but Anson Isaacson, former Ideal Toy Company vice president, was brought in as chief operating officer and chairman of the executive committee.

In 2 years, losses had reached almost $6 million. This was a terrible drain on a firm whose revenues were not much more than $10 million a year. But loans were renegotiated at higher interest rates, and major creditors agreed to a delay in payment over a 3-year period. After the last several years of profligate expansion of sales staff and product lines, Isaacson began a strong economy drive.

He made a major change in the selling mechanism. In place of company salespeople, he fired the sales staff and switched to manufacturers' representatives. Manufacturers' representatives are independent sales representatives who handle a number of noncompeting lines of various manufacturers and charge a fixed commission, usually 5 or 6 percent on all sales made. They are somewhat less expensive than a company sales force and should be able to contact more dealers. Gilbert had less control over them, however, and their customer service for Gilbert could be erratic. In addition, major cuts were made in factory personnel, with the result that administrative and operating expenses were reduced from $10 million to $4.7 million for 1964. In June of 1964, A. C. Gilbert, Jr. died; Mr. Wrather became chairman of the board, and Mr. Isaacson president.

For the 1964 Christmas season, 20 new toys were added to the depleted line. Encouragingly, sales picked up almost 7 percent, to $11.4 million. The company would have registered a profit for the year, but Isaacson insisted on dumping excess inventory to enhance future years' profits, so a loss was registered of $1.9 million.

The expectations of Isaacson and the Gilbert Company now rested on the fall and Christmas selling season of 1965. This was to be the year the company turned around and reached for its new potential. To this end, the product line was again revamped and a heavy advertising and point-of-purchase display program budgeted. Television advertising centered on a 52-week schedule of Saturday morning Beatles cartoon shows, and $2 million was committed for this. In addition, the Gilbert Company furnished some 65,000 animated displays free to dealers at a cost of $1 million.

Early indications for 1965 were favorable. By July 1, Isaacson predicted a net profit for the year. The order backlog was $12 million in July, and losses for the first 6 months of the year (toymakers characteristically incur losses through most of the year until the peak Christmas business is realized) were only half those for the same period in 1964.

Isaacson's optimistic prediction, however, proved wrong. The heavy promotional expenditures did bring sales of $14.9 million, the best since the early 1950s, and a 30 percent increase over the preceding year. However, losses were up to $2.9 million, mostly because of heavy returns on a 007 racing auto set, which was then handled exclusively by Sears, as well as other racing sets. These racing sets turned out to be poorly engineered and constructed, poorly packaged, and overpriced.

As the company's financial condition continued to worsen. Anson Isaacson began his rounds to find the financing necessary to keep the company alive. The multimillion-dollar rescue loan that he finally obtained made virtually all the assets subject to liens to secure such indebtedness and was contingent on the company's making a profit in 1966.

It did not make a profit in 1966. Instead, the announced loss was $12,872.000. The once proud A. C. Gilbert Company went out of business in February 1967. Gabriel Industries acquired certain of Gilbert's assets, including Erector sets and chemistry sets, for about $17 million. This was paid to the financial institutions holding Gilbert's indebtedness.

Figure 13.1 depicts Gilbert's last 6 years.

HOW DID IT HAPPEN?

We can group the mistakes that Gilbert made into two broad categories: *lack of recognition of the problem* until late, and *frantic reactions once the problem was recognized*, resulting in successive mistakes until the end. Each of these will be discussed in more detail, and the specific mistakes under these categories identified.

Gilbert failed to recognize that the toy environment was changing, and that the changes were causing an ever-worsening problem. Diminishing sales from the peak years of the 1950s apparently did not alert the company

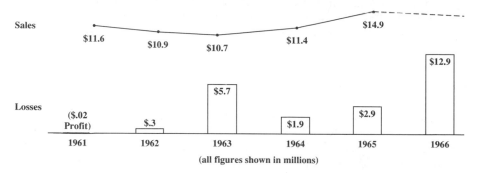

Figure 13.1

that there was a problem needing investigation and some adjustment in business strategy.

We have previously noted how major changes in advertising and distribution of toys were occurring and were only belatedly recognized by Gilbert. One change in toy demand that should have been quickly detected was that tabletop slot-car auto racing sets, almost unknown 10 years before, were now outselling toy trains. Gilbert should have been in this market near the outset. Instead, not until the mid-1960s were its racing sets introduced. And these were poorly engineered, fragile, and overpriced—their returns in 1965 practically scuttled the company.

Apparently, not until the end of the 1961 selling season, when the company barely made a profit, was there any awareness of a possible problem. At this point, frantic and poorly thought-out actions were commenced. With the serious loss of 1962, there was no longer any doubt that there was a problem.

Frantic actions took place with the product line. This had remained relatively unchanged for decades. Suddenly, in 1 year, the line was greatly expanded—more than 50 new toys were added, not only directed to the traditional target market of 6- to 14-year-old boys, but now also for girls and for preschool children. Furthermore, the toys were different from what the company had been used to making—lower priced, lower quality, and geared to large-volume sales. This placed great strain on the company's engineering and production capabilities. The almost inevitable result was poorly designed toys of not very good quality and of disappointing customer appeal. More than this, the company's unique niche as a quality toy maker of high-level educational toys was abandoned, and the company flung itself into the fiercely competitive marketplace against better experienced and mostly larger competitors.

INFORMATION SIDELIGHT

THE PROCESS OF CHANGE IN ORGANIZATIONS

We can identify certain steps that should normally be followed by top management in responding to major forces dictating change:[2]

1. Awareness of a problem
2. Diagnosing the cause of the problem
3. Examining alternative solutions to the problem
4. Making a preliminary choice for a new course of action
5. Testing the preliminary choice on a small scale before making a permanent choice
6. As a result of the test results or pilot run, the proposed solution is either accepted and adopted on a wider scale, or rejected and another alternative is considered.

Effective management is quick to recognize emerging problems, hopefully before they have become serious and are drastically affecting sales and profits. Considerable attention is given to determining the cause(s) of the problems. This may involve collecting more information, perhaps through a research study or various internal analyses. After determining cause, alternative solutions can then be identified, their pros and cons evaluated in view of the resources of the organization, and one selected. If there are doubts concerning the chosen alternative, it may be introduced on a small scale—perhaps in one or two departments or locations—before proceeding further with it or else testing another alternative.

These, then, are the steps for prudently coping with major change. Crises develop when the first step is not recognized early enough, before sales and profits are drastically affected. Therefore, crisis management can usually be avoided. But if a crisis should develop, the other steps represent the most systematic and effective approach to dealing with it.

Subsequent actions did nothing to restore the image of the reputable toymaker. A company and brand image is precious; a good image is not easily developed but can be torn down rather quickly.

Toy buyers were critical of the company's product changes and of its packaging:

Gilbert had a natural in its Erector sets. Instead, they neglected it. They used to offer sets up to $75 packaged in metal boxes. Now the most expensive is only

---

[2] For more discussion of such steps, see Larry Greiner, "Patterns of Organization Change," *Harvard Business Review*, May–June 1967, pp. 119–130; and William F. Glueck, *Management*, 2nd Ed. (Hinsdale, Ill.: Dryden, 1980), pp. 418–442.

$20, the parts are flimsy, and it's in an oversized cardboard box. They did the same thing to their chemistry sets. You can't store anything in those oversize see-through packages.[3]

Gilbert had high hopes for its new All Aboard series, consisting of landscaped panels that fit together to form a tabletop train layout. But:

It's a real good idea, but the quality is poor. The locomotive and cars are cheap and lack detail.[4]

Gilbert's doll series was overpriced, poorly made, and incomplete, because no changes of clothes were offered. This was at the time when additional wardrobes were the major appeal of many dolls, as well as a source of extra profits.

Incredibly poor timing was the lot of the company in attempting to compete with fad items. For example, in 1965, spy items were especially popular, with spy and secret agent movies and television series having high audience ratings. So Gilbert introduced such spy figures as Man from U.N.C.L.E., James Bond, and Honey West. The only trouble was that they did not reach the market until after Christmas Day in 1965, obviously too late for the selling season. Such timing was inexcusable and reflected drastic problems in the planning and operations of the company; the ground had been laid for this situation in 1964.

Successive errors were piled on each other. After the ill-conceived product line expansion of 1963 that resulted in $5.7 million in losses, an austerity campaign was put in effect in 1964, with major cutbacks made in engineering and production—expenses were consequently reduced more than 50 percent for 1964. But such austerity hardly led to the planning and production efficiencies needed for the quick introduction of fad items.

Other aspects of the austerity were less obvious but consequential. The company switched from having its own sales force to contracting for independent manufacturers' representatives to handle its selling efforts.

Although this move was expected to increase dealer coverage while not adding to the cost of selling, dealers did not like the new arrangement: "It used to be that you could call a Gilbert salesman and get service on a problem. Now the reps just want to get the order," disgruntled dealers were saying.[5]

---

[3] Art Detman, Jr., "Toymaker, A.C. Gilbert Co., Poor Loser?" *Sales Management*, May 1, 1966, p. 27.

[4] Ibid., p. 28.

[5] Ibid.

In attempting to widen its distribution to supermarkets, discount stores, and other aggressive promotional retailers, Gilbert made certain concessions that were to cost dearly, such as guaranteeing the sales of its products to some of these demanding outlets. By guaranteeing sales, the company assumed the burden of poor selling efforts, markdowns, and product write-offs of anything unsold after the Christmas season. Guaranteeing sales is usually a last-ditch effort by a new manufacturer trying to gain entry in the marketplace. Offering an unknown brand, such a supplier is totally dependent on retailers and may be forced to accept the conditions demanded by some. Gilbert was not a small unknown firm trying to crack the marketplace. In 1963, it still had a quality image, was widely known, and had good distribution, even though not as wide as desired.

A final dramatic mistake came in 1965. After the austerity of 1964, the spigots were reopened, and with a vengeance. More new toys were added. Of more significance, a massive television advertising campaign and point-of-purchase display program were instituted. Here was a company with sales of just over $11 million facing the specter of insolvency; yet, almost 30 percent of sales was budgeted for a massive promotion effort. The lack of success, resulting from poor judgment of products, distribution, and timing, laid the groundwork for the company's demise. The image of a reliable producer of high-quality toys had been lost. The $6.25 million last-resort financing that Isaacson managed to come up with in 1966 could no longer support the company's efforts to regain a viable niche in the market.

WHAT CAN BE LEARNED?

Learning Insight. *It does not take long to destroy a company.*

Perhaps the most important thing to be learned from Gilbert's experience is that it does not take long for a supposedly healthy and long-experienced company to come to its end. A series of successive bad decisions coming in the space of a few years can destroy all the gains built up by decades of successful operation. And we saw something similar with W. T. Grant: a rash expenditure binge destroyed the decades-old enterprise.

Learning Insight. *Again, firms need to give close attention to their environment and how it is changing.*

Gilbert needed to assess changing conditions better and more quickly. Such assessment should have included changes in consumer demand and buying patterns, as well as competitive actions. The changes occurring were not difficult to detect. They were obvious to all—consumers, retailers, and manufacturers alike. But Gilbert continued to operate as if the status quo could be maintained, as if everything were unchanging. It is worth repeating: It is important to be constantly alert and responsive to change.

Learning Insight. *Problems need to be recognized quickly before they reach the crisis stage.*

In a dynamic environment, problems will inevitably arise. Some portend to be serious; other are minor or transitory. The seriousness and duration of other problems may be difficult to predict; here, the prudent executive needs to at least consider the worst scenario. A declining market share or competitive position should be a red flag waving that something is amiss that needs to be seriously addressed. What is the cause of the worsening situation? Is it something we need to aggressively act upon? In a time of steadily increasing demand for toys, to have sales remain static or decline, strongly suggests something is wrong, even though profitability may still not be an obvious problem. Gilbert blundered seriously in not recognizing the changing toy market and its failings long before the drastic decline in sales and profits for 1961.

Learning Insight. *Crisis management should guard against reacting too quickly, without careful analysis of alternatives and their implications.*

A firm must beware of reacting too quickly, without careful analysis of alternatives. This is the height of misguided crisis management. Problems need to be carefully identified, and probable solutions or adjustments to them weighed in view of the particular strengths and resources of the firm. In Gilbert's case, hasty actions only compounded past mistakes. The whipsawing was particularly deadly to the company—drastically cutting costs to the bone one year, then in a wild spree, budgeting $3 million for advertising and promotional displays at a time when the firm was on the verge of bankruptcy, and this amount constituting almost 30 percent of sales.

Learning Insight. *At all costs, a firm must zealously guard a good-quality image.*

The major strength of the firm was its quality image. In no way should this have been sacrificed to bring out a proliferation of "cheap" new products similar to competitors. By expanding hastily with such products, the company's production and quality-control capabilities were disregarded. The flood of poorly made products in one selling season destroyed the quality image that had been built up and maintained for over 50 years. A quality image is difficult to attain, but as we see here, it can be destroyed in only a few months. Maintaining Gilbert's quality image should have been given the highest priority; all decisions should have been made with this in mind.

UPDATE

Although the Gilbert Company has folded, never to return to life, we can happily note that the Erector set has survived. As described earlier, Gabriel Industries, a large toy manufacturer that also makes Tinker Toys, acquired the Erector asset at the liquidation of Gilbert. In 1977, nearly 600,000 Erector sets, ranging in price from $1 for a 45-piece pocket set to $40 for a deluxe 450-piece set, were sold around the world.

In August of 1978, Gabriel and its Erector set subsidiary were purchased by CBS for $27.1 million. The senior vice president of Gabriel predicted: "A hundred years from now, I think you'll still be able to buy an Erector set . . . long after everyone here is gone."[6]

FOR THOUGHT AND DISCUSSION

1. What controls should Gilbert have had to remain alert to changing market conditions? What research would have helped?
2. Do you think Gilbert was right in expanding its target market in 1963? Why or why not?
3. Evaluate the advertising efforts of 1965 and the point-of-purchase display expenditures.
4. Discuss the pros and cons of changing management quickly when adversity sets in.

INVITATION TO ROLE PLAY

1. As an assistant to the president, what would you have advised Gilbert to do at the end of 1962 when the first drastic decline in profit occurred?
2. As a management consultant, what would you have advised at the end of 1963?

---

[6] "The Nuts and Bolts of Erector Set Firm," *Cleveland Plain Dealer*, September 10, 1978, Sec. 2-1.

14

Contrast—the Classic Confrontation: Harley Davidson Versus Honda

In the early 1960s, a staid and unexciting market was shaken up, was rocked to its core, by the most unlikely invader. This intruder was a smallish Japanese firm that had risen out of the ashes of World War II, and was now trying to encroach on the territory of a major U.S. firm that had in the space of 60 years destroyed all of its U.S. competitors, and now had a firm 70 percent of the motorcycle market.

Yet, almost inconceivably, in half a decade this market share was to fall to 5 percent, and the total market was to expand many times over what it had been for decades. A foreign invader had furnished a textbook example of the awesome effectiveness of carefully crafted marketing efforts. In the process, this confrontation between Honda and Harley Davidson was a harbinger of the Japanese invasion of the auto industry.

HARLEY DAVIDSON: THE OPPORTUNITY UNNOTICED

Historical Background

Harley Davidson motorcycles date back to 1903 when the Harley and Davidson families, in a 10-by-15 foot wooden shed in the Davidson backyard, built motorcycles in evenings and weekends. Members of both families participated in the endeavor, aided by a few other people, notably Ole Evinrude, who became a well-known manufacturer of outboard motors. The first year they sold four motorcycles, the next year eight. Production continued to increase, aided by a demand that was greater than could be filled, as motorcycles began replacing horses. By 1915, Harley Davidson was producing 18,000 machines a year, and another brand, Indian, joined it in dominating the U.S. two-wheel machine industry. With America's entry into World War I, practically all of Harley Davidson's production went to the military.

However, the boom collapsed with peacetime. The horseless carriage, particularly Ford's Model T, was tough competition. A motorcycle with a sidecar could never provide the comfort and convenience of the Model T. And Ford priced his cars so low that they cost little more than Harley Davidson motorcycles, and sometimes even less. The situation did not improve during the depression years of the 1930s. Rather than making motorcycles inexpensive to appeal to consumers' reduced incomes during the 1930s, Harley Davidson and its major competitors, Indian and Henderson, made motorcycles more luxurious and more powerful—and, of course, more expensive. A deluxe model with a sidecar in 1930 sold for as much as $2000—all the Spartan comfort of two wheels at more than the price of most automobiles.

World War II again buttressed the motorcycle industry, with Harley Davidson selling 90,000 machines alone. But motorcycles played only a minor role in this war, where the emphasis was on other types of motorized equipment. The peacetime booming economy still found the motorcycle industry on the sidelines. Sales increased much less in proportion than did the sales of automobiles. And now motorcycles were being purchased by some of the wrong people—drifters, gangs of hoodlums, and other undesirables.

In 1953 the Indian Motorcycle Company folded. This was the largest motorcycle manufacturer to fail; others, such as Henderson, Yale, Merkel, Minnesota, Pope, and Thor, preceded Indian. Now only Harley Davidson was left to make motorcycles in the United States, where once there had been 114 makers of motorcycles.

The Public's Perception of the Motorcyclist. Over the decades, the motorcycle became synonymous with black-leather jackets and deviant and even violent behavior. This perception dates back to the late 1920s and the 1930s, years of hard times and high unemployment, when a gypsy lifestyle was embraced by some as they roamed over the country untethered by job or responsibilities, often dirty, sometimes drunken, always noisy as their machines roared through city streets. Regardless of the number of motorcyclists who actually fit that description, and regardless of the general invalidity of it, the idea stuck.

The years after World War II reinforced the idea. In 1947 in Hollister, California, a town of 4800 people, a gang on big, black Harley Davidsons rolled into town, converging on the open taverns, and by evening had torn up the town. The outnumbered police, gathering volunteer deputies and aided by vigilante bands of outraged citizens, met them in a pitched battle that left 50 people injured. The episode led to a widely screened movie, *The Wild One*, starring Marlon Brando, in which a gang of hoodlum motorcyclists roam the country, contemptuous of law and order, and take over a small town. As the *New York Times* reported:

> A little bit of the surface of contemporary American life is scratched in Stanley Kramer's "The Wild One" . . . and underneath is opened an ugly, debauched and frightening view of a small, but particularly significant and menacing element of modern youth.[1]

In subsequent years, the antics of motorcycle gangs, particularly Hell's Angels, increased the public's negative image of motorcyclists. In 1966 a Florida police official was quoted:

> These punks with their cycles and their Nazi trappings have it in for the world— and for everyone in it. They're a menace, a damned serious menace, that's growing bigger every year.[2]

The Invasion. Sales in the United States were around 50,000 per year during the 1950s, with Harley Davidson, Britain's Norton and Triumph, and Germany's BMW accounting for most of the market. By the turn of the decade, the Japanese firm Honda began to penetrate the U.S. market. In 1960 less than 400,000 motorcycles were registered in the United States. While this was an increase of almost 200,000 from the end of World War II 15 years before, it was far below the increase in other motor vehicles. But by 1964, only four years later, the number had risen to 960,000; two years later it was 1.4 million; and by 1971 it was almost 4 million.

As we examine in depth in the next section, Honda instituted a distinctly different strategy to expand the demand for motorcycles. The major elements of this strategy were lightweight cycles and an advertising approach directed toward a new customer. Few firms have ever experienced such a shattering of market share as did Harley Davidson in the 1960s. (Although its market share declined drastically, its total sales remained nearly constant, indicating that it was getting none of the new customers for motorcycles.)

Reaction of Harley Davidson to the Honda Threat

Faced with an invasion of its staid and static U.S. market, how did Harley Davidson react to the intruder? They did not react! At least not until far too

---

[1] Bosley Crowther, *New York Times*, December 31, 1953, p. 9:2.
[2] Lee Gutkind, *Bike Fever* (Chicago: Follet Publishing, 1973), pp. 38–39.

late. Harley Davidson considered themselves the leader in full-size motorcycles. While the company might shudder at the image tied in with their product's usage by the leather jacket types, it took solace in the fact that almost every U.S. police department used its machines. Perhaps this is what led Harley Davidson to stand aside and complacently watch Honda make deep inroads into the American motorcycle market. The management saw no threat in Honda's thrust into the market with lightweight motorcycles. Their attitude was exemplified in this statement by William H. Davidson, the president of the company and son of the founder.

> Basically, we don't believe in the lightweight market. We believe that motorcycles are sport vehicles, not transportation vehicles. Even if a man says he bought a motorcycle for transportation, it's generally for leisure-time use. The lightweight motorcycle is only supplemental. Back around World War I, a number of companies came out with lightweight bikes. We came out with one ourselves. They never got anywhere. We've seen what happens to these small sizes.[3]

Eventually Harley recognized that the Honda phenomenon was not an aberration, and that there was a new factor in the market. The company attempted to retaliate by offering an Italian-made lightweight in the mid-1960s. But it was far too late; Honda was firmly entrenched. The Italian bikes were regarded in the industry to be of lower quality than the Japanese. Honda, and toward the end of the 1960s other Japanese manufacturers, continued to dominate what had become a much larger market than ever dreamed.

What Went Wrong for Harley Davidson?

Harley Davidson's error was one of omission. It took no action, made no commitment—an approach that was to turn out rash and costly. Its problems did not come from misguided expansion. Its problems came from a null decision, the lack of aggressiveness, an unwillingness to change anything. We can identify Harley's problems under what we might term the "three C's" syndrome of failure.

The "Three C's" Syndrome of Failure. Firms that have been well entrenched in their industry and that have dominated it for years often fall into a particular syndrome that leaves them vulnerable to aggressive and innovative competitors.

---

[3] Tom Rowan, "Harley Sets New Drive to Boost Market Share," *Advertising Age*, January 29, 1973, pp. 34–35.

The "three C's" that are detrimental to a front-runner's continued success are:

Complacency

Conservatism

Conceit

We can define *complacency* as smugness; a self-satisfied firm, content with the status quo, is no longer hungry and eager for growth. This term describes Harley in the 1950s and into the 1960s, even while Honda was intensifying its American invasion. The last major U.S. competitor, Indian, had closed its doors in 1953. There was no competitor within sight who might contest Harley's share of the market for large motorcycles; Harley was the lone survivor, and it had a comfortable captive market, the police. Even the bad image continuing to plague the civilian motorcycle user could not dent the complacency of Harley.

Conservatism characterizes a management that is wedded to the past, to the traditional, the way things have always been done. There is no need to change because nothing is different today. And to a complacent management the environment seemed static, with little growth potential. There was no need for any strategy changes from the satisfactory ways of the past: big machines, expensive options—profitable—all aimed at the hard-core motor-cyclist. The possibility that the market might be far greater than the hard-core user of big, expensive machines was never even considered.

Finally, *conceit* can further reinforce the myopia of the managerial perspective: conceit for present and potential competitors. A belief that "we are the best," and "no one else can touch us" can easily permeate an organization when everything has been going quietly for years. It must have given Harley management great satisfaction to think of themselves as the best of the 100-plus former manufacturers of motorcycles. A feeling of self-confidence and a disdain for potential competitors is easy to come by, especially back in the 1950s and early 1960s when the potential competitor was a small Japanese upstart.

With the three C's syndrome of failure, there is no incentive to undertake aggressive and innovative actions. There is disinterest in some important facets of the business, particularly in quality control, customer relations, and servicing. Furthermore, there is no incentive to develop new products, and there is an aversion to sharp promotional activities. With such a syndrome, a firm sets itself up for a fall to an aggressive and hungry competitor, no matter how small and unknown the competitor might be at first.

Harley, in defense of its conviction that there was no market for light-weight cycles, was quick to cite how it had attempted to introduce them twice, and failed badly both times. It tried once in 1925, and again in 1949.

"Therefore, how could the market want these now?"

In retrospect, a major reason for the failures was that it had priced the lightweights only a little below the heavier motorcycles, and most people consequently saw the heavier machines as the better values. But, more than this, Harley should have recognized that no market is static and unchanging. America's tastes were changing by the late 1950s. A greater interest was being shown in smaller cars and in economy of operation. The Edsel also failed in the late 1950s as consumers spurned its high horsepower and size and turned to the smaller and more economical imported cars. The way was paved for an aggressive and ingenious David to confront Goliath and leave him sprawled in the dust.

THE HONDA MOTORCYCLE INVASION

Soichiro Honda was the son of a blacksmith. When he was three years old, his father gave him a pair of pliers. It remained his favorite possession. He only went to the tenth grade in school, but he had great mechanical ability and received his first patent when he was 14. He became an auto mechanic and by the time he was 21 had opened a garage where he became known as the man who could fix anything. By the time he was 27, his garage had grown to the point where he had 50 employees.

Honda was not only a fixer, he was also a creator. He bolted an old Curtis airplane engine into an auto chassis and had a racing car that nobody could beat. He designed his own piston rings and by World War II had developed the finest piston rings in Japan. His entire output was taken for military vehicles. Near the end of the war, a bomb demolished his factory. He was then 41, with almost all his money gone.

Honda began looking for other ventures. He purchased 500 small war-surplus gasoline engines that had been used to power communications equipment. He mounted these on standard bicycles. While crude and difficult to start, they sold rapidly in a country with little transportation. After the engines were gone, Honda designed and built his own engine, and later also began producing frames and wheels. By 1949, his plant was manufacturing all the basic components and was assembling Honda motorcycles. These early cycles could go 45 miles per hour, getting up to 200 miles per gallon of gas. In 1950 Honda produced 3600 motorcycles. In only two years he employed 1000 men in a plant 100 times larger than he had before. In 1959, Soichiro Honda decided to invade the American motorcycle market.

The Japanese Invasion

Honda's introduction of the lightweight motorbike in the United States did not have a very auspicious beginning: only 167 units were sold during the first year. Motorcycle experts laughed at the puny Japanese machines. But such derision and skepticism were to change quickly. In 1960, sales were 22,100 units, increasing in only five years more than tenfold to 270,000 units in 1965. By 1965, Honda had 80 percent of the expanding U.S. market, and Harley Davidson was still selling about 35,000 units per year.

While Honda enjoyed steady growth after 1965, it was not as dramatic as during the real growth years from 1963 to 1965. Sales increased to 650,000 units by 1974, but market share steadily declined from 80 percent in 1965 to 45.6 percent in 1977. However, this was still the major share of the U.S. market, which Honda now was contesting with other Japanese firms. Market shares for the leading motorcycle makers in 1977 were as follows:

Honda	45.6%
Yamaha	18.9
Suzuki	10.7
Kawasaki	14.4
Harley Davidson	5.7

In few annals of business history had an invader come into an entrenched market and so quickly gained mastery. How could this have happened?

The Invasion Strategy. Soichiro Honda's philosophy has been widely stated:

> If you turn out a superior product, it will be patronized by the public. Our policy is not simply to turn out a product because there is demand, but to turn out a superior product and create a demand.[4]

To move beyond Japan and open up the export market, Honda thought that his machines would need an international reputation, and that this could best be gained on the international racing circuit. In June 1954 he went to the Isle of Man to enter his machines in the oldest of the international racing classics. He was shocked to learn that the European competition was fielding models with three times the horsepower of the Hondas. By 1961, however, Honda won world championships in the 125-cc (cubic centimeter) and 150-cc engine classes.

But it took more than racing trophies to open the U.S. market. At best only a limited number of bikes would have been sold to motorcycle buffs. So Honda moved his attack on the United States and international markets to a different level, a level never before achieved in the industry, and advertising was given the key role in this.

---

[4] *Journal of Commerce*, November 6, 1965, p. 23.

Promotional Strategy. The Grey Advertising Agency was commissioned to handle the U.S. promotion. The task assigned was to win social acceptance for the motorcycle and its rider. The basic thrust of the communications strategy was to create a fresh image for the Honda motorcycle and to educate the general public to a new mode of transportation.

Honda wanted to promote the idea that riding a motorcycle is fun. A basic theme of advertising in the early 1960s was "Holidays and Honda days," and "Go happy, go Honda." To promote this theme, Honda had to buck the negative perceptions of motorcyclists as the black-leather-jacketed characters widely publicized in a continuing negative press. Most Americans had never ridden on or driven a motorcycle, and the negative image of motorcyclists stood in the way of Honda, who wanted to attract a large new market.

Social acceptance was finally achieved by heavy promotion of the theme, "You meet the nicest people on a Honda." Early advertisements showed nine totally different kinds of people—old, young, casual, formal, but they all had in common the fact that they were nice, acceptable people, and they were all riding a Honda. One ad read:

> You meet the nicest people on a Honda. It's largely a question of personality. A Honda is easygoing, dependable. Makes few demands. Prices start at around $215. And it runs all day on a nickel's worth of gas. That's the kind of friend to have. Frugal. How about one in your family? World's biggest seller.

Despite the quiet tone of this ad, it puts over the Honda story through words like "nice," "easygoing," "friend," "family," and "frugal."

Ads with this theme were placed in magazines, network TV, spot radio, newspapers, outdoor farm publications, and direct mail. The media chosen were designed to reach nontraditional bike owners, people who might never have thought of owning any vehicle with less than four wheels. Ads were placed in magazines such as *Life*, *Look*, *Saturday Evening Post*, and *Sports Illustrated*.

People already sold on motorcycles were not overlooked either, as many ads were also placed in magazines for cycle enthusiasts. Commercials were run on the top 40 radio stations favored by young people. Newspapers were used in key markets as well as large space advertising in more than 225 college newspapers where the message was stressed that Honda had the answer to campus parking problems. Even billboards were used in a unified program to give Honda maximum public exposure.

The major target of the promotional efforts was the young. Honda and Grey Agency believed that with the increasing number of World War II babies growing up, products that would assert their individuality could become popular. The new lightweight bikes of Honda were introduced as such a product (the Mustang was also introduced about this time, riding the youth crest). While it was expected that many parents would oppose the purchase of a motorcycle, it was thought that their resistance could be overcome by the advertising.

The buyers were primarily young males between 16 and 26: college students, young professionals, and others getting started in their white-collar careers. Studies showed that teenagers were becoming the largest group of owners, with 32 percent of the first-time purchasers under 20.

While there were other factors in the strategy that contributed to the success of Honda, the importance of the advertising campaign can hardly be overemphasized. Honda succeeded in selling the idea that it was smart and sophisticated to ride a motorcycle through their "nice people" advertising. American and European makers alike credited this advertising campaign with sparking the enormous growth of the entire industry. Indeed, in the annals of advertising there are few such examples of the effectiveness of the mass media in radically changing mores and social acceptability in such a short period of time.

The Product Strategy. Honda invaded the U.S. market with small (50 cc), light-weight bikes that could go miles on a thimbleful of gasoline, and that could be purchased for less than $300 when most of the other motorcycles cost $1500 and more. Furthermore, a customer had six snappy colors to choose from in three different models, at a time when most other motorcycle makers offered no more than two or three models and color choices. The little Hondas could go 55 miles per hour for 180 miles on 30 cents worth of regular gas. And the product quality was impressive. A top executive of a British motorcycle firm examined a Honda machine in 1961 and made a widely quoted statement: "When we stripped the machine, frankly, it was so good it frightened us. It was made like a watch, and it wasn't a copy of anything."[5]

As Honda began to dominate the U.S. market, it expanded the product line, aiming to have a model for every potential rider. By 1965, 14 different motorcycles were available, ranging from a light 50 cc to a fast 305 cc. In 1966 a larger 450-cc bike was added to compete with the Harley Davidson models, but the bulk of the Honda sales in 1965 was in the 150-cc and smaller models.

But the potential for trade-up sales spurred Honda to offer larger models, and a few years later there were models available up to 1100 cc, fully as large as any Harley Davidson. As people traded up to get bikes with more horsepower, they looked to Honda for the larger motorcycles, not Harley Davidson. One study found that 40 percent of those with light machines were buying heavier ones.

[5] Gutkind, *Bike Fever*, p. 160.

Production Advantage. Honda had certain inherent advantages in its effective strategy to invade the U.S. market. Japanese labor was much less expensive than American, contributing to competitively lower production costs. In addition, the size of the Japanese home market afforded a substantial advantage over any American producer. The demand for motorcycles in Japan was in the neighborhood of two million machines a year. This large sales base made it possible to keep production high and unit costs low. Consequently, motorcycles could be exported at prices unmatchable by foreign producers.

Handling Service Problems. A servicing problem emerged as sales began to mushroom. Growth was so rapid that not enough trained mechanics were available. Parts warehouses encountered severe shortages. The problem for a time became so bad that the growth of Honda was jeopardized, and there was the potential for a long-term image problem and loss of customer loyalty. To Honda's credit, once the problem was recognized, immediate corrective actions were taken. More mechanics were quickly trained, more parts warehouses were opened, existing warehouses were enlarged, and dealer inventories were maintained at more adequate levels. There was no serious long-term harm to Honda.

Distribution Strategy. Honda continued its innovative approach to the U.S. market in its distribution strategy and choice of dealers. Previously, most motorcycle dealers were located on the outskirts of cities, often in seedy neighborhoods where the leather-jacketed crowd felt more comfortable. Dealerships tended to be dirty and noisy places and rather undesirable neighbors. Honda spurned this approach and often located its dealers in the center of town. New York City for some time had a dealer on Madison Avenue, only three blocks from Grand Central Station and its concentration of commuter traffic. By 1965 more than 1500 Honda dealers were located in every state, making the product readily available. Most of these locations were where the traditional motorcyclist would hardly feel at ease. This was 19 percent of a national total of 8000 dealers, and it compared with Harley Davidson's 880 dealers, or 11 percent.

In addition to selling and servicing Hondas, another plum was offered dealers as Honda sought to tap a different customer—the person who preferred to rent—at least at first—rather than buying. By 1965 rentals amounted to some $40 million. In addition to providing extra income, many of those who rented eventually bought. Rentals provided a good way to try out a new form of transportation and to determine how easy it was to handle, and how economical and convenient these vehicles really were. The general public would never rent the large, expensive Harley Davidsons, but many were keen to rent the light and easy-to-handle Hondas.

Reactions to Looming Problems. In 1966 total sales of motorcycles slumped. Although Honda sales increased, they were less than projected, and Honda was concerned. The cause was not difficult to pinpoint. Activity in the Vietnam War was increasing and more 18–25-year-olds were being drafted. This was the group that comprised 50 percent of the Honda market. Adding to the problem, banks were becoming more reluctant to finance purchases for draft-age buyers.

Such problems, of course, were external factors in the environment, presumably conditions that Honda or any other motorcycle maker could do little about. But Honda did. Amid a slumping market, Honda actually increased advertising expenditures from $6 million to $7 million. They mapped out a campaign aimed primarily at the undraftables. One such target was women.

And such a natural this was. The inexpensive, light, easy-to-manage motorbike was attractive for women. They could buy or rent at convenient and comfortable dealerships, where service was no problem. The image had changed so that housewives, students, young professionals all could feel compatible. And more and more women were induced to turn to this new mode of transportation.

Ingredients of Success

The successful incursion of an unknown foreign invader into a long-established traditional market appeared easy. It took only a few years to accomplish. This experience should be sobering for many firms—competitive entry can be easy for the innovative outsider with a wider perspective who is willing to accept some risks.

Practically everything that Honda did during the 1960s has escaped criticism. All the elements of the strategy seemed to mesh beautifully. There were a few servicing problems during a period of the most rapid growth, but these were quickly identified and corrected. We might question the dogged perseverance of Honda in gearing itself to winning international racing competitions, and doing so successfully. How relevant were such trophies to the consumer Honda was hoping to woo?

Let us examine what appear to be the key ingredients to the Honda success.

Willingness to Beard the Lion. For any upstart firm to try to beard an entrenched competitor is perilous indeed. When the newcomer is an unknown foreign firm attempting to gain entry to the home ground of its formidable foe, and when the foe has been well entrenched for decades, and when the entrenched firm has driven out all the other domestic competitors over the years, the chances of any kind of success appear quite small. In this situation a willingness to beard the lion is a key ingredient of success.

While the attack could have failed, there was sufficient confidence in the planned strategy that the risks were considered worthwhile. This was no reckless and foolish charge; it was carefully crafted, and while the premises that guided it—namely that the market for motorcycles could be greatly expanded to nontraditional users—were unproven as yet, they were reasonable and worth testing.

Identifying the Potential for Expanding the Market. How did Soichiro Honda arrive at his vision of a widely expanded potential market? While we cannot know for sure, we can make some reasonable assumptions. He did not use an extensive marketing research study. Though such might have confirmed what was already known about the characteristics of the present market, it probably would not have uncovered the widened perspective. It might even have discouraged any such efforts to expand the market because of the negative impressions that motorcycles had with the general public and the sheer audaciousness of the idea that the average person could enjoy two-wheel transportation.

Most likely, Soichiro Honda recognized that the light motorcycles he had been manufacturing should be adaptable to commuter traveling in the United States, just as they were being used in Japan. While America was a far different country, with less traffic and more affluence, should not economy and ease of transportation and parking also be desirable there? The product was available, and it was far different from existing competitive products.

Such reasoning seems to violate a solid marketing principle that customer needs and wants should be firmly ascertained, and then products developed to best serve these needs and wants. But sometimes there are exceptions to cherished principles.

Effective Use of Advertising. The negative image of the black-leather-jacketed cyclists was erased and a positive image of upwardly mobile youth and common folk substituted. Mass-media advertising was the main force in changing the image, and in doing so highlights one of the best examples we can ever find of the effectiveness of advertising. While the budget used to achieve such results was unheard of for the industry, the $6 or $7 million spent per year was certainly modest by today's perspectives—when a single-minute commercial during a Super Bowl game cost more than $1 million for the air time, not counting the production costs.

Complementing and reinforcing the effective advertising campaign was the coordination of all facets of the strategy and operations. The product was light, pretty, comfortable, nonthreatening to ride, and inexpensive; dealers were recruited who were far removed from the dirty and noisy establishments on the outskirts of towns; product quality was emphasized; and servicing was convenient and more hassle-free than generally encountered with automobiles.

Honda was even careful to shy away from words that had a negative connotation. For example, headgear were not called "crash helmets," which conveyed something negative and rather fearful, but were called "safetywear." And the word "motorcycle" was never used in an advertisement because it was still thought to have a negative image; instead, the Hondas were described as "two-wheeled motoring sport."

Honda was the precursor or trailblazer for the Japanese cars that were soon to flood the U.S. market, capitalizing on a growing public image of quality and economy.

HARLEY DAVIDSON VERSUS HONDA: WHAT CAN BE LEARNED?

In the space of a few years a long-standing U.S. industry came to be dominated by the Japanese. This phenomenon was to occur in other industries as well in later years. The skill of the Honda takeover should have warned other smug American industries; but, alas, most of them, if they paid any attention to this struggle, would have considered the results a fluke. After all, in the 1950s people associated most Japanese goods, as well as products made in other Far Eastern countries, to be poorly made with cheap labor and far below the level of American or European-made goods. Honda blazed the trail that changed that misperception.

Learning Insight. *The "three C's" syndrome—complacency, conservatism, and conceit—make a firm particularly vulnerable to competitors.*

It is possible for the most unlikely firm to rise and become an aggressive and major factor in an industry. The inclination of the dominant firm in an industry, however, is to underestimate, belittle, or disdain the competition, and not even deign to react or respond to the initial puny efforts of the competitor.

The "three C's" attitudes, which originate from top management, can permeate an entire organization—from production workers to sales staff to those who service customers. The consequences are a reduced commitment to consistency of quality, an aloofness to customer needs and concerns, and a lack of innovativeness in seeking new markets and improved products. There is decreased emphasis on pricing for good value and more on maximizing per-unit profits. And the foundation is laid for vulnerability to the aggressive competitor "foolish enough" to invade a seemingly static market and its entrenched firm.

What can an organization do to guard against this dangerous syndrome? In general, these are the best tools:

1. **Bring fresh blood into the organization.** This step is applicable to all levels of staff and managerial personnel. New people bring with them diverse experiences that result in new ideas and different perspectives from those who have long been with the organization. However, these new people must be listened to if their presence is to have any impact on the three C's syndrome.

2. **Monitor the environment and be alert to any changes.** Such monitoring can be formal (perhaps through the systematic use of marketing research) or informal. Every executive can do his or her own monitoring. Generally, monitoring takes three directions:

   a. Keep abreast of the latest statistics and other information in industry and general business publications.

   b. Obtain feedback from customers, dealers, and sales staff about environmental changes and any unmet needs and possible opportunities and dangers.

   c. Be receptive to new ideas from wherever they may come.

In general, the executive needs to cast a wide net, to pull in information and ideas from as many diverse sources as possible. Customer feedback is an important source of such monitoring, but it will not often provide the forward-looking insights that may be critical. For example, a survey of Harley Davidson customers, their dealers, and their shops probably would not have yielded much value since most of these customers would not have realized the attractiveness of lightweight motorbikes. Perhaps a better monitoring of dealers, however, might have led Harley Davidson more quickly to recognize the seriousness of the Honda threat.

Receptivity to new ideas is the most important ingredient if desirable changes are to be made. Where an organization has grown accustomed to a certain way of doing business, any changes can be traumatic and unwelcome.

3. **Always keep a strong commitment to customer service and satisfaction.** The successful and dominant firm must especially beware of slipping here. A systematic survey of customers to measure their satisfaction can be a useful tool. The boxed information describes how customer feedback can be obtained.

4. **Maintain continuing corporate self-analysis.** It is difficult to sell healthy firms on the need for such an analysis; with sick firms the

nced is more obvious. Such self-analysis should be particularly directed to the marketing efforts of the firm and should be comprehensive. In particular, answers should be sought for these questions:

What are we doing right?

What could we do better?

Self-analysis needs to be objective. Care must be taken to minimize defensiveness and obstructionism from involved executives. While no one relishes having his or her performance evaluated and scrutinized more closely than before, it is in the best interest of the firm, and of all involved, to detect promptly any deficiencies or any unmet opportunities. A *marketing audit* is the term most often used for such self-analysis.

Learning Insight. *Any industry or market may have untapped potential—but only an innovative approach can harvest it.*

The notion of untapped potential may appear unlikely in supposedly mature industries where sales have been on a plateau for years. Such an industry not only appears to offer no growth potential, but it also appears unlikely to attract new competition. How could any industry offer less growth and be less likely to attract competition than the old motorcycle industry?

Not only stagnant industries may find untapped potential—it can lie anywhere. A growing industry may find new customers other than those presently cultivated, and thereby improve its growth rate. Of course, not all companies and industries can discover untapped potential. Perhaps it is out there, but no one recognizes it or is able to develop it. Sometimes unsuspected opportunities can be found in even stranger places than motorcycles.

Church and Dwight was a small, family-owned firm that made Arm & Hammer baking soda. It had the dubious distinction of being a 125-year-old one-product company. Though its baking soda had almost 100 percent market dominance, sales were declining. In 1970, the company conceived the idea of using Arm and Hammer to eliminate foul odors, and it really did absorb them. Church and Dwight began a TV campaign touting the benefits of using Arm & Hammer inside refrigerators. The results of this innovation? In four years, sales doubled and profits tripled.

There is also the classic example of Listerine. An old product, it was originally sold as a mild external antiseptic. Sales were static until in the 1920s, someone came up with the idea of promoting Listerine as a mouthwash.

INFORMATION SIDELIGHT

USE OF CUSTOMER SURVEYS FOR MEASURING SATISFACTION

For a retail firm, attitude surveys can be made by interviewing customers leaving the store or department, perhaps those without a package, under the assumption that such people did not find what they wanted or were in some other way not satisfied. Brief questionnaires inviting customer opinions may be inserted in packages or in monthly statements. The samples need not be large. They should, however, be systematic and continuous; otherwise, trends in attitudes go unnoticed and danger areas may not be spotted until serious erosion of old customers occurs.

More ingenuity may be required by manufacturers to obtain feedback on customer attitudes, but this is not usually difficult. Customers can always be invited to express their opinions and their satisfaction or dissatisfaction. The more serious complaints or the strongest customer feelings will be brought to light.

Direct measures of customer satisfaction have these particular advantages:

1. Trends can be established for customer attitudes, and problems can be detected before they become serious.
2. Goodwill can be gained by continuing efforts of this kind (the company will gain the reputation of "the firm that cares").
3. Time and expense need not be great.
4. Unfulfilled customer needs and wants may be revealed, and these may suggest opportunities to be tapped.

Customer panels can be useful in obtaining clues for various facets of customer satisfaction. Where the panel is used systematically, the firm may detect changes in its customer-satisfaction effectiveness before they become serious. However, these panels of customers suffer from the flaw of not always being representative of customers in general.

A firm can better maintain and improve competitive position if it closely monitors customer satisfaction. Direct measures, as in the surveys described, are far superior to any indirect estimates, such as from profits, sales, and market share. The latter lack sensitivity because many other determinants, such as environmental elements, quality of competition, and economic factors affect sales, profits, and market share.

As these examples illustrate, new potential may lie in two areas:

1. Finding new customers
2. Finding new uses

Honda essentially used the first approach. It modified the conventional motorcycle to make it attractive to entirely different customers. Arm & Hammer and Listerine found success with the second approach: they promoted new ways for old customers to make greater use of the products.

Learning Insight. *Mass-media advertising can be a powerful tool. It can even change an image for the better.*

We saw in the Gilbert case how easy it is to tear down a good public image. But it is usually extremely difficult to build up an image. But Honda proved that an image can be improved with the right advertising and a coordinated strategy execution.

Usually the effectiveness of mass-media advertising is difficult to measure. We can determine the attention-value of certain ads in relation to other ads, but their real impact on sales is more difficult, often impossible, to measure since so many factors affect sales other than advertising. Competitive efforts and prices, dealer displays and in-stock conditions, customer attitudes, the economy, and even the weather play major roles. Furthermore, there are thousands of commercial messages competing for the average person's attention. Many of these are screened out and do not even consciously register. Consequently, greater and greater expenditures are necessary for advertising to have any impact. In the United States advertising expenditures are well over $100 billion a year. One firm, Procter & Gamble Company, alone spends almost $1 billion a year. In the 1990 Super Bowl game, a 30-second time slot cost $700,000. Are these firms getting their money's worth?

Yet Honda, with only modest expenditures for advertising, achieved extraordinary impact and effectiveness. The keys, of course, were the uniqueness of the messages, their tapping of latent consumer needs, and their adroit presentation of clean-cut images of the persons who ride Hondas. This is a great example of the effective role advertising *can* play—but practically never does. The coordination of the other elements of the strategy with the advertising reinforced the effective image change.

FOR THOUGHT AND DISCUSSION

1. We have suggested that complacency, conceit, and conservatism led to Harley's vulnerability. How could such an organizational flaw have been prevented?
2. Could Honda have successfully entered the market with big motorcycles in 1960?
3. How could Harley have anticipated the competitive incursion of Honda, or some similar firm?

INVITATION TO ROLE PLAY

It is 1962. As one of the senior executives of Harley Davidson, you have been given the assignment of developing plans to counter the competitive thrust of Honda. What marketing strategy would you recommend, and why?

15

Contrast—International Management Group: Managing Athletes

In a previous case, we saw how Hyatt Legal Clinics showed its winning ways in promoting a *service*, rather than a tangible product. Here we have another success in the nonproduct sector. Mark McCormack and his International Management Group was an innovator in managing the affairs and the promotability of athletes and celebrities. The independence and eccentricities of such individuals create unique management problems, but the rewards have proven to be great indeed. Let us examine the notable success story in the managing and promoting of athletes and encounter some of the most famous athletic personalities of the last several decades. As with most of our success stories, the credit must go to one individual—the shape maker, innovator, and risk taker.

MARK McCORMACK AND THE FOUNDING OF INTERNATIONAL MANAGEMENT GROUP (IMG)

When he was a young boy, Mark wanted to become a baseball player. However, he was hit by an automobile and suffered a skull facture when he was six, and this prevented him from ever playing contact sports. Mark's father, a successful farm journal publisher, encouraged the boy to take up golf, and he immediately was taken with the game.

Among the golf partners of his youth was an elderly man who had a summer home near the McCormack family in the Dunes area of Michigan.

INFORMATION SIDELIGHT

UNIQUE CHARACTERISTICS OF SERVICE BUSINESSES

Table 15.1 shows the growth in number of establishments and in sales volume of certain consumer- and business-service firms in the 10-year period from 1967 to 1977. Services are playing an ever-more important role in our total lifestyle as we have more leisure time and more discretionary income.

Service businesses typically have several distinctive characteristics that distinguish them from those that handle products; these can create problems as well as opportunities.

Services are *intangible*. They cannot be sampled—that is, touched, tasted, or seen—before being purchased. This means they must be bought on faith, with uncertain future benefits.

Services are *people-dependent*. That is, the persons offering them have a far more crucial role in customer satisfaction than typically is the situation with products. And there usually is a limit to how many clients or customers can be handled, since a dentist can only treat so many people, a lawyer or a financial adviser counsel so many clients.

Services usually are *nonstandard*, and as a result tend to be unpredictable. Just as dining out experiences may differ from one time to another, even at the same restaurant, so may other services vary in the degree of satisfaction and competence.

Services tend to be *perishable*. They cannot be stored and used another time. For example, an idle dentist cannot regain the lost time, nor can an underutilized financial or estate planning adviser.

Many services face *fluctuating demand*. Hotel occupancy, theater attendance, ski lifts, restaurants, and tax preparers all face wide fluctuations in demand. This situation, along with the perishability of services, poses intriguing challenges for firms trying to reduce the extremes of demand and maximize efficiency.

The service of managing highly paid, proud, and eccentric athletes and other celebrities present particular challenges. Not only must their needs and wants be catered to, but it is especially important that the service provided be seen as desirable and well handled—by the celebrities, and by the corporate clients ready to pay well for their names and promotional presence.

He was Carl Sandburg. Mark spent part of a summer organizing the papers of the Pulitzer Prize winner, biographer, and poet. He did not know then the enormous stature of the man; he considered him just a good neighbor. But he had his first exposure to celebrities. Today, McCormack cherishes the books the famous man autographed for him during his adolescent and teen years.

McCormack won the Chicago prep school golf championship when he was a student at the Harvard School of Boys, and later he played on the William and Mary golf team. Among the teams challenged was Wake Forest. And playing for Wake Forest was their star, Arnold Palmer.

Table 15.1   Number and Sales volume of Selected Consumer- and Business-Service Establishments, 1967–1977

Kind of Business	Number of Establishments (Thousands)		Sales volume (Millions)	
	1967	1977	1967	1977
Hotels, motels, etc.	87.0	70.7	$ 7,039	$18,453
Personal services (e.g., laundry, dry cleaning, beauty shops, barber shops, photographic, shoe repair, funeral, alterations)	498.9	512.1	11,750	18,433
Automobile repair and other automotive services	139.2	200.2	7,028	21,576
Motion picture theaters	18.8	11.8	3,476	2,606
Amusement, recreation services, except motion picture (e.g., dance halls, theatrical presentations, bowling, billiards, commercial sports)	96.0	165.0	4,827	18,537
Business services (e.g., advertising agencies, consulting firms, credit bureaus, computer services, stenographic services, research firms, employment agencies, telephone answering services, armored-car operations)	200.0	458.2	22,000	54,500

Sources: U.S. Census of Business—Selected Services, 1967 and 1977.

McCormack graduated from William and Mary in 1951 and then went on for his law degree at Yale. He joined a Cleveland law firm at an annual salary of $5400, but he found himself more interested in golf than in practicing law. He participated in four U.S. Amateur Championships and played well enough to qualify for the 1958 U.S. Open in Tulsa, Oklahoma. It was there after a practice round that pro golfer Gene Littler asked him to examine an endorsement contract. McCormack was amazed at how one-sided the contract was and began to involve himself in negotiating contracts for golfers.

In 1959, McCormack formed National Sports Management, Inc., with the objective of booking playing dates and appearances for 16 golfers, one of whom was Palmer. A year later, in 1960, Palmer asked McCormack to be his agent. Their deal was sealed with a handshake. At that time Palmer earned about $60,000 a year. However, with McCormack as his financial manager/

agent, within two years Palmer was making more than $500,000 annually through licensing arrangements, books, articles, radio and TV appearances, golf franchises, exhibitions, and an array of golf-related industries. Soon after, Palmer asked McCormack to manage a relatively unknown player from South Africa, named Gary Player, and a chubby Ohioan golfer, Jack Nicklaus. In a few years, these three were to dominate pro golf.

In 1961, McCormack founded the International Management Group, and growth intensified. Soon he was representing most of the top golfers of the world. Now he realized that IMG needed to branch out into other areas if it was to grow further.

It was natural to expand into other individual sports. In tennis, such big names as Rod Laver and John Newcombe were signed up; in skiing, the famous Jean-Claude Killy; and Jackie Stewart in auto racing. Signing up athletes in team sports, such as football was a natural extension. Next the decision was made to represent nonathletes, and cartoonist Hank Ketchum, author of Dennis the Menace, as well as other talent in modeling, songwriting, and announcing, became part of the IMG stable. Going beyond individuals, IMG began representing and negotiating television and commercial rights for the sponsors of such prestigious events as Wimbledon and the British Open.

Diversification did not stop at that point. Consulting, promotional, and merchandising plans and activities were provided for purely business organizations, such as Rolex, Sears, Seagram, Wilkinson Sword, AT&T, and British American Tobacco Company. The tie-in of IMG's athletic clients with the promotional needs of such firms was a natural and mutually beneficial. "We're showing corporations how to use sports to sell their products," McCormack explains.[1] IMG further expanded into the largest independent producer and packager of sports programming in the world. Sports events, specials, and series appearing on television included The Superstars, The Superteams, Games People Play, Challenge of the Sexes, and Battle of the Network Stars.

By the early 1980s, IMG and its various divisions was managing the affairs of some 400 clients from the world of sports, business, and the professions. Annual revenues were over $200 million. And an office network had been established with 15 offices located around the world, from Hong Kong to New Zealand, from Monte Carlo to London. Such offices enabled IMG clients to stay in contact with IMG representatives at all times as they toured outside their home countries.

As a result of his successful services, McCormack attracted a wide range of famous clients. The most notable has to be Pope John Paul II, whom he

[1] IMG brochure, n.d., p. 5.

obtained as a client in the spring of 1981. The Vatican wanted somebody to handle the commercial aspects of the Pope's visit to England, Wales, and Scotland and to avoid the widespread merchandising of trashy, unofficial items. A few years before, a papal visit to Ireland had brought the Vatican all sorts of problems from vendors selling cheap junk to ineffective sound systems for sermons and celebration of masses.

IMG was able to provide the Vatican with good quality merchandise for sale at profits to help defray the cost of the trip. Special emphasis was given to such commemorative items as books, videotapes, statues, gold watches, and bricks inscribed with "To commemorate the visit of Pope John Paul II to Great Britain 1982." This last item was bought by homeowners for $7 and used to replace a brick in their home. Now McCormack is known around the world as the Pope's agent.

SERVICES

For Individuals

The foundation of IMG's success is its variety of services tailored to meet the individual needs of its clientele. Most of these have been celebrity athletes who typically have a relatively short period of high income, and whose income may come from different activities throughout the world. IMG not only represented these clients in their particular sports, but greatly enhanced their earning power through the marketing of their names. Clients could thus earn income from commercials and various licensing agreements that far exceeded their tournament winnings.

In addition, through its subsidiaries IMG managed many financial matters for its clients such as investing their money, paying their bills, arranging for adequate insurance, legal services, tax planning and tax return preparation, and retirement advising. One of the many ways in which IMG protected an athlete's assets from erosion was through tax planning techniques such as recommending to some athletes that they move their homes from high-tax countries to lower tax countries. Tennis star Bjorn Borg, at the time the world's highest paid athlete who under McCormack's guidance was making an estimated $5 million a year, was advised to move from Sweden where taxes were as high as 85 percent to Monte Carlo where taxes were paid only on income earned in Monaco.[2] Legal services might involve collecting money from foreign sources, the use of a client's name and likeness, and the development and use of trademarks.

---

[2] Candace E. Trunzo, "Choosing a Financial Planner," *Money,* April 1982, p. 52.

For Corporate Clients

Corporations quickly realized the promotional and public relations benefits of sponsoring events such as track meets, ski races, equine events, golf tournaments, and a variety of other athletic events including the Olympics. However, every sport is not compatible with every manufacturer. For example, IMG account executive, Mary Hambrick noted: "It would be foolish for a potato chip maker to sponsor a horse-jumping event, despite the fact that people who like horses eat snack food too. We could find a sport in which the fans eat more or even the majority of potato chips. The key is matching the sport and the product as closely as possible."[3] IMG developed the expertise to create a mutually beneficial relationship between sponsor and event.

More than 50 international companies were using IMG's services, which involved reviewing the firm's existing programs and, when appropriate, proposing ways to make them more efficient and effective. Long-term marketing and public relations plans were developed and tailored to the firm's objectives. Plans were then created for the tactical use of sports to solve individual sales, distribution, and corporate image problems. IMG "helps customers assess the potential value of sport as leisure-time opportunities presented to them from the outside. And it implements . . . and oversees the details of a promotion, right down to and including on-site supervision when it is called for."[4]

In addition to sponsoring events, IMG worked closely with businesses for corporate outings and pro-ams, which give companies the opportunity to introduce their associates and customers to well-known personalities from highly visible sports. Such activities gain exposure and credibility, and can build personal relationships with hard-to-reach customers, as well as giving the opportunity to show "you are important to us."

Fee Structure

The fees IMG charged its clients appear to have varied from person to person based on their service requirements. Published articles state a range from 20 to 50 percent of gross income for athletes, averaging $30,000, whereas corporate clients were paying a flat fee of $8000.[5] Although the fees appear high, they are normally tax deductible and this reduces the net of tax cost considerably for these high-income clients.

McCormack explains these considerable fees this way: "It's a question of how good a job you can do. If I were to pick the 25th leading tennis player in

[3] Julie Howell Turner, "The Midas Touch," *Spur*, September–October 1982., p. 56.
[4] IMG brochure, p. 26.
[5] Trunzo, "Choosing a Financial Planner," p. 52.

the world . . . and say to him, 'I can get you a $1 million-a-year contract with Ford Motor Company, and there is no way he can get that $1 million without me, then 90 percent might be a fair price on that deal.'"[6]

INGREDIENTS OF SUCCESS

The managing and promoting of athletes, which began with Arnold Palmer asking Mark McCormack to manage his affairs, was a new idea for the 1960s. Part of the popularity of agents for athletes today stems from the success that IMG achieved. So we have an innovative concept melded to an execution that was mutually satisfactory. Success was not surprising because a latent need was only awaiting the proper execution.

We need to be more specific, however, about the successful managing of athletes. Even with the latent need, a poor execution would undoubtedly have scuttled the concept or at least delayed its widening appeal. McCormack's strategy involved these three facets:

1. Developing a stable (or inventory) of personalities, mostly athletes, who could provide a quality promotional offering for business customers.
2. Providing a strong incentive for celebrity clients to be affiliated with IMG.
3. Providing integrated services for both clients and customers.

These three facets mesh together and reinforce each other. Before discussing them in more detail, let us clarify what we mean by "clients" and "customers." The clients are the individual celebrities—mostly athletes—who use IMG as an agent to increase their income and provide financial and other services. The customers are business firms who can (1) use IMG celebrities as promotional tools to further their public image and promote their products; (2) use IMG planning and execution for various sporting events also to further the public image and promote the products of the firm; (3) or both.

IMG uses great care in providing athletes to business firms. These individuals are chosen carefully and some rather well-known people are turned down as clients. For example, Wilt Chamberlain was not accepted as a client because his promotional possibilities were seen as limited to only demonstrating the amount of legroom in a small car commercial. McCormack saw such a limited utilization as not worthwhile. Athletes in some team sports were found to be less effective and desirable as promotional entities. This was particularly true for football and basketball in which most of the athletes

[6] Robert Cubbedge, "Is This Man Going to Take Over Pro Tennis?" *Tennis*, February 1981, pp. 47–48.

were not thought to have the appeal of an Arnold Palmer, a Bjorn Borg, or a Jean-Claude Killy. Because of such selectivity, IMG's athletes have been very effective promoters for most business firms. And the amount that firms have been willing to spend to have athletes represent them multiplied greatly by the late 1970s. Arnold Palmer conveyed the charisma and great public popularity that made him particularly valuable. His low-key sincere approach and his great recognizability, though he is no longer a winner on the PGA regular tour, made him most effective in promoting an array of products from Cadillacs to Penzoil motor oil. By the early 1980s, Palmer reportedly was making more than Borg through his various business and personal appearance ventures: between $7 million and $10 million a year.[7] The success of some of IMG's client athletes and the increasing publicity IMG was receiving through the press and word of mouth brought great credibility and further enhanced business.

As demand for the services of IMG's individual clients increased because of corporate interest, the athletes benefited greatly in supplemental income that often far exceeded their regular earnings. And the array of financial services that IMG provided freed clients from worrying about such matters, knowing that these were in expert hands, and permitted concentration on their profession.

Although other agents have provided some of the services of IMG to their clients, IMG has been unique in the array of integrated services it can provide, both for its individual clients and for its business firm customers. Lawyers, insurance specialists, accountants, financial analysts, and investment advisers all are provided under one roof of services. For corporate customers, IMG was able to provide a complete package consisting of both the planning and the execution of sporting events and publicity efforts. Such an integrated service package, along with a history of considerable expertise in a variety of sports-related endeavors, has given IMG a powerful competitive advantage over a scattering of much smaller agents and promoters.

The initial success of McCormack in promoting his golf clients was creatively evolved and expanded. Other sports stars in both individual and team sports were a natural extension. Then other types of celebrities who were not athletes rather logically followed. Selling his clients' promotional appeal to business customers naturally evolved into providing more managerial services for such customers, notably in planning, executing, and even creating sporting events of various kinds that could be sponsored by firms.

From personal financial planning for individual clients, a major diversification effort reached beyond athletes and other celebrities to corporate executives. Most recently, IMG has inaugurated efforts to provide its financial planning to the more general public and has teamed up with a bank to form

---

[7] Hal Lebovitz, "What Makes Mark Run?", *Cleveland Plain Dealer*, March 6, 1983, p. 2B.

a joint venture whereby "each customer of the new service would be assigned a professional banker and a financial planner to manage the account."[8] This venture is considered a first in the financial world.

Finally we are left with the question: Is the major ingredient of IMG's success the drive and personality of Mark McCormack? Is he the vital ingredient in developing clients and customers and in keeping both happy? I think not. Despite his 18-hour working days and his travels of nearly 300,000 miles a year, and his "stamina of a marathon runner and genius for organization and detail,"[9] I do not believe that today this growing and creative venture depends on one individual, and probably it has not since the early 1960s when the major golfers of the world sought him as their agent.

One individual can certainly make an impact, as we have seen time and time again in these success stories. But if the individual builds well and develops an effective organization—as McCormack seems to have done—the enterprise should be able to continue its course much as a plane on auto pilot, at least until major external changes arise.

WHAT CAN BE LEARNED?

In this case we have strong confirmation of how inspirational leadership and innovative strategy execution can be powerfully applied to other than tangible products. This corroborates the evidence of the earlier case of Hyatt Legal Services.

Learning Insight. *An innovative business strategy can be found far beyond the traditional tangible product emphasis.*

Mark McCormack has proven that athletes can be successfully marketed and that they can have great promotional, publicity, and public relations value to a business firm. For this they can be worth millions in fees. Testimonials are nothing new in advertising; indeed, testimonials have been used since the early decades of this century. But McCormack has brought the use of celebrities—especially the superstars of sports—to a level far beyond merely appearing in an advertisement or commercial and extolling a product that they perhaps never used. McCormack's athletic celebrities are involved in endorsements, public appearances in behalf of firms, apparel and related licenses, and in other ways increase the value of their services.

---

[8] John Fuller, "Financial Planning Offered to Wealthy," *Cleveland Plain Dealer,* July 27, 1983, p. 5B.

[9] IMG brochure, p. 5.

Learning Insight. *A strategy using celebrities can give a business firm a powerful stimulus, competitively as well as internally.*

In particular, the superstar can help a firm in the following ways:

1. As an image builder—when a firm is identified with a well-known, successful, and popular athlete, some of the esteem and excitement rubs off on the firm and its public image. Positive associations can buttress stodgy public awareness.

2. Strengthening customer, supplier, and employee relations—by getting a famous athlete to act as a company spokesperson, a firm can strengthen its relations with its outside affiliates as well as its own employees. All can take some pride in this association. Not the least of these benefits is the powerful motivational tool that can be provided by the personal appearance of the celebrity. For example, for some $20,000 IMG will furnish a celebrity sports star such as Arnold Palmer to play a few holes of golf or a few tennis matches. Important customers, suppliers, and company personnel and executives can participate, and long afterward they may still be saying, "Do you know what Arnie said about my chip shot?" or "When Arnie and I were teeing off . . ."[10]

3. The biggest incentive for a corporation to use high-priced athletic talent is as a promotional tool. If the athlete by endorsing and recommending the product can increase sales, then this is an uncontroversial decision and well worth virtually any expenditure to obtain the endorsement. For example, in 1980, the Italian tennis wear firm, Fila, paid for a one-year advertising campaign using Borg's name and picture (including one day of his time to shoot the ad), at $50,000 per commercial. Why would a firm pay so much for a Borg endorsement? Fila eventually signed Borg to a five-year contract, and during the last three years of the agreement, Fila's sales climbed from $35 million to $53 million.[11]

Learning Insight. *A major challenge of a nonproduct strategy is to gain credibility and trust with clients and customers through providing a perceived sufficient value for the offerings.*

Much depends on faith that the service expectations will be realized. This poses the major challenge to any firm involved with a service strategy: to serve the needs of its present and potential customers sufficiently according to their expectations, and to do so better than competitors can. An agency relationship with clients such as IMG's must provide perceived tangi-

---

[10] Turner, "The Midas Touch," p. 59.
[11] "A Word from the Sponsors," *Time*, June 30, 1980, p. 60.

ble benefits to its clients and customers to justify high fees. Otherwise it will easily be replaced. In general, IMG did a superlative job of this. But there were some who disputed the value. For example, Jack Nicklaus was lost as a client in 1971. Perhaps Nicklaus felt that he was not being represented as well as Palmer was. This may have been particularly disturbing to Nicklaus because by the beginning of the decade he had dethroned Palmer as the number 1 golfer in the world, yet Palmer was still receiving more attention. In Jack's case, then, relative tangible benefits was the criterion for acceptance or nonacceptance of the client–agent relationship.

Learning Insight. *A nonproduct strategy should provide a unique and quality offering.*

We see the desirability of providing a unique and quality offering, in this case, people. This quality strategy is by no means the only approach to business success, because certainly some products and firms have found success with a low-priced bargain image, as we know from some previous cases. Still, uniqueness combined with a quality image may be most important for a nonproduct strategy when the customer has to purchase on faith from an intangible and relatively unstandardized offering and is highly dependent on the persons offering the service. A unique and quality offering is more likely to meet with customer approval in these circumstances, especially when dealing with high-income clientele and major business firms. But the quality appeal must be maintained by scrupulous controls.

Learning Insight. *Once successful, a nonproduct strategy can often be effectively expanded in other directions.*

IMG illustrates the potency of a constantly evolving firm. Diversification and modification of a highly successful format to tap other opportunities should be the rule for any such firm. The firm that is content to rest on its laurels repudiates opportunities for transference of its successful strategy to related areas. Controlled growth according to the lines of proven strength may offer substantial additional rewards.

FOR THOUGHT AND DISCUSSION

1. Discuss the promotional impact of using prominent athletes and other celebrities versus using ordinary people in commercials.
2. Do you see any limit of the fees that celebrities can command, as well as their effectiveness in promotional activities?

INVITATION TO ROLE PLAY

As an IMG executive charged with developing the promotional effectiveness of runners, how would you plan and execute this athletic sector development? Be as specific and creative as you can.

Four

LACK OF ADEQUATE CONTROLS

16

Contrasts in the Battle of Hamburgers: Burger Chef and McDonald's

Such a simple product: a hamburger. What can any reasonably efficient operation do to hurt a hamburger, and jeopardize business? But, alas, we face the vivid contrast between the great success of McDonald's, the premier hamburger maker, and an also-ran, Burger Chef.

The differences between the success and failure of the two firms is hardly one of resources: McDonald's did not have vastly superior financial and managerial resources with which to command mass-media advertising and to open hundreds of additional outlets. In fact, Burger Chef was acquired by General Foods Corporation in 1967 when General Foods was a $3 billion corporation lacking neither resources nor know-how about the marketing of food. Our look at the differences in the two corporations will uncover some important learning concepts with far wider applicability than simply the jockeying of fast-food behemoths.

PART A   BURGER CHEF—WHY NOT ANOTHER McDONALD'S?

In 1967, General Foods Corporation acquired Burger Chef Systems, a fast-food franchising operation of some 700 units, for $16 million. In less than four years, General Foods amassed a pretax loss of $83 million from the venture, while, during the same period, McDonald's net income rose 285 percent. There were some marginal fast-food franchisors that collapsed during this period in which there appeared to be a saturation of hamburger, chicken, and other restaurants. But General Foods was no marginal firm. It was the nation's largest manufacturer of convenience foods, with sales approaching $3 billion. It was an astute and aggressive marketer and the country's third largest national advertiser, spending over $150 million a year. It had an unbroken string of annual sales increases dating back to 1935. With such backing for an already established and growing franchise chain, how could disaster strike, and in just a few years?

THE GENERAL FOODS COMPANY

General Foods traces its beginning back to C. W. Post Cereals in 1895. It was incorporated in 1922 as the Postum Cereal Company, manufacturers of Post cereals and Postum beverage. In 1925, the firm began consolidating with other companies, including the Jello-O Company and the Maxwell House Coffee Company. In 1929 the Postum Cereal Company changed its name to General Foods.

The company continued to grow and diversify through internal development of new products and by acquisition and mergers with other firms. By 1965 its sales were $1.5 billion and net earnings over $177 million. Well-known brands of this major processor and marketer of packaged food products included Maxwell House, Yuban, and Sanka coffees; Jell-O desserts; Bird's Eye frozen foods; Post cereals; Swans Down cake mixes; Baker's chocolate; Minute rice; Kool-Aid soft drink mixes; Gaines pet foods; Tang breakfast drink; and Log Cabin syrup.

During the 1960s, however, some performance indicators showed deterioration. While sales revenues increased steadily, profit margins on sales began declining from the high of 6.5 percent in 1963. Returns on stockholders' equity were also showing declines. Still, in 1966 when a new man, C. W. "Tex" Cook, came in as chairman and chief executive, and Arthur E. Larkin became president and chief operating officer, General Foods stood at the forefront of the packaged foods industry with net profits at 6 percent of sales. Of six major food categories, General Foods led sales in all but cereals, with no competitor even close in instant coffee, desserts, and dog food.

Tangible problems emerged in 1968 when the Federal Trade Commission forced General Foods to divest of its S.O.S. soap-pad business, which it had acquired in 1957. Chairman Cook bitterly took umbrage at this decision:

> They laid down some pretty severe strictures regarding what we could and could not do for "X" number of years. For instance, they made it very clear that we were precluded from touching anything of consequence that went through the supermarket on a national basis. Similarly, they would frown on something that depended very heavily on consumer advertising. So that we were almost

directed away from the kinds of things where our experience and expertise had, over the years, given us most of our benefits.[1]

To add to the problems connected with antitrust action, three of General Foods' biggest divisions began running into trouble. The Birds' Eye Division lost ground to Green Giant Company, which developed ready-to-cook vegetables in plastic bags that could be dropped directly into boiling water. Supermarkets were bringing out their own branded products, which they sold below the prices of General Foods' national brands. Consumer acceptance of these *private brands* cut into General Foods' market share and profit margins.

The sales of Maxwell House Division, which generated more than a third of General Foods' sales revenues, leveled off. This sales decline reflected changing consumer tastes, particularly those of young adults, whose consumption of coffee was less than that of their parents.

Changes in consumer tastes also caused the dry cereal market growth to slow markedly. As a result of a massive promotion by competitor General Mills, General Foods' Post Division (Post Toasties, Grape Nuts, 40% Bran Flakes, etc.) was displaced from second place (behind Kellogg).

Faced with governmental constraints, a tangible loss of profit momentum, and an eroding market share, General Foods began seeking diversification in directions compatible with the company's expertise in food-related activities. During the mid-1960s, food sold away from home was growing at twice the rate of food sold in stores for home consumption.

The decision to acquire Burger Chef Systems, an Indianapolis-based chain of 700 (mostly franchised) fast-food hamburger restaurants, seemed reasonable and expeditious. Six Rix roast-beef sandwich restaurants were also acquired at that time. 1968 was a boom year, and companies like McDonald's were growing at rates in excess of 25 percent a year. Burger Chef was operating in 39 states and selling a million hamburgers per day. Expectations for the fast-food business were high.

Burger Chef under General Foods

A vigorous expansion program was undertaken for Burger Chef. By March 1969, not much more than a year after the acquisition, there were 900 outlets operating across the country. That same month, Burger Chef moved into Canada with an outlet in Toronto.

By December 1969, there were 1022 outlets in the United States and 29 in Canada. One year later, there were more than 1200 outlets in the United States and 36 in Canada, representing an increase of over 70 percent in three

[1] "The Rebuilding Job at General Foods," *Business Week*, August 25, 1973, p. 50.

INFORMATION SIDELIGHT

PRIVATE BRANDS

Wholesalers and retailers often use their own brands—commonly referred to as private brands—in place of or in addition to the branded goods of manufacturers. Private brands, although offered at lower selling prices than nationally advertised brands, typically give dealers more per-unit profit since they are bought on more favorable terms, partly reflecting promotional savings. Some firms, such as Sears, Penney, and A & P, stock mostly their own brands. As a result they have better control over repeat business, since satisfied customers can repurchase the brand only through the particular store or chain.

Since private brands directly compete with manufacturers' brands, sometimes at a better price, why do manufacturers sell some of their output to retailers under a private brand? Some manufacturers do so to minimize idle plant capacity, arguing that if they refuse business with private label seekers, someone else will get the business. Other manufacturers welcome private brand business because they lack the resources and know-how to enter the marketplace effectively with their own brands.

years. Some 84 percent of the outlets were franchised and 16 percent operated by Burger Chef. Advertising expenditures averaged $2.5 million a year.

General Foods lost several of its key executives in its fast-food acquisitions. The founder of Burger Chef left to pursue other interests shortly after the acquisition. Another key executive had a heart attack. Other departures for various reasons resulted in an almost complete management turnover during the first two years. But this seemed to pose no severe problems, because General Foods supplied the new management for its acquisition from its own ranks.

The bad news, when it came, was sudden and shocking. In January 1972, General Foods announced a write-down amounting to $83 million pretax dollars, nearly $1 a share after taxes. General Foods informed its stockholders that it was cutting back its ambitious expansion into fast food. It closed all 70 of its Rix roast-beef restaurants. It closed 100 of the 1200 Burger Chef units and announced it was writing off many more. The faster General Foods tried to expand its fast-food operation, the bigger the problems became.

Forbes magazine questioned how so big a company could go so wrong in as simple a business as frying hamburgers and slicing roast beef. In an interview with *Forbes's* reporters, President Larkin explained: "We couldn't get enough people to come into our stores. The kids didn't want roast beef and later the adults didn't want it either. Roast beef was just a fad." Regarding the Burger Chef operation, Larkin admitted the problem was simply management: "The key man had a heart attack. We sent one of our own men and he just did not know his way around this kind of operation."[2]

Struggle for Survival

For 19 consecutive years, General Foods managed to achieve gains in per-share earnings. But the hamburger and roast-beef disaster broke the trend in 1972. The viability of the multibillion dollar company was not in danger, and the company was still profitable despite the fast-food drain. However, Burger Chef's substantial losses hurt the image of the company, especially with its major food chain customers. This image further suffered when General Foods cut back on some customer services in order to absorb the fast-food losses.

Arthur Larkin, the heir apparent for the chairman's position, took an early retirement. As part of the companywide efficiency drive, salaried personnel were cut by 10 percent, and General Foods took a hard look at its total operation.

While other aspects of the corporation were also causing problems, the biggest rebuilding job continued to be the Burger Chef chain. The total number of units was pruned to about 1000, and more attention was given to clustering these in major markets to obtain a more efficient sharing of advertising expenditures. More thorough screening and training of franchise owners and managers was instituted. A new building design, new logo, more emphasis on product quality, a more varied menu, and even a new plastic wrapper to keep hamburgers warm longer, were belatedly introduced. Yet, it seemed likely the fast-food division was years away from making a major contribution to General Food's earnings.

POSTMORTEM

Burger Chef seemed such a perfect acquisition in 1968. How could such a compatible union go wrong? In retrospect, a fast-food operation is vastly different from the marketing of packaged food in supermarkets. There were major differences in promotional efforts, in competition, in facilities, and, most important, in management controls. Unfortunately, General Foods did not realize this until much of the damage was done.

No single event can be selected as the cause of the Burger Chef debacle; rather, it was a combination of factors. But these factors were by no means hidden; they were obvious and should have been identified and corrected by management. At the time of the acquisition, Burger Chef suffered from a lack of distinction and identity. McDonald's had its golden arches, Kentucky

[2] "The Bigger They Are . . . " *Forbes*, February 15, 1972, p. 21.

Fried Chicken had its easily recognized red and white colors, and most of the other successful fast-food establishments were readily identified. Burger Chef, on the other hand, had an undistinguished red and yellow sign that was not universally used, and when used it was inconspicuous among the multitude of other signs proliferating along commercial strips. The outlets themselves were modestly constructed, some with walk-up windows, but few with sit-down accommodations. There was little uniformity in design among the mostly franchised operations.

At the time of acquisition, Burger Chef had a considerable disadvantage in that its 700 outlets were thinly dispersed and spread over 39 states. A major metropolitan area might have only a handful of restaurants, in contrast to McDonald's and some of the other major franchisors. Supervision of such a widespread network was difficult and costly, and the benefits of concentrated promotional efforts, which could have been shared among a number of outlets at relatively low cost, were lost, leaving the competitive advantage to those firms with greater concentration of outlets. The better policy would have been a slower geographical expansion, on a market-by-market basis.

The quality of food and the limited assortment available also contributed to the poor market performance. At a time when competitors were adding fish sandwiches, double- and triple-decker hamburgers, onion rings, and fruit pies to their menu, Burger Chef stood pat. In addition, food quality varied with franchisee and area.

Company spokesmen admitted their selection of franchisees, and their training of them, was questionable. Interest in a Burger Chef franchise, satisfactory character references, adequate financial standing, and some experience in running a filling station or whatever, were all that was necessary for approval. Although new franchise holders were sent to a training school for a brief period, there was no on-the-job training to familiarize them with hiring people, to teach them how to be hospitable, how to handle the problems of a teenage gathering place, and so on.

Major emphasis in the Burger Chef operation was on expanding the number of outlets just as rapidly as possible. In the process, existing outlets and their problems were ignored. As a result, location mistakes, problems of controlling quality of product and service, and other problems were not corrected for the new units being established. The expansion was coming on top of an unstable and even wobbly base.

An economic recession in 1969–1971 should have discouraged pell-mell expansion, or at least caused some introspection and review of the overall marketing strategy for this division. During this time some of the marginal fast-food franchisors went out of business. But the stronger ones survived with little ill effects. With the formidable resources of General Foods, Burger Chef should have strengthened its market share, focusing on upgrading and improving the outlets it had instead of enlarging its number of mediocre establishments. As president Larkin said: "We moved too far, too fast, under the pressure of the times."[3]

UPDATE

Late in 1981, General Foods sold The Burger Chef subsidiary to Hardee's, a Canadian-owned hamburger fast-food firm with 1396 U.S. outlets. At the time Burger Chef had been pruned to 676 units and, after five years of losses, was finally showing a small profit. The sale to Hardee's resulted in a charge against earnings for General Foods of $12.5 million. The loss was regarded as acceptable to be rid of a burr that had plagued it and that, while showing a profit, was still yielding a lower return on investment than most of its other divisions. The acquisition was viewed by Hardee's as providing additional sales and earnings growth potential to its already substantial fast-food operation.

By the mid-1980s, there was rapid growth in the fast-food restaurant industry in the number of outlets and the variety of offerings. Some 10,000 new franchise chain outlets were opened in nearly two years, 1984 and 1985. New chains were coming on the scene, while the older ones continued to expand. While certain market areas were becoming saturated, considerable expansion was occurring in the international market and in nontraditional domestic sites, such as military bases, college campuses, and various other institutions.

The general public was showing a new concern for nutrition and weight consciousness, and such chains as Burger King and Wendy's emphasized low-calorie menus. Demand for chicken and seafood was increasing, "gourmet" hamburgers, gourmet pizza (nontraditional toppings on a thin crust), and gourmet croissants were doing well. Ethnic food restaurants, particularly Mexican, were finding strong demand.

While General Foods failed with its Burger Chef acquisition, in recent years large food-related corporations eagerly diversified successfully into fast-food restaurants. Pepsico had Pizza Hut and Taco Bell; General Mills owned Red Lobster; Pillsbury was successful with its Burger King and Godfathers chains; and RJR Nabisco had Kentucky Fried Chicken.

And still, McDonald's remained at the top of the heap, with 1989 sales of $5.97 billion and net profits of 707 million.

---

[3] Marylin Bender, "At General Foods, Did Success Breed Failure?" *New York Times*, June 1, 1972, pp. 111–118.

PART B   McDONALD'S: SUCCESS WITH SUCH A SIMPLE PRODUCT

Ray Kroc faced a serious dilemma. He was 57 years old and all his life had dreamed of becoming rich. And how he had tried. Ever since he came back from World War I (at 15, he had falsified his age when he joined), he had worked hard at getting rich. He played piano with dance bands; he sold paper cups for Lily-Tulip; and moon-lighted at a Chicago radio station (WGES) playing the piano, arranging the music programs, and accompanying singers. The Florida land boom in the mid-1920s brought him from Chicago where he tried selling land. A year later he returned to Chicago almost broke. Lily-Tulip gave him back his old job, and he stayed there more than 10 years. In 1937, he stumbled onto a new gadget, a simple electric appliance that would make six milkshakes at the same time. He quit Lily-Tulip again, made a deal with the inventor, and soon became the world's exclusive agent for the Price Castle Multi-Mixer. Over the next 20 years he traveled all over the country peddling it. He earned a fair living, but did not become rich.

Now Kroc had stumbled onto the opportunity of a lifetime. But he needed $1.5 million to make it work. Unfortunately, he had neither money nor credit. His main source of income had dried up when he was forced to sell his mixer business for $100,000 to pay for a divorce. Now his total assets, including his house, were $90,000.

PRELUDE

In 1954 Kroc received an order for eight Multi-Mixers from a hamburger stand in San Bernardino, California. The order was unusual enough that he decided to get a firsthand look at an operation that needed to make 48 milkshakes at a time.

Maurice and Richard McDonald had come to California from New England in 1928, thinking California was the land of opportunity. They opened their first restaurant in Pasadena in 1940, and in 1948 opened a self-service hamburger stand in San Bernardino. They had trouble staffing their restaurant after World War II: unskilled job seekers were primarily drunks and drifters. Dick McDonald recalled thinking:

> Let's get rid of it all. Out went dishes, glasses, and silverware. Out went service, the dishwashers, and the long menu. We decided to serve just hamburgers, drinks, and french fries on paper plates. Everything prepared in advance, everything uniform.[4]

---

[4] "What McDonald's Had, the Others Didn't," *Forbes*, January 2, 1973, p. 26.

These operations proved so successful that they had offers to buy them out or work out franchising deals. But they were conservative and cautiously sold only six franchises in California while passing up other deals. The brothers lived in a small town, netted $75,000 a year, and were afraid of getting too big.

When Ray Kroc arrived, he was amazed. He saw crowds of people waiting in line under the Golden Arches. He estimated the hamburger stand's gross at $250,000 a year. He was even more impressed with the speed of service and the cleanliness. The McDonald's served a standard hamburger for 15 cents, and the french fries, kept warm under infrared heat lamps, were always fresh and crispy. Since customers moved in and out quickly, only a small facility was needed to generate the substantial sales volume.

Ray Kroc badly wanted in on this business. He hounded the McDonald brothers for two days until they relented and allowed him to sell franchises. The agreement was to charge 1.9 percent of revenues for each franchise, of which Kroc got 1.4 percent and the McDonald brothers 0.5 percent.

At first Kroc was most interested in expanding the chain in order to sell more Multi-Mixer machines. But by 1960 he had sold 200 franchises, providing him gross franchise income of about $700,000 per year. He had taken a partner, Harry Sonneborn, a former vice president of Tastee Freez, who was drawing $100 a week. Kroc's secretary was taking her wages in stock. (When she retired, she had an estimated 1 million shares of McDonald's stock.)

Sonneborn convinced Kroc to take a wholly new approach. All new franchises would be tenants: the company would select the site, build the store, provide the equipment, and rent the total package to an operator. McDonald's would receive the rental from the lease as well as the franchising fee. A great plan, but it required money—about $1.5 million. And with Kroc's meager assets, bank credit was unattainable.

FRANCHISING

Franchising is a contractual arrangement in which the franchisor extends to independent franchisees the right to conduct a certain kind of business according to a particular format. Although the franchising arrangement may involve a product, a common type of franchise involves a service, with the franchisors providing a carefully developed, promoted, and controlled operation.

Franchising dates back at least to the turn of the century. General Motors very early established its first independent dealer to sell and service automobiles. Coca-Cola and the other soft-drink makers granted franchises to their independent bottlers. By 1910, franchising was the principal method of marketing automobiles and petroleum products. By 1920 it was used by food, drug, variety, hardware, and automotive parts firms. The major growth of franchising began after World War II. Soft ice cream outlets typified this growth: in 1945 there were 100 soft ice cream stands in the United States; by 1960 there were almost 18,000. Franchise sales of goods and services comprise almost 30 percent of all retail sales, with half a million franchise establishments in the United States employing over 4 million workers.[5]

Fast-Food Restaurant Franchising

Franchised fast-food restaurants have made a major impact on the food service industry since World War II. Employment in fast-food franchising by the 1970s accounted for almost 30 percent of total franchising employment and for over 30 percent of all persons employed in eating and drinking places in the United States.

Advantages of Franchising

A firm has two major advantages in expanding through franchised outlets rather than company-owned units. First, expansion can be rapid because the franchisees are putting up some or most of the money; almost the only limitations to growth are the need to screen applicants, to find suitable sites for new outlets, and to develop the managerial controls necessary to ensure consistency of performance. Second, more conscientious people normally can be obtained to operate the outlets, since franchisees are entrepreneurs with a personal stake in performance rather than hired managers.

The major advantage to a franchisee or licensee is the lower risk of business failure or, to put it positively, the greater chance of success. The entrepreneur has a business with proven consumer acceptance and wider recognition. The franchisee can also benefit from well-developed managerial and promotional techniques and from group buying power.

ONWARD TO SUCCESS

Ray Kroc got the money he needed and propelled McDonald's to a huge success. In only 22 years his firm reached the billion-dollar milestone. It took corporations such as IBM and Xerox 46 and 63 years, respectively, to reach this milestone. And Kroc boasted in his autobiography that the company is responsible for the making of over 1000 millionaires—the franchise holders.[6]

---

[5] U.S. Department of Commerce, *Franchising in the Economy, 1972–1979* (Washington, D.C.: Superintendent of Documents, U.S. Government Printing Office, 1979), pp. vi, I.

[6] Ray Kroc and Robert Anderson, *Grinding It Out: The Making of McDonald's* (New York: Berkley Publishing, 1977), p. 200.

Kroc obtained the $1.5 million from several insurance companies. As a premium on the loan, they took 20 percent of the company; this they later sold for a $7 million profit. A year later, Kroc bought out the McDonald brothers, paying them $2.7 million for everything—trademarks, copyrights, formulas, the Golden Arches, and the name. The brothers took their money and quietly retired to their hometown in New Hampshire. A few years later, when Sonneborn's health began to fail, Kroc offered him $10 million in cash, and $100,000 a year for life, and Sonneborn retired to Florida.

Figures 16.1 and 16.2 show the extraordinary growth of McDonald's in number of outlets and in sales from 1955 to 1975. An investment of $5000 in McDonald's in 1967 was worth $100,000 by 1973.

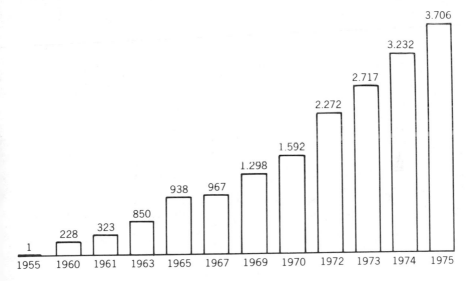

Figure 16.1. McDonald's Corporation, number of outlets 1955–1975.

THE STRATEGY

Ray Kroc saw a "strategic window" in catering to "budget-conscious families on wheels who want quick service, clean surroundings, and high-quality food."[7] This was seen as an alternative to drive-ins with car hops, jukeboxes, tipping, waiting, and food of inconsistent and questionable quality. Kroc defended his approach because

[7] Carol White and Merle Klingman, " 'Hamburger,' McDonald's Takes It Seriously," *Advertising Age*, May 22, 1972, p. 117.

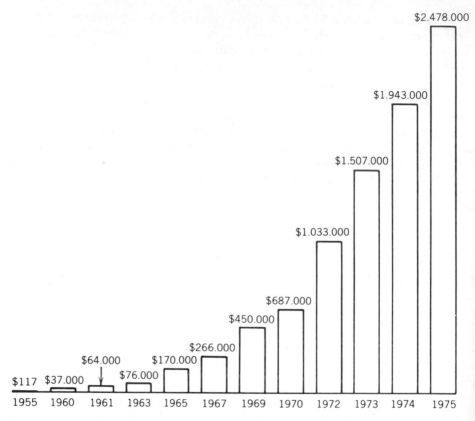

Figure 16.2. McDonald's Corporation, sales growth analysis 1955–1975 (figures in thousands of dollars)

. . . all of those things create unproductive traffic in a store and encourage loitering that can disrupt customers. This would downgrade the family image we wanted to create for McDonald's. Furthermore, in some areas the vending machines were controlled by the crime syndicate, and I wanted no part of that.[8]

As the executive vice president, Fred L. Turner, said, "We want young families in the tricycle and bicycle neighborhoods—the station wagon set, or one car going on two."[9]

During the company's early years, Ray Kroc used the company airplane to spot good locations; he would fly over a community looking for schools

[8] R. Kroc and R. Anderson, *Grinding It Out*, p. 200.
[9] "McDonald's Makes a Franchise Sizzle," *Business Week*, June 15, 1968, p. 107.

and church steeples and follow with site surveys. The company favored above-average-income and residential areas, preferably near shopping centers. New store sites should contain 50,000 residents within a three-mile radius. This changed by the 1970s when marketing research revealed that three-fourths of McDonald's customers stopped by in conjunction with some other activity. As a consequence, stores were located according to pattern of customer activity and traffic flows.

Kroc offered the public a clean family atmosphere in which service was quick and cheerful. Cleanliness of outlets, including the toilets, and friendliness of sales-people became major competitive advantages. These characteristics were not obtained without great pains. At Hamburger University, a special McDonald's training school for managers and owners, heavy emphasis was given customer service. A 350-page operating manual required adherence to strict standards, not only in preparation of food but also in care and maintenance of the facilities. For example, the manual called for door windows to be washed twice daily. There was even an employee dress code, with men required to keep their hair cropped to military length and their shoes highly polished. Women were to wear dark, low shoes, hair nets, and only very light makeup. All employees wore prescribed uniforms.

Food preparation was completely standardized: a pound of meat was to have less than 19 percent fat; buns were to measure 3½ inches wide, no more than one-quarter ounce of onions was permitted per hamburger, and so on. The holding time for each of the cooked products was set by corporate headquarters: french fries, 7 minutes; burger, 10 minutes; coffee, 30 minutes—after these time limits the products were thrown out. Company auditors scrutinized this part of the operation to ensure that all food served was of the same quality.

Consistency in adhering to these high standards was inherent in the management strategy. Store operation was closely supervised by strong regional offices to prevent damage to the reputation of the system from weakness in one restaurant. Field consultants made two three-day inspections of each outlet every year, grading operators on quality, cleanliness, quick service, and friendliness. This grading system could determine whether an existing operator would be granted desirable additional franchises. On rare occasions, a franchise could be terminated if prescribed standards were not met.

Franchises were granted store by store. This contrasted with most other franchisors who granted area franchises to large investors who promised to establish a given number of outlets within a specified period. Although the rate of growth was rapid, there were few problems with substandard conditions at either company-owned or franchised outlets.

McDonald's rigorously analyzed potential sites to ensure each unit the maximum chance for success; failures because of poor locations were few.

The distinctive buildings and the arches made a McDonald's unit visible from a distance.

McDonald's was one of the biggest users of mass-media advertising of any retailer, budgeting over $50 million each year. Who is not familiar with the jingle "You Deserve a Break Today"? How successful has this mass advertising been? In a survey of schoolchildren in the early 1970s, 96 percent identified Ronald McDonald, ranking him second only to Santa Claus.

THE MATURING YEARS

In 1968 Ray Kroc stepped aside and appointed 35-year-old Fred Turner president of the company. Turner had been Kroc's understudy for several years, starting as a cook and working his way up.

Despite Turner's allegiance and admiration for Kroc, he began instituting a number of changes in established policies. The red-and-white tile exteriors were replaced with dull-brown brick, more plate glass windows, and a shingled roof. The garish neon Golden Arches gave way to a more sedate logo. The interiors were modified so that people could more comfortably eat on the premises, and the hamburger stands were now called restaurants. Certain outlets were permitted more flexible decor, such as a nautical theme in Boston and a campus theme at UCLA.

As McDonald's gained financial strength, efforts were made to increase the number of company-owned units. An aggressive buy-back policy encouraged old franchise-holders to sell out to McDonald's. Company stores proved to be more desirable because of their higher profitability and more centralized control. In 1968, McDonald's owned only 15 percent of the outlets, but by 1974 40 percent were company owned.

As choice highway locations became scarce, McDonald's moved into downtown locations and shopping malls, zoos, office buildings, hospitals, and even a high school. Central city locations involved some adjustments. Salaries and occupancy costs were higher, and selling hours shorter with little business on weekends. But much higher volume—averaging twice the volume of the suburban stores—offset these drawbacks. Along with the central city expansion came the overseas market. By 1980, 1050 stores were located abroad, of which 250 were in Japan and 50 in England; 19 percent of total company sales volume came from this international operation.

McDonald's continued with its traditional Saturday morning television ads promoting Ronald. According to a McDonald's official, "It takes only one child to influence a meal out."[10] McDonald's also developed ads aimed at specific segments to the public, such as blue-collar workers, a group that had

---

[10] Christy Marshall, "McDonald's '79' Plan: Beat Back the Competition," *Advertising Age,* February 2, 1979, p. 88.

been hard for McDonald's to draw. Special promotions and giveaways aimed at children also influenced sales—for example, Kid's Day, featuring free sundaes, premiums in "play value" packages, and even a "Fun Bus" that takes schoolchildren on field trips with, of course, a stop at a McDonald's restaurant for lunch.

The traditional product offering of McDonald's is simplicity itself. In the early days, the product line was only hamburgers, french fries, milkshakes, and soft drinks. The first successful menu expansion came with the Filet-o-Fish in 1962, invented by an operator in Cincinnati, Ohio, located in a large Catholic neighborhood and faced with weak Friday sales. Before introducing the sandwich chainwide (not until 1965), McDonald's developed standards on how long to cook it, what type of breading to use, how thick to make it, and the kind of tartar sauce to use. It was then test-marketed, being offered on Fridays in a limited number of outlets. Similarly, chicken was intensively tested, beginning in 1971, and not made generally available until 1981. Even the Big Mac was tested for several years before being made widely available.

The most notable success with product expansion was the breakfast menu. The Egg McMuffin was first tested in 1972, with other breakfast items added shortly after. Initially, breakfast menus were tested in Chicago, Pittsburgh, and Washington, D.C. They proved so successful there that the breakfast menu became available nationwide in 1976 and by 1977 accounted for 10 percent of the company's sales. A major advantage of these breakfast sales is that they bring additional business during a time when these outlets would otherwise be idle. In addition, the breakfast menu lured older customers not previously attracted to the restaurant. In 1977, only one year after introduction of the breakfast menu, patronage from customers over 35 years of age jumped from 18 percent to 22.5 percent. Thoroughly testing a few selected menu additions has been a hallmark of the product strategy. The company uses its company-owned stores to test-market new-product candidates before making them more widely available.

KEYS TO SUCCESS

Many franchise firms faded in the late 1960s and 1970s because of oversaturation. Competitors established more outlets than the market could support, and marginal operations faltered. Some franchisors failed because of difficulty in obtaining qualified franchisees or licensees. McDonald's believed that a key factor for success was for a licensee initially to work full time in the business. The unsuccessful franchisors failed to attract or insist on licensees who met prescribed qualifications. They tended to be interested primarily in getting the initial franchise fee. Business was viewed as a quick-buck scheme, to be milked dry with the franchisor then exiting.

Poor site selection plagued some operations. Too fast an expansion led to indiscriminate site selection, sometimes influenced by opportunistic realtors. Another factor leading to poor locations was lack of capital to purchase the more desirable sites.

When business and the economy are going well, ineffective management controls are not always readily apparent. However, when the economy experiences a downturn and competition intensifies, lack of effective controls can be fatal.

In order to gain quick public attention and recognition, many fast-food franchisors used the name of either an entertainer or a professional sports figure to lure potential licensees: Minnie Pearl's Chicken, Here's Johnny Restaurant (Johnny Carson), Al Hirt Sandwich Saloon, Broadway Joe's (Joe Namath), Jerry Lucas Beef'n Shake, and Mickey Mantle's Country Cookin' Restaurant. Although the public would pay to see the entertainer or sports figure perform, they do not necessarily frequent a fast-food outlet simply because of the famous name—unless the food and service warrant their patronage.

The ingredients of success for McDonald's were simple, but few competitors were able to emulate them:

- A brief menu of consistent quality with hundreds and thousands of outlets.
- Strictly enforced and rigorous operational standards for service, cleanliness, and all aspects of the operation.
- Friendly employees, despite a high turnover of personnel because of the monotony of automated food handling.
- Heavy mass-media advertising, d'rected mostly to families and children.
- Identifying a fertile target market—the family—and directing the strategy to satisfying it: product, price, promotional efforts, and site locations.

McDONALD'S AND BURGER CHEF: WHAT CAN BE LEARNED?

In most areas of operation, Burger Chef compared poorly with McDonald's. It lacked image, consistency in its product, and a diversified product line. Its promotional expenditures—$2.5 million annually during the growth years versus $50 million for McDonald's—were insufficient to bring it recognition. It had neither a well-planned and organized selection procedure for franchisees nor a training program to assure efficient operational procedures. Its controls and auditing compared in no way with the thoroughness and strictness practiced by McDonald's.

There is nothing exotic about success. It consists simply of doing customer-pleasing things better and more consistently than the competition. A unique product is not an essential ingredient for success, although it can certainly help. But a hamburger is a hamburger is a hamburger.

Franchising is significantly different from other types of business operations, and the differences present powerful opportunities as well as lurking dangers. Rapid growth is possible through franchising—far more rapid than a firm can achieve on its own, even with substantial resources. Because somebody else is putting up most or all of the capital for an outlet, the major requirements for expansion are finding and wooing sufficient investor-licensees and locating attractive sites for additional units. Both requirements can be met *carelessly* in the quest for wild expansion or *carefully* for controlled expansion.

In franchising, a few poor operations hurt the other outlets since all operate under the same format and logo. This is similar to the situation of any chain operation (a few bad stores can hurt the image of the rest of the chain), but a franchise system is composed of independent entrepreneurs who tend to be less controlled than the hired managers of a chain operation.

Learning Insight. *The benefits of rapid growth may be illusory.*

The rapid growth made possible through a franchise system can be its downfall. Because growth in the number of units can occur easily and quickly, it is tempting to rush headlong into opening more units to meet the demand of prospective licensees. Emphasis on growth often means that existing operations are ignored. As a consequence, they are undercontrolled, and emerging problems do not receive adequate attention. Screening of people and locations tends to become superficial. Eventually the bubble bursts, and the firm is forced to recognize that many outlets are marginal and must be drastically pruned. Growth must be prudent and controlled in order to achieve adequate assimilation.

Learning Insight. *Controlled growth requires tight controls.*

All firms need to maintain tight controls over far-flung outlets in order to be sufficiently informed about emerging problems and opportunities, to optimize their use of resources, and to maintain a desired image and standard of performance. In a franchise operation, tight controls are all the more essential since franchisees often are independent entrepreneurs rather than hired managers.

The establishment of a control process requires three basic steps:

1. Standards of performance must be set and communicated to those persons involved.
2. Performance should be checked against these standards.
3. Corrective action should be taken when needed.

Burger Chef's performance would have been greatly improved had it set up standards for the quality and preparation of food, cleanliness and service, menus, general operations, and personnel. Also helpful would have been accounting standards for budgeting, cost or expenses, size of servings, number of employees, payrolls, and the like. Better-run franchised operations have extensive standards and specifications for all aspects of their operations in minute detail—remember the 350-page operating manual of McDonald's?

When standards are specifically designated and communicated to those responsible for adhering to them, the next step of the control process can be imposed—measuring performance against the standards. Performance is best measured by outside auditors, inspectors, or district and home-office executives visiting the premises unannounced, perhaps with a checklist in hand, and grading actual against expected performance. All aspects of the operation should be checked—from the grease content of the french fries to the soap supply in the restrooms.

After deviations from the standards are identified and their importance assessed, measures should be taken to correct the situation, perhaps through better training, more motivation, or even threat of dismissal or demotion. Although franchise operations involve independent owners of outlets, the franchisor still has authority to impose sanctions on deviant behavior. Such sanctions typically consist of warnings, placing on probation, and finally, if performance still does not meet standards, removing the franchise.

Learning Insight. *All firms need to develop a distinctive image, and they must guard against a negative one.*

A unique and distinctive image is highly important in a competitive environment. Distinction is not always easy to achieve, especially where many competitors have already adopted the more obvious possibilities. Burger Chef was unable to achieve any distinction. Distinction can come from a design or logo, a roof, or a building style; it can come from a menu, services, or the promotional approach; it can even be achieved by appealing to a different segment of the market.

The hardest task in achieving a distinctive image is with a commodity-type product, such as grain, beef, or chicken. Since such products can hardly be differentiated from competing brands, it is difficult to advertise a particular brand effectively. But it is possible. Consider the case of Perdue Chickens.

Frank Perdue produced and marketed chickens. He differentiated his product in two ways:

1. He fed his chickens special feed. Along with high-nutritional ingredients, he added some marigold flowers, giving the broiler a golden-yellow appearance instead of the usual pale flesh color.
2. He sold fresh rather than frozen birds. Consumers considered his chickens to be more flavorful and desirable than competitors' frozen birds. Eventually more than 600 vehicles left Perdue facilities each day to ensure fresh produce in all the markets served.

By 1980 Frank Perdue was spending $5,000,000 a year on advertising and appearing in his own commercials. Perdue chickens dominated the New York City market area, and, indeed, the Northeastern United States, accounting for 20 percent of total retail sales of almost $2 billion.

Worse, of course, than an unexciting image is a negative image, such as the one Nestle developed and which we will examine later in this book.

Learning Insight. *Imitation should not be disdained.*

A willingness to imitate may appear inconsistent with the need to develop a distinctive image, but it need not be so. McDonald's management and operational procedures were not unknown; indeed, they were highly publicized. It required no genius to recognize the merits of McDonald's operational procedures or to put these procedures into effect. But most of the other fast-food operations—such as Burger Chef, and even Burger King in its early years—either failed to imitate the successful strategy or did so only belatedly.

When a firm has developed a proven and successful format, why not imitate it? Creativity can be reserved for other aspects of the operation. A firm can still maintain its own distinctive image while basing its operations on successful management and control practices.

Learning Insight. *In diversifying, a firm should seek a strategic fit.*

Strategic fit refers to the mutually reinforcing effects that different business activities can have on the organization's overall effectiveness. Sometimes this idea is graphically referred to as "2 + 2 = 5"; that is, the sum of the benefits of the combined operations is more than if they had remained separate.

Several forms of fit can be recognized. *Product-market fit* is obtained when the different products can use the same distribution channels, sales promotion techniques, and can be sold to the same customers with the same sales force. *Operating fit* results from economies of purchasing, warehousing, overlapping of technology and engineering, production compatibility, and the like. *Management fit* occurs when existing management know-how and experience can be effectively transferred to the newly acquired activities. The common thread of strategic fit can provide a unifying focus and the company can build on joint managerial, financial, and technological strengths.

The popularity of conglomerate mergers, in the late 1960s, the early 1970s, and later in the 1980s, involving little or no fit or similarity, cast doubt on the necessity for fit. Some of these conglomerates have been successful: for example, International Telephone and Telegraph (ITT) products and subsidiary companies range from Sheraton Hotels, Wonder Bread, and Avis Rent-a-Car to finance companies, chemicals, lawn care, and even business schools.

But other conglomerates found that trying to manage many unrelated product markets and technologies brought severe problems, as with the General Foods and the Burger Chef operation. In some cases, such acquisitions resulted in "2 + 2 = 3" (for example, Mobil Oil and its Marcor [Montgomery Ward] acquisition). Many conglomerates, after the initial acquisition spree, have been forced to sell off some of their subsidiaries in order to get on the profit track again.

With the benefit of hindsight we can question the judgment of General Foods' decision to diversity into a fast-food franchised restaurant operation. While fast-food marketing at first appeared within General Foods' experience in food marketing, in retrospect it proved dissimilar and difficult for General Foods' executives to manage effectively.

We conclude that, although a common thread or strategic fit is not absolutely essential for all of a firm's business activities, it increases the probability of successful assimilation and synergy.

FOR THOUGHT AND DISCUSSION

1. Playing the devil's advocate (one who takes the opposing viewpoint for argument's sake), criticize the acquisition of Burger Chef by General Foods as thoroughly as you can.

2. Would you advocate changing the name of Burger Chef? Why or why not?

3. How do you account for the reluctance of competitors to imitate successful examples of other firms in their industry?

4. To date, McDonald's has shunned diversification into other related and unrelated food retailing operations. Discuss the desirability of such diversification efforts.

INVITATION TO ROLE PLAY

1. Assume the role of the General Foods' executive responsible for Burger Chef after the acquisition. Be as specific as you can in formulating a management strategy for the growth of this venture.

2. As a McDonald's executive, you are strongly in favor of significantly expanding the menu offerings. In particular, you have been very critical of the slow (four to five years) testing of the breakfast menu before its widespread adoption. Array as many arguments as you can for expanding the menu in specific ways. Be prepared to defend your position against other skeptical executives.

17

Contrasts in the Personal Computer Industry: Osborne and Apple

In this chapter we examine two of the most rapidly growing firms ever seen in the U.S. economy. The sales of one firm rose from $774,000 to $583 million in only six years; the sales of the other rocketed to $100 million in only 18 months. Fantastic success stories. But one firm could not maintain its level of success, and sales plummeted as fast as they had risen. The other firm maintained its growth and market position for almost a decade in an environment of rapid change before encountering problems that it stoutly set out to overcome.

What underlying factors accounted for such contrasts? And what transference do they have to other firms, perhaps in more sedate industries?

PART A   OSBORNE COMPUTER: THE ILLUSION OF SUCCESS UNLIMITED

Rarely does a new firm hit the jackpot—a meteoric rise surpassing the most optimistic expectations of founders and investors. In the heady excitement anything seems possible. It appears that the enterprise is invincible. Alas, sometimes such stars come tumbling back to earth, and reality. Perhaps there is no better example in modern business annals than the almost vertical rise and collapse of Osborne Computer Corporation. Founded in 1981, the business was booming at a $100 million clip—in barely 18 months. But on September 14, 1983, the company sought protection from creditors under Chapter 11 of the Bankruptcy Code.

ADAM OSBORNE

Adam Osborne was born in Thailand, the son of a British professor, and spent his earliest years in India. His parents were disciples of a maharishi, although he was educated in Catholic schools. Later he was sent to Britain for schooling, and in 1961 at the age of 22 he moved to the United States. He obtained a Ph.D. in chemical engineering at the University of Delaware and then worked for Shell Development Company in California.

Osborne and Shell soon parted company, the bureaucratic structure frustrating him. He became interested in computers, and in 1970 he set up his own computer consulting company. The market for personal computers began to mushroom in the mid-1970s, and he emerged a guru. He had a computer column, "From the Fountainhead," for *Interface Age*, and he began making speeches and building a reputation. He wrote a book, *Introduction to Microcomputers*, geared to the mass market. When it was turned down by a publisher, Osborne published it himself and sold 300,000 copies. By 1975 his publishing company had put out some 40 books on microcomputers, nearly a dozen of which he had written himself. In 1979 he sold his publishing company to McGraw-Hill, but agreed to stay as a consultant through May 1982.

Osborne was thus in a position to take full advantage of the growth of the microcomputer industry. But he also angered many in the industry by his stinging criticisms and bold assertions. In particular he spoke out sharply against the pricing strategies of the personal computer manufacturers, contending that they were ignoring the mass market by raising prices with every new feature added.

Osborne himself was the subject of some of the most colorful copy of the industry. Tall and energetic, he possessed a strong British accent to go along with his volubility, charm, and supreme confidence. He epitomized the new breed of entrepreneurs drawn to the epicenter of high-tech industry, the Silicon Valley in California.

Early in 1981, Osborne put his criticisms and assertions to the test. To a chorus of skeptics he announced plans to manufacture and market a new personal computer priced well below the competition. His first machines were ready for shipping by that July, and before long the skeptics were running for the hills. Osborne was showing that he was a doer, and not merely a talker.

THE OSBORNE STRATEGY

Osborne discerned a significant niche in the personal computer market. "I saw a truck-size hole in the industry, and I plugged it," he said.[1] He hired

---

[1] "Osborne: From Brags to Riches," *Business Week*, February 22, 1982, p. 86.

Lee Felsenstein, a former Berkeley radical, to design a powerful unit that weighed 24 pounds, could be placed in a briefcase, and was small enough to fit under an airline seat. It was the first portable *business* computer; the other portable computers were much less sophisticated. Portable computers are a subset of personal computers. As the name implies, they are lightweight and relatively easy to carry. Actually, there are three categories of portable computers recognized by the industry : (1) hand-held computers, (2) portable computers, which have a small screen, limited memory, and weight 10 to 20 pounds; and (3) transportable computers, which have bigger screens and memories, and weigh more than 20 pounds. Osborne Computer was in the third group.

Osborne priced his computer at $1795, hundreds of dollars less than most other business-oriented computers. He was able to sell for this price by running a low-overhead operation. For example, he hired Georgette Psaris, then 25, and made her vice president of sales and marketing, putting her office in a chilly former warehouse. He achieved economies of scale and capitalized on the declining prices of semiconductor parts. Assembled from standard industry components, the display screen was small, only five inches across, and there was no color graphics capability. Osborne himself admitted, "The Osborne had no technology of consequence. We made the purchasing decision convenient by bundling hardware and needed software in one price."[2]

To cut costs on software, Osborne, in a drastic departure from other personal computer makers, relied entirely on independent software companies to provide programs written in the popular programming language. To reduce software costs still further, Osborne gave some software suppliers equity in the company. As a result, Osborne provided almost $1500 worth of software packages as part of the $1795 system price.

Osborne had a flair for showmanship. One of his first triumphs was in the 1981 West Coast Computer Faire in San Francisco. In place of the rather ordinary booths and displays of the other computer makers, he took a substantial part of his venture capital to build a Plexiglass booth that towered toward the ceiling. The Osborne Company logo, the "Flying O," dominated the show.

He believed that mass distribution was a key to success. By 1982 he had signed an agreement with Computerland Corporation, the largest computer retailer. This extended Osborne's distribution by doubling in one swoop the number of retail stores carrying his computer. The Osborne 1 proved to be a hot item, with sales hitting $10 million by the end of 1981, the first year of

---

[2] Thayer C. Taylor, "Osborne Bytes the Distribution Bullet," *Sales & Marketing Management*, July 4, 1983, p. 34.

operation. By the end of 1982, after only 18 months of operation, annual sales soared to $100 million. There were predictions that "most of the Osborne management team would be millionaires by the time they're 40 or even 30."[3] At this point the bare-bones operating style was abandoned.

By 1983, some 750 retail outlets stocked the company's portables: the Computerland chain, Xerox's retail stores, Sears' business centers, and various department stores. Early in 1983, the company added 150 office-equipment dealers with experience in selling the most advanced copiers, enabling Osborne to reach small and medium-size businesses. While Osborne was not the originator of the portable computer, he was the first to sell such computers in mass quantities. He expanded the targeted market greatly, from key people in data processing departments to every office desk.

MARCHING INTO 1983

By early 1983, Osborne began to loosen his grip on the company, under pressure from his investors. The investors felt that the growing operation—it already had 800 employees—required professional management instead of Osborne and his early hirees. Osborne was an entrepreneur and not an administrator, and the two abilities are quite different. To protect its front-running position—estimated at an 80-90 percent market share—the company hired Robert Jaunich II, president of Consolidated Foods, to become president and chief executive officer. Adam Osborne moved up to chairman. Jaunich turned down offers at Apple and Atari because he felt these firms would not give him enough control. He also sacrificed a $1 million incentive to remain at Consolidated Foods. Obviously he felt strongly that the opportunities and potential of Osborne far surpassed his other options.

Jaunich moved quickly to decentralize the management structure. Georgette Psaris, vice president of marketing, became vice president of strategic planning. Joseph Roebuck, lured from Apple Computer where he was marketing director, replaced her. Fred Brown, the director of sales for Osborne, became vice president of sales, and David Lorenzen, a consultant for Osborne, became director of marketing services, with responsibility for dealer-support programs.

The distribution strategy, on which Adam Osborne prided himself as being one of the strengths of the venture, was refined. The company continued using computer-store outlets, but added alternative channels as well. A major addition was Harris Corporation's computer systems division to act as a national distributor for major firms. Harris was a $1.7 billion minicomputer firm with 70 salespeople and 1200 support personnel, including sys-

---

[3] Steve Fishman, "Facing Up to Failure," *Success*, November 26, 1984, p. 48.

tems analysts, in its computer systems division. To protect Osborne's smaller clients, Harris agreed to handle only large orders of 50 units or over.

Other sales targets were United Press International (UPI), the news service, to sell Osborne portables to its 1000 subscriber newspapers as personal workstations. Brown, the vice president of sales, began exploring other distribution possibilities, including independent sales organizations, airlines, and hotel chains.

As competitors started to enter the portable market, offering cheaper and fancier machines than the Osborne 1, the firm readied itself to broaden its product line. It prepared an even cheaper version of the Osborne 1, the Vixen. It unveiled an Executive 1 in the spring of 1983, with an Executive 2 planned for late summer. These models offered more storage capacity and larger screens than Osborne 1. The Executive 1 was able to serve as a terminal to communicate with a mainframe, thereby enabling users to work with larger data bases and handle more complicated jobs. The Executive 1 had a $2495 price tag that included $2000 worth of software, covering word and data processing. The Executive 2, at $3195, was promoted as compatible with IBM's hot-selling personal computer, the IBM PC.

In 1982, Osborne spent $3.5 million on advertising, including $1.5 million in consumer magazines, $500,000 on spot TV, and $1.5 million in business publications. Plans were made to continue heavy advertising in order to reinforce the product differentiation. The sales force was expanded to keep pace with the growing firm. An 8-person sales force was to be supplemented by an additional 30 to 40 people, thereby permitting more specialized selling. Instead of being generalists selling to all types of customers, sales were organized by specialists concentrating either on retail or nonretail accounts. Brown explained this rationale:

> Retailers . . . need help on such things as point-of-sale displays to stimulate the guy who comes in off the street. Dealers call on purchasing and data-processing departments and need advice on direct mail campaigns.[4]

The sky seemed the limit. Osborne predicted revenues of $300 million for 1983. And when he made one of his frequent trips abroad, he was received by ambassadors and prime ministers, most of whom wanted stock in his company. He was the head of one of the fastest-growing companies Silicon Valley had ever seen—growing even faster than Apple.

---

[4] Taylor, "Osborne Bytes . . . ," p. 36.

Premonition

The first premonition of trouble came to Adam Osborne on April 26, 1983. He was giving a seminar in Colorado when he received a call. "Over the weekend considerable losses were discovered," he was told. "That's not possible," he is reported to have said.[5] But in the few days Adam was away from the office, the bad news built.

The news that earlier profit figures were in error came at a particularly bad time. On April 29 a public stock offering, designed to raise about $50 million, was planned that would have made the top executives of Osborne rich. Adam Osborne had to wonder how news of losses instead of profits would affect the stock offering.

In the first two months of the fourth fiscal quarter (the fiscal year ended February 1983), pretax profits were reported that were $300,000 ahead of company projections. In February the company racked up an all-time high in shipments, and with supposed high profit margins. Projections for February profits were in the neighborhood of $750,000, and the future seemed euphoric. But it was all an illusion.

By late March the results for February showed, instead of the projected profit, a loss of more than $600,000, reflecting charges against new facilities and heavy promotional spending. For the entire fiscal year there was a loss of $1.5 million, despite revenues slightly more than $100 million.

The worst was yet to come. On April 21, Jaunich learned that the company would have a $1.5 million loss for the February quarter, and a $4 million loss for the full year, brought about chiefly by excessive inventories of old stock, liabilities in software contracts, and the need for greater bad debt and warranty reserves. Although Jaunich planned to move ahead with the stock offering, the attractiveness of stock in the company was rapidly diminishing. But worse news was to come. On April 24, new projections showed that losses would be $5 million for the quarter and $8 million for the year, thanks to further unrecorded liabilities and more inventory problems.

That same day Jaunich decided to scrap the offering, despite heavy pressure to find another underwriter to bring the stock to market. Every report made the situation appear blacker. The final report for the year showed a loss of more than $12 million. Heavy losses continued over the next months, as further adjustments in inventories and reserves became necessary. Adam Osborne's house of cards was collapsing.

Osborne had had no trouble attracting seed money from venture capitalists before; indeed, venture capital firms were clamoring to participate. But when the company's earnings came to light, the funding dried up. A few investors still had hopes, and Osborne found another $11 million in June.

[5] Fishman, op. cit., p. 51.

But the firm could not find an additional $20 million which the company considered necessary to speed a needed competitive product from drawing board to market.

Black Friday. Osborne resorted to sporadic employee layoffs beginning in the late spring as the company desperately tried to improve its cash flow. But the climax came on Friday, September 16. On the previous Tuesday the company had filed for protection from creditor lawsuits under Chapter 11 of the federal Bankruptcy Code. The company did so after three creditors filed two lawsuits saying Osborne owed them $4.7 million. Osborne's petition stated that it owed secured and unsecured creditors about $45 million whereas its assets were $40 million.

Osborne's employees expected the worst when a meeting was abruptly called in the company cafeteria. They soberly listened as top management announced that more than 300, about 80 percent of the remaining company staff, were to be immediately "furloughed." Final paychecks were issued, and workers were given two hours to empty their desks and vacate the company offices.

News of the company's Chapter 11 filing and near shutdown shocked the industry, although Osborne's recently sagging sales and consequent need for cash were well known. The company made strenuous efforts to raise money, especially after the July shipments turned soft. But venture capitalists fled from the industry shakeout; the market was not able to support 150-plus microcomputer companies.

POSTMORTEM

Internal Factors

Adam Osborne was an entrepreneur, not a professional manager. Perhaps this accounted for most of the problems that befell his company. Often, it seems, the entrepreneurial personality is incompatible with the manager-type person who must deal with the nitty-gritty details and day-to-day controls over operations. Osborne had never managed more than 50 people, but the organization had grown to almost 20 times that size. He operated with a "fire-fighting" perspective, with no advance planning. "I had no professional training whatsoever in finance or business management," Osborne admitted.[6]

The board of directors of Osborne and the venture capitalists who contributed to the fledgling enterprise brought about sufficient pressure that

---

[6] Jaye Scholl, *Barron's*, July 26, 1984, p. 26.

Adam Osborne stepped aside and turned over the operating responsibilities to a professional manager, Robert Jaunich, early in 1983. But apparently the switch was too late to rectify the damage already done. Perhaps six months earlier . . . ?

Some of the mistakes can be explained by the heady excitement that accompanied the geometrically rising sales. Other mistakes can be credited to simple miscalculations—of which any firm can be guilty—about the impact of competitors of all kinds, and particularly the rapidity with which the awesome IBM could enter the market and dominate it.

Lack of controls was the most obvious failing of the company. Managers did not know how much inventory they had. They did not know how much they were spending, or needed to spend. Ironically, information management was sorely lacking in a company whose product was primarily geared to aiding information management. Other examples of incompetence were unrecorded liabilities, such as bills never handed over to the accounting department; inadequate reserves established for the shutdown of a New Jersey plant that was producing computers with a 40 percent failure rate; and insufficient funds set aside to pay for a new European headquarters on Lake Geneva in Switzerland.

Lack of controls permitted expenses to run rampant. "Everybody was trying to buy anything they wanted," said one former Osborne employee.[7] When Jaunich finally took over the managerial reins, he clamped down hard on expenses, but it was too late.

By spring of 1983, miscalculations had reduced cash flow to a trickle. Osborne made the mistake of announcing the new computer, the Executive, too soon. Upon learning of the new machine in April, many canceled their orders for the Osborne 1, resulting in heavy inventory write-offs. Compounding the problems, the Executive was delayed and not ready for initial shipments until May. April was a month with practically no sales.

Other companies, notably Kaypro and Compaq, entered the market with low-priced computers and at least as much bundled software. But the biggest impact was from IBM. Its personal computer, introduced in late 1981, quickly became the industry standard against which other competitors were judged. Osborne was slow in reacting and adopting IBM's state of the art technology and equally slow in developing a model compatible with the IBM personal computer at home or in the office. While Osborne waited, scores of other computer companies jumped to produce IBM-compatible computers. Hardly a year after coming to market the formerly popular Osborne computer with its tiny screen was obsolete.

---

[7] Eric Larson and Ken Wells, "Shaken Osborne Computer Seeking Suitor in the Face of Possible Failure," *Wall Street Journal*, September 12, 1983, p. 35.

Another new product was obsolete before it was introduced—the Vixen, originally scheduled for introduction in December 1982. It was 10 pounds lighter and cheaper than the Osborne 1. A poorly designed circuit board caused production delays, and the project was finally scrapped as company resources were redirected to an IBM-compatible unit with a larger screen. It was difficult to cope with production delays and the speed with which IBM took over the personal computer market.

External Factors

The environment for personal computer makers was becoming unhealthy by 1983. A major shakeout for the more than 150 small manufacturers in this industry was inevitable. A factor behind the proliferation of firms was a tidal wave of venture capital. Early winners such as Apple Computer dazzled investors and led to the perception of a "can't lose" industry. It was almost too easy to start a new computer company. "As a result, a whole series of 'me too' companies started. They are developing products that do not have a unique feature or competitive advantage. They don't stand a chance," one venture capitalist said.[8]

While demand by businesses and consumers for small computers was increasing, so was cutthroat competition. Price-cutting and shrinking profit margins were inevitable. Dealers' shelves could hardly accommodate more than a few brands.

The first presentiment of worsening problems for the industry came early in 1983 when three big manufacturers of low-priced home computers—Atari, Texas Instruments, and Mattel—reported first-half losses totaling more than half a billion dollars. Makers of higher-priced computers tried to dissociate themselves from this low-end calamitous environment. But other well-known companies such as Victor Technologies, Fortune Systems, and Vector Graphics all reported shocking losses for the second quarter. Even Apple Computer saw its stock price sink nearly 34 points between June and September 1983.

Texas Instruments' 99/4A home computer, which sold for $525 when introduced in 1981, retailed for $100 by early 1983. Yet, each 99/4A cost about $80 in parts and labor not including TI's overhead expenses, dealer profits, and marketing costs.

Other computer makers were desperately struggling to revamp their production and marketing efforts. For example, Vector Graphic, after losing $1.7 million in the second quarter of 1983, obtained a new $7 million line of credit to help tailor its computers to such specialty markets as agriculture.

---

[8] "Trouble in Computer Land," *Newsweek*, September 26, 1983, p. 73.

UPDATE

Under Chapter 11 of the federal Bankruptcy Act, a company continues to operate, but has court protection against creditors' lawsuits while working out a plan for paying its debts. By the end of 1984 Osborne was emerging from bankruptcy with most of its debts paid and two new machines to sell. Its retail network had shrunk from 800 dealers to about 50. Suppliers now demanded cash on delivery. And the firm was anathema to venture capitalists who lost $31 million when the company collapsed. Gone are the factories, the 1000-worker payroll, and the swank executive offices. But the lean, trimmed-down company had $10 to $30 million worth of tax credits to offset future income taxes. Its name and still-extant dealer network in Europe was a plus. Perhaps the biggest challenge it now faced was redeveloping its retail network. "Competition for shelf space is hot even for companies with no strikes against them. Retailers were left with a bad taste when the company went Chapter 11," noted an executive of a 40-store chain. The new president was Ronald J. Brown, the former vice president of international operations who engineered the company's restructuring.

Adam Osborne left the company to try his entrepreneurial talents in the marketing of software, as well as organizing a defense against investor lawsuits. He wrote a book (publishing it himself) called *Hypergrowth: The Rise and Fall of the Osborne Computer Corporation* (with John Dvorak), soundly criticizing Robert Jaunich. Georgette Psaris, Osborne's former vice president, noted: "I've gone from being a multimillionaire to being in the hole,"[9] but she joined Adam Osborne in his new entrepreneurial endeavor.

PART B   APPLE COMPUTER: CONTROLLED GROWTH OF INNOVATIVE TECHNOLOGY

Apple Computer . . . Steven P. Jobs . . . 28, Single . . . College dropout . . . saw potential in fellow computer freak's home-built personal computer. With partner started production in 1976 in family garage on $1300 from sale of calculator and VW minibus. Went public in 1980. . . . Has 7.5 million Apple shares worth $225 million.[10]

In perhaps the greatest success story of the last half-century, this young man, who was 21 when he turned entrepreneur, became a multimillionaire and one of the richest individuals in America in just a few years. Jobs is the

---

[9] Ibid., p. 74.
[10] "The Richest People in America—The *Forbes* Four Hundred," *Forbes*, Fall, 1982, p. 110.

youngest of all those who accumulated their great wealth without inheritance.

INDUSTRY BACKGROUND

In the early 1970s it became obvious that survival in the computer industry requires a large market share and broad customer base. Computers ranged from small units to the very large mainframes affordable only by well-heeled firms. The industry was dominated by one company, IBM, with 70 percent of the market. All the other firms in the industry were scrambling for small shares. IBM seemed to have an unassailable advantage because it had the resources for the greatest marketing and research and development expenditures in the industry. A firm with a masterful lead in a rapidly growing industry has an increasing command over resources in comparison with its competitors who must be content to chip away at the periphery of the market.

The computer industry had experienced rapid technological change since the early 1960s. By the early 1970s, however, the new technology involved peripheral accessories rather than major changes in main units.

Before the advent of microelectronics technology, which made smaller parts possible, computers were costly and complicated. It was not economically feasible for one person to interact with one computer. The processing power existed in a central data processing installation, and for those who could not afford to have their own computer, time-sharing services were available.

The "small" or minicomputer industry began in 1974 when a few small firms used memory chips to produce small computer systems as do-it-yourself kits for as low as $400. These proved popular and other companies built microcomputers designed for the affluent hobbyist and small-business person. In 1975 microcomputer and small-business computer shipments went over the $1 billion mark. The mainframe market was maturing and the microcomputer industry was beginning its rocketing ascendancy.

In 1975, the first personal computer reached the market. Personal computers are easy-to-use desktop machines based on microprocessors, have their own power supply, and are priced below $10,000. By using various software packages, these computers can serve the needs of businesses and a variety of professionals such as accountants, financial analysts, scientists, and educators, as well as the sophisticated individual at home. The big three minicomputer makers in 1977 were Data General, Digital Equipment, and Hewlett-Packard. It should be noted that the minicomputer grew up without IBM, the company that dominated mainframe computers and accounted for two-thirds of all computer revenues in 1976.

THE MARKET FOR SMALL COMPUTERS

By 1977 there were three identifiable segments within the microcomputer market: (1) hobbyists, (2) home users, and (3) professional and small-business users. Table 17.1 shows an industry analysis of this market in 1977. The greatest number of customers was in the hobby segment. A complete hobby system could involve a $2000 investment or more. The systems were sold by mail order and through approximately 300 retail stores.

Table 17.1   Estimates of the Market for Personal Computers, 1977

		Potential Market	
Segment	Units	Percent Share	Price Range
Hobby	40,000	57.1	$1,000 to $ 5,000
Home	20,000	28.6	$ 500 to $ 1,000
Professional/business	10,000	14.3	$5,000 to $20,000
Total	70,000	100.0	

Source: "Home Computer Sales Ready to Take off," *Industry Week,* Nov. 7, 1977, p. 98. Reprinted by permission of *Industry Week,* copyright © Penton/IPC, Inc., Cleveland, Ohio.

The home segment was comprised mainly of those interested in video games. During 1977 Commodore introduced the Commodore PET, priced at $495, especially for this market. National Semiconductor and Tandy's Radio Shack also targeted products to this consumer, with distribution through computer stores, consumer electronic shops, and department stores.

Available for the professional and small-business segment were the IBM 5100, Wang 2200, Hewlett-Packard 9830 series, and the Datapoint 2200, with prices ranging from $5000 to $20,000. At that time, there was nothing lower priced that could provide the needed level of reliability. Lack of software and an inadequate network of field service offices were problems for this market segment. Because of these deficiencies, most of this segment relied on time-sharing.

In summary, in 1977 as Jobs and his Apple were making the initial market entry, the hobby market was mature, with little growth. The consumer market seemed ripe for growth but lacked computer equipment simple enough for home use to achieve mass penetration. For the professional and business sector, the potential was real, but two obstacles existed: (1) product capabilities and prices were not attractive enough for this market, and (2) service, support, and efficient distribution were also lacking. Computers were needed that were more user-oriented and lower priced.

STEVEN JOBS

Few multimillionaires were more unpromising in their youth than Steven Jobs. He was a loner in school, and his family had to move once because the boy refused to go back to his junior high school. At Homestead High School in Los Altos, California, Jobs became enchanted with technology. He often went to Hewlett-Packard lectures after school. One day he boldy called the president, William Hewlett, to ask for some equipment for a machine he was building. Hewlett was impressed, gave him the equipment, and helped arrange summer employment. While at Homestead High School, Jobs became acquainted with Stephen Wozniak, also profoundly interested in technology.

After graduating from high school, Jobs went to Reed College in Oregon, but dropped out before the first semester was over. He decided college was not for him, and he experimented for a year with fruitarianism and Hare Krishna. Next he took a job at Atari, a small electronics firm only two years old. Steve soon left Atari. With the money he had saved, he took a trip to India and spent the rest of 1974 trying to decide what to do with his life.

Meanwhile, Wozniak went to the University of Colorado and DeAnza College in Cupertino. After a year of designing software, he enrolled at the University of California at Berkeley. He dropped out in 1975 to become an engineering designer at Hewlett-Packard. In his free time he worked at building a small computer, something that had fascinated him from his childhood when his father taught him to design logic circuits.

Jobs often visited Wozniak where he was building small computers and circuits to show other computer buffs. At one such visit Jobs envisioned the potential that Wozniak devices might have in the marketplace, and the germ of the idea was born that was to make the two college dropouts multimillionaires.

THE BEGINNING

In March 1976 Jobs and Wozniak formed a partnership and by June were selling pint-size circuit boards. They pestered electronics suppliers for credit; they even tried to get backing from Atari and Hewlett-Packard but were unsuccessful. The two young men finally raised $1300 by selling Jobs's Volkswagen bus and Wozniak's Hewlett-Packard hand-held calculator. They purchased $10,000 in parts on credit and soon found that orders for their circuit boards outnumbered their ability to manufacture them. By that summer they were well into the design of an advanced version, which they called the Apple II, a personal computer. By the end of 1976, sales were $200,000 with a 20 percent net income—all this from a $1300 investment.

In late 1976 and early 1977, Jobs and Wozniak made some major moves.

They placed a technical article in a leading trade journal that gave them considerable visibility. They established a distribution agreement with several computer retailers. They persuaded an attorney to provide legal services in a pay-later plan. But they still needed vastly more capital if they were to tap what seemed to them an almost unlimited potential, and they badly needed marketing expertise.

Jobs called a major semiconductor company in the area to find out who did their advertising. The agency, Regis, McKenna, at first refused to consider Apple as a client because of their insistence on a pay-later plan. But Jobs continued to pester Regis, and the ad agency finally agreed to the proposition and remained the Apple agency until 1986.

Jobs and Wozniak found the answer to their financial and marketing needs in A. C. Markkula, marketing manager of Intel Corporation, a leading semiconductor manufacturer. He was made an equal partner in return for his services and a $250,000 personal investment. (Markkula is now also one of the *Forbes's* Four Hundred Richest People in America.)

Markkula helped arrange a credit line with Bank of America. The firm, beginning to look impressive at this stage, attracted the attention of strong financial venture capitalists. Two such financial backers were Venrock Associates (the Rockefeller family) and Arthur Rock. Apple now had over $3 million, enough to begin major production.

THE CHARGE OF APPLE

In March 1977 Apple incorporated and moved out of a garage into a plant. The Apple II was introduced at a trade show in April and was an instant success. It was the first fully programmable personal computer. It was designed to function as a home system and was simple enough for a beginner but easily adaptable to the expert programmer. The name "Apple" was chosen because it was believed that computers intimidated the lay user, but "Apple" conveyed a friendly and ordinary image that could be targeted to the home user.

The total marketing budget for 1977 was $162,419, close to the total sales of the previous year. Sales for 1977 surged to $774,000, but the amazing growth caused corporate structural problems. The company leadership needed to be formalized, with a president and chairman. Jobs and Wozniak balked at the day-to-day operating responsibilities. They nominated Markkula as chairman and brought in Michael Scott, president of National Semiconductor, to be president. Scott saw the growth potential of Apple and took a 50 percent pay cut to come on board. Jobs became vice chairman, and Wozniak vice president of research and development. The firm remained privately held and primarily employee-owned until December 12, 1980, when it made a $96.8 million public offering. The stock was snapped up and rose quickly in market value. Three years after the founding, Jobs and his colleagues were multimillionaires.

Growth burgeoned again in 1978 as the Apple II found wide acceptance among small businesses and professionals. The international market opened up as IT&T agreed to handle overseas sales of Apple computers. Sales for 1978 were almost 8 million.

By 1979 Apple and its major competitor, Tandy, dominated the market for personal computers. Apple had 500 retailers selling its computers in the United States, whereas Tandy with its Radio Shacks had 8000 outlets. Because of its retail network, Tandy led the personal computer industry, but Apple was second and closing fast. Many other computer makers were gearing up to invade the personal computer market, with rumors that mighty IBM might soon put in an appearance, too. Atari, a company gaining success in the video arcade market, was ready to invade, and Texas Instruments entered the market early in the year. By the end of 1979, approximately 30 companies were making personal computers.

In 1979 Apple added 100,000 square feet of manufacturing capacity to its 22,000 square feet in order to keep pace with the growing market potential and not lose market share to eager competitors. Apple sales in 1979 rose to almost 48 million, a sixfold increase over the previous year. Apple was now marketing through five independent distributors who in turn sold to dealers and other customers.

In 1980 the Apple II was still selling well at $1435 for the basic model. This same year the company introduced the more expensive and heralded Apple III. The new computer was targeted to the small business and professional market and not meant for the home, but this Apple was plagued with one technical flaw after another. Overheating problems in the main circuit board resulted in a lab overhaul, leaving 850 U.S. dealers empty-handed because of the unavailability of the Apple III. Fortunately, many customers turned to the II. The company was forced to recall the 1400 units it had sold to be reengineered. It was not brought to market again until November 1981. If the Apple II had not been held in such high esteem, the Apple III debacle could have jeopardized the entire company.

In March, Apple set up its own network of four regional replenishment centers. It now controlled its entire channel of distribution except the 800 retail outlets. The market budget for 1980 reached $12.1 million. Some 135,000 Apple IIs were sold, with total year sales reaching $117 million and a 12 million net profit.

The Apple III fiasco resulted in some changes in 1981. The product manager of the Apple III and president Scott resigned, and 40 employees were dismissed. The Apple III, redesigned and vigorously tested, was reintroduced with some sales success.

In the fall, IBM came into the market. Apple, now ahead of Tandy in the race for market share, became IBM's target. To increase customer and dealer service, Apple opened three more distribution centers. The Apple II was upgraded and named the Apple II plus. About 15,000 units per month were sold through 1981. Total sales in 1981 were $334.7 million, again a phenomenal increase.

Sales in 1982 again increased spectacularly. Net sales rose 74 percent to $583.1 million, and earnings increased by 56 percent. Although more than 100 manufacturers had entered the personal computer market, Apple pulled ahead with a 24 percent market share. The company strengthened its retail distribution network, increased its research and development expenditures, and spent more for marketing. It added two service centers to bring the worldwide total to 12.

The entry of IBM, however, cast shadows over the optimism of Apple. *Forbes* analyzed the situation in the following terms:

> Apple's essential problem is that it could find itself squeezed from below by Atari, Commodore, and Tandy, and from above by the big battalions of IBM, Xerox, H-P, and others.[11]

In 1983 Apple unveiled its new computer. "Lisa," a $10,000 unit that Apple hoped would attract the corporate market. Late in 1983 the Macintosh was introduced, aimed at the home and professional markets. While the aggressive efforts of IBM blunted the impact of these new products, nevertheless, in the 1977 through 1982 period, Apple achieved an extraordinary success story (see Figure 17.1).

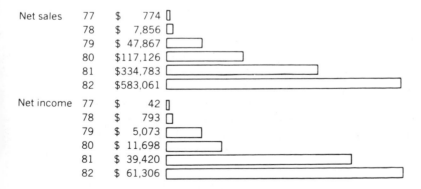

Figure 17.1 Sales and income, Apple Computer, 1977–1982 (in thousands of dollars). (*Source:* Company annual reports.)

[11] Kathleen K. Wiegner, "Tomorrow Has Arrived," *Forbes*, February 15, 1982, p. 119.

INGREDIENTS OF SUCCESS

Environmental

The success of Apple might be attributed to having the right idea at the right time. But this is far too simplistic. It took no genius to recognize that there was a latent demand for a simple personal computer. But it took a young computer buff, Wozniak, to design the computer and an entrepreneurial whiz to maneuver the idea and the early prototypes into a half-a-billion-dollar company, wedging in through entrenched, well-heeled, experienced, and aggressive competitors.

The following conditions created a favorable environment for introduction of the personal computer:

- Interest in computers was growing among business people and the general public, while the need to improve business productivity through better information flow and analyses was becoming more apparent.
- Simple equipment offering reliability was not available.
- Lack of programming knowledge was a big deterrent for many potential users. People wanted a product that would let them program without being computer experts.
- Microcomputers were available in the market in the form of kits, so the technology and interest was emerging.
- Software was lagging behind the hardware, and manufacturers such as Commodore and Heath were entering the market unaware of this gap. The situation was aggravated by an incompatibility of language support.

Strategy Coups

Apple responding to almost all the environmental needs of the market with its Apple II. For the first time the end user had access to a low-priced small computer that was easy to use but with the technical capabilities of a more expensive minicomputer. Software was no longer an obstacle because the company made available to consumers its own programs; and a number of enterprising firms began supplying software packages designed specifically to work with Apple systems. The product was given a friendly, nonthreatening name and logo. It was compact, light and trim, and easily portable. The case for the keyboard and video display was light plastic instead of metal. The video display was smaller than a television but large enough to provide good resolution and clear print. The whole product was light-colored and attractive, rather than the austere and formidable black and silver colors of such brands as Tandy. The instruction manual made it easy to understand the system and the software. The instructions were an early key to success because they added to the ease of operation the "user-friendliness." All these features reinforced the perception that the computer was easy to use: a friendly computer with a high-quality image at an affordable price.

The company decided to manufacture the Apple with the highest quality control standards possible. A reputation for high quality quickly followed, and Apple was able to command a price premium and maintain its market lead over a host of scrambling competitors.

Apple detected the need to shift the target market for its personal computers away from the general public and home use to which most personal computer firms were catering. Consumers were disillusioned with a lack of suitable software, a fear of machines, and a growing recognition that they did not need such sophisticated machines. Instead, Apple saw professionals and small businesses as the main market. Accordingly, it shifted gears and emphasized software, encouraging independent software developers as well as its own developers to design software products for a vast array of potential users.

Apple's pricing policies also aided its entry into the personal computing-for-profit market. For example, while Tandy offered a 4000-character memory system for $499, Apple offered the II with 16,000-character memory for $1195 or 48,000-character memory for $1495. These products, much more suited to the computing needs of the small business firm, especially in view of the wide array of software now becoming available, were still attractively priced.

Apple's distribution channels and strategies also proved appropriate for the professional and business market. Apple created strong ties to 750 to 800 independent retail outlets, such as Computerland, Inc. It provided toll-free software hotlines for users, a monthly newsletter, and a magazine that focused on different applications in each issue. A cooperative advertising program reimbursed dealers for 3 percent of their dollar purchases. By using these marketing efforts directed primarily to dealers, Apple overturned a key computer industry marketing law established by IBM: that selling computers requires armies of direct sales people schooled in hand-holding of the end user.

Apple kept its margins high and direct sales costs low by using this method of distribution. By 1981 it eliminated the intermediaries by selling directly to retailers through its own regional support centers. The objectives were better inventory control and better access to end users. The company gave direct training to dealers through sales seminars entitled "Apple Means Business." Apple provided dealers with structured presentations that they could use to educate end users. It also equipped dealers to handle same-day walk-in repairs and free replacement of equipment if needed.

Apple's promotional efforts reinforced the other strong ingredients of the strategy. User friendliness was continually stressed. The name Apple fostered wide recognition of the company and product. Heavy emphasis was placed on television. A recognizable and authoritative spokesman, Dick Cavett, helped make millions of people aware of Apple, long before any competitor attempted to achieve such public awareness. In unaided tests in 1981, 79 percent of consumers, asked to name "a company that makes personal computers," named Apple. Since professionals are among the general public, this high awareness proved effective in tapping this market.

Handling Great Growth

The ability of Jobs and the organization he created to handle the phenomenal growth—from $200,000 in 1976 to $583 million in sales in 1982—is one of the most remarkable growth episodes of U.S. business. This growth is the more remarkable since it was accomplished without loss of control of the company or serious dilution of ownership. Table 17.2 compares the six key growth years of Apple with those of K mart and McDonald's during their most rapid growth. Apple's growth rate far surpassed the others, despite their being outstanding successes and the dominant influences in their industries. Of course, a small firm can much more easily double and triple its sales from year to year than larger firms with a much greater base. But McDonald's, even in its embryonic years, did not come close to matching the growth of Apple.

Apple did, of course, have some problems in handling its growth. Management of creative employees is an important and often difficult task because such people tend to be nonconformists. Jobs attempted to encourage a creative, risk-taking spirit, one in which high motivation and embracing of challenges prevailed. He used techniques that deviated from orthodox management thinking with its insistence on formal lines of authority and well-designated policies. But infighting and power struggles caused the departures of several key people, most notably Stephen Wozniak, co-founder of Apple, and Michael Scott, the former president. Apple was described as disorganized and incompetent in its management.

The problems with Apple III, which could have scuttled the company, were perhaps caused by the loose management controls and bickering, or may simply have reflected the strains of great growth amid fantastic market potential and the eagerness to tap the potential before competitors.

Not the least of the success factors for Apple was its handling of adversity. The significant failure of the Apple III was dealt with as well as was possible. The danger with any highly heralded product that fails because of quality problems is the potential damage to the rest of the product line. Such

Table 17.2 Comparisons of Growth in Sales for Kresge (K mart), McDonald's, and Apple during the Six Greatest Growth Years

Year	Sales (in Millions of Dollars)	Percent Change from Previous Year
	Kresge	
1965	851.4	25
1966	1090.2	28
1967	1385.7	27
1968	1731.5	25
1979	2185.3	26
1980	2558.7	17
	Apple	
1977	0.8	286
1978	7.9	915
1979	47.1	510
1980	117.1	145
1981	334.8	186
1982	583.1	74
	McDonald's	
1965	35.4	37
1966	42.7	21
1967	53.7	26
1968	97.8	82
1969	143.3	47
1970	200.3	40

Source: Company records.

danger is especially acute for the new firm with little tradition of quality to sustain it.

But Apple handled this quality dilemma very well. As soon as the magnitude of the problems with Apple III surfaced, it withdrew the product, despite extensive preintroductory promotional efforts. The product was not reintroduced until many months later when the problems were corrected. A potential catastrophe was averted.

UPDATE—ANOTHER SWINGING PENDULUM

Apple, as had Nike, encountered trouble maintaining its pattern of success. By 1985 and 1986 problems at the core of Apple were evident. One involved a major personality conflict, others showed up in operating statistics.

In mid-1983, John Sculley came to Apple as president, leaving the presidency of the Pepsi Cola subsidiary of PepsiCo, Inc., and passing up a chance to become chairman of the $7.5 billion conglomerate. He was intrigued by the challenge and opportunity of personal computers, and he was impressed with the charismatic Steven Jobs.

Sculley soon felt the reluctance of chairman Jobs to let him run the company. In the spring of 1985, Apple faltered, incurring its first quarterly loss ever. In addition, the MacIntosh Division with which Jobs was most directly involved experienced chronic developmental delays. At this point, Sculley persuaded Apple's directors to remove Jobs from operating responsibilities and turn these completely over to him.

Relegated largely to a titular role as chairman, Jobs informed Apple's board on September 12, 1985, that he was starting a new company that would work closely with universities in developing a computer system to fill their research needs, and that five key Apple people would join him. The board was outraged and demanded Jobs' resignation. Amid a highly publicized legal confrontation, there were allegations that Jobs had abrogated his fiduciary responsibilities as chairman and had taken trade secrets with him.

In terms of sales and profit performance, sales were $1.9 billion in 1985, up 51 percent from the year before, while profits were $69.7 million, an 86 percent improvement over a rather poor year. But there were some ominous portents. Market share, expressed as a percentage of worldwide sales of computers costing $1000 to $10,000, slipped from almost 19 percent to less than 11 percent in only two years. The nine-year-old Apple II contributed 65 percent of Apple's revenues and most of its profits, and this in an industry priding itself on rapid technological advances. The Lisa, designed to tap the business segment of the market, failed along with the Apple III. The MacIntosh, the company's hope for the future, sold at only one-fourth the level of company expectations. And Apple's stock price, which had been as high as 63 in 1983, managed only to climb into the 30s from a low of 14 during the great stock market rally. President Sculley predicted 1986 sales would only match those of 1985, although he did expect that severe cost-cutting would boost profits. He pledged to make Apple products compatible with IBM personal computers, which had come to dominate the business market.

While the company remained a major factor in the personal computer industry, it still needed to regain a solid position in the business market, the fastest-growing area for personal computers. Without this, Apple would have to content itself with the slower-growing education and home markets, and perhaps never become a major computer company. In an attempt to recapture some of its lost momentum, Apple budgeted $50 million for advertising in 1986 and changed the advertising agency to BBDO. The company announced that it expected to introduce more new products over the coming year than it had in the previous 10 years. By 1990, sales were $5.3 billion and profits were $454 million, and Apple was the largest supplier of personal computers in the United States.

APPLE AND OSBORNE, THE GREAT CONTRASTS: WHAT CAN BE LEARNED?

We have examined two rapidly growing entrepreneurial endeavors—one which made venture capitalists and other investors ecstatic, and the other which graphically illustrated the risks inherent in new enterprises.

Learning Insight. *Venture capital is usually available for the "right kind" of concepts.*

Perhaps the first thing we can learn from these two cases is that venture capital is available for the idea that can be persuasively presented to well-heeled investors. Apple could have achieved only limited success without the investment of outsiders convinced that it stood on the threshold of opportunity. And the success of Apple made additional venture capital available for other new high-tech enterprises, such as Osborne.

For any small business an aggressive and attractive concept helps in winning seed money. Many venture capitalists look more at the person than the idea: "Nearly every mistake I've made has been because I picked the wrong people, not the wrong idea," says Arthur Rock, a renowned venture capitalist.[12] Venture capital exists; some $1 billion a year is flooding into venture capital for innovative entrepreneurs from pension funds, corporations, and wealthy individuals.

Let us also consider several insights that affirm ones discussed earlier in this book. That they are again relevant confirms their significance.

Learning Insight. *The financial rewards of entrepreneurship can be great indeed.*

In Chapter 4 we noted the rewards coming to the founders of Nike, and how in less than a decade both Phil Knight and his old mentor, Coach Bill Bowerman, became multimillionaires. Apple provides an even more notable example of the quick attainment of great wealth, this time in less than five years. The trigger to such wealth lies in taking a private enterprise public. To do this successfully, the business must have an attractive concept, an idea that seems innovative in a perceived growth area, as Apple did; or the enterprise must be seen as having an attractive similarity to another suc-

---

[12] John Merwin, "Have You Got What It Takes?" *Forbes*, August 3, 1981, pp. 60–61.

cessful newcomer, as Osborne appeared to have. After a brief period of burgeoning sales, such an enterprise when taken public can command strong investor interest and a high offering price.

Learning Insight. *Embrace growth opportunity, but beware of uncontrolled growth.*

Apple proved that great growth is possible, that it can be managed without losing control, even if the organization and human relations may be a bit flaky during some of the wildly escalating years. It shows that we "need to run with the ball" when we get that rare opportunity. But there are times when caution is required. We saw another firm, Korvette, that was unable to cope with the demands of increasing size, even though its growth rate was far less than Apple's. And we know that Osborne could not cope with its heady growth.

Risks lie on all sides as we reach for these opportunities. When a market begins to boom and a firm is unable to keep up with demand without greatly increasing capacity and resources, it faces a dilemma: stay conservative in the expectation that the burgeoning potential will be short lived, and thereby abdicate some of the growing market to competitors, or expand vigorously and take full advantage of the opportunity. If the euphoria is short lived, and demand stops exponential increases, or even tapers off, the firm is left with expanded capacity, more resource commitment than is needed, high interest and carrying costs, and perhaps even a jeopardized viability because of overextension. This is the dilemma that firms such as Apple and Osborne, Nike and Adidas, and K mart and Woolworth faced, and there is no firm answer or solution to it. Decision making in the chaotic times of technological breakthroughs and environmental changes is risky, challenging, and tremendously exciting.

Regardless of the commitment to a vision of great growth, a firm must build in organizational, accounting, and financial standards and controls, or find itself on treacherous footing. Inexperienced entrepreneurs tend to fall into the quicksand of expanding operations faster than they can build up the organization and controls necessary for larger enterprises. As a result, costs get out of hand, inventory buildup becomes an albatross, customer accounts may imprudently be allowed to become excessive and overdue, and, in the excitement of increasing sales, assumed profits in reality are losses. Tight controls, especially over inventories and expenses, are essential.

Learning Insight. *Build an image of quality, and guard it zealously.*

The great importance of guarding a quality image is vividly illustrated with Apple. In only a few years it established a quality product among its many competitors. But it stood to lose all with its inferior Apple III. Drastic action was required if the company's reputation was not to be tarnished, perhaps irrevocably, especially with IBM standing in the wings. Apple quickly withdrew the product and made restitution to all purchasers without delay. All firms should heed this example. To find excuses, to try to dismiss the reality of a defective product, is flirting with disaster. If the problems cannot be quickly remedied, for the sake of customer relations and protection of the vital quality image, any such product should be withdrawn immediately.

Learning Insight. *In an industry with rapidly changing technology, heavy commitments to research and development are necessary.*

Youthful industries are often characterized by rapidly changing technology. Technological breakthroughs can come at any time, from any firm. The competitor who lags in research and development (R&D) faces serious problems that may well jeopardize its continuing in the industry. Technological breakthroughs may bring improvements or modifications that make existing products obsolete, or they may increase production efficiency and lower costs. Figure 17.2 shows the increasingly heavy expenditures for R&D by Apple from 1977 to 1982, as it sought to avoid vulnerability and to achieve further breakthroughs.

1977	$ 100
1978	$ 600
1979	$ 3,600
1980	$ 7,300
1981	$20,956
1982	$37,979

Figure 17.2 Apple research and development expenditures, 1977–1982 (in thousands of dollars). (*Source:* Company annual reports.)

Learning Insight. *For new and rapidly growing firms, tight controls of expenditures and inventories are crucial.*

We saw in the Osborne example the disaster possible in not keeping a close rein over costs. Such a tight rein requires prompt and complete recording and reporting of all expenditures, of inventories, of orders and transactions. It requires operating budgets, so that actual results can be compared to budgeted figures, with any expense overages to be carefully considered and well supported. Authorization for expenditures must be established and enforced to prevent runaway spending sprees.

The temptation with rapidly growing firms is to disregard expenditures, assuming that they will easily be covered by the burgeoning revenues. The temptation is to disregard mounting inventories, since they will likely soon be depleted. In the heady optimism of rapid growth, it is difficult to throttle spending, and careful recording of such spending is likely to be of low priority. Yet, as we saw with Osborne, looseness of controls during exuberant growth may well pave the way for major losses and eventual disaster. Especially when the profitability of sales is not even firmly established.

Learning Insight. *New and rapidly growing industries are often characterized by particularly keen competition.*

New and rapidly growing industries present dangers far greater than those facing the entrant to more mature industries. Unless entry to the industry is exceedingly difficult because of high start-up costs or secure technological expertise, the new, rapidly growing industry is attractive to all kinds of firms and a host of investors. Such new industries are usually characterized by rapid product improvements and by severe price-cutting. A firm in such an industry must beware of the potential shakeout. It may be better to resist expanding so fast that it becomes vulnerable to overcapacity and excessive inventory when the trauma of price-cutting begins. Competition invariably results in price-cutting as production efficiencies and technological improvements are advanced by competing firms. Where many firms enter the industry, the marginal ones will fall by the wayside, leaving the field to the more able firms with better management and greater resources. During the shakeout period, however, virtually all firms may find themselves losing money because of the severe price competition and the dumping of excess inventories. A stayer must be prepared to weather some rough times before the industry stabilizes.

Learning Insight. *The advantage of uniqueness may be transitory and quickly countered by competitors.*

Uniqueness is usually transitory. Osborne had a unique product offering in its early months. But it vastly underestimated how quickly that uniqueness would be matched by competitors.

Learning Insight. *The possibility of cannibalization must be prudently considered.*

The Osborne example shows the dangers of cannibalization carried to the extreme. *Cannibalization* refers to the process by which one product of the firm takes sales away from other products of the firm. Generally, the success of a new product to some extent is at the expense of other products in the line, but hopefully there will be enough new business to increase total sales. In Osborne's case, the foolish announcement of the new Executive computer—before it was even ready to go to market—practically killed sales for the older Osborne 1. Encountering a month and more of virtually no sales is more than most firms can endure.

On the other hand, to be so concerned about cannibalization that needed product improvements and additions are delayed or withheld from the market can also be costly. The classic example of the dangers of such delays is that of Gillette. It procrastinated in introducing its higher-quality stainless steel blade for fear that this blade, which afforded more shaves than its highly profitable super blue blade, would seriously cannibalize the other product. Only when aggressive competitors introduced their own stainless steel blades did Gillette do so. Because of this hesitance in bringing forth an innovation and improvement in shaving, Gillette's market share of the double-edge blade market fell from 90 percent to 70 percent. The loss in competitive position was never fully regained.

INFORMATION SIDELIGHT

STRATEGY COUNTERING BY COMPETITORS

Some strategies are easily duplicated or countered by competitors. Price-cutting is the most easily countered. it is easy to match a price cut, and it sometimes can be done within minutes. Similarly, a different package, such as bundling, or an extended warranty, are easily matched by competitors. The low price of Osborne and its bundling of software, and even the portability of its product, were quickly and easily met by competitors, with profits severely affected.

Other strategies are not so easily duplicated. Most such strategies pertain to either service considerations or a strong and positive company image. A reputation for quality and dependability is not easily countered, at least in the short run. A good company or brand image is hard to match since it usually results from years of good service and satisfied customers—and here, of course, Osborne was hampered by its newness.

The best strategies are those that offer something not easily countered, that have lasting effect, and that are reasonably compatible with the present image and resources of the company. In a volatile industry comprised of mostly new and unproved firms, however, such insulation from competitors is rarely achieved. Strategy countering has to be expected and euphoric expectations tempered.

FOR THOUGHT AND DISCUSSION

1. What kind of controls would you advise Osborne to have set up to prevent the debacle that befell it?
2. Did Osborne Computer have any unique strengths that could have enabled it to survive in this hotly competitive industry?
3. What factors account for the surge of competitors in the portable computer field? Should this have been anticipated by a prudent executive?
4. Discuss and evaluate the pros and cons of a heavy growth commitment for a small innovator in
   a. A personal computer adaptation
   b. Running shoes
   c. Discount-concept retailing
   d. A fast-food restaurant

INVITATION TO ROLE PLAY

1. Place yourself in the role of Adam Osborne in late 1982. Sales are exceeding the wildest expectations. Yet you sense that IBM will soon be a factor in this market, as well as many smaller firms. Plan your strategy for 1983 to protect the viability of your enterprise and pave the way for further growth.
2. As a management consultant you have been called in by Robert Jaunich in late spring of 1983. Company losses are mounting. You have been charged with developing recommendations to save the company.
3. As an entrepreneur seeking venture capital for a new and innovative personal computer, what persuasive arguments would you propose for a $500,000 initial request for funds? How would you counter the skeptic's query of how you could possibly compete with the might of IBM?

18

The Yugo:
A Socialist Fiasco
in a Competitive
Environment

The Yugo was introduced in the U.S. market with what seemed a significant differential advantage: it was the lowest priced car available in America. The Yugo, as the name implies, was a product of Yugoslavia, an Eastern European Socialist republic. Its failure in the United States typifies the problems that Socialist firms have competing in Western capitalist markets. The particular orientation of Socialist firms and their work forces—which emphasizes protected jobs and uniformity of status—makes it difficult to compete in the harsher climate of private enterprise and a market economy.

While the flaws of socialism are apparent in this case, and can be given major blame for the troubles of Yugo, we find learning insights of broader applicability.

THE DECISION

It was early 1985. Malcolm Bricklin, 46, had raised $10 million and formed a company called Yugo America. He planned to import the Zastava Yugo 55, a small, boxy, front-wheel-drive car from Yugoslavia. He hoped to put it on sale in the Northeast by summer for a startling $3990, this at a time when the average sticker price was $11,500. It would cost about $1000 less than the next cheapest car on the market, the Suzuki Sprint, which Chevrolet was selling in some western states. The low-end market had recently been neglected by the Japanese because of import quotas that encouraged them to export higher price cars to the United States.

Bricklin was an entrepreneur, and Yugo America was a subsidiary of his Bricklin Industries. To date, he had no history of success in the auto industry. On the contrary, Bricklin had unsuccessfully tried to sell the Subaru 360, another minicar, back in 1969. He later started a factory in Nova Scotia to build a sports car that bore his name. But that venture also failed. Two strikes already. But there would be a third strike to come: more recently he had taken over the import and sale of the foundering Fiat X1/9 and Spider sports cars. He even changed the Fiat nameplate to the more glamorous Bertone and Pininfarina nameplates, and still the cars did not sell.

Undaunted by his past failures, Bricklin thought he at last had a real gem of an opportunity with his Yugo. He envisioned the Yugo, if promoted rightly to have a potential one million customers in the United States. But he was fearful of emphasizing "cheap": "People don't want anything cheap," he said. "It has to be perceived as a smart buy, like getting something real good on sale."[1]

With what seemed like shrewd wisdom, he turned to Leonard Sirowitz, 52, a New York adman who created many memorable Volkswagen Beetle ads in the 1960s. Sirowitz saw an "uncanny" parallel between the highly successful Beetle and the Yugo. The Beetle was homely; it was the cheapest car on the road at the time; and it was marketed not to the blue-collar worker but to the 1960s equivalent of the yuppie. At that time, Sirowitz's ads turned the public's fascination from chrome and tail fins and gas guzzlers, to the character and frugality of the VW Beetle. Now he faced this challenge.

Sirowitz had something else going for him. In the 1960s, he was instrumental in overcoming the American public's suspicions of unfamiliar foreign products. In that decade, "Made in Japan" raised serious questions about quality. His ads helped Sony sell its portable TVs, and played a major role in changing the perception of Japanese products of all kinds from low quality to high quality.

In 1985, it appeared that the image of the Yugo would need similar doctoring. Since it was a Communist country, Yugoslavia's image was one more akin to breadlines and shoddy consumer goods. Yet, as Bricklin and Sirowitz reasoned, the Yugo, which for five years had been produced by Yugoslavia's leading car manufacturer, Zavodi Crvena Zastava—mostly for domestic consumption where it appeared sturdy enough to survive notoriously rough roads—should surely be a dependable product for U.S. streets and highways. Already, Bricklin's Yugo America had spent $1.5 million to get the car ready for U.S. emissions and safety tests, and had sent a nine-foot telex to the factory requesting detailed cosmetic changes.

---

[1] Jaclyn Fierman, "Can a Beetle Brain Stir a Yearning for Yugos?" *Fortune*, May 13, 1985, p. 73.

The factory knew of the stakes in this U.S. introduction. The country was in desperate need of dollars to meet its foreign debt payments as well as import needs. The trade deficit in 1985 had been significantly increased by Yugoslavia's large purchases of airliners from Boeing and McDonnell Douglas. Debts to Western banks now totaled $24 billion, and there was a serious need to lessen this The Yugo could provide the key to achieving this goal. The factory stood to make up to $2800 for each car sold. (Yugo America expected to earn $200 to $300 per car.)

Because of the importance of this venture, the Zastava factory developed two assembly lines: one for those cars slated for domestic consumption; the other for cars slated for exportation. And the best and most experienced workers were assigned to this second production line. The factory was thus able to assure Bricklin that only cars of superb quality would find their way to the U.S. market.

Crvena Zastava had been making automobiles for about 30 years, mostly under license from other, larger auto firms in other countries. The Yugo was essentially a Fiat front-wheel-drive design dating back to the early 1970s. In 1984, the company turned out only 171,000 cars, and exported 47,000 of these to Europe, Africa, and the Middle East. That year the U.S. market promised a rich opportunity. But the 130-year-old Serbian conglomerate, which also made weapons, looked even beyond the U.S. market. It planned to quadruple its exports by 1989 to worldwide markets.

Of the million potential customers that Bricklin saw for the Yugo, he envisioned some would be normal purchasers of used cars, but who now could be induced to instead buy a new car costing less than many used cars do. He saw another large potential group of purchasers to be suburbanites who needed a second or even a third car for basic transportation around town. He thought other purchasers would include those who had been shocked out of the new car market by the average $11,500 sticker price. Altogether, expectations were that sales should reach at least 100,000 units a year near term, then 250,000 after several years—not as great as the heady days of the Beetle, one of the best-selling cars in history, but still a satisfactory showing for both Yugo America and Yugoslavia.

ACTION

By November 1985, Bricklin decided to cancel a planned $10 million ad campaign because of overwhelming demand for the cars. His dealers had already received more than 8000 orders since August. Shipments were running far behind demand, as only 1558 had been shipped. At the current rate, the company would receive 100,000 orders by August 1986, although it planned to import only 40,000 cars this first year. The company could earn $16 million its first year, and Bricklin was now planning a public stock offering. His sales projections reached 70,000 cars for model year 1987, and 250,000 for model year 1988. He planned to continue selling the Yugos each year for under $4000, including such extras as power brakes. Cheap labor kept the prices low: Yugoslav workers earned only $1 an hour.

Despite the early success, Bricklin believed that a full range of cars was needed to be competitive. Consequently, he planned to expand the product line to include larger autos in 1986–1991. The basic Yugo GV was a four-passenger two-door hatchback with a 1.1 liter, four-cylinder engine. By June 1986, he planned to introduce a GVS model, which added sports trim to the GV model. By June 1987, the GVX was to be introduced, which would have a larger engine for better performance. In June 1988, a convertible was to be introduced for the youth market. Also planned for 1988 was the Yugo 103, a larger four-door hatchback. By 1989, the Yugo 104 was planned, this being an upscale notchback sedan the size of the Honda Accord. And shortly after this, the TCX was planned to be introduced, this a two-seat, four-wheel drive sports car to sell for under $10,000. With such a broad product line, Bricklin saw the Yugo's success as assured.

Except for slower than expected deliveries from Yugoslavia, which the factory assured him would be corrected, no problems loomed. Bricklin and his Yugo had apparently found a strategic window, one that had been abandoned by the Japanese, and he was prepared to make the most of it. As a final coup, in a December issue, *Fortune* magazine's fifth annual roster of Products of the Year listed the low-priced Yugo as one of the top seven.[2]

STORM CLOUDS

By the early months of 1986, competition was beginning to emerge in the low-priced car sector. These cars were termed minis—cars selling for under $6000 fully equipped and with engines smaller than 1.2 liters. One industry expert, J. D. Power and Associates, predicted sales of cars priced below $6500 would account for about 12 percent of the total U.S. market by 1991. The three principle competitors for 1986 appeared to be Chevrolet's Sprint (expected to sell 60,000 at $5380); South Korea's Hyundai, which was already selling Canada's most popular import; the $4800 Pony, and Yugo. But the $3,990 price of the Yugo still seemed the dominant force in this minicar market.

However, two widely publicized reports appearing in February and March of 1986 brought serious image problems to Yugo, and even placed its viability in the competitive U.S. market in jeopardy. That the sentiment regarding the Yugo could change from high positive to seriously negative

---

[2] "Products of the Year," *Fortune*, December 9, 1985, pp. 106–112.

shows the risks in competing in a capitalistic market, and the need for utterly reliable products.

The February 1986 *Consumer Reports (CR)* gave a scathing criticism of the Yugo. First of all, *CR* noted that it was virtually impossible to buy a Yugo for $3990. Dealer preparation charges, destination charges, and other essential add-ons most likely would bring the price to about $4650. The following is directly quoted from *CR*:

> Is low price sufficient justification for buying the Yugo? We don't think so. Over-all, the Yugo scored below every other small car we've tested in recent years. It's heavy for its size, and though its tiny engine revs willingly enough, it delivers weak performance and unimpressive fuel economy. Handling was competent and braking was very effective, but comfort, ride, shifting, heating, and the design of the controls were below par.
>
> Our Yugo was a sorry sample indeed. We note 21 defects attributable to sloppy assembly or incomplete dealer preparation. Oil dripped from the engine and coated the underbody as we drove. When it contacted the hot exhaust system, the car filled with acrid smoke. Despite several attempted repairs by the dealer, with "factory" assistance, the oil continued to leak, and the car continued to smoke and smell. The clutch chattered. The brakes squealed, and every so often they dragged so badly that we could barely coax the car to 45 mph on level pavement. The speedometer clicked. The hood became loose. The reception of the official Yugo radio was so poor that we played tapes most of the time. The rear-window washer quit. The ignition switch had to be replaced. And two bolts holding the transmission were loose.[3]

The report further described this as a dated car, painfully reminiscent of Fiats of a decade earlier. Serious questions were raised as to the safety of such a small car. After additional denunciations, the CR article concluded: "If $4400 is the most you can spend on a car, we think you'd get better value from a good used car than a new Yugo."[4]

The following Information Sidelight presents the issue of *responsibility for quality,* or Who is to blame for poor quality?

As if this critical commentary by *Consumer Reports* was not enough, a month later the results of federal crash tests hit the new media. The National Highway Traffic Safety Administration, in releasing the results of the tests for 1986, said that the two-door hatchback Yugo ran up the worst scores of all the cars tested.[6]

---

[3] "How Much Car for $3,990?" *Consumer Reports*, February 1986, pp. 84–86.

[4] Ibid.

[6] Reported, among other media, in "Yugo Results Poor in Crash Tests," *The Washington Post*, March 13, 1986, p. E1.

INFORMATION SIDELIGHT

RESPONSIBILITY FOR QUALITY

As products have become more complex, and as the assembly line has divorced workers from the pride of making something from start to finish, problems with defects and poor quality have become widespread. In no other industry have such problems received the critical attention of the auto industry. In the last several decades we know that U.S. car makers have confronted an invasion of good quality imports, especially from Japan. As they have doggedly tried to raise their poor image of quality in customers' minds, recriminations have been raised as to whom is to blame for the persistence of poor quality of American products.

Management blames the workers for their indifference. And the phrase, "Beware the Monday car," has become widely accepted.

But some workers point the finger at management:

I don't believe it is inherent in human nature to do a lousy job. . . . We on the line take our cue from those in the home office. If they don't really care about quality, they can't expect us to either.[5]

Workers also blame overemphasis on production and poor management for all such problems.

In Yugoslavia, similar passing the buck takes place, only on a bigger scale if that is possible. In recent years the quality of U.S. cars has improved, and defects are less common than a decade ago. A more concerned management and labor help account for this, since the idea has finally been accepted that U.S. car makers face serious competitive pressures to improve quality or lose ever-more market shares and jobs to foreign competitors. Whether a similar transformation of quality orientation can take place in Yugoslavia after decades of a Communist work ethic seems doubtful at this point.

CONSEQUENCES

In June 1986, Bricklin postponed indefinitely a first public offering of common stock. Sales, which had rather modestly been estimated at 40,000 for the year, did reach 35,900, but this was by no means a robust picture. Hyundai's Excel, a South Korean import, was the big winner in minicars this year, racking up 168,882 in sales. This was a record for a first-year imported car. The previous record dated back to 1958, when the French Renault Dauphine sold 48,148.

For 1987, the advertising budget was increased to $20 million, up from $13 million in 1986, and several new models were introduced. While Yugo

---

[5] Martin Douglas, "Auto Workers Can Only Do as Well as Head Office Permits." In *Management for Productivity,* edited by John R. Schermerhorn, Jr. (New York: Wiley, 1984), p. 441.

sales rose modestly in 1987 to 48,812, still this was far below the projections of 70,000.

Bricklin Industries in early 1987 obtained the sole U.S. distributorship for another small foreign car, this time the Proton Saga from Malaysia. Bricklin estimated he could sell 100,000 Sagas during the initial year in the United States, and 250,000 a year by 5 years. He planned to spend $10 million to modify the car for the American market. It would sell for $5,000–$8,000, with the U.S. debut planned for early 1988. This car would complement the Yugo line and provide dealers with a more extensive offering, as well as an alternative to the faltering Yugo.

In an attempt to improve Yugo's severely eroded quality image and increase sales, a 12,000 mile or 1-year warranty package was offered as part of the 1988 strategy. The warranty covered all parts and labor costs for wear items and adjustment items. A 4-year or 40,000-mile warranty in addition covered labor and parts for the engine and transmission. More models were to be introduced, including a convertible and a sporty model. The advertising and promotional budget was boosted to $48 million for 1988. Toughness and reliability were emphasized in a new TV ad campaign. The theme line was "The toughest, most dependable cars a little money can buy."

Despite these efforts, 1988 was not a good year. Projections back in 1985 had been for 250,000 sales by 1988. And actually sales started out fairly strong, but by the latter part of the year, monthly sales were running at less than half the previous year's pace, and were to reach a total of only 32,000. Table 18.1 shows the projections and actual sales for the Yugo during these years.

In mid-1988, Bricklin sold out his interest in the parent firm, Global Motors, to an investment baking firm. He had invested heavily in trying to adapt the Proton Saga to the U.S. market. This forced him to delay the introductions of badly needed additional Yugo models.

Table 18.1   Expectations and Actual Sales of the Yugo

	Expected Sales (units)	Actual Sales
1986	40,000	35,959
1987	70,000	48,812
1988	250,000	32,000
1989	250,000	10,500

On January 30, 1989, Yugo America along with its parent, Global Motors, filed for bankruptcy, listing assets of $30.5 million and liabilities of $49.9 million. The filing was in response to threats by an Ohio Liquidator to dump several thousand Yugos on the market below wholesale cost. The Ohio firm had taken the cars as part of a complicated financial arrangement Global had undertaken to raise enough cash to continue operations.

The financial difficulties were triggered by the sudden sales collapse in 1988. While lack of new and more attractive models was certainly a factor in this sales decline, an increasing number of lenders were showing reluctance in financing the riskier first-time buyers attracted to the car.

Zastava Bails Out Its American Distributor

Most of the original Yugo management team was now gone. Zastava, the Yugoslavian producer, recognizing the need to try to continue to penetrate the U.S. market, now invested capital to keep Yugo America afloat, while it readied a new GVC convertible and all-new subcompact hatchback models that it hoped would be more attractive to the American consumer. It announced it would honor all car warranties. Yugo America at the time of the bankruptcy filing owed its dealers $2.5 million in rebates and reimbursements for warranty repairs going back 3 months. Zastava tried to help the 260 remaining dealers sell 16,000 unsold 1988 Yugo cars. It planned to build more 1989 cars if demand exceeded the supply. The manufacturer intended to concentrate on 1990 models, which were to include a convertible, automatic transmission for some models, and the Yugo 103, a four-door model with a larger fuel-injected engine than the Yugo GV.

Yugo America emerged from Chapter 11 bankruptcy in December 1989, thanks to the intervention of Zastava. It was now a wholly owned subsidiary of the Yugoslavian manufacturer. Sales for 1989 had been virtually nonexistent, with only 10,500 cars sold. The subsidiary was still $125 million in debt, and under the terms of its reorganization plan, creditors were told that partial payments on the debt would only be resumed if U.S. sales rise to 20,000 a year. Two new models were planned for early introduction, both having larger and more sophisticated engines. Plans were to launch a $10 million advertising campaign to help revive sales, with major emphasis on its low prices.

A major problem was to woo back dealers who dropped the Yugo cars after the company filed for bankruptcy-law protection in January 1989. The number of dealers at the beginning of 1990 was 185, down from 350 two years before. "We probably need 270 dealers in the United States for the brand to be viable," said John A. Spiech, Yugo's new president and chief executive officer.[7] A one-quarter page ad appeared on January 23, 1990, in the *Wall Street Journal*, aimed at recruiting dealers. The message of the advertisement: "Yugo Is Here to Stay . . . Permanently."

[7] Jacqueline Mitchell, "Yugo America Sets $10 Million for Ads to Revive Car Line," *Wall Street Journal*, January 8, 1990, p. B3.

ANALYSIS

We have examined other cases—notably the Edsel and Gilbert—where poor quality proved an albatross, something not be overcome. While we still await the final demise of the Yugo, the probability of its survival in the American market is low. How does the Yugo differ from the earlier cases? It shows graphically the deficiencies of firms in Socialist economies and their particular vulnerabilities in competing in Western markets. The contrasts of Eastern and Western management styles and work ethics are stark, and worth describing. We can learn from the institutionalized limitations of Eastern European firms.

The Socialist Business Environment

The bureaucratic central planning that characterizes Socialist/Communist countries—though it minimizes unemployment, maintains relative income equality, provides housing and health care, and even higher education for the most promising—does not present the spur for efficiency that capitalism does. Workers and managers alike have little incentive and experience in initiative and innovative thinking.

The result is that consumer choice is limited. Since there is little compe tition, products are functional and not stylish; there is nothing to motivate improving them or innovating; and the products often are of poor quality, defective, and otherwise third rate by Western standards. Factories and stores are bogged down with more workers than needed, with workers unconcerned about doing a good job or grooming themselves for advancement. With income equality endemic in the goals of socialism, the compensation of the top executive of a firm may be no more than three or four times higher than the lowliest worker. Consequently, incentives for managers are meager compared to those in capitalist firms. Management skills have lagged in such an environment and have been further thwarted by the dependence on bureaucratic central planning.

For the workers, the best are permitted no pay increases or incentive bonuses over the most incompetent. In such an atmosphere of egalitarianism, why should any person work harder than his or her peers, who can hardly be fired no matter how poorly they work? For decades, Socialist workers have known no other work ethic than simply spending their time on the job in the easiest way possible. An old adage, jokingly repeated throughout Eastern Europe, asserts: "They pretend to pay us and we pretend to work." While the self-interested pursuit of profits provides powerful incentives for individual efforts and drives resources toward their higher-paying use in capitalist societies, this condition does not exist under socialism.

If you were to visit a factory in an Eastern European country today (and while changes appear to be forthcoming as these countries grapple with discarding the communist mantle, it may take years for widespread changes to take place in the work ethic and managerial competence), you would find far too many workers, many of them in thinly disguised idleness. A typical retail store will have more employees than customers. And in the ingenuity of requiring the most employees possible, a simple sales transaction may involve three or four different stations and their separate workers.

Is it any wonder that such firms have difficulty competing against Western firms? Is it so surprising that Yugo cars, despite the two separate assembly lines, were merely representative of the built-in inefficiencies of Socialist economies?

Given the inability of most Socialist products to compete in Western markets with attractive product features, technological superiority, or quality the only option then becomes one of competing on the basis of lowest price. Actually, competing in world markets as the lowest-price producer is not even possible for most such firms, because of the inefficiencies due to the Socialist policies of full employment, no layoffs, and no incentives. Even with low-priced labor, Socialist factories are not low-cost producers. But in order to get badly needed Western currencies, a Socialist government, such as Yugoslavia's, can subsidize export production and assist in the costs so that these products can indeed be offered at the lowest prices in export markets.

So we have the Yugo as the lowest-price new car available in the United States. Is this a strong competitive advantage? Unfortunately, it promises no lasting advantage. A low price, if effective in winning customers, can be easily matched or countered by competitors. In Yugo's case, while it stubbornly maintained the lowest price, it had a growing number of competitors—both foreign and domestic—entering the scene with cars of better quality, technologically superior, and priced only modestly more than the Yugo.

Low price, then, as a competitive advantage, is highly vulnerable. An advantage based on other considerations—such as dependability, quality, technological advances, styling, even the glamour of a respected foreign brand—is not so easily countered by competitors.

Were Domestic Deficiencies Also Evident?

So far we have blamed the producer for the problems besetting the Yugo. But was Bricklin and Yugo America exonerated from all blame? We think not. Their expectations were far too rosy for an unknown car from an unproven manufacturer in a Socialist country. A longer trial period with more careful attention to the warranty and servicing work by fewer well-chosen dealers might have saved the Yugo from its devastated quality image. It may never be able to overcome this poor image so quickly formed. Undoubtedly,

Bricklin was surprised at the poor quality of the cars and their technological obsolescence. But he should have given defect-prevention top priority. In his haste to expand, he assumed away such possible problems—and laid the groundwork for the future difficulties of the Yugo.

Quality Control

Given that the Zastava factory was soon aware of the quality problems—and Yugo America should have been protesting these—could not improved *quality control standards* have corrected the situation before it got out of hand and permanently damaged the image of the car? Perhaps, and we discuss this further in the following Information Sidelight. We need to recognize that for a complex product such as a car, quality control can be costly if it is done so thoroughly that few defects are passed on. Certainly in the absence of more careful and motivated workers, quality control standards need to be beefed up.

But not only at the factory. The U.S. dealers should also have assumed more responsibility for quality control. After all, the final preparation and servicing was done by dealers before delivery to customers; a more systematic and thorough examination of each car before delivery should have uncovered many of the worst and most immediate defects. A knowledgeable service department was needed by each dealer, both for the preparation stage and for later, when customers brought back the cars for servicing and to have any newly discovered problems taken care of.

Worker Motivation

Finally, we come to worker motivation. Could not the factory, despite its Socialist setting, have developed better employee motivation? The separate assembly line should have been a source of worker pride for those so selected. Apparently this was of no consequence, nor was any other type of motivation evident. But even in Socialist countries, where pay scales are rigid with no incentive for superior performance, still other methods of motivation are possible, such as recognition, token honors and awards, and even more prestigious assignments.

CONCLUSION: CAN A SOCIALIST FIRM COMPETE IN A CAPITALISTIC MARKETPLACE?

The Yugo typifies the Socialist/Communist firm, and its serious weaknesses. With a few rare exceptions, it also typifies the strategy of most such firms when they try to export to Western countries: they compete as the lowest-

INFORMATION SIDELIGHT

QUALITY CONTROL AND QUALITY ASSURANCE

With quality control, the various components of products (or services) are checked to determine if they meet prescribed standards. The purpose of quality control is to minimize or eliminate defects before the customer is exposed to them. In addition to safeguarding a quality image, effective quality control can reduce waste and rejects.

Most firms do not inspect every item, as this is believed to be too costly and time consuming. Rather, a random sample is taken of the output—this sample could be as low as 1 percent of the items. Under such statistical quality control, the great majority of output will not be carefully inspected.

Another limitation of conventional quality control is that it does little to indicate how to avoid defects in the first place. *Quality assurance* is the process of preventing defective products, not simply detecting them after the fact. It has come into prominence with the success of the Japanese in bringing a new level of quality to all kinds of products. Interestingly, the Japanese advances in the achievement of consistent quality were introduced by an American consultant, W. Edwards Deming, three decades ago. He taught the Japanese these principles:

1. tally defects
2. trace them to the source
3. make corrections
4. record what happens afterward

From such attention paid to quality assurance, quality-control circles have arisen, as described in an Information Sidelight in the Chrysler case. Employee involvement in quality is essential for quality assurance to work. Even more important is higher management dedication and commitment, and encouragement and tangible appreciation of employees' contribution to quality maintenance.

The problems of the Yugo suggest the inability of the manufacturer to wholeheartedly embrace the concept of quality control and quality assurance. This attitude was fostered by the conditioning of the domestic customers from decades of past experiences: to expect poor quality under socialism and to accept it as a way of life, with little complaint.

priced brand in their class. Is change likely? While Eastern Europe is frenetically trying to reshape itself to a market-oriented economy, this will require a lengthy process of adjustment.

The biggest problem in such an adjustment may well be in engineering technology. In many Socialist industries this lags Western firms by one to three decades. Catching up may be a long, slow process. Still, efficiency should be improved, and worker motivation increased. Yet, this also will not come easily with workers steeped in the Socialist work ethic. But it can be done, as the following example of Hungarian workers exposed to Western management shows:

> In the Fall 1988, Levi Strauss, in a joint venture with four Hungarian firms, opened a factory for making blue jeans in a town of 40,000 in southern Hungary. This proved to be a model of what could be accomplished by Western management and Socialist workers. Under the agreement, Levi Strauss had total control over production and marketing, and as a joint venture the factory was exempt from many of the restrictions that other Hungarian employers faced.
>
> Motivational tactics included wages more than twice the average for Hungarian garment workers, and the work force achieved production levels considered remarkable by Hungarian experts, and even by Western observers. The workers, most of them young women with no previous garment experience, were approaching the world production record for the 51 plants operated by Levi Strauss worldwide. Wages were based directly on how much an employee produced. In the clamorous neon-lit sewing room, the pace appears breakneck. No one stands idle, amazing Hungarian economists and managers.
>
> Three workers have been fired, this being so unusual that it caused a scandal that reached national news. Three-month contracts can be terminated if employees work at less than 60 percent efficiency. Some of the workers complain that they're treated like slaves, and others that no one could last more than four or five years at the pace. But high compensation spurs them on.
>
> By contrast, a neighboring knitwear factory is beset with the problems common to much of Hungarian industry: a huge, outmoded plant producing low-quality goods; a badly paid, sluggish work force; and a top-heavy organization (of 600 employees, one-quarter work in the office). The value of production per employee is one-tenth that at the Levi Strauss factory.[8]
>
> How long will it take to change a decades-long work ethic? Under the right circumstances, perhaps not as long as some think.

WHAT CAN BE LEARNED?

While the problems of the Yugo emanate mostly from a different environment and depict the weaknesses of socialism, American managers can learn from these difficulties.

Learning Insight. *A poor-quality image is haunting.*

This insight is nothing new; but perhaps repetition is needed, since so many firms repeat this mistake of minimizing the importance of quality, dependability, and a reputation or image for such quality. As noted before, a

---

[8] Compiled from several sources, including Alexandra Shelley, "Hungary Sees Profit in Levi's," *International Herald Tribune*, May 15, 1989, pp. 1 and 13.

bad reputation will not easily be overcome. It lingers powerfully, even when the problem is corrected. And this posits the fundamental maxim: A firm's reputation for quality and dependability must be safeguarded at any cost of effort or expenditure. To lose this, as Edsel and Gilbert did, and as Yugo has more recently, is a burden that cannot be escaped easily or quickly, and may be life threatening to the product and the enterprise.

Learning Insight. *A competitive advantage based on lowest price is the most vulnerable and the most easily countered.*

It is not difficult to lower a price. It is not difficult to introduce a stripped-down model to match a competitor's low price. It is much more difficult to try to counter other competitive strengths such as good service, dependable quality, style, or technological features. Consequently, any brand or firm that only attempts to be competitive on the basis of lowest price, has but a short-term and tenuous advantage.

Learning Insight. *Worker and management motivation can be an advantage or a major obstacle.*

On the one hand, an organization of highly motivated executives and workers has a distinct competitive advantage. We would expect such a firm to have better productivity, alertness to ideas for improvement, and strong continuing efforts to maintain or improve quality. On the other hand, a poorly motivated work force cannot be relied on for consistent defect-free output, will not give maximum effort for good productivity, and will hardly contribute new ideas and innovativeness.

Learning Insight. *Motivation does not solely or even optimally depend on compensation; people are motivated, often more so, by other factors.*

Individuals are motivated by many different things, of which compensation is but one. Recognition, good working conditions, opportunity for advancement—these are only a few of the things that motivate people. Even the fairness and competence of the supervisor can be a powerful factor in motivating workers to their best efforts. (See the following Information Sidelight for a more detailed discussion of *worker motivation.*)

It is true that firms in Socialist countries lack some of the motivational tools that capitalistic firms enjoy. But other means of motivation are available. But first, management has to recognize the desirability of motivating the work force to its best efforts.

INFORMATION SIDELIGHT

WORKER MOTIVATION

Motivation refers to how strongly an individual wants to do his or her job well; it refers to the desire to succeed. Much research has focused on motivation, and a number of theories developed. Its importance in the workplace is undeniable. How to achieve it consistently is the challenge.

In our society we know that motivation varies greatly among individuals. Some persons are self-starters; others are motivated by certain job-related factors such as money, working conditions, an understanding supervisor, status, and even harsh criticism. Motivation for assembly-line workers, especially when unionized, has presented particular challenges. Exceeding the group norm for speed and careful work may not be acceptable. But efforts can certainly be made to increase the group norms through worker participation, empathetic and nonadversarial management, and encouraging a team attitude toward company objectives. Certainly, pride in the company, the job, and the products is to be sought.

While motivation is a complex topic, and an everlasting challenge, certain practical management tactics help:

Pride and identification with the company can be fostered, so that company goals become individual goals.

Employees' self-esteem can be enhanced by inviting their participation in solving problems, publicly recognizing accomplishments, and explaining the importance of what they are doing.

A feeling of security can be promoted by building a work environment that reduces uncertainty, often best achieved by keeping communications channels open regarding any pending changes.

By just and empathetic supervision, a nonadversarial atmosphere of fairness can be gained.

Could the workers in a socialist economy be motivated to be more productive and conscientious? While management faces constraints in the use of incentive pay, promotional opportunities, the ability to discipline and terminate under most circumstances, could not workers be motivated in other ways to do a superior job? For example, could not their sense of pride have been stimulated by the opportunity to produce for the U.S. market? "Only the best" were chosen for this assembly line—could not that have been a source of pride, of teamwork, of commitment to the firm and to the country?

Learning Insight. *The route to dependable quality takes great effort and constant follow-up.*

As discussed in the earlier Information Sidelight, quality control is no panacea. The temptation is to skimp on quality control because it is expensive. Both the inspections and the pulling out of defective products are costly and time consuming. The common practice of statistical quality control, with only a small sample of the output given careful inspection, hardly prevents defective products from going out. But to inspect every item may be an unreasonable alternative. And quality control still does not get at the cause of any difficulties so that these can be corrected; for this, a quality assurance program must be put in place.

The firm wanting to safeguard its quality reputation may need to use more expensive and strict quality control standards and quality assurance procedures. Despite the higher costs, safeguarding an image and lessening future complaints and costly handling of returned goods may mandate greater controls. The issue becomes one of short-term cost savings versus longer-term benefits in image and adjustment costs. Too many firms have erred in the direction of short-term cost considerations at the expense of long-term customer satisfaction and loyalty.

FOR THOUGHT AND DISCUSSION

1. Would increasing the warranty have helped Yugo's problems? Why or why not?
2. How best can Yugo America in 1990 tackle its image problem of cheap and poor quality?
3. While we are given only sketchy information about the Communist factory, Zastava, what do you think might have been done to improve worker performance given the constraints of no incentive pay, and very limited disciplinary powers?

INVITATION TO ROLE PLAY

Place yourself in the position of Bricklin in 1985. You have the contract as sole importer of Yugo cars to the United States. With hindsight, what would or could you have done to eliminate or minimize the quality-control problems of the foreign import? Be as specific as you can, and defend your reasoning.

Five

ETHICAL AND SOCIAL RESPONSIBILITY PROBLEMS

19

Nestle's Infant Formula— Consequences of Ignoring Social Issues

When a firm is a huge international conglomerate, with diversifications into many product lines, bad publicity and negative public reactions about a single product seemingly should be no particular cause for alarm. The inclination is to ignore such a "minor" problem, and it should go away.

But the expectations of Nestle went awry. The attitudes of the general public toward the firm continued to worsen, exacerbated certainly by a negative press and vocal protestors. Far from diminishing over a few weeks and a few months, the situation worsened over years. And far from affecting only the particular product involved—infant formula marketed to underdeveloped countries—other products and other divisions of the company became the object of virulent protests. Nestle had for too long ignored assaults on its public image, and now the road back to public acceptance was slow and rocky.

BACKGROUND

The Trouble Begins

By the early 1970s, suspicions were arising that powdered infant formula manufacturers were contributing to the high infant mortality in less-developed Third World countries by their aggressive marketing efforts directed to people unable to read the instructions or use the product properly because of their living conditions. The possible link between infant formulas and mortality through product misuse began to be discussed by medical professionals, industry representatives, and government officials at a number of international conferences. But public awareness of the problem had not surfaced as yet.

Then, in 1974, a British charity organization, War on Want, published a 28-page pamphlet, *The Baby Killer*. In it, two multinationals, Nestle of Switzerland and Unigate of Britain, were criticized as engaging in ill-advised marketing efforts in Africa. With the printing of this short publication, the general public became not only aware of the problem, but increasingly concerned.

This concern was to intensify less than a year later. A German-based Third World Working Group reissued a German translation of *The Baby Killer*, but with a few changes. Although the British version criticized the entire infant formula industry, the German activists singled out Nestle for "unethical and immoral behavior" and retitled their version *Nestle Kills Babies*.

The accusation enraged executives at Nestle headquarters, and they sued the activists for defamation. The trial lasted 2 years and focused worldwide attention on the issue. Though Nestle won the lawsuit, the court advised the firm to review its current marketing practices. "We won the legal case, but it was a public relations disaster," one Nestle official admitted. "The baby-killing accusation was a natural for antiwar groups and others looking for a cause. The company was dealing with the situation on a scientific and nutritional level, but the protestors were dealing on an emotional and political level."[1]

The Nestle Company

The Nestle Company, formally known as Nestle Alimentana, S.A., is headquartered in Vevey, Switzerland. It is a giant worldwide corporation, with sales of $12.5 billion 1983. It owns or controls extensive interests in numerous companies of the food and cosmetics industries in various parts of the world. Products include instant drinks (coffee and tea), dairy products, cosmetics, frozen foods, chocolate, and pharmaceutical products. In addition, it holds interests in catering services, as well as restaurant and hotel operations such as the Stouffer Corporation, which was acquired in 1973. By 1980, Nestle was marketing its products in Europe, Africa, North America, Latin America, the Caribbean, Asia, and Oceania. Its three top-product groups were dairy products, instant drinks, and culinary/sundry products. Infant

---

[1] Kevin Higgins, "Infant Formula Protest Teaches Nestle a Tactical Lesson," *Marketing News*, June 10, 1983, p. 1.

foods, including the controversial infant formula, and dietetic products accounted for considerably less than 10 percent of total conglomerate sales.

Nestle's appetite for acquisition has continued unabated in recent years. In 1975, it purchased food processor Libby, McNeill & Libby. In 1979, it acquired Beech-Nut, the baby-food producer. Other purchases of note include CooperVision, a contact lens maker, such well-known candy brands as Chunky, Bit-O-Honey, Raisinettes, Oh Henry, Goobers, and Sno Caps, and most recently, Hills Bros. Coffee Company, and Carnation.

The Infant Formula Industry

Nestle first developed and marketed a milk food used to nourish premature infants in 1867. This was in response to the urgent need of premature infants who were unable to take any food. Borden also introduced a similar sweetened and condensed milk.

Infant formula foods are somewhat more recent, developed in the early 1920s as an alternative to breast-feeding. Infant formula is a specially prepared food for infants (under 6 months) and is based on cow's milk. It is scientifically formulated to approximate the most perfect of all infant foods, human breast milk. Today, a number of different artificial milk products are available for infants, and these range in nutritional value from very high (humanized infant formula) to very low (various powdered, evaporated, and sweetened condensed milks).

Sales of infant formula had increased sharply after World War II and hit a peak in 1957, with 4.3 million births in developed countries. From this point on, births started a decline that continued into the 1970s. The result was a steep downturn in baby formula sales and profits. Therefore, the industry began searching for new business. This was found in the Third World countries where the population was still increasing: the less developed countries of Africa, South America, and the Far East.

Total industry sales for infant formula alone, excluding all other commercial milk products, is about $1.5 billion. Of this, an estimated $600 million comes from the less developed countries. Hence, this market segment comprises a significant total potential.

Nestle maintained a strong market share—some 40 to 50 percent—of the Third World market for baby formula. Competitors included three U.S. firms, American Home Products, Bristol Myers, and Abbott Labs, which shared 20 percent of the market. Foreign firms accounted for the remainder. In 1981, the market was estimated to be growing at 15–20 percent per year.[2]

---

[2] Kurt Anderson, "The Battle of the Bottle," *Time*, June 1, 1981, p. 26.

THE ISSUE: MISUSE OF THE PRODUCT, AND MARKETING PRACTICES

> If your lives were embittered as mine is, by seeing day after day this massacre of the innocents by unsuitable feeding, then I believe you would feel as I do that misguided propaganda on infant feeding should be punished as the most criminal form of sedition, and that these deaths should be regarded as murder.[3]

This lone indictment from a doctor in 1939 evolved from a single cry into a crescendo of protest against the infant formula industry.

Incapability of the Market to Use the Product Correctly

A large number of Third World consumers live in poverty, have poor sanitation, receive inadequate health care, and are illiterate. Therefore, misuse of infant formula would seem inevitable. Water is obtained from polluted rivers or a common well and is brought back in contaminated containers. A refrigerator is considered a luxury item, and fuel is very expensive.

Consequently, powdered formula may be mixed with contaminated water and put into unsterilized bottles and nipples. In addition, mothers are tempted to dilute the formula with excess water so that it will last longer. An example was cited by one physician at a Jamaican hospital of malnutrition of two exclusively bottle-fed siblings, 4 months and 18 months old, respectively. A can of formula would adequately feed a 4-month-old baby just under 3 days. However, their mother so diluted the formula as to feed the two infants for 14 days. The mother was poor and illiterate, had no running water or electricity, and had 12 other children.[4]

Studies have given three reasons for the trend to less nursing and more bottle feeding in the less developed countries.[5]

First, a changing sociocultural environment. This consists of urbanization, changing social mores, and increased mobility in employment. Infant formula was seen as representing social mobility and a symbol of highly regarded modern products and medical expertise. The smiling white babies pictured on the fronts of formula tins suggested that rich, white mothers

[3] As quoted in Cicely D. Williams, "The Marketing of Malnutrition," *Business and Society Review,* Spring 1980–81, p. 66.

[4] U.S. Congress, Senate, Committee on Human Resources, Subcommittee on Health and Scientific Research, *Marketing and Promotion of Infant Formula in the Developing Nations,* Hearing, 95th Congress, 2nd Session, May 23, 1978 (Washington, D.C.: Government Printing Office, 1978), p. 6.

[5] Prakash Sethi and James E. Post, "Public Consequences of Private Action: The Marketing of Infant Formula in Less Developed Countries," *California Management Review,* Summer 1979, pp. 35–48.

feed their babies this product and that, therefore, it must be better. High-income consumers in these less developed countries were the first to use infant formula in imitation of Western practices. Bottle-feeding was looked upon as a high status practice, and lower-income groups readily followed.

Second, the health care professional. Many hospitals and clinics endorsed the use of infant formula. A mother's first experience with a hospital may be to deliver a baby. Therefore, any products or gifts received there carry medical endorsement. Also, hospital practices are perceived as better and deserving of emulation. Babies are routinely separated from their mothers for 12 to 48 hours and are bottle-fed whether or not the mothers plan to breast-feed.

Third, the marketing and promotional practices of infant formula manufacturers, which we will discuss shortly.

In 1951, approximately 80 percent of all 3-months-old babies in Singapore were being breast-fed; by 1971, only 5 percent were. In 1966, 40 percent fewer mothers in Mexico nursed 6-month-old babies than had done so 6 years earlier. In Chile in 1973, there were three times as many deaths among infants who were bottle-fed before 3 months of age than among wholly breast-fed infants. Other statistics of increased illnesses and higher death rates of bottle-fed infants were plentiful.[6]

Quality Control Problems

Nestle had some serious quality control problems in its production of the formula in its far-flung plants:

In April 1977, the Colombian General Hospital encountered an increase in mortality at the premature ward. Bacteria was traced to a Nestle factory. But 25 deaths occurred before the cause was found.

Also in 1977, the Australian Department of Health reported that 134 infants had fallen seriously ill as a result of being fed contaminated infant milk formulas produced by Nestle. Government officials estimated 20 million pounds of contaminated milk had been exported to Southeast Asian countries.

The Australian story started in 1976. The Nestle Tongala plant noticed an increase in bacterial counts in samples of infant milk powder. Inspection revealed cracks in the spray drier used to turn liquid milk into powder form. The bacterium was found to be a variant of salmonella that causes severe gastroenteritis. The State Health Department was not informed, and Nestle attempted sterilizing the equipment without halting production; but the bac-

---

[6] For more such statistics, see Leah Margulies, "Bottle Babies: Death and Business Get Their Market," *Business and Society Review*, Spring 1978, pp. 43–49.

terium continued to be discovered. The drier was kept in operation for a full 8 months after the contaminants were found.[7]

Perspective of Criticisms of Misuse

In fairness to Nestle, the critics who condemned the company and other infant food manufacturers for even attempting to market in underdeveloped countries disregarded any benefits of such products over the alternatives. The problem of water contamination also affects the alternatives to commercial infant foods. Such alternatives are various "native" cereal gruels of millet/rice used as weaning foods. The nutritional quality of these gruels tends to be low, and this deficiency is in addition to contamination of the water and containers used to cook the material. Furthermore, the millet/rice often has microbiological contamination. Although it is true that infant formula mixed with contaminated water and containers presents dangers, commercial formulas are more nutritious than local foods and are closer to breast milk than native weaning foods; they are therefore easier to digest. A further rebuttal to the critics is that not all people in less developed countries face water contamination. Millions can safely mix powdered formula with local water without water contamination.[8]

Criticisms of Nestle's Marketing Practices

Nestle has undoubtedly been an aggressive marketer in many Third World countries. Its promotional efforts have been directed to physicians and other medical personnel as well as consumers. Direct consumer promotion of infant formula has taken many forms. Media have included radio, newspapers, magazines, and billboards—even vans with loudspeakers have been used. It has widely distributed free samples, bottles, nipples, and measuring spoons. In some countries, direct customer contacts have been made through "milk nurses," and these have been the subject of particular criticism.

Nestle employed about 200 women who were registered nurses, nutritionists, or midwives. These professionals were often nicknamed, "milk nurses." Critics maintained that these milk nurses were actually sales personnel in disguise who visited mothers and gave product samples in an attempt to persuade mothers to stop breast-feeding. With their uniforms giving them great credibility, this practice was condemned as being too persuasive for naive consumers.

---

[7] Reported in Douglas Clement, "Nestle's Latest Killing in Bottle Baby Market," *Business and Society Review,* Summer 1978, pp. 60–64.

[8] John Sparks, "The Nestle Controversy—Anatomy of a Boycott," Public Policy Education Fund, Inc., June 1981.

INFORMATION SIDELIGHT

THE USE OF MISSIONARY SALESPEOPLE (DETAIL PEOPLE)

Missionary salespeople—these are called detail people in the drug industry—are commonly used by many firms to provide specialized services and cultivate customer goodwill. They generally do not try to secure orders.

Missionary salespeople are employed by manufacturers to work with their dealers. They may put up point-of-purchase displays, train dealer salespeople, provide better communication between distributor and manufacturer, and, in general, try to have their brand more aggressively promoted by the dealer. In the drug industry, the detail people leave samples and explain research information about new products to the medical professionals to encourage prescriptions and recommendations for their brands.

Promotion to physicians and other medical personnel has also been controversial. This type of promotion has generally involved the use of detail people who discuss product quality and characteristics with pediatricians, pediatric nurses, and other related medical personnel. (The use of *detail people*, who are a type of missionary sales representative, is common practice, as described in the Information Sidelight.) Materials such as posters, charts, and samples were made available to physicians, hospitals, and clinics without charge. Physicians and other hospital personnel have also received company-sponsored travel to medical meetings.

Critics felt that the promotion of infant formula had been too aggressive and had contributed to the decline in breast feeding. Despite increased criticisms, however, sales of infant formula in poor countries continued to escalate. It had become the third most advertised product in The Third World, after tobacco and soap. And it was generally recognized that new mothers in such countries were most susceptible to advertising. A 1969 study of 120 mothers in Barbados found that 82 percent of the ones given free samples later purchased the same brand, whether the samples were received from the hospital or at home.[9]

In summary, the criticisms of promotional practices were:

Bottle-feeding contributes to infant mortality in less developed countries.

Baby-booklets ignore or deemphasize breast-feeding.

Media promotions are misleading in encouraging poor and illiterate mothers to bottle-feed rather than breast-feed their infants.

---

[9] Reported in "A Boycott Over Infant Formula," *Business Week*, April 23, 1979, pp. 137–140.

Advertising portrays breast-feeding as primitive and inconvenient.

Free gifts and samples are direct inducement to bottle-feed infants.

Posters and pamphlets in hospitals, and milk nurses are viewed as "endorsement by association," or "manipulation by assistance."

Prices of formulas at the milk banks are still too high for many consumers, who are then tempted to dilute the formula.

THE SITUATION WORSENS FOR NESTLE

With the publication of the two articles, *The Baby Killer* and *Nestle Kills Babies*, and the subsequent lawsuit by Nestle, which received worldwide publicity, two groups were formed and solidified the opposition that was to lead to boycotting Nestle products and services: the Interfaith Center on Corporate Responsibility and the Infant Formula Action Coalition (INFACT).

Since the early 1970s, various agencies had been trying to reduce the promotion and advertising practices of infant formula companies. These agencies included the Protein Advisory Group in 1970 and 1973, the World Health Assembly in 1974, and the World Health Organization (WHO) in 1978.

As a byproduct of the growing condemnation of the industry, Nestle and other firms began to make some changes in their promotional practices, at least on paper. The changes were brought about under the auspices of the International Council of Infant Food Industries (ICIFI), which was formed in 1975 by nine infant-food manufacturers, including Nestle. The changes included the following: product information would always recognize breast milk as best; infant formulas would be advertised as supplementary and recommend that professional advice be sought; nurse's uniforms would be worn only by professional nurses.

But the self-regulation apparently was not sufficient to allay the criticisms. Documentation by the International Baby Food Action Network confirmed over 1000 violations of the "code" since 1977. Some critics compared "asking for self-regulation was like asking Colonel Sanders to babysit your chickens."[10]

With continued reported violations, a boycott was organized in the United States in July 1977, and soon spread to nine other countries. It was to last until January 26, 1984, in the United States and Canada, with other countries following suit.

Nestle was singled out as the sole object of the boycott because of its 50-percent worldwide market share and the adverse publicity that had cen-

---

[10] "Killer in a Bottle," *The Economist*, May 9, 1981, p. 50; and Douglas Clement, pp. 60–64.

tered on it more than other firms who were engaged in the same business practices.

The demands of INFACT and the boycotters were:

1. Stop the use of milk nurses altogether.
2. Stop distributing all free samples.
3. Stop promoting infant formula to the health care industry.
4. Stop consumer promotion and advertising of infant formula.

The public image of Nestle was now heading for the "pits" and could no longer be ignored by management. Indeed, as the following Information Sidelight suggests, a firm's *public image* ought to be zealously safeguarded and never permitted to erode as Nestle's did.

INFORMATION SIDELIGHT

THE PUBLIC IMAGE

The public image is a composite of how an organization is viewed by its various publics: its customers, suppliers, employees, stockholders, the financial institutions with which it is associated, the communities in which it dwells, and the government, both local and federal. To these groups must be added the press, which cannot always be relied upon to deliver an objective and unbiased report, but is influenced by the firm's reputation.

How controllable is the public image? Some would argue that a reputation is durable and not easily changed. But we know better. It can take years for an organization to build a reputation for quality, good service, and care and responsibility. Yet such a reputation, no matter how well established it may seem, can be quickly torn down by a lapse in quality control as with Gilbert, in product safety, or in concern for customer service, satisfaction, and welfare. Or by a lapse in community or environmental good neighborliness.

The boycott soon had the support of over 450 local and religious groups across America, and proponents claimed it was the largest nonunion boycott in U.S. history. Boycott activity was strongest in Boston, Baltimore, and Chicago, where INFACT established an office with five full-time staffers. Thousands of signatures were gathered on various petitions urging removal of Nestle products from supermarket shelves. Some grocers acquiesced, agreeing to remove such products as Taster's Choice from their shelves. The boycott also hit college campuses. With the slogan, "Crunch Nestle," boycotts were encouraged on products ranging from milk chocolate to tea, coffee, and hot chocolate. The college boycott reportedly began at Wellesley College and soon spread to others, such as Colgate, Yale, and the University of Minnesota.

This boycott was undoubtedly effective, not only directly in causing lost business and profits for the company, but in crystallizing public opinion against the company and in invoking governmental response. The following examples demonstrate this effectiveness.

The government of New Guinea enacted stringent laws to curb the artificial feeding of babies in the summer of 1978. Bottles and nipples now could only be obtained by prescription. Other countries also began introducing legislation to reduce the promotion of breast-milk substitutes.

In May 1981, WHO adopted a restrictive ad code that applied only to the infant food industry. A portion of Article 5 of the Code states, "There shall be no advertising or other forms of promotion to the general public of products within the scope of this code."[11] The products covered were infant food formulas and other weaning foods.

The European Parliament in France voted overwhelmingly for strict enforcement of the WHO Code throughout the 10-nation Common Market. The European Parliament also placed responsibility on Common Market firms for the actions of their subsidiaries abroad in observing the WHO Code.

NESTLE FIGHTS BACK

Nestle's first efforts to combat vituperative accusations resulted in more harm than good, as we have seen. As its public image continued to worsen, the worldwide boycott finally surfaced in 1977. Now Nestlé could no longer ignore the protests and hope they would go away. Obviously, they were not going to go away. Initial strategy at this point was to treat the boycott and widespread protests as a public relations problem. The public relations department of the firm was upgraded into the Office of Corporate Responsibility. The world's largest public relations firm, Hill & Knowlton, was hired to assist. Over 300,000 packets of information were mailed by Nestle to U.S. clergymen, informing them that they were wrong in their denunciations of Nestle. Finally, Daniel J. Edelmon, a renowned public relations specialist, was hired. He advised the company to keep a low profile and to try to get third-party endorsement of its actions.

Finally, in 1981, after failing to improve its image and mute the critical cries against it, Nestle dismissed its two public relations firms and took on the task of reestablishing its reputation itself. Ignoring the situation had not

[11] "World Health Organization Drafts Restrictive Ad Code," *Editor & Publisher*, April 11, 1981, p. 8.

helped; public outcries, rather than lessening, had increased. And efforts to denounce the critics angrily had only exacerbated the situation. Now the firm was ready to try a new tack in efforts to establish its credibility as a humane and responsible corporate citizen.

One of the first steps was to endorse WHO's Code of Marketing for Breast Milk Substitutes a step three other U.S. manufacturers did not make until 2 years later. The code, which imposed only voluntary compliance, banned advertising to the general public, as well as distribution of samples to mothers.

Next, Nestle sought an ethical group to work with in vouching for its compliance with the code, and found it in the Methodist Task Force in Infant Formula.

Nestle's relations with the press had been abysmal. For example, in the first 6 months of 1981, the *Washington Post* published 91 articles critical of Nestle. In the company's multifaceted attempt to rebuild its image, the policy for dealing with the media was changed to an "open door, candid approach."[12]

The most effective restorative strategy finally adopted was the establishment of a 10-member panel of medical experts, clergymen, civic leaders, and experts in international policy to monitor Nestle's compliance with the WHO code publicly and to investigate complaints against its marketing practices. This Nestle Infant Formula Audit Commission (NIFAC) gained credibility with the acceptance of the chairmanship by Edmund S. Muskie, former secretary of state, vice presidential candidate, and Democratic senator from Maine. The Commission was established in May 1982.

This so-called Muskie Commission worked with representatives of WHO, International Nestle Boycott Committee (INBC), and UNICEF to resolve conflicts in four areas of the WHO code. Points of contention were educational materials, labels, gifts to medical and health professionals, and free or subsidized supplies to hospitals. These were resolved, and Nestle agreed that, on educational material distributed, social and health aspects of formula versus breast-feeding would be addressed. Its infant formula labels would clearly state the dangers of using contaminated water and the superiority of mother's milk. Personal gifts to health officials (which smacked of bribery and seeking of preferential treatment) were banned. Finally, free samples of formula distributed to hospitals were to be limited to supplies going to mothers incapable of breast-feeding their children.

At last, after years of an adversarial posture, which had only resulted in a growing crescendo of criticisms and boycotting, with bitter accusations that the company was causing the deaths of millions of Third World babies

---

[12] "Fighting a Boycott," *Industry Week*, January 23, 1984, p. 54.

because of its marketing practices, the situation was improving. "We have all learned a lesson . . . ," said Rafael D. Pagan, Jr., president of the Nestle Coordination Center for Nutrition. "Companies should be sensitive and listen carefully to what consumers and members of the general public are saying. When problems surface, they should seek a dialogue with responsible leaders and try to work out the problems together."[13]

Early in 1984, after a decade of confrontation with protestors and 7 years of boycotting, most groups agreed to a suspension of their boycott. Although some diehards refused to accept the conciliatory efforts of Nestle, several large groups—the American Federation of Teachers, the American Federation of Churches, the Federation of Nurses & Health Professionals, the United Methodist Church, and the Church of the Brethren—had either withdrawn from the boycott or decided not to join it.

The company admitted, however, that perhaps 20 obdurate boycott leaders and 50,000 followers in the United States may never stop ostracizing the company no matter what Nestle does.[14]

The results in lost business for Nestle because of the infant food controversy are impossible to pinpoint. Estimates ranged up to $40 million in lost profits as direct results of the boycott. However, lost business could have been far greater than this, with some coming in the years before the boycott began, as consumers turned to alternative brands from firms with better reputations. Even during the years of the boycotts, not all consumers were militant protestors; but they could certainly take their business elsewhere as sort of a silent protest. Admittedly, infant food accounted for only 3 percent of total Nestle sales worldwide. But other Nestle products were blackened to an unknown degree by the embattled public image of this one minor part of the total business. One of the more obvious negative consequences of the boycotts was the loss of meetings and convention business at Stouffer facilities, with some planners opting to schedule at other locations to avoid any association with negative publicity.

Table 19.1 shows the sales and profits for the Nestle conglomerate during some of these years. As you can see, by the late 1970s, profits were declining from the years before the protests had become so pronounced. By 1981, however, sales and profits were rising substantially, partly as the result of acquisitions. Looking at total sales and profit figures, we cannot measure how much is the direct effect of the confrontation; more important, we can only guess at the extent of unrealized potential.

---

[13] Kevin Higgins, "Nestle Gains Formula Accord: Product Boycott Is Suspended," *Marketing News*, February 17, 1984, p. 5.

[14] "Fighting a Boycott," p. 55.

Table 19.1   Nestle Sales and Profits, 1974–1983 (In thousands of Swiss Francs)

Years	Sales	Profits
1974	16,624,000	742,000
1975	18,286,000	799,000
1976	19,063,000	872,000
1977	20,095,000	830,000
1978	20,266,000	739,000
1979	21,639,000	816,000
1980	24,479,000	638,000
1981	27,734,000	964,000
1982	27,664,000	1,098,000
1983	27,943,000	1,261,000

Sources: Company annual reports.

ADDENDUM: ANOTHER NESTLE SCANDAL

On February 17, 1988, two former top executives of the Beech Nut Nutrition Corporation were found guilty of violating federal laws by intentionally marketing phony apple juice intended for babies.

The previous November, the company itself pleaded guilty to 215 felony counts and admitted to willful violations of the food and drug laws by selling adulterated apple products from 1981 to 1983. While the apple juice, the best-selling product of Beech-Nut, was labeled "100% fruit juice," it was actually a blend of synthetic ingredients, a "100% fraudulent chemical cocktail," as one interviewer testified.[15]

Beech-Nut is the second largest U.S. baby food manufacturer and is a subsidiary of Nestle, which acquired it in 1979. The company was founded in 1891, and had always stressed purity, high quality, and natural ingredients in its marketing programs and company philosophy.

How could such a reputable company have strayed so far from its reputation and, indeed, its heritage?

Background. In 1977, Beech-Nut signed an agreement to buy apple concentrate from Interjuice Trading Corporation, a wholesaler whose prices were about 20 percent below the market. Such a low price should have aroused suspicions of adulteration, and it did. Beech-Nut chemists concluded that the Interjuice product was probably extensively adulterated, and maybe even entirely ersatz. In 1978, several Beech-Nut employees were sent to inspect

---

[15] Chris Welles, "What Led Beech-Nut Down the Road to Disgrace," *Business Week*, February 22, 1988, p. 124.

Interjuice's plant, but were not given access to all the facilities, and in particular, the concentrate processing unit. Some years later suspicions were verified that this was a huge national bogus concentrate operation. And Beech-Nut was by far its biggest customer.

While the scientists urged the company to stop buying from Interjuice, top Beech-Nut executives demurred. The company was on the verge of bankruptcy. Products containing apple concentrate accounted for 30 percent of Beech-Nut's sales, and the savings from the cheap concentrate were helping to keep the company alive.

After a desperate search for a buyer, the company was sold to Nestle in 1979 for $35 million. Nestle invested an additional $60 million, and hiked marketing budgets, but the losses continued.

In early 1981, Jerome LiCari, director of research and development, mounted a major effort to improve adulteration testing. By August, he and his fellow scientists believed they had an irrefutable case against their supplier. But their concerns were ignored, and LiCari was even threatened with termination by John Lavery, the chief of operations. LiCari then went to company headquarters and met with the president, Neils Hoyvald, but still no action was taken.

Matters came to a head in June 1982 when a private investigator, hired by apple processors, offered conclusive proof of the bogus concentrate, and asked Beech-Nut to join other juice makers in a lawsuit against the supplier. But Beech-Nut refused, and continued selling products made from the phony concentrate for months despite warnings by the Food and Drug Administration and the New York State Agriculture Department. The company was later charged with stalling the investigation until it could unload its $3.5 million inventory of tainted apple juice products.

Nestle lawyers vigorously defended Neils Hoyvald and John Lavery, hoping to remove some of the onus of the corporate guilty plea in November, but the efforts failed.

Consequences. The lawsuit and scandal cost Beech-Nut an estimated $25 million in fines, legal costs, and slumping sales. Negative publicity led to market share dropping about 20 percent in 1987, and new record losses resulted for the year.

Fortunately for Nestle, most of the bad publicity focused on Beech-Nut, and not on Nestle as the parent company. None of the legal action involved Nestle or Nestle executives. But, of course, the profit travails of a subsidiary impact on the parent. And Nestle executives must have shuddered at the possibility of its involvement with adulterated apple juice being publicized and related to the infant formula scandal.

Analysis. In probing into what led to this blatant disregard for ethical and even legal considerations and, of course, the public image consequences, we need to determine just what could have led responsible executives to this pathway of destruction. Were they honorable men? There is no evidence that they were not. They were hardly hardened and conscienceless individuals pursuing a program for personal gain. Why then?

We are forced to conclude that unethical and illegal acts can be undertaken by essentially honest and well-respected individuals. This defies our darker musings, but it is true. Here we have a company in serious financial straits. The opportunity is presented to save millions of dollars in adulterated ingredients that would not easily be detected. What a temptation! Health and consumer safety apparently was not a major consideration here: the adulterated ingredients were hardly life-threatening—just dishonestly promoted. So, if we have a little cheating, how bad is this, really? Such could well have been the reasoning of the executives involved.

In situations like this, it is easy to rationalize. Another flawed rationalization is that there was no good, solid proof that the concentrate was not authentic. Lacking this, why should we suspect the worst? But the clues were there for any objective observer:

- 20 percent lower cost than any alternatives—how would this be, without something amiss?
- The lack of full disclosure by the supplier.
- The almost certain proof of adulteration by the Beech-Nut research and development department.

The defense maintained that positive proof was lacking that the concentrate was bogus. But should not a grave suspicion require further intense investigation? A laissez-faire or hands-off policy by top management of a serious charge—especially when millions of dollars of inventory are involved, suggesting conflict of interest—can hardly be condoned.

So, the public image can be vulnerable—and should be vulnerable—to less than ethical practices, whether they directly impinge on public health and welfare, as did the infant formula, or whether they involve "merely" a major misrepresentation.

WHAT CAN BE LEARNED?

The Nestle debacle should be sobering for many firms. It should raise some real concerns about the possibility of damage to the public image—damage that can be difficult to rebuild. Specifically, the following are major lessons to be learned from this experience.

Learning Insight. *A public image is always vulnerable; it needs protection at all costs.*

A reputable image, or at least one that is neutral and not negative, can be quickly besmirched. A firm should not underestimate the power of social awareness and activist groups. Furthermore, the large firm is the more vulnerable—even if other firms in the industry are engaged in the same practices—and is the most desirable target for activist groups. Size brings with it greater visibility and public recognition than is the case with smaller competitors. This makes it the target of choice: the goal is to bring down the giant. And public sentiment—be it on the athletic field, in business, or wherever—is not on the side of the big and powerful.

Learning Insight. *Beware of the power of a hostile press.*

A bad press can both arouse and intensify negative public opinion. It can fan the flames. A firm cannot plan on the press being objective and unbiased in such reporting. The press tends to be eager to find a "fault object," and when this is a large and rather impersonal firm, the likelihood is all the greater that bad actions or the negatives of a particular situation will be emphasized far more than the positive and helpful side of the issue. Although infant formulas had many benefits and were a positive health influence in many situations, publicity focused almost exclusively on alleged abuses.

Learning Insight. *A besmirched reputation is not easily overcome.*

Nestle's expectations that the controversy would die out were certainly squashed by the duration and increasing virulence of the protest movement. Without constructive efforts by Nestle in the early 1980s, the gathering strength of the protest movement probably would have resulted in ever-greater boycotting, and most likely in restrictive legislation by many countries. Thus, a tarnished reputation is not suddenly going to become bright and shiny just because of the passage of time. Some sort of strong positive efforts must be made by the firm to try to restore its image—or it will not be improved.

Learning Insight. *Public relations efforts by themselves will seldom improve a negative public image.*

Public relations is not the answer when certain aspects of a firm's operation are the focal points of criticism. The act must be cleaned up first. The public relations efforts of Nestle were notoriously impotent, despite hiring two of the largest and most expensive public relations firms in the world. Without improving the operations under question, no amount of public relation statements—even mailing some 300,000 pamphlets to clergy propagandizing Nestle's position—could produce positive and lasting results.

Learning Insight. *Marketing efforts in particular have strong potential to impact on the public image.*

Many of Nestle's problems emanated from its marketing efforts in Third World countries. Normally, such marketing efforts would be viewed as effective; under different circumstances they could even have been lauded as models for introducing a new and improved product. But here they were seen as far too effective in swaying a naive population in not wholly desirable directions. A firm's marketing efforts are the most visible aspects of its operation. This visibility can sometimes be a curse, as it was with Nestle.

Suggested Reactions with a Darkening Public Image

The Nestle example gives us helpful insights as to how best to react to smears and protests. Ignoring the problem seems ill-advised if the protests are severe enough and the issue is inflammatory. And certainly, alleged culpable loss of life—whether from chemical dumps or spills or from the ill-advised use of infant formula—is inflammatory enough.

Direct confrontation and an adversarial stand is seldom effective either. As Nestle found out the hard way, its court case, even though won by Nestle, only increased the negative publicity and fueled the protestations. Even if the weight of evidence is on the firm's side, the propaganda and one-sided criticisms of the opposition will likely win over the general public.

So it seems more prudent for the firm that unwittingly falls into the snare of public image problems regarding its social role to approach the situation with a spirit of cooperation and constructive participation with opposing groups, despite some diehard activists who may refuse all efforts at conciliation. We cannot fault the efforts of Nestle in 1981–1983 in working with the more reasonable critics. But we can severely fault the company for waiting so long to take such constructive actions.

Many firms need a greater sensitivity to potential problem areas involving corporate social performance. They need to try to anticipate potential problems and nip them quickly. Failing this, an organization should strive to resolve as many of the objections as it can—even if this means assuming the burden of an inequitable compromise position. The consequence otherwise may be a gradually deteriorating image problem, even if the negative public perceptions are not fully based on facts.

A firm doing business in sensitive areas needs to prove that it is a responsible corporate citizen and not an insensitive giant organization. More attention to the public image mix may well prevent the type of image problems that bedeviled Nestle for years.

FOR THOUGHT AND DISCUSSION

1. Faced with activist protestors, do you think a firm has any recourse but to yield to their complete demands? Is there any room for an aggressive stance?
2. Could the public relations efforts of Nestle have been used more effectively?
3. Do you think Nestle was unfairly picked on? Why or why not?

INVITATION TO ROLE PLAY

1. As the staff assistant to the CEO of Nestle, you have been asked to develop a position paper as to the desirability of withdrawing infant formula from the market in Third World countries. Discuss the pros and cons of such a move, and then make your recommendations and support them as persuasively as you can.
2. You are the manager of a Stouffer hotel. A delegation of clergy and lay people have approached you with the threat of boycotting your premises. Be as persuasive as you can in trying to dissuade them from doing so.
3. As the research director of Beech-Nut, Mr. LiCari, given the lack of receptivity of top management, did you have any other recourse?

20

The Dalkon Shield— Mishandling The Public Trust

It is February 29, 1984. Three company executives have been summoned to appear in federal district court before Judge Miles Lord in Minneapolis, Minnesota. They are E. Claiborne Robins, Jr., A. H. Robins Company president and CEO; Dr. Carl D. Lunsford, director of research; and William A. Forrest, Jr., the company's general counsel. With them in the courtroom are a horde of lawyers.

To the three executives' acute shock, embarrassment, and anger, they hear Judge Lord publicly chastise them and their company for their conduct regarding the marketing of the Dalkon Shield, an interuterine birth control device.

For some months Judge Lord had been involved with a combined suit against the company by seven women who had been seriously injured by the Shield. The investigation delved into past Dalkon Shield litigation and the legal tactics employed by Robins for over 10 years. The stinging rebuke noted:

> And when the time came for these women to make their claims against your company, you attacked their characters. You inquired into their sexual practices and into the identity of their sex partners. You ruined families and reputations and careers in order to intimidate those who would raise their voices against you. You introduced issues that had no relationship to the fact that you had planted in the bodies of these women instruments of death, of mutilation, of disease. . . . Another of your callous legal tactics is to force women of little

means to withstand the onslaughts of your well-financed team of attorneys. You target your worse tactics at the meek and the poor. . . . You have taken the bottom line as your guiding beacon and the low road as your route.[1]

Judge Lord also ordered a search of the company's files. Court-appointed officials found strong evidence that the company had covered up its knowledge of the Dalkon Shield's dangers.

The Robins officials retaliated by bringing a lawsuit against Judge Lord—which they subsequently lost.

Between 1971 and 1975, Robins had sold more than 4 million Dalkon Shield IUDs in 80 countries of the world. In so doing, it had ignored ever-increasing concerns of physicians and others about its effectiveness and safety. In the United States alone, more than 2 million women were fitted with the inadequately tested contraceptive device by doctors who believed the optimistic claims of the company. As a result, thousands of women suffered serious damage caused by the Shield—from pelvic infection to sterility, miscarriage, and even death.

This became one of the biggest business blunders of all time, made so much worse by a firm that at first blinded itself to any danger, then tried to cover it up . . . until finally the dam burst.

How could a respected management, one with the reputation of a multigenerational family firm at stake, have accepted such risks with an untested new product in the crass pursuit of short-term profits? And how could it in a panic over impending lawsuits, have so deceived itself, as well as the medical profession and the general public, into believing that nothing was wrong, that others—that is, physicians themselves—were to blame?

INTRAUTERINE CONTRACEPTIVES (IUDs) AND THE DALKON SHIELD

Interest in birth control, and in particular, IUDs as a form of contraception, goes back to ancient times, although most efforts were perilous and unreliable. Medical reports in the 1920s noted many cases of pelvic infection and inflammation with the crude IUD devices available then, and they were generally discredited.

In the early 1960s interest in birth control greatly increased because of two factors. First, fears had begun to emerge of an overpopulated world. These fears seemed justified as a billion people had been added to the world's population between 1930 and 1960. While most of the fears centered on the developing nations of Africa, Asia, and South America, the United

---

[1] Miles W. Lord, "A Plea for Corporate Conscience." Speech reprinted in *Harpers*, June 1984, pp. 13–14.

States was also experiencing a population growth, reaching the psychological milestone of 200 million in the 1960s.

And second, the first oral contraceptive was approved by the Food and Drug Administration in 1960, and was enthusiastically received by both women and the medical profession. However, worries began to surface about the Pill. Some of these concerned its side effects, such as blood clotting. Of even more concern was the possibility of long-term risks for women using the powerful birth-control hormone for as many as three decades of childbearing years.

After decades of being discredited, two developments in the 1960s spurred interest in IUDs. One was the discovery of a new, malleable, inert plastic from which IUDs could be made, and the second was the development of a new molding process. Two new IUDs were patented in 1966: the Lippes Loop and the Saf-T-Coil.

Meantime, Hugh J. Davis, an associate professor of gynecology at Johns Hopkins, and Irwin Lerner, an inventor, came up with an idea for a new IUD—on Christmas Day, 1967. Initial results looked good, and Lerner applied for a patent in 1968. In shape this new IUD resembled a shield, and was a dime-size, crablike plastic device with a string attached for removal by the physician.

On February 1, 1970, the *American Journal of Obstetrics and Gynecology* published an article by Davis based on his testing at Johns Hopkins Family Planning Clinic of 640 women who had worn the device, named the Dalkon Shield. Davis cited 5 pregnancies, 10 rejections, 9 removals for medical reasons, and 3 removals for personal reasons. He reported a pregnancy rate of 1.1 percent. The article impressed many doctors because of such favorable statistics and because it was tested at the prestigious School of Medicine. As a result, many became interested in obtaining the device for their own patients.

Davis and Lerner decided to market the device themselves, and the Dalkon Company was formed in 1969. They worked to refine the product; and by April 1970, they introduced a new, improved device, which made the Shield more flexible and thinner, with barium sulfate added to strengthen the plastic, while retaining its flexibility. However, lacking a sales organization, the owners quickly realized that the Shield would have to be distributed by an established corporation.

Schmid Laboratories turned down the idea, but then Upjohn made an offer. However, at a medical meeting in Bedford, Pennsylvania, another company was attracted, A. H. Robins. On June 12, 1970, after three days of negotiating, Robins topped the Upjohn offer and bought ownership rights to the Dalkon Shield for $750,000 plus consulting fees and a royalty of 10 percent on all U.S. and Canadian net sales. (That figure ultimately came to nearly $1.2 million.)

THE A. H. ROBINS COMPANY

A. H. Robins Company, headquartered in Richmond, Virginia, was a relatively small company ($135 million in sales at the time), but it had subsidiaries in more than a dozen foreign countries. It was best known for such products as Robitussin cough syrup, Chap Stick lip balm, and Sergeant's Flea and Tick collars. It was no fly-by-night company: for more than a century it had been a solid business citizen.

In 1860, Albert Hanley Robins opened a small apothecary shop in downtown Richmond. In 1878, he expanded into manufacturing: while A. H. Robins handled walk-in business selling the patent medicines of the day, his son and daughter-in-law had a small pill-rolling operation upstairs.

So the mom-and-pop undertaking continued until 1933, when a grandson, Edwin Claiborne Robins, took over management with dreams of expanding. He stopped selling medicines directly to the public and turned instead to selling prescription drugs to physicians and pharmacists. The first such product was a stomach remedy, Donnatel, which still remains a major product. After World War II, the company became a major manufacturer of mass-marketed prescription and non-prescription drugs. In 1963, with net sales of $47 million and profits near $5 million, the firm went public. In the process, E. Claiborne Robins, Sr., turned his family into one of the wealthiest in Virginia. In 1978, E. Claiborne Robins, Jr., became president and CEO.

Since 1965, the company had been interested in the birth control market, and particularly in intrauterine devices, although it had never made or sold a medical device or gynecological product before and had no obstetrician or gynecologist on its staff. It had considered buying the rights for the Lippes Loop, but then the Dalkon Shield opportunity surfaced.

The potential for IUDs as a group seemed attractive. But perhaps the biggest plus for IUDs was that they did not require filing a new-drug application (NDA) with the Food and Drug Administration. Since the agency only had jurisdiction over drugs and not over medical devices (which was how IUDs were classified), a manufacturer did not have to file an NDA demonstrating that it had established relative safety with reliable and sufficient clinical and animal testing. Thus the lengthy research and safety testing of the Dalkon Shield could be avoided. (On May 28, 1976, the Medical Device Amendments were enacted to bring medical devices under the supervision of the Food and Drug Administration, but these amendments came five years after the Dalkon Shield was first brought to market.)

Robins quickly made plans to bring the Shield to market, and its assembly was assigned to the Chap Stick division. The company saw an urgent need to get into the market before potential competitors could rush in. In January 1971, just six months after it acquired the rights, the Dalkon Shield was ready for national distribution. The profitability potential was intriguing: the production cost was only about 25 cents, while the Shield was priced at $4.35. While there were some quality control problems, they were deemed not to be particularly serious.

Promoting the Dalkon Shield

An aggressive marketing strategy was put in place. Several hundred salesmen were trained to contact physicians. The advertising itself was directed at both the medical professionals—physicians as well as agencies and clinics that provided IUDs—and women directly to persuade them to accept the Shield if their physicians should so recommend, and even to request and insist on the device if their physicians were skeptical. Consequently, in addition to advertising in medical journals, *Family Circle*, *Mademoiselle*, and similar magazines carried Dalkon Shield advertising.

Robins wanted to position the Shield as a superior product. It was promoted in 1970 as a modern superior IUD, with the lowest pregnancy rate (1.1%), lowest expulsion rate (2.3%), and the highest continuation rate (94%). Other promotional literature stated that it was the only IUD anatomically engineered for optimal uterine placement, fit, tolerance, and retention.

In the ads in major medical journals, Dr. Davis (the original researcher and coinventor) was impressively noted as a research physician with citations from the articles he had published. Not disclosed was his financial interest in the product, and that he was hardly the objective and unbiased researcher deemed essential to sound medical research.

The Shield proved to be a popular product in the contraceptive market. By 1972, an estimated 12,000,000 IUDs were in use worldwide, with 3,000,000 in the United States. And the Shield was in the forefront: some 1,146,000 were sold in 1971, with an estimated market share of 40 percent. In one month, April 1972, some 88,000 women were fitted with the Shield.

But physician complaints began to mount. Many of them in the early months focused on the difficulty of inserting the Shield—later these complaints would assume a more serious nature.

Despite all objections, by August 1973, more than 5 million pieces of promotional literature had been printed. The sales pitch did not change: "No general effects on the body, blood, or brain . . . safe and troublefree . . . the safest and most satisfactory method of contraception . . . truly superior."[2] A new, smaller Shield had been brought out, and this was especially directed to women who had never borne children. However, no safety and effectiveness testing was ever done with this new version.

---

[2] Morton Mintz, *At Any Cost: Corporate Greed, Women, and the Dalkon Shield* (New York: Pantheon Books, 1985), p. 75.

Storm Clouds

In June 1973, Henry S. Kahn, a researcher working for the Center for Disease Control, headed a study to assess the safety of IUDs in general. In a survey of physicians in the United States and Puerto Rico, some surprising and troubling things surfaced. There seemed to be a significant correlation between the Dalkon Shield and the incidence of women hospitalized for a complicated pregnancy. He suggested that a more detailed investigation was warranted. At about the same time, Representative Fountain was chairing a subcommittee investigating whether or not medical devices should be subject to the same kinds of controls as regular drugs.

In the months that followed, more serious problems came to light, including some Shield-related deaths. In October 1973, the Robins Company changed its package label of the Shield to include the warning, "Severe sepsis with fatal outcome, most often associated with spontaneous abortion following pregnancy with the Dalkon Shield *in situ,* has been reported. In view of this, serious consideration should be given to removing the device when the diagnosis of pregnancy is made with the Dalkon Shield *in situ.*"

Robins convened its own Ob-Gyn Advisory Panel in February 1974, to evaluate information on cases of spontaneous septic abortion among women who became pregnant with the Shield in place. The panel finally concluded that there was inadequate information to establish a cause-and-effect relationship.

But problems continued to multiply. The Shield had a multifilament tail, compared with the monofilament tails used in all other IUDs. This tail was shown in several studies to be an excellent harbor for bacteria. In a letter dated May 8, 1974, Robins informed over 125,000 doctors that the Dalkon Shield should be removed immediately if a patient became pregnant and, if this was impossible, to perform a therapeutic abortion. The letter did not advise removal of the Shield from nonpregnant women. The company also stated that it felt the problems shown with the Shield were common to all IUDs. This letter was reported in the *Wall Street Journal,* and Robins quickly issued a press release stating that it had no intention of canceling production of the Shield.

There were more deaths, and by the end of June 1974, the Food and Drug Administration asked (not ordered) Robins to cease marketing the Shield. Bowing to public pressure, the company announced that it would cease marketing the Shield until FDA tests were finalized. However, it still insisted that women who were currently using the Shield were in no danger. Meanwhile, the directors of Planned Parenthood and federally funded Family Planning Programs urged the discontinuance of the Shield.

In October 1974, a preliminary report from the FDA concluded that the Shield was as safe as any other IUD, and attributed the problem to the fact that the Shield was the newest IUD on the market and was still undergoing a "shakedown" period. In December 1974, Alexander Schmidt, then commissioner of the FDA, announced that Robins could continue to market the Shield as long as accurate records were kept of all wearers.

The Climax

Robins was never to remarket the device. Where the FDA failed, the judicial system took over. By March 1975, 186 suits had been filed against Robins. Also in March, the first judicial award was made: $10,000 compensatory and $75,000 punitive damages against Robins. In May, a $475,000 judgment was awarded to the estate of a woman who had died while using the Shield. In August 1975, Robins formally announced that it would not remarket the Shield, but it still insisted that women who had had it inserted previously were in no danger.

Not until September of 1980, six years after the problems with the Shield had begun to surface, did Robins finally send a letter to 200,000 doctors urging them to remove the device from all women who were still using them. The company stated that a "new" study showed that other problems, such as an infection called pelvic actinomycosis, were more likely the longer the device was worn. This move followed a $6.8 million judgment in Colorado in June 1980, in which $600,000 was awarded in compensatory damages and $6.2 million in punitive damages. The punitive award was of serious concern to the company since Robins's liability insurance covered only compensatory damages.

By 1980, 4300 suits were pending against Robins. Some attorneys were spending their entire time suing Robins; this became so popular a cause that a newsletter was published covering IUD litigation, and four-day yearly seminars were held so that more experienced lawyers could instruct on how best to sue Robins.

The 1981 annual report noted that 2300 cases were still pending, while 4200 cases had been settled. Up to now, the company and its insurer (Aetna) had paid out $98 million for Dalkon Shield litigation. Lawsuits continued to multiply and they became increasingly expensive for the company to deal with. For example, the average settlement in 1976 was $8,000; in 1984, the average was in the $400,000 range.

As 1985 approached, Robins's sales had continued to climb, reflecting the strength in its other product lines and its international operations. Profits had risen more grudgingly because of the heavy legal costs—until 1984. (See Table 20.1 for the trend in sales and profits, as well as for a chronology of major events.)

In 1984, hounded by ever-mounting legal costs and judgments, and the running out of liability insurance coverage from Aetna, Robins took an

Table 20.1   Trend in Sales and Profits, 1970–1984; and Chronology of Major Events

	Sales (000,000)	Profits (000,000)	Profits as Percent of Sales	Major Events
1970	132.6	15.7	11.8	June 12, 1970, Robins buys the Dalkon Shield
1971	151.4	19.1	12.6	Jan. 1971, Robins begins to market it
				April 1972, peak month for number of women fitted with the Shield
1973	189.2	25.4	13.4	October 1973, Robins puts warnings on packages
				June 1974, Robins suspends Shield sales in U.S.
1975	241.1	26.6	11.0	April 1975, Robins suspends Shield sales in other countries
1977	366.7	26.8	7.2	
1979	386.4	44.7	11.6	June 1980, $6.8 million judgment against Robins
1981	450.9	44.2	9.8	
1983	563.5	58.2	10.3	
1984	631.9	(461.6) loss		February 1984, Judge Miles Lord chastises Robins in Minneapolis court
				October 1984, Robins urges removal of all Shields
				Robins establishes $615 million reserve for claims

August 21, 1985, Robins files for bankruptcy

extraordinary charge of $615 million as a Reserve for Claims. This resulted in a paper loss of $461.6 million in 1984. In August 1985, Robins filed Chapter 11 bankruptcy. Under Chapter 11 bankruptcy, all litigation against a company is stayed while the company and its creditors attempt to devise a plan to pay the bankrupt company's debts. E. Claiborne Robins, Jr., said the action was necessary to protect the company's economic vitality against those who would destroy it for the benefit of a few. Attorneys for the victims found this action to be fraudulent and in bad faith, and an attempt by Robins to escape responsibility for the thousands of injuries the Shield had caused.

Not even Aetna was to escape unscathed. In 1986, a group of former Dalkon Shield users sued Aetna, charging that it had conspired with Robins to keep the alleged health hazards of the IUD from the public. The women claimed that Aetna also participated in intentional destruction of evidence that would have helped the plaintiffs prove the dangers of the device.

A bidding war developed for the troubled Robins Company. Rorer Group, a Pennsylvania pharmaceutical concern, made the first offer. Late in 1987, Sanofi, a French drug maker, made another takeover proposal. A week later, American Home Products Corporation joined the fast-developing bidding war. On January 20, 1988, the bid by American Home Products was accepted. John Stafford, chairman and CEO of American Home Products, was interested in Robins because of the tax advantages and the acquisition of two popular consumer brands: Robitussin and Dimetapp. "Franchises that powerful come along every few decades," he said.[3] And American Home could deduct its funding of Dalkon Shield liabilities from federal taxes.

American Home offered Robins' shareholders $700 million in American Home stock, and agreed to pay $2.15 billion in cash to the trust fund of claims. The final modification had the two top executives of Robins each giving $5 million in exchange for protection against being sued personally over the Shield. This plan, Robins's fourth in its 29 months of bankruptcy proceedings, was the first to receive endorsement from both the company's shareholders and the committee representing the Shield claimants.

POSTMORTEM

Here we see a company in extremis. Its conduct led a well-regarded firm with 100-year history down the road to bankruptcy; but even worse, the innocent public was brutalized. How could this have happened? After all, these were not deliberately vicious men: they were well intentioned, albeit badly misguided. Perhaps their worse sin was that of trying to ignore and then cover up the increasingly apparent serious health problems with their product, doing this to such an extent that a federal judge castigated them and their company on corporate immorality. How could this situation—in which everyone lost but lawyers—have possibly been permitted to get so out of hand?

It began innocently enough, and in accordance with sound business strategy. Robins recognized an emerging opportunity: the birth control market. While competitors were already in the oral contraceptive market, the

---

[3] Michael Waldholz, "American Home Expects Most of its Price for A. H. Robins Will be Tax-Deductible," *Wall Street Journal,* January 21, 1988, p. 1.

IUD sector of this market was virtually untapped, yet seemed to offer enormous potential. This sector appeared to be in the early stages of development, with no serious competitors as yet. But the likelihood of strong competitive entry could not be ignored, and Robins thus saw the need to enter this IUD market quickly and secure a major share of it—that is, beat competitors to the punch. Again, we have to recognize that this is textbook business strategy.

In accordance with the desirability of quickly entering the market, many decisions were made with little deliberation. One such decision was to assign production of the Dalkon Shield to the Chap Stick division of the company. Any similarity of the two products was remote at best; but this assignment seemed a matter of expediency, and a means of offering lower labor costs. And it might be argued that with such a new and unique product, there was not much more compatibility with any other division of the company.

Now we come to the point where Robins deviated from sound business strategy. It was entering a market in which it had no previous experience whatsoever, one in which health dangers ought to have been carefully evaluated. Yet Robins had not a single obstetrician or gynecologist on its staff. The company also neglected to conduct its own testing of the product, relying instead on the limited research that had been done by the Dalkon Shield's inventors. Robins did not question their research and testing, flawed though it soon proved to be. Rather, it rushed the product to market, thankful that the Food and Drug Administration did not have to be involved. Good judgment would have mandated confirmation of the safety of the product by independent parties. But this would have taken time, time that Robins was fearful of spending.

Recognizing an emerging and spectacular strategic opportunity, Robins proceeded to pursue it with single-minded determination. Unfortunately, such determination ignored prudent and even ethical considerations. For example, much of the product information and advertising that was used was taken from Davis and Lerner's admittedly biased research, and the financial interest that these two "researchers" had in the Dalkon Shield was ignored, and certainly never publicly mentioned. Physicians were thereby misled into thinking the research was objective and unbiased.

The impressive research figures cited in the ads were soon to conflict with studies done by others. As one example, Robins's ads originally claimed that the Shield had a low pregnancy rate of 1.1 percent; but later studies showed pregnancy rates varying from 5 to 10 percent. But Robins continued to use the 1.1 percent rate in its advertising until late 1973, when the claimed pregnancy rate was revised upward.

Other advertising claims attested to the safety and superiority of the Dalkon Shield, that "it was generally well tolerated by even the most sensitive women," and that no anesthetic was required. Only after many physicians complained about the difficulty of insertion was the advertising literature changed in November 1971, by removing the statement that no anesthetic was required. But the claim of being safe and superior went unchanged.

Robins continued to ignore reports of major problems—such as massive bleeding, pelvic inflammatory diseases, miscarriages, and even deaths—that kept coming in over the years following the introduction of the Shield.

Admittedly, the term "safety" was relative: Was the Shield as safe or safer than the Pill? After all, the Pill was known not to be completely safe—it could cause serious side effects. Still, the evidence was mounting that there were significant dangers associated with the Shield, dangers beyond reasonable risk. And these Robins opted to ignore for far longer than was prudent and ethical.

The Robins Company maintained that its product was safe—and it proclaimed so publicly. But evidence suggests that the company knew otherwise. Internal memos indicated that the company knew of potential danger less than a month after it acquired rights to the Shield. And more internal company memos were to surface during subsequent litigation: two to three truckloads of incriminating papers.

The basic component of Robins's strategy now became strictly defensive: to cooperate when necessary, but to spend most of its time on lobbying Congress and defending itself against lawsuits. Major concern was thus on legal and not ethical considerations regarding its past actions.

So, what seemed at first to be an unassailable strategy was found seriously wanting. Was the company guilty of subordinating everything to the profit maximization goal, in an end-justifies-the-means perspective? Or did it simply panic, faced with a calamity of extraordinarily severe consequences, and resort to the defense mechanism of denial?

Roger L. Tuttle, a former A. H. Robins attorney, believed the latter:

> I've got to believe that had they known early on what they were dealing with they wouldn't have touched it with a 10-foot pole. It was just that one step led to another, until they had the grenade spinning in the middle of the floor.[4]

Regardless, the dire consequences to the company and to its innocent customer victims represents a classic example of a monumental management mistake that should have been handled better.

---

[4] Mintz, *At Any Cost*, pp. 51–52.

WHAT CAN BE LEARNED

The Robins Company's actions seemed exemplary, at first:

1. Identify a business opportunity or strategic window.
2. Find or develop a product to tap this strategic window.
3. Beat competition in being the first to capitalize on this opportunity.

But there was one basic difference with other effective strategies: health and safety was more at stake with this particular product. And this should have necessitated a more cautious approach to tapping the window of opportunity to assure that the product had no risks to customers. Yet with Robins, health and safety considerations were ignored in a single-minded pursuit of profits. Everything else was secondary to this profit orientation. (The following Information Sidelight discusses *the major incentives for questionable practices*.)

Does our business system necessarily motivate firms toward such a profit-at-any-cost perspective? The answer is no. A firm, as we will see in our next case, can be scrupulously honest and prudent in protecting health and safety considerations of its customers—and in so doing, protecting its reputation or public image—even at the cost of severe current diminishment of profits.

Learning Insight. *A firm today must zealously guard against product liability suits.*

Any responsible executive now has to recognize that product liability suits, in the increasingly litigious environment of today, can bankrupt a firm. The business arena has become more risky, more fraught with peril for the unwary or the naively unconcerned. Consequently, any firm needs careful and objective testing of any product that can even remotely impact on customer health and safety—and this must be undertaken even if product introduction is delayed and competitive entry encouraged.

Learning Insight. *Suspicions and complaints about product safety must be thoroughly investigated.*

We should learn unequivocally from this case that immediate and thorough investigation of any suspicions or complaints must be undertaken—regardless of the confidence management may have in the product or of the glowing recommendations of persons whose objectivity could be suspect. To procrastinate or ignore poses what should be unacceptable risks.

INFORMATION SIDELIGHT

INCENTIVES FOR QUESTIONABLE PRACTICES

The perception that unethical and shady practices will yield more sales and profits (or are necessary even for reasonable profits) still prevails. Given this attitude, several factors or conditions can be identified that tend to motivate less than desirable practices, whether illegal or merely ethically questionable:

- *Overemphasis on Performance.* In most firms performance is measured by sales and profits. Job promotion and higher pay depend on achieving greater sales and profits. This is true not only for individual employees and executives, but for departments, divisions, and the entire firm. The value that stockholders and investors, creditors, and suppliers place on a firm depends to a large extent on growth. And the evidence of growth is increasing sales and profits. The better the growth rate, the more money available for further expansion by investors and creditors at attractive rates. Suppliers and often customers are more eager to do business. Top-quality personnel and executives are also more easily attracted. This emphasis on quantitative measures of performance, however, has some negative potential consequences.

  > Men are not measured on the basis of their moral contribution to the business. Hence they become caught up in a system which is characterized by an ethic foreign to and often lower than the ethics of man. There is always the temptation for the business person to push harder even though there are infractions of the "rules of the game."[5]

- *Intensity of Competition.* An intensely competitive environment, especially if coupled with an inability to achieve a competitive advantage in the normal course of business dealings, can motivate unethical behavior. The actions of one or a few firms in such an industry may generate a follow-the-leader situation, requiring the more ethical competitors to choose lower profits or lower ethics.
- *Expediency, Indifference, or Both.* The attitude of expediency and indifference to customers' best interests accounts for some questionable practices. These attitudes, whether permeating an entire firm or affecting only a few individuals, are more prevalent in firms with many small customers and when repeat business is relatively unimportant, such as in certain areas of consumer goods and services, including used cars, home repairs, and recreational land. Here, unfortunately, deceptive practices and even fraud are not uncommon.

[5] Robert J. Holloway and Robert S. Hancock, *Marketing in a Changing Environment* (New York: Wiley, 1968), p. 212.

Learning Insight. *If the worst happens, and lawsuits begin to mount, a salvage strategy is best undertaken, regardless of costs.*

Robins faced a crossroads in 1974. Scary reports of problems and lawsuits were flooding in. How should the company react? One course of action was to tough it out, trying to combat the bad press, denying culpability, and resorting to the strongest possible legal defense. This Robins opted to do. At stake was its reputation, its economic life, and the welfare of tens of thousands of women.

The other recourse was what we might call a salvage strategy: recognition and full admission of the problem, and removal of the Shield from more than 4 million women amid a full-market withdrawal. Expensive, yes, but far less risky for the viability of the company, and certainly for the health of those women involved.

Neither strategy is without major costs. But the first course of action puts major cost consequences in the future, where they may turn out to be vastly greater. The second course of action poses an immediate impact on profitability but may save the company and its reputation and return it to profitability in the future.

Learning Insight. *This is an era of* caveat vendidor—*let the seller beware.*

Businesses today have to recognize that this is no longer an age of caveat emptor—let the buyer beware. Such ruled the business environment for many decades, but now the pendulum has swung to *caveat vendidor*—let the seller beware. Products or business practices that are perceived as not in the best interest of the public are subject to reprisals—be these in customer resentment and public outcry, or in lawsuits. Woe to the firm that does not recognize this or underestimates the environmental constraints.

FOR THOUGHT AND DISCUSSION

1. Can a firm guarantee complete product safety? Discuss.
2. Design a strategy for the Dalkon Shield that would have minimized the problems Robins eventually faced. What might be some concerns with such a strategy?
3. After this disaster, do you think Robins could ever have regained a sufficiently respected image to be a viable business under the same management? Why or why not?

INVITATION TO ROLE PLAY

You are the public relations director for Robins in late 1972. Some disquieting information has come to you about far higher than expected physician complaints about the Shield. Top management has so far been unconcerned about such reports, especially in view of Food and Drug Administration complacency.

Develop a plan of action for dealing with potential product safety problems that can be persuasively presented to top management.

CHAPTER 21

Contrast—Johnson & Johnson's Tylenol: Regaining Public Trust

It is September 30, 1982. On the fifth floor of Johnson & Johnson's (J & J) headquarters in New Brunswick, New Jersey, Chairman James E. Burke is having a quiet meeting with President David R. Clair. The two top executives of the company liked to hold such informal meetings every two months. They would talk over important but nonpressing matters that they usually did not get around to dealing with in the normal course of events. Today, both men had reason to feel good, for J & J's sales and earnings were up sharply and the trend of business could hardly have been more promising. They even had time to dwell on some nonbusiness matters that sunny September morning.

Their complacency and self-satisfaction does not last long. Arthur Quill, a member of the executive committee, bursts into the meeting. Consternation and anguish flood the room as he brings word of cyanide deaths in Chicago that are connected to J & J's most important and profitable product, Extra-Strength Tylenol capsules.

THE PRODUCT

The success of Tylenol in the late 1970s and early 1980s had been sensational. It was introduced in 1955 by McNeil Laboratories as an alternative drug to aspirin and one that avoided the side effects of aspirin. In 1959, Johnson & Johnson acquired McNeil Laboratories and ran it as an independent subsidiary.

By 1974, Tylenol sales had grown to $50 million at retail, primarily achieved through heavy advertising to physicians. A national consumer advertising campaign was instituted in 1976, and this proved very effective. By 1979, Tylenol had become the largest selling health and beauty aid in drug and food mass merchandising, breaking the 18-year domination of Procter & Gamble's Crest toothpaste. By 1982, Tylenol had captured 35.3 percent of the over-the-counter analgesic market. This was more than the market shares of Bayer, Bufferin, and Anacin combined. Table 21.1 shows the competitive positions of Tylenol and its principal competitors in this analgesic market. Total sales of all Tylenol products went from $115 million in 1976 to $350 million in 1982, a whopping 204 percent increase in a highly competitive market. As such, Tylenol accounted for 7 percent of all J & J sales. More important, it contributed 17 percent of all profits.

Then catastrophe struck.

Table 21.2 Market Shares of Major Brands—Over-the-Counter Analgesic Market, 1981

Brand	Percent of Market
Tylenol	35.3
Anacin	13
Bayer	11
Excedrin	10.1
Bufferin	9

Source: "A Death Blow for Tylenol?" Business Week, October 18, 1982, page 151.

THE COMPANY

Johnson & Johnson manufactures and markets a broad range of health care products in many countries of the world. Table 21.2 shows the various categories of products and their percent of total corporate sales. In 1981, J & J was number 68 on the Fortune 500 list of the largest industrial companies in the United States, and it had sales of $5.4 billion. It was organized into four industry categories: Professional, Pharmaceutical, Industrial, and Consumer. The Professional Division included products such as ligatures, sutures, surgical dressings, and other surgical-related items. The Pharmaceutical Division included basically prescription drugs, while the Industrial area included textile products, industrial tapes, and fine chemicals.

The largest division was the Consumer Division, and this consisted of toiletries and hygiene products, such as baby care items, first aid products,

Table 21.2 Contribution to Total Johnson & Johnson Sales Of Product Categories, 1983

Product Classification	Sales (Millions)	Percent of Total Company Sales
Surgical and First-Aid Supplies	$1,268	21%
Pharmaceuticals	1,200	20
Sanitary Napkins and Tampons	933	16
Baby Products	555	9
Diagnostic Equipment	518	9
Tylenol and Variants	460	8
Other (includes hospital supplies, dental products, contraceptives	1,039	17
TOTAL	$5,973	100%

Source: "After Its Recovery, New Headaches for Tylenol," Business Week, May 14, 1984, page 137.

and nonprescription drugs. These products were marketed primarily to the general public and distributed through wholesalers and directly to independent and chain retail outlets.

Tylenol was one of the major brands included in the Consumer Division. It is an acetaminophen-based or nonaspirin analgesic. It was the most profitable product for Johnson & Johnson in the early 1980s.

Through the years, J & J had assiduously worked to cultivate an image of responsibility and trust. Its products were associated with gentleness and safety—for all customers, from babies to the elderly. The corporate sense of responsibility fully covered the products and actions of any firms that it acquired, such as McNeil Laboratories.

THE CRISIS

The catastrophe started on a Wednesday morning in late September, 1982. Adam Janus had a minor chest pain so he purchased a bottle of Extra-Strength Tylenol capsules. He took one capsule, and was dead by midafternoon. Later that same day, Stanley Janus and his wife also took capsules from the same bottle—both were dead by Friday afternoon. By the weekend four more Chicago-area residents died under similar circumstances. The cause of death: cyanide, a deadly poison that can kill within 15 minutes by disrupting the blood's ability to carry oxygen through the body, thereby affecting the heart, lungs, and brain. The cyanide had been used to contaminate Extra-Strength Tylenol capsules. Dr. Thomas Kim, chief of the critical care unit of Northwest Community Hospital in Arlington Heights, Illinois, noted, "The victims never had a chance. Death was certain within minutes."[1]

Medical examiners retrieved bottles from the victims' homes and found another 10 capsules laced with cyanide. In each case the red half of the capsule was discolored and slightly swollen, and the usual dry white powder was replaced with a gray substance that had an almond odor. One of the capsules had 65 mg of cyanide—a lethal dose is considered to be 50 mg.

The McNeil executives learned of the poisonings from reporters calling for comment about the tragedy—calls came from all the media, and then from pharmacies, doctors, hospitals, poison control centers and hundreds of panicked consumers. McNeil quickly gathered information on the victims, causes of deaths, lot numbers on the poisoned Tylenol bottles, and outlets where they had been purchased, dates when they had been manufactured, and the route they had taken through the distribution system.

After the deaths were linked to Tylenol, one of the biggest consumer alerts ever took place. Johnson & Johnson recalled batches, while consumers were advised not to take any Extra-Strength Tylenol capsules until the mystery was solved. Drugstores and supermarkets across the country pulled Tylenol products from their shelves; it soon became virtually impossible to obtain Tylenol anywhere.

In tracking down the mysterious contamination, it was quickly determined that the poisoning did not occur in manufacturing either intentionally or accidentally. The poisoned capsules came from lots manufactured at both McNeil plants. Therefore, the tampering had to have happened in Chicago since poisoning at both plants at the same time would have been almost impossible. The FDA suspected someone unconnected with the manufacturer had bought the Tylenol over the counter, inserted cyanide in some capsules, then returned the bottles to the stores. Otherwise, the contamination would have been widespread, and not only in the Chicago area.

At this point, Johnson & Johnson was virtually cleared of any wrongdoing. But the company was stuck with having one of its major products publicly associated with poison and death, no matter how innocent it was. Perhaps the task of coping with the devastating impact of the tragedy would have been easier for Johnson & Johnson if the perpetrator were conclusively identified and caught. This was not to be, despite a special task force of 100 FBI agents and Illinois investigators who chased down more than 2000 leads and filed 57 volumes of reports.[2]

---

[1] Susan Tifft, "Poison Madness in the Midwest," *Time*, October 11, 1982, p. 18.
[2] "Tylenol Comes Back as Case Grows Cold," *Newsweek*, April 25, 1983, p. 16.

COMPANY REACTION

Johnson & Johnson decided to elevate the management of the crisis to the corporate level. A game plan was developed that company executives hoped would ensure eventual recovery. The game plan consisted of three phases: Phase I was to figure out what had actually happened; Phase II was to assess and contain the damage; and Phase III was to try to get Tylenol back into the market.

The company that had always tried to keep a low profile now turned to the media to provide it with the most accurate and current information, as well as to help it prevent a panic. Twenty-five public relations specialists were recruited from Johnson & Johnson's other divisions to help McNeil's regular staff of 15. Advertising was suspended at first. All Tylenol capsules were recalled—31 million bottles with a retail value of over $100 million. Through advertisements promising to exchange tablets for capsules, through 500,000 Mailgram messages to doctors, hospitals, and distributors, and through statements to the media, J & J hoped to demystify the situation.

With proof that the tampering had not occurred in the manufacturing process, the company moved into Phase II. Financially it experienced immediate losses amounting to over $100 million, the bulk of this coming from the expense of buying unused Tylenol bottles from retailers and consumers and shipping them to disposal points. The cost of sending the telegrams was estimated at half a million, while the costs associated with expected product liability suits were expected to run in the millions.

Of more concern to the management was the impact of the poisoning on the brand itself. Many predicted that Tylenol as a brand could no longer survive. Some suggested that Johnson & Johnson reintroduce the product under a new name to give it a fresh start and thus rid itself of the devastated brand image.

Surveys conducted by Johnson & Johnson about a month after the poisonings seemed to buttress the death of Tylenol as a brand name. In one survey 94 percent of the consumers were aware that Tylenol was involved with the poisonings. Although 87 percent of these respondents realized that the maker of Tylenol was not to blame for the deaths, 61 percent said they were not likely to buy Tylenol in the future. Even worse, 50 percent of the consumers said they would not use the Tylenol tablets either. The only promising result from the research was that 49 percent of the *frequent* users answered that they would eventually use Tylenol.[3]

The company found itself in a real dilemma. It wanted so much to keep the Tylenol name; after all, the acceptance had been developed by years of advertising. Now, was it all to be destroyed in a few days of adversity? On

---

[3] Thomas Moore, "The Fight to Save Tylenol," *Fortune*, November 29, 1982, p. 48.

the one hand, if Tylenol was brought back too soon—before the hysteria had subsided—the product could die on the shelves. On the other hand, if Johnson & Johnson waited too long to bring the product back, competitors might well gain an unassailable market share lead. The marketing research results were not entirely acceptable to Johnson & Johnson executives. One expressed the company doubts: "The problem with consumer research is that it reflects attitudes and not behavior. The best way to know what consumers are really going to do is put the product back on the shelves and let them vote with their hands."[4] But what was the right timing?

Johnson & Johnson decided to rebuild the brand by focusing on the frequent users, and then to expand to include other consumers. It hoped that there was a core of loyal users who would want the product in both its tablet and capsule forms. In order to regain regular user confidence, television commercials were run informing the public that the company would do everything it could to regain their trust. The commercials featured Dr. Thomas Gates, medical director of McNeil, urging consumers to continue to trust Tylenol: "Tylenol has had the trust of the medical profession and a hundred million Americans for over twenty years. We value that trust too much to let any individual tamper with it. We want you to continue to trust Tylenol."[5]

Johnson & Johnson also tried to encourage Tylenol capsule users to switch to tablets, which are more difficult to sabotage. In an advertising campaign it offered to exchange tablets for capsules at no charge. In addition, it placed 76 million coupons in Sunday newspaper ads good for $2.50 toward the purchase of Tylenol.

Finally, a tamper-resistant package was designed to prevent the kind of tragedy that occurred in Chicago. Extra-strength capsules were now sold only in new triple-sealed packages. The flaps of the box were glued shut and were visibly torn apart when opened. The bottle's cap and neck were covered with a tight plastic seal printed with the company name, and the mouth of the bottle was covered with an inner foil seal. Both the box and the bottle were labeled, "Do Not Use If Safety Seals Are Broken." This triple-seal package cost an additional 2.4 cents per bottle, but Johnson & Johnson hoped it would instill consumer confidence in the safety of the product and spur sales. In addition, the company offered retailers higher-than-normal discounts—up to 25 percent on orders.

Consumers who said they had thrown away their Tylenol after the scare were given a toll-free number to call, and they received $2.50 in coupons

[4] Ibid., p. 49.

[5] Judith B. Gardner, "When a Brand Name Gets Hit by Bad News," U.S. News & World Report, November 8, 1982, p. 71.

too—in effect a free bottle, since bottles of 24 capsules or 30 tablets sold for about $2.50.

Over 2000 salespeople from all Johnson & Johnson domestic subsidiaries were mobilized to persuade doctors and pharmacists to again begin recommending Tylenol tablets to patients and customers. This was similar to the strategy initially used when the product was first introduced some 25 years before.

The Outcome

Immediately after the crisis, J & J's market share plunged from 35.3 percent of the pain reliever market to below 7 percent. Competitors were quick to take advantage of the situation. Upjohn Company and American Home Products Corporation were seeking Food and Drug Administration permission to sell an over-the-counter version of ibuprofen, a popular prescription pain reliever. Upjohn also granted marketing rights for its brand, Nuprin, to Bristol-Myers Co., maker of Bufferin, Excedrin, and Datril. Upjohn's prescription brand, Motrin—a stronger formulation than Nuprin—was generating some $200 million in 1982, making Motrin the company's biggest-selling drug. And lurking in the wings was mighty Procter & Gamble Company (P & G), the world's heaviest advertiser. P & G was launching national ads for Norwich aspirin and was test-marketing a coated capsule containing aspirin granules.

Yet, there were some encouraging signs for J & J. *Psychology Today* polled its readers regarding whether Tylenol would survive as a brand name. Ninety-two percent thought Tylenol would survive the incident. This figure corresponded closely with the results of another survey conducted by Leo Shapiro, an independent market researcher, just two weeks after the deaths occurred, in which 91 percent said they would probably buy the product again.

Psychology Today tried to get at the roots of such loyalty, and roused comments such as these:

A 23-year-old woman wrote that she would continue to use Tylenol because she felt that it was "tried and true."

A 61-year-old woman said that the company had been "honest and sincere."

And a young man thought Tylenol was an easy name to say.[6]

Such survey results presaged an amazing comeback. J & J's conscientious actions paid off. By May 1983, Tylenol had regained almost all the mar-

[6] Carin Rubenstein, "The Tylenol Tradition," *Psychology Today*, April 1983, p. 16.

ket share lost the previous September; its market share reached 35 percent, and it was to hold this until 1986, when another calamity struck.

New industry safety standards had been developed by the over-the-counter drug industry in concert with the Food and Drug Administration for tamper-resistant packaging. Marketers under law had to select a package "having an indicator or barrier to entry, which if breached or missing, can reasonably be expected to provide visible evidence to the consumer that the package has been tampered with or opened."[7] Despite toughened package standards, in February 1986, a Westchester, New York woman died from cyanide-laced Extra-Strength Tylenol capsules. The tragedy of $3\frac{1}{2}$ years before was being replayed. J & J immediately removed all Tylenol capsules from the market and offered refunds for capsules consumers had already bought.

Now the company made a major decision. It decided no longer to manufacture any over-the-counter capsules because it could not guarantee their safety from criminal contamination. Henceforth, the company would market only tablets and so-called caplets, which were coated and elongated tablets that are easy to swallow. This decision was expected to cost $150 million. The president explained: "People think of this company as extraordinarily trustworthy and responsible, and we don't want to do anything to damage that."[8]

By July 1986, Tylenol had regained most of the market share lost in February, and it now stood at 32 percent.

INGREDIENTS OF SUCCESS AND THE CONTRAST WITH ROBINS

Johnson & Johnson, in its handling of the Tylenol problem, was truly a business success. It overcame the worst kind of adversity, that in which human life was lost in association with one of its products. In only a few months it recouped most of its lost market share, and regained its public image of corporate responsibility and trust. Admittedly, the injury to customers was by no means as great as that perpetrated by Robins and its Dalkon Shield; still the public limelight was more intense and the trauma of the deaths greater because of the way they occurred. What accounted for the success of J & J in overcoming the adversity?

We can identify five significant factors:

1. Keeping communication channels open.
2. Taking quick corrective action.

---

[7] "Package Guides Studied," *Advertising Age*, October 18, 1982, p. 82.

[8] Richard W. Stevenson, "Johnson & Johnson's Recovery," *New York Times*, July 5, 1986, pp. 33–34.

3. Keeping faith in the product.
4. Protecting the public image at all costs.
5. Aggressively bringing back the brand.

Effective communication has seldom been better illustrated. It is vital to gain rapport with the press, to enlist their support and even their sympathy. And this is not easily done, for the press is inclined to sensationalize, criticize, and take sides against the big corporation. Johnson & Johnson gained the needed rapport through corporate openness and cooperation. In the early days of the disaster it sought good two-way communication, with the media furnishing information from the field, while J & J gave full and honest disclosure of its internal investigation and corrective actions. For good rapport, company officials need to be freely available and open to the press. Unfortunately, this usually goes against the natural bent of executives so that a spirit of antipathy often is fostered—as it was with Robins, but not so with J & J during its time of greatest trial.

When product safety is in jeopardy, quick corrective action must be taken, *regardless* of the cost. This usually means immediate recall of the affected product, and such action can run into many millions of dollars. Even if the fault lies with only an isolated batch of products, a firm prudently may have to consider recalling them all, since the problem and danger can quickly become transferable to all items of that brand. Robin's grudging and delayed recall of the Shield simply exacerbated the problem and led to costs many times greater than would have occurred if the recall had taken place years before when the problems were first brought to light.

Johnson & Johnson kept faith with its products and brand name, despite experts who thought the Tylenol name should be abandoned and that public trust could never be regained. Of course, the company was not at fault, there was no culpability, no carelessness. The cause was right. With Robins the situation was vastly different: the company was culpable, with research carelessness heaped on callous disregard for real and potential health problems associated with the product. Admittedly, in keeping faith with a product there is a thin line between a positive commitment and recalcitrant stubbornness to face up to any problem and accept any blame. Without J & J's faith in Tylenol, there would have been no chance of resurrecting the product and its market share.

Johnson & Johnson strove to protect its public image of being a socially responsible and caring firm. (The following Information Sidelight discusses *social responsibility* and presents the J & J credo regarding this.) If there was to be any chance for a fairly quick recovery from adversity, this public image had to be guarded—no matter how beset it was. While the plight of Tylenol was well known, the corrective actions were prompt and thorough, and many people were thus assured that safety was restored. We should note

INFORMATION SIDELIGHT

SOCIAL RESPONSIBILITY AND THE JOHNSON & JOHNSON CREDO REGARDING IT

We can define social responsibility as the sense of responsibility a firm has for the needs of society, over and above its commitment to maximizing profits and stockholder interests. The following "Credo" of J & J illustrates the wide circle of corporate social responsibility that more and more firms are beginning to accept.

JOHNSON & JOHNSON'S CREDO[9]

We believe our first responsibility is to the doctors, nurses, and patients, to mothers and all others who use our products and services. In meeting their needs everything we do must be of high quality. We must constantly strive to reduce our costs in order to maintain reasonable prices. Customers' orders must be serviced promptly and accurately. Our suppliers and distributors must have an opportunity to make a fair profit.

We are responsible to our employees, the men and women who work with us throughout the world. Everyone must be considered as an individual. We must respect their dignity and recognize their merit. They must have a sense of security in their jobs. Compensation must be fair and adequate, and working conditions clean, orderly, and safe. Employees must feel free to make suggestions and complaints. There must be equal opportunity for employment, development, and advancement for those qualified. We must provide competent management, and their actions must be just and ethical.

We are responsible to the communities in which we live and work and to the world community as well. We must be good citizens—support good works and charities and bear our fair share of taxes. We must encourage civic improvements and better health and education. We must maintain in good order the property we are privileged to use, protecting the environment and natural resources.

Our final responsibility is to our stockholders. Business must make a sound profit. We must experiment with new ideas. Research must be carried on, innovative programs developed and mistakes paid for. New equipment must be purchased, new facilities provided, and new products launched. Reserves must be created to provide for adverse times. When we operate according to these principles, the stockholders should realize a fair return.

here that for the public image to be regained under adverse circumstances, the corrective actions must be well publicized. Public relations efforts and good communication with the media are essential for this. Of course, it helps when the fault of the catastrophe is clearly not the firm's.

[9] Source: Company recruiting brochure.

Johnson & Johnson did a superb job of aggressively bringing back the brand. In so doing, all efforts had to be coordinated: efforts to safeguard the public image had to be reasonably successful; the cause of the disaster needed to be conclusively established; the likelihood of the event happening again had to be made virtually impossible. Then aggressive promotional efforts could fuel the recovery.

Johnson & Johnson's efforts to come back necessarily focused on correcting the problem. Initially it designed a tamper-resistant container to prevent the kind of tragedy that had occurred in Chicago. Extra-strength capsules were now to be sold only in new triple-sealed packages. Later in 1986, when another death occurred, the company dropped capsules entirely, and offered Tylenol only in tablet form.

With the safety features in place, J & J then used heavy promotion. This included consumer advertising, with the theme of safety assurance and company social responsibility. J & J offered to exchange tablets for capsules at no charge. It offered millions of newspaper coupons good for $2.50 toward the purchase of Tylenol. Retailers were also given incentives to back Tylenol through discounts, advertising allowances, and full refunds for recalled capsules with all handling costs paid. These efforts directed to consumers and retailers alike bolstered dealer confidence in the resurgence of the brand.

WHAT CAN BE LEARNED?

Any company's nightmare is that its product might be linked to death or injury. Such a calamity invariably results in fear and loss of public confidence in the product and the firm. At worst, such a disaster can kill a company, as happened with some canned-food firms whose products were contaminated with the deadly botulism toxin. And we cannot forget the grudging demise of Chevolet's rear-engine Corvair, whose lack of safety was the object of Ralph Nader's best-selling book, *Unsafe at Any Speed*. And we saw the delayed but serious consequences to Robins. Even at best, years of time and money invested in a brand may be lost, with the brand never able to regain its former robustness. In the throes of the catastrophe, J & J executives grappled with the major decision of abandoning the brand, at the height of its popularity. The decision could have gone either way. Now with hindsight, the correctness of the decision not to abandon was unmistakably correct; but at the time how was one to know? And this leads us to our first Insight.

Learning Insight. *In event of a catastrophe, heroic efforts may still save the brand, although the costs may be staggering.*

Even though J & J successfully brought back Tylenol, the cost was in the hundreds of millions of dollars. But the company size, over $5 billion in sales from a diversified product line, enabled it to handle the costs without jeopardy. A smaller firm would not have been able to weather this. This would have been especially difficult without a broad product line.

Learning Insight. *Whenever product safety is an issue, the danger of lawsuits must be reckoned with.*

As we suffered with the last case, litigation brought Robins into bankruptcy and eventual takeover. Legal action finally was effective in curbing its abuses and procrastination in the absence of strong government regulation. This recourse upheld the rights of the general public, even though lawyers were perhaps the biggest beneficiaries. With J & J, the danger of litigation was muted, although hundreds of millions of dollars in lawsuits were still filed. But in the absence of corporate neglect, the swift constructive reaction, and the fact that the company could hardly have guarded against the actions of a madman, it escaped the worse scenario regarding litigation. Still, suits accused J & J of failing to package Tylenol in a tamperproof container, and the legal expenses of defending itself were not inconsequential. The threat of litigation must be a major consideration for any firm today. Even if the organization is relatively blameless, legal costs can run into the millions. And no one can with certainty predict the decisions of juries.

Learning Insight. *Other firms may also be vulnerable to actions taken against their competitor.*

While other firms in the industry stand to gain a competitive advantage with something like this, they and firms in related industries need to be particularly vigilant—because of the tendency toward "copycat crimes." By November, a month after the deaths, the Food and Drug Administration had received more than 270 reports of chemicals, pills, poisons, needles, pins, and razor blades in everything from food to drinks to medications. Fortunately, no deaths resulted from these incidents. But FDA Commissioner Hayes worried: "My greatest fear is that because of the notoriety of the case and the financial damage to the company, someone else will take out his or her grudges on a product and do something similar."[10] Actually, the Tylenol

---

[10] "Lessons That Emerge from Tylenol Disaster," *U.S. News & World Report*, October 18, 1982, p. 68.

case was not the first time products had been deliberately contaminated. Eyedrops, nasal sprays, milk of magnesia, as well as foods and cosmetics have all been targets of tampering. An Oregon man was even sentenced to 20 years in prison for attempting to extort diamonds from grocery chains by putting cyanide in food products on their shelves.

Learning Insight. *It is possible to bounce back from extreme adversity.*

Certainly, one of the major things we can learn from this case is that it is possible to bounce back from extreme adversity. Before the Tylenol episode, this was not realized by most experts: the general opinion was that severe negative publicity resulted in such an image destruction that recovery could take years. The most optimistic predictions were that Tylenol might recover to about a 20–21 percent market share in a year;[11] the pessimistic predictions were that the brand would never recover and should be abandoned. Actually, in eight months, Tylenol had regained almost all of its market share, to a satisfactory 35 percent. For such a recovery, a firm has to manifest unselfish concern, quick corrective action, and unsparing spending. And it must have a base of a good public image before the catastrophe.

FOR THOUGHT AND DISCUSSION

1. Did J & J move too far in recalling all Extra-Strength Tylenol capsules? Would not a sufficient action have been to recall only those in the Chicago area, thus saving millions of dollars? Discuss.
2. How helpful were the marketing research survey results in the decision about whether or not to keep the Tylenol name?
3. "We must assume that someone had a terrible grudge against J & J to have perpetrated such a crime." Discuss.

INVITATION TO ROLE PLAY

Assume this scenario: It has been established that the fault of the contamination was accidental introduction of cyanide at a company plant. How would you as CEO of J & J have directed your recovery strategy? Be sure to give your rationale.

[11] "J & J Will Pay Dearly to Cure Tylenol," *Business Week*, November 29, 1982, p. 37.

CHAPTER 22

Conclusions—What Can Be Learned?

In considering mistakes, two things are worth noting: (1) even the most successful organizations make mistakes but survive as long as they can maintain a good "batting average," and (2) making mistakes can be an effective teaching tool, thereby enabling a firm to avoid similar errors.

We can make a number of generalizations from mistakes, as well as from contrasting successes. Of course we need to recognize that management as is true of the social sciences, is a discipline that does not lend itself to laws or axioms. Examples of exceptions to every principle or generalization can be found. However, the business executive does well to heed these insights. For the most part, they are based on specific corporate experiences and are transferable to other situations and other times.

INSIGHTS REGARDING OVERALL ENTERPRISE PERSPECTIVES

Importance of Public Image

The impact, for good or bad, of the public image was a common thread through a number of cases. For example, the Edsel, Gilbert, Korvette, Grant, Coors, Burger Chef, the Yugo, Nestle, Robins, and Johnson & Johnson.

The Edsel and the Yugo were haunted by early product defects and could never overcome the poor quality image. With Gilbert we saw how quickly a superior image, a quality image, one built up from decades of well-conceived toys, could be cut down. In Gilbert's case, two or three years of an image-destructive strategy ruined the company. The Coors image or mystique proved vulnerable because of a nonaggressive strategy and the onslaught of strong competitors. Nestle tried to ignore a damning reputation having to do with only one part of its diverse and worldwide operation, but found the image problem to be both durable and transferable to all other aspects of its operation. And Robins and its Dalkon Shield catastrophe shows the fallacy of trying to ignore product problems having to do with health by denials and legal maneuverings.

Other image problems stemmed from a hazy or indistinct image, or else trying to upgrade an image. Burger Chef's lack of a distinctive image placed it at a major disadvantage vis-à-vis McDonald's and other successful fast-food operations, just as the fuzzy images of Grant and Woolco hurt them against the solid and undeviating discounting image of K mart. Korvette lost its positive image as a reliable discounter offering greater values than most other firms when the food and furniture operations became questionable. When it tried to upgrade, the low-price, discount image remained and thwarted efforts to move to a higher-quality operation.

But there were some successes in protecting and enhancing an image. The ability of Johnson & Johnson to regain its image of trust and product safety, after the severest kind of adversity must be reckoned as one of the great success stories. So also must Honda be accorded great credit for its total reversal of the image of people who rode motorcycles.

The importance of a firm's public image is undeniable. Yet firms continue to disregard this and act in ways detrimental to such an important asset, or else ignore the constraints or opportunities that an image affords.

What should our business be? An organization's business, its mission and purpose, should be thought through, spelled out clearly, and well communicated to those executives involved in policy-making. This is especially true for an organization endeavoring to grow. Otherwise, the organization lacks unified and coordinated goals and objectives, which makes running it like trying to navigate relatively unknown terrain without a map.

However, it is prudent judgment to choose safe rather than courageous goals. Mayer, in his presidency of Grant's, wanted the company to grow from $1 billion in sales to $2 billion in barely four years—a courageous goal but hardly safe and prudent. And then there were the Savings and Loans, perhaps the worst abuses of business judgment this country has ever seen.

Determining what a firm's business is or ought to be is a starting point for specifying goals. Several elements help determine this.

The *history of the organization* cannot be disavowed, since it affects employees, suppliers, and customers alike. In view of its history, Grant was unable to translate its future business definition to that of a high-quality and fashion-oriented department-store operation. And some S & Ls completely disavowed their tradition in the quest for wild speculations of all kinds. The firm's *resources* and *distinctive abilities and strengths* must play a major role in determining its goals. It is not enough to wish for a certain status or position if the firm's resources and competence do not warrant this. To take an extreme example, a railroad company can hardly expect to transform itself into an airline, even though both may be in the transportation business.

Finally, *competitive and environmental opportunities* ought to be considered. The inroads of foreign car makers in the United States reflected environmental opportunities for energy-efficient vehicles and the lack of formidable U.S. competition in this area.

Image can be a lodestone for the organization wishing to expand or upgrade its operation. Improving an image can be a long process requiring great patience and strong resources. For many firms the best course may be to go with the present image rather than radically try to change it. An alternative is to introduce a different brand or a different division, anything to escape the negative or fuzzy image. Occasionally, however, an image can be upgraded. But it takes an inspired type of advertising and strategy, as Honda was able to accomplish in improving the image of motorcyclists.

A favorable image can be an offensive weapon, insulating the organization from most of the rigors of competition, permitting it to charge higher prices, to recruit better employees, to obtain easier financing, and to smooth the way for product expansion or diversification. Such an image needs to be zealously guarded, as Apple was quick to do when one of its products experienced problems, and as J & J was able to do. A good image can be quickly destroyed through an episode of poor quality control or servicing.

Power of the media. In a number of cases we would see or suspect the power of the media. Coca-Cola, the Edsel, the Yugo, Nestle, Robins, and Johnson & Johnson are the most obvious examples. This power is most often used in a critical sense—to hurt a firm's public image. The media can fan a problem or exacerbate an embarrassing or imprudent action. In particular, with well-known firms this can trigger the *herd instinct*, with increasing numbers of people joining in with protests and public criticism. But it is possible to use the media in a positive role, as J & J effectively was able to do.

We can make these key generalizations regarding image:

1. It is important to maintain a stable, clear-cut image and undeviating objectives.
2. It is very difficult and time-consuming to upgrade an image.
3. An episode of poor quality control has a lasting stigma.
4. A good image can be quickly lost if a firm relaxes in an environment of aggressive competition.

5. Well-known firms are particularly vulnerable to critical public scrutiny, and must be prudent in decisions and actions that can affect their reputation.

Success Does Not Guarantee Continued Success

That success does not guarantee continued success or freedom from adversity is a sobering realization that must come from examining these cases. Many of the organizations described were notably successful. Some of them had exhibited enviable growth records; some had grown to such a large size that they dominated their industry. Yet they succumbed to grievous mistakes, some while at the very pinnacle of their success. How could this possibly have happened to these firms—firms with such experience, momentum, and resources, both financial and managerial, behind them?

We are forced to conclude that, far from ensuring continued success and mastery, success may actually promote vulnerability. The "three C's" syndrome of complacency, conservatism, and conceit often blanket the leading firms, such as Harley Davidson, in its dominance of the motorcycle industry. We suggest that a constructive attitude of never underestimating a competitor can be fostered by:

- Bringing fresh blood into the organization for new ideas and different perspectives
- Establishing a strong and continuing commitment to customer service and satisfaction
- Conducting periodically a corporate self-analysis designed to detect weaknesses as well as opportunities in their early stages
- Continually monitoring the environment and being alert to any changes

The environment is dynamic, sometimes with subtle and hardly recognizable changes, at other times with violent and unmistakable changes. To operate in this environment, an established firm must constantly be on guard to protect its position. Let us examine several internal tools for doing so.

Management by exception. In controlling diverse and far-flung operations, it becomes difficult to closely monitor all phases of the operation. Successful managers are content to direct their attention to significant performances that deviate from the expected at *strategic control points*. Ordinary operations and less significant deviations can be handled by subordinates. With this approach to control, the manager is not overburdened by a host of details.

Major advantages of management by exception are, first, management efficiency can be improved by freeing time and attention for the most important problems and parts of the job, such as planning, and second, subordinates are permitted more self-management.

In the Korvette example, attention should have been given to deviations from expected performance at important parts of an individual store operation. Deviations that should have received attention included markdowns and shrinkage, merchandise turnover, sales per square foot, and the various categories of expenses. These strategic control points should have been evaluated not only by store but by individual departments. The trends should have been noted. Are conditions getting better or worse? Are we becoming more vulnerable in certain areas of our operation?

Need for environmental monitoring. A firm must be alert to changes in the business environment: changes in customer preferences and needs, in competition, in the economy, and even in international events such as nationalism in Canada, OPEC machinations, changes in Eastern Europe, or in Japanese productivity and quality control advances. Edsel failed because it did not recognize the trend away from big, high-horsepower cars toward smaller, more economical ones. Gilbert did not recognize changes in the toy industry, which should have been obvious to any alert observer. Penney did not comprehend that the retail environment had changed greatly over three or four decades, and that unchanging policies were no longer appropriate. Harley Davidson, Coors, and Adidas also did not heed changes, even though some of these should have been obvious.

How can a firm remain alert to subtle, insidious, as well as more obvious changes? A firm must have *sensors* constantly monitoring the environment. The sensor may reside in a marketing or economic research department, but in many instances such a formal organizational entity is not really necessary to provide primary monitoring. Executive alertness is essential. Most changes do not occur suddenly and without warning. Feedback from customers, sales representatives, and suppliers, keeping abreast of the latest material and projections in business journals; and even simple observations of what is happening in stores, advertising, prices, and new technologies can provide sufficient information about the environment and how it is changing. But it is surprising and disturbing how many executives overlook or disregard important changing environmental factors that presage changes in their present and future business.

The following are generalizations regarding vulnerability to competition:

1. Initial strategic advantage tends to be rather quickly countered by competitors.
2. Countering by competitors is more likely to occur when an innovation is involved than when the advantage concerns more commonplace effective management and marketing techniques.
3. An easy-entry industry is particularly vulnerable to new and aggressive competition, especially in an expanding market. In such

new industries, severe price competition usually will weed out marginal firms.

4. Long-dominant firms tend to be vulnerable to upstart competitors because of their complacency, resistance to change, and myopia concerning a changing environment. Careful monitoring of performance at strategic control points and comparison of similar operating units and their trends in various performance categories can detect weakening positions and alert management can take corrective action before competitors intrude.

5. In expanding markets it is a delusion to judge performance by increases in sales rather than by market share: an increase in sales may hide a deteriorating competitive situation.

Need for Growth Orientation—But Not Reckless Growth

The opposite of a growth commitment is a status quo philosophy, not interested in expansion or the problems and work involved. With Penney, there was an unwillingness to change traditional ways of doing things that were stifling growth. For Gilbert, contentment with status quo seemed to have reached an extreme until a drastically worsening sales and profit picture and a takeover by new management hastened the company on its path of ill-conceived expansion efforts.

In general, how tenable is a low-or-no-growth philosophy? Although at first glance it seems workable, upon closer inspection such a philosophy can be seen as sowing the seeds of its own destruction, unless reversed before too late. More than 3 decades ago the following was pointed out:

> Vitality is required even for survival; but vitality is difficult to maintain without growth, at least in the American business climate. The vitality of a firm depends on the vigor and ambition of its members. The prospect of growth is one of the principal means by which a firm can attract able and vigorous recruits.[1]

Consequently, if a firm is obviously not growth-minded, its ability to attract able people diminishes so that it is vulnerable to competition. Customers see a growing firm as reliable, eager to please, and getting better all the time. Suppliers and creditors tend to give preferential treatment to a growth-oriented firm, because they hope to retain it as a customer and client when it reaches large size.

But an emphasis on growth can be carried too far. Somehow the growth must be kept within the abilities of the firm to handle it. Some of the exam-

---

[1] Wroe Alderson, *Marketing Behavior and Executive Action* (Homewood, Ill.: Irwin, 1957), p. 59.

ples show how firms can grow rapidly without losing control; other cases—such as some members of the Savings and Loan industry, and Campeau, the epitome of unsound leveraged buyouts—show how growth can be an instrument of corporate downfall.

McDonald's is an example of the achievement of rapid growth through franchised units rather than company-owned outlets. However, other franchised fast-food operations expanded just as fast and either went out of business or had to cut back drastically and rid themselves of marginal operations. What was the secret of McDonald's handling of rapid growth, while the supposedly shrewd General Foods Corporation's subsidiary, Burger Chef, could not? The key was very tight controls, careful screening of prospective franchisees as well as new locations, and monitoring existing units even during the excitement of opening new ones.

Apple and Nike, on the one hand, show that geometric annual growth is possible without losing control of operations. Although Apple had some growing pains, it was able to overcome them and remain a major player in the rapidly evolving technology of personal computers. Nike experienced almost as rapid growth as Apple, but it had a major problem: the uncertain life cycle of the running boom. It met this challenge by building a very flexible operation, and it also positioned itself to move into related product areas before the running bubble could burst.

Osborne, on the other hand, illustrates the large number of problems associated with growth: no controls established over inventories, expenses, and most other aspects of the operation. As a result, expenses ran amuck, inventory buildup was out of hand, and the incurring of huge losses was not even realized until too late for remedial action.

Perhaps manufacturers such as Nike and Apple can handle rapid growth better than retailers. A geographically expanding retailer has to develop sufficient controls and standards for far-flung operations. Personnel requirements are far greater, also. For example, Nike grew to a half-billion-dollar corporation with less than 3000 employees, and Apple with less than 4000. A retail enterprise of the same size employs tens of thousands.

We saw two contrasting examples of rapidly growing retailers. On the one hand, Korvette, the innovator and early leader in discounting, could not cope with its growth and at the height of its success, faltered. On the other hand, K mart, the imitator rather than the innovator, had the organizational strength to facilitate its growth and become and world's largest discounter and the second largest retailer. And K mart did this while keeping its organization, store facilities, and merchandise plans and controls as simple as possible.

Beware of growth at any cost. W. T. Grant is a classic example of the fallacy of a growth-at-any-cost philosophy. There is prestige in being one of the biggest firms in the industry, prestige especially for top management. Great market share and sales can be achieved if the firm is willing to commit huge expenditures for advertising, or open millions of square feet of selling space as Grant did. Sales increase from such efforts—for as long as the money holds out. Eventually comes the realization that profits are adversely affected, there is a towering debt, liquidity has been lost, and the very viability of the enterprise is jeopardized. And more recently, we saw the extremes of the growth-at-any-cost mentality in the wild expansion on borrowed capital of Campeau and the risk-be-damned excesses of certain Savings and Loans. Profitability and good financial judgment must not be sacrificed to the siren call for growth.

We can make these generalizations about the most desirable growth perspectives:

1.   Growth targets should not exceed the abilities of the organization to assimilate, control, and provide sufficient managerial and financial resources. Growth at any cost—especially at the expense of profits and financial stability—must be shunned. In particular, tight controls over inventories and expenses should be established and performance should be monitored promptly and completely.

2.   The most prudent approach to growth is to keep the organization and operation as simple and uniform as possible, to be flexible in case sales do not meet expectations, and to keep the break-even point as low as possible, especially for new and untried ventures.

3.   Concentrating maximum efforts on the expansion opportunity is like an army exploiting a breakthrough. The concentration strategy usually wins out over more timid competitors who diffuse efforts and resources. But such concentration is not without risk.

4.   Rapidly expanding markets pose dangers from both too conservative and overly optimistic sales forecasts. The latter may overextend resources and jeopardize viability should demand contract; the former opens the door to more aggressive competitors. There is no definitive answer to this dilemma, but the firm should be aware of the risks and the rewards.

5.   A strategy emphasizing rapid growth should not neglect other aspects of the operation. For example, older stores should not be ignored in the quest to open new outlets. Basic merchandising principles, such as inventory control and new merchandise planning, should not be violated. Otherwise, the sales coming from expansion are built on a shaky foundation, growth is not assimilated, and an illusion is created of strength and success.

6.   Decentralized management is more compatible with rapid growth than a centralized organization since it puts less strain on home

office executives. However, delegation of decision making to field executives must be accompanied by well-defined standards and controls and executed by high-caliber field personnel.

7. In the quest for rapid growth, the integrity of the product and the reputation of the firm must not be sacrificed. This should be a major consideration when customers' health and safety may be jeopardized. Today the risk may extend beyond that of customers to the very viability of the firm.

Innovation

Innovation led to the great success of Apple and Honda. With Apple, product innovation came from humble surroundings and seemingly unpromising individuals—two college dropouts. The innovative product, aggressive strategic efforts, and identification of the most potent customer group brought great success despite the fact that the mightiest of competitors, IBM, was lurking on the periphery.

With Honda the innovation was partly product; a lightweight, classy model of the old motorcycle. But the important innovation involved changing the image of the motorcycle and catering to an entirely different customer group through effective advertising and revamping the method of distribution.

In the nonproduct area, we saw two significant innovations, Hyatt Legal Clinics and International Management Group, who focused their efforts on unmet customer needs and developed service packages to effectively meet these. The success of these two firms shows clearly that innovation is not limited to technology.

As desirable as innovative-mindedness is for organizations, major changes are difficult to accomplish in most. This is particularly true for larger and older organizations; major changes usually come from smaller and younger firms. Furthermore, as we saw with the Penney Company, innovation is particularly difficult to foster in an organization firmly espousing promotion from within. Such a policy tends to restrict new ideas and wide perspectives.

Resistance to change. People as well as organizations are naturally reluctant to embrace change. Change is disruptive, it destroys accepted ways of doing things and familiar authority and responsibility relationships. It makes people uneasy, since their routines are disrupted and their interpersonal relationships with subordinates, coworkers, and superiors are modified. Previously important positions may be downgraded. And the person who views him- or herself as highly competent in a particular job may be forced to assume unfamiliar duties amid the fear that the new assignments cannot be handled as well. And when the change involves wholesale terminations in a major downsizing, as Campeau foisted on his Allied and Federated buyouts, the resistance and fear of change becomes all the greater, to the extent that personnel efficiency may be seriously jeopardized.

Normal resistance to change can be combated by good communication with participants about forthcoming changes. Without such communication, rumors and fears assume monumental proportions. Acceptance of change is facilitated if employees are involved as fully as possible in planning the changes, if their participation is solicited and welcomed, and if assurance is given that positions will not be impaired, only changed. Gradual rather than abrupt changes also make a transition smoother.

In the final analysis, however, making needed changes and embracing different opportunities should not be delayed or canceled because of their possible negative repercussions on the organization. If change is desirable, it should be initiated. Individuals and organizations can adapt to change—it just takes a bit of time.

We can make these generalizations regarding innovation:

1. Opportunities often exist when a traditional way of doing business has prevailed in the industry for a long time.
2. Opportunities often exist when there are gaps in serving customers' needs by existing firms.
3. Innovations are not limited to products, but can involve services, as well as such elements as the method of distribution.
4. For industries with rapidly changing technologies—often new industries—heavy research and development expenditures are usually required if a firm is not to be left behind by competition.

Power of Judicious Imitation

Some firms are reluctant to copy successful practices of their competitors; they want to be leaders, not followers. But successful practices or innovations may need to be embraced in order to survive. Sometimes the imitator outdoes the innovator. Success can lie in doing the ordinary better than competitors.

K mart and Nike, on the one hand, were imitators. They recognized an effective strategy and rose to dominate their industries. On the other hand, competitors of McDonald's, including Burger Chef, ignored McDonald's successful format, even though the high standards and rigid controls were obvious to all. Such disavowal probably was due to lackadaisical management. It is no easy task to develop high standards and controls and to insist that they be followed. We can make this generalization:

It makes sense to identify the characteristics of successful competitors (and even similar but noncompeting firms) that contribute most to their success, and then adopt them if compatible with the resources of the imitator. Let someone else do the experimenting and risk-taking of innovating. The imitator faces some risk in waiting too long, but this usually is far less than the risk of an untested product or operation.

Necessity of Prudent Crisis Management

Crises are unexpected happenings that pose threats, ranging from moderate to catastrophic, to the organization's well-being. With the Gilbert Company, poor crisis management resulted in frenetic efforts to correct a suddenly realized crisis and vastly exacerbated the problem. With Robins, a denial of the extent of the crisis until far too late resulted in the downfall of the company. Johnson & Johnson, however, handled a crisis of the worst possible kind with prompt and judicious actions.

Most crises can be avoided if precautions are taken and if the organization is alert to changing conditions, has contingency plans for dealing with them, and practices risk avoidance. For example, it is only prudent to stipulate that all the key executives of a division or of the firm do not travel on the same air flight; it is prudent to insure key executives so that their incapacity will not endanger the organization; it is prudent to set up contingency plans for a strike, an equipment failure or plant destruction, unexpected economic conditions, or a serious lawsuit. Some risks can be covered by insurance; others need good planning done in a calm atmosphere. The mettle of any organization may be severely tested by an unexpected crisis. But such crises need not cause the demise of the company if alternatives are weighed and actions taken only after due deliberation.

Above all, however, crises usually necessitate some changes in the organization and the way of doing business. Such changes can be hasty, disruptive, and ill-advised, as with Gilbert. At the other extreme, they may be too few and too late. The middle ground is usually best. And with advance planning, the trauma can be minimized and effective solutions more likely to be forthcoming.

Importance of Organizational Compatibility

Organization is often taken for granted for an established firm. The role of the organization in the success or failure of the enterprise or of a particular venture or division tends to be downgraded in favor of the supposedly more important strategic planning and decision-making functions. But sometimes organizational problems can dominate the mistake.

With Korvette, the mistake was in not recognizing that an organization must change as a firm grows to relatively large size. One person can no longer oversee all the important aspects of the operation. Now authority must be delegated, new executive levels and responsibilities created, the use of staff improved. Not to have recognized such requirements strikes us as unsophisticated and naive; yet it is a rather common phenomenon for the person who exhibits great ability and innovation in founding a firm to be seriously flawed in coping with large size.

Although Edsel's mistakes were varied, the crucial one may well have been its establishing a separate organization to sell and service Edsels, thereby greatly increasing the breakeven point, managerial problems, and the need to find and maintain an adequate dealer force. Had such an organizational mistake not been made—who knows?—we might still have Edsels on the market today.

W. T. Grant had a well-established organization and one suitable for a large-size operation. But the violent growth placed demands upon it with little prior warning and proved to be beyond its ability to cope. Consequently, it could provide neither sufficiently trained personnel for the great growth nor enough research and store-planning staff people to adequately handle increasing selling space by millions of square feet a year. The fault was not so much the organization, which was otherwise adequate, as the severe growth demands suddenly thrust upon it. K mart's organization, however, handled its great growth smoothly and with few problems. Its management development efforts kept pace with the expansion needs, and financial and other resources were more than adequate for the carefully controlled rapid expansion. And we saw how Campeau practically destroyed successful organizations by his placing them in hock for billions of dollars of debt.

The organization should be considered in major decisions. Its capabilities must be compatible with any new role in which it is placed. It is a resource that can be constraining if demands for expansion are not to exceed its capability of meeting them. Otherwise, change and growth may have to be slowed until the organization can be built up to achieve desired compatibility with expectations. But, an organization bulging with capable and ambitious people may almost demand serious growth efforts, lest its strength be dissipated as the able abandon it for better opportunities.

Desirability of Systematic Evaluations and Controls

Organizations need feedback to determine how well something is being done, whether improvement is possible, where it should occur, how much is needed, and how quickly it must be accomplished. Without feedback or performance evaluation, a worsening situation can go unrecognized until too late for corrective action. That was apparently the situation with Gilbert. For some reason, sales declines and loss of competitive position up to 1961 did not arouse any particular concern; certainly, no serious attempt was made to find the causes and take action accordingly.

As firms become larger, the need for better controls or feedback increases, because top management can no longer personally monitor all aspects of the operation. This was where Eugene Ferkauf found the Korvette operation too much for him, but he was unable to install adequate controls and reorganization in time to prevent overwhelming problems. The trend toward diversification and mergers, which often results in loosely controlled decentralized operations, also makes timely feedback on performance critical.

The need for careful financial and expense controls seems irrefutable. After all, if costs and inventories get severely out of line—and what can be worse, when this is not recognized until too late—then the viability of the firm can be jeopardized. Yet when firms are new and rapidly growing, as Osborne Computer was in its brief flirtation with stardom, such controls may be overlooked. Even older firms, when they embark on a vigorous expansion program, may be complacent to worsening financial and inventory problems; and they can be just as vulnerable as newer firms, as the W. T. Grant Company found to its horror.

Performance standards are another means of control crucial to large and far-flung operations. Unless operating standards and procedures are imposed—and enforced—the results are likely to be lack of uniformity of performance, great unevenness of quality and service, and a lack of coordination and continuity among the different units; instead of a tight ship, a very loose and undisciplined one will be the natural consequence. The lack of standards regarding facilities, personnel, managerial and franchisee selection, food preparation, and service and maintenance was a major contributor to Burger Chef's problems, especially when competing with McDonald's, whose insistence on tight and rigorously enforced standards was the strongest of all business firms.

Necessity of Long-Term Strategy Objectives for Management of the 1990s

The desperate situation of Chrysler, and to a lesser extent the rest of the U.S. auto industry and a number of other major industries, brought to light a disturbing realization. The prevalent management thinking with its emphasis on short-term profit objectives was vulnerable to aggressive foreign firms that were willing to sacrifice for the short term in building for the future. As we saw in the Chrysler case, the diminishing relative productivity of large parts of U.S. industry could be attributed to numerous factors, some of which management had little or no direct control over, such as government regulations and tax policies. Still, substantial blame must lie with a management unwilling to commit enough resources to research and development, use the newest technologies for modern plant and equipment, and work more closely with labor, encouraging a teamwork approach. Management in certain industries, especially the auto industry, must also be faulted for complacency about quality control and customer complaints and dissatisfaction. A columnist in an editorial in a major newspaper commented about the U.S. automaker's plight as follows:

> Perhaps the public's apathy toward the current plight of the American auto companies . . . suggests . . . that the industry today is paying for yesterday's arrogance and dishonesty in dealing with its customers. Did your new car in 1965 turn out to be a lemon? Tough luck, but you were on your own. And did your 1971 automobile turn from shiny beauty into a rusty monstrosity inside of two or three years, only to have the manufacturer and his dealer shrug off the tragedy?[2]

Perhaps we can learn from these past sins of omission. Not only should long-term strategy objectives involve investment goals and labor incentives aimed at increasing productivity, but customer satisfaction should also be given priority attention:

> The rules for the auto industry are the same as the rules for people. You've got to be basically nice and lead a reasonably decent life if you want others to love you and if you want to make claims to their loyalty in times of trouble.[3]

In two other cases, we saw the contrast in management thinking of short-term profit objectives versus long-term objectives. Robins, with its Dalkon Shield dilemma, focused its attention and strategy on safeguarding short-term profits as much as possible. Eventually it lost everything because of the contemptible reluctance to pull an unsafe product off the market. Johnson & Johnson, in the middle of its catastrophe, was willing to sacrifice short-term profits. And its besieged product, Tylenol, not only survived but prospered in the years ahead.

INSIGHTS REGARDING SPECIFIC STRATEGY ELEMENTS

Strengths and Limitations of Advertising

We can gain several insights regarding the power and effectiveness of advertising from the various cases. But they leave some unanswered questions, and some contradictions. On the one hand, major advertising and promo-

---

[2] George E. Condon, "No Tears Are Wept at Auto-Makers' Plight," *The Cleveland Plain Dealer*, May 18, 1982, p. 3-B.
[3] Ibid.

tional expenditures were made for the Edsel, but the car flopped. On the other hand, an equal level of commitment for the Mustang is associated with an outstanding success. And then we have Coca-Cola with its $100 million greater expenditure than Pepsi, all the while with market share steadily declining. Does advertising have much relationship with success?

There are striking examples of the effectiveness of advertising. Honda successfully used it to change a negative image—with modest expenditures of a few million dollars a year. The advertising campaign of Pepsi—the Pepsi Generation and the Pepsi Challenge—are models of the most effective use of advertising. Joel Hyatt effectively parlayed himself as a concerned antithesis of the negative public image of lawyers, and led his legal clinics to become one of the largest law firms in the United States, and in so doing may well build on his own public image toward a major political career.

We can draw these conclusions:

> There is no assured correlation between expenditures for advertising and sales success. However, given that the other elements of the strategy are relatively attractive, advertising can be an effective tool in generating demand and bringing about the attitude change.

Advertising induced consumers to go to dealers showrooms to look at the Edsel. It performed its primary objective of gaining attention and interest for the product so that consumers would examine it more closely. With the Mustang they liked what they saw; with the Edsel they did not—it is as simple as that.

Planning and budgeting advertising presents some problems. Certain advertisements and campaigns are more effective than others. Other campaigns with higher budgets somehow fall short of expectations. Therein lies the great challenge of advertising. One never knows for sure how much should be spent to get the job done, to reach the planned objectives of perhaps increasing sales by a certain percentage, or gaining market share. Despite the inability to measure directly the effectiveness of advertising, aggressively promoting competitors usually need to be countered, as Coors belatedly found out.

Limitations of Marketing Research

Marketing research is usually touted as the key to better decision making and the mark of sophisticated professional management. It is commonly thought that the more money spent for marketing research the less chance for a bad decision. But heavy use of marketing research does not always help the situation, as we saw with the Edsel and Coca-Cola.

Marketing research does not guarantee a correct decision. At best, marketing research increases the "batting average" of correct decisions—maybe only by a little, sometimes by quite a bit. To be effective, research must be current and unbiased. The several million dollars spent on Edsel marketing research came to naught. Most of the research on consumer preferences and attitudes was done several years before the Edsel came on the market, and the decision to use the name Edsel was made despite its negative connotation to many people. From the Edsel example we can further conclude that planning and long lead time do not assure success, especially when based on faulty premises.

And the several million dollars in taste-test research for Coca-Cola can hardly reassure us about the validity of marketing research. Admittedly, results of taste tests are difficult to rely on, simply because of the subjective nature of taste preferences. But the Coca-Cola research did not even uncover the latent and powerful loyalty toward tradition, and gave a completely false "go" signal for the new flavor.

It is wrong, however, to view all marketing research and planning as useless. Some of the flawed studies might have been worthwhile with better planning. Lee Iacocca used marketing research to identify the most promising markets for the Mustang, guide the design of the car, and determine its price. Marketing research could have provided Coors with early feedback that customers did not like the hard-to-open cans and increasingly preferred low-calorie beer.

Many successful firms chronicled in this book used little formal research. The great successes of Nike and Apple relied on entrepreneurial hunch rather than sophisticated research. So did Joel Hyatt and Mark McCormack of IMG. Ray Kroc of McDonald's recognized a good thing when he saw it, although McDonald's later relied heavily on research, especially for its site selections. Kresge's major move into K mart also came without formal research. Harry Cunningham on his own conducted a two-year investigation that was a far cry from a formal and sophisticated marketing research study. However, Batten of Penney commissioned a two-year formal research study that led to major policy changes.

Why have we not seen more extensive use of marketing research? Consider the following major reasons:

1. Most of the founding entrepreneurs did not have marketing backgrounds and therefore were not familiar and confident with such research.

2. Available tools and techniques are not always appropriate to handle some problems and opportunities. There may be too many variables. They may be intangible and incapable to precise measurement. Much research consists of collecting past and present data that although helpful in predicting a stable future are of little help

in charting revolutionary new ventures. But the higher risks for such ventures are often offset by the potential for great rewards.

GENERAL INSIGHTS

Impact of One Person

In many of the cases one person had a powerful impact on the organization. William Batten fostered major changes at Penney. Harry Cunningham of Kresge completely turned a mediocre and conservative variety-store chain into the most aggressive and largest discounter, with a growth rate almost unparalleled in retailing. Ray Kroc of McDonald's converted a small hamburger stand into the world's largest fast-food restaurant operation, and maintained its successful format against all comers. The accomplishments of Lee Iacocca are well known, both with the Mustang and with his later rejuvenation of Chrysler.

We have encountered some great entrepreneurs: Steven Jobs of Apple, Phil Knight of Nike, Joel Hyatt and his legal clinics, Mark McCormack and his managing and promoting of athletes through International Management Group. These individuals, most of them young, conceived and built thriving corporations from scratch.

One person can also have a negative impact on an organization. Eugene Ferkauf was the force behind the development and growth of Korvette. He was heralded as one of the outstanding merchants in U.S. history, but he could not adapt himself or his organization to the challenges of large size. And how can we forget Adam Osborne, and Robert Campeau? The impact of one person, for good or ill, is one of the marvels of history, whether business history or world history.

Prevalence of Opportunities for Entrepreneurship Today

The recent successes of Nike and Apple show that opportunities and rewards for entrepreneurship were never better. Despite the maturing of our economy and the growing size and power of many firms in many industries, there still is abundant opportunity. Such opportunity exists not only for the change maker or innovator, but even for the entrepreneur who only seeks to do things a little better than existing, and complacent, competition.

Venture capital to support promising new businesses is increasing— some $1 billion a year. We are in the midst of the greatest boom in new stock issues and new company formations since the late 1960s.

Of course, we know that not all of us have what it takes to be an entrepreneur. It takes more than the "great idea." Nolan Bushnell, founder of

Atari in 1972 with $500, says: "A lot of people have ideas, but there are few who decide to do something about them now. Not tomorrow. Not next week. But today."[4] Dreamers do not make entrepreneurs; doers do. The great venture capitalists look at the person, not the idea. Typically they distribute their seed money to resourceful people, who are courageous enough to give up security for the unknown consequences of their embryonic venture, who have great self-confidence, and who demonstrate a tremendous will to win.

Role of Greed

We can define greed as an extreme desire to amass wealth; it might even be seen as rapaciousness or plundering. Are there any examples of greed in these cases? Certainly some of the S & L excesses would smack of such. Campeau's acquisitive drive suggests greed outweighing good judgment. Some of the corporate raiders in the leveraged buyout frenzy of the 1980s were bent on plundering their targets.

Does ambition and a strong growth commitment constitute greed? Was Ray Kroc greedy for much greater size and growth for McDonald's? Were Phil Knight and Steve Jobs greedy in the quest for great growth and glory for their fledgling enterprises?

Can we say that greed comes into play when the great quest for growth hurts somebody—perhaps customers, investors or creditors, or employees— and therefore exceeds reasonable expectations of ethical and socially responsible behavior? Then extreme ambition becomes negative, whereas ambition should be positive and a spur for our society. Now we find that Nestle's and Robins' disregard for the health and safety of their customers shows greed outweighing concern for the common good. Greed then becomes the antithesis of the free enterprise system and of the ambition that fuels it.

Socialist Shortcomings

The Yugo case showed the particular vulnerabilities of Eastern European firms: vulnerabilities in technological backwardness, in worker motivation, and in managerial competence. Their deficiencies result in quality that is poor and inconsistent, and in products that are subpar in technology, attractiveness, and competitive stature. Because of these shortcomings, such firms usually are forced to try to compete only by offering the lowest prices in the industry. And this creates the continuing public image problems of low quality.

U.S. firms can learn from the Yugo example of the desirability of not being the lowest-priced firm because of the image it fosters of low quality.

---

[4] John Merwin, "Have You Got What It Takes?" *Forbes*, August 3, 1981, p. 60.

They can learn the importance of quality control and assurance, and worker motivation. The Yugo represents the worst of manufacturer mistakes, which all firms should seek to avoid.

FINALLY

We learn from mistakes and from successes. Yet every management problem seems cast in a somewhat different setting, requiring a different strategy. One author has likened business strategy to military strategy:

> . . . strategies which are flexible rather than static enhance optimum use and offer the greatest number of alternative objectives. A good commander knows that he cannot control his environment to suit a prescribed strategy. Natural phenomena pose their own restraints to strategic planning, whether physical, geographic, regional, or psychological and sociological.[5]

And:

> Planning leadership recognizes the unpleasant fact that, despite every effort, the war may be lost. Therefore, the aim is to retain the maximum number of facilities and the basic organization. Indicators of a deteriorating and unsalvageable total situation are, therefore, mandatory. . . . No possible combination of strategies and tactics, no mobilization of resources . . . can supply a magic formula which guarantees victory; it is possible only to increase the probability of victory.[6]

Thus we can pull two concepts from military strategy to help guide business strategy: the desirability of flexibility due to an unknown or changing environment, and the idea of a basic core that should be maintained under all circumstances. The first suggests that the firm should be prepared for adjustments in strategy as conditions warrant. The second suggests that there is a basic core of a firm's business that should be unchanging; it should be the final bastion to fall back on for regrouping if necessary. Grant and Korvette abandoned their basic strengths, and had nothing to fall back on. Harley Davidson stolidly maintained its core position, even though it let expansion opportunities slither away.

In regard to the basic core of a firm, every viable firm had some distinctive function or "ecological niche" in the business environment:

---

[5] Myron S. Heidingsfield, *Changing Patterns in Marketing* (Boston: Allyn and Bacon, 1968), p. 11.

[6] Ibid.

Every business firm occupies a position which is in some respects unique. Its location, the product it sells, its operating methods, or the customers it serves tend to set it off in some degree from every other firm. Each firm competes by making the most of its individuality and its special character.[7]

Woe to the firm that loses its ecological niche.

FOR THOUGHT AND DISCUSSION

1. Design a program aimed at mistake avoidance. Be as specific, as creative, and as complete as possible.
2. How would you build into an organization the controls to assure that similar mistakes will not happen in the future?
3. Which would you advise a firm to be: an imitator or an innovator? Why?

INVITATION TO ROLE PLAY

You have been assigned the responsibility of assuring that your firm has adequate sensors of the marketplace. How would you go about developing such sensors?

---

[7] Alderson, *Marketing Behavior*, p. 101.